The Changing Academic Profession

The Changing Academy – The Changing Academic Profession in International Comparative Perspective 1

Series Editors
William K. Cummings, *The George Washington University, Washington, USA*
Akira Arimoto, *Kurashiki Sakuyo University, Kurashiki City, Okayama, Japan*

Editorial Board
Jürgen Enders, *University of Twente, Enschede, the Netherlands*
Amy Metcalfe, *the University of British Columbia, Vancouver, Canada*
Christine Musselin, *CSO Research Interests Higher Education and Research, Paris, France*
Rui Santiago, *University of Aveiro, Portugal*
Simon Schwartzman, *Institute for Studies and Labour and Society, Rio de Janeiro, Brazil*
Ulrich Teichler, *University of Kassel, Germany*
Charles Wohluter, *Northwest University, South Africa*

Scope of the series

As the landscape of higher education has in recent years undergone significant changes, so correspondingly have the backgrounds, specializations, expectations and work roles of academic staff. The Academy is expected to be more professional in teaching, more productive in research and more entrepreneurial in everything. Some of the changes involved have raised questions about the attractiveness of an academic career for today's graduates. At the same time, knowledge has come to be identified as the most vital resource of contemporary societies.

The Changing Academy series examines the nature and extent of the changes experienced by the academic profession in recent years. It explores both the reasons for and the consequences of these changes. It considers the implications of the changes for the attractiveness of the academic profession as a career and for the ability of the academic community to contribute to the further development of knowledge societies and the attainment of national goals. It makes comparisons on these matters between different national higher education systems, institutional types, disciplines and generations of academics, drawing initially on available data-sets and qualitative research studies with special emphasis on the recent twenty nation survey of the Changing Academic Profession. Among the themes featured will be:

1. Relevance of the Academy's Work
2. Internationalization of the Academy
3. Current Governance and Management, particularly as perceived by the Academy
4. Commitment of the Academy

The audience includes researchers in higher education, sociology of education and political science studies; university managers and administrators; national and institutional policymakers; officials and staff at governments and organizations, e.g. the World Bank.

For further volumes:
http://www.springer.com/series/8668

Ulrich Teichler • Akira Arimoto
William K. Cummings

The Changing Academic Profession

Major Findings of a Comparative Survey

Springer

Ulrich Teichler
INCHER, University of Kassel
Kassel, Germany

William K. Cummings
Graduate School of Education and HD
George Washington University
Washington, DC, USA

Akira Arimoto
Research Institute for Higher Education
Kurashiki Sakuyo University
Kurashiki, Okayama, Japan

ISBN 978-94-007-6154-4   ISBN 978-94-007-6155-1 (eBook)
DOI 10.1007/978-94-007-6155-1
Springer Dordrecht Heidelberg New York London

Library of Congress Control Number: 2012956295

© Springer Science+Business Media Dordrecht 2013
This work is subject to copyright. All rights are reserved by the Publisher, whether the whole or part of the material is concerned, specifically the rights of translation, reprinting, reuse of illustrations, recitation, broadcasting, reproduction on microfilms or in any other physical way, and transmission or information storage and retrieval, electronic adaptation, computer software, or by similar or dissimilar methodology now known or hereafter developed. Exempted from this legal reservation are brief excerpts in connection with reviews or scholarly analysis or material supplied specifically for the purpose of being entered and executed on a computer system, for exclusive use by the purchaser of the work. Duplication of this publication or parts thereof is permitted only under the provisions of the Copyright Law of the Publisher's location, in its current version, and permission for use must always be obtained from Springer. Permissions for use may be obtained through RightsLink at the Copyright Clearance Center. Violations are liable to prosecution under the respective Copyright Law.
The use of general descriptive names, registered names, trademarks, service marks, etc. in this publication does not imply, even in the absence of a specific statement, that such names are exempt from the relevant protective laws and regulations and therefore free for general use.
While the advice and information in this book are believed to be true and accurate at the date of publication, neither the authors nor the editors nor the publisher can accept any legal responsibility for any errors or omissions that may be made. The publisher makes no warranty, express or implied, with respect to the material contained herein.

Printed on acid-free paper

Springer is part of Springer Science+Business Media (www.springer.com)

Contents

1	**Introduction**		1
	1.1 The Scope of the Study		1
	1.2 The Predecessor Survey of the Early 1990s		2
		1.2.1 The Carnegie Initiative and the Design of the Study	2
		1.2.2 The Synthesis of Results	3
		1.2.3 An Additional Interpretation	5
		1.2.4 Follow-Up Thoughts	6
	1.3 Diverse Issues to Be Addressed in the Analysis of the Academic Profession		7
		1.3.1 'Academic'	7
		1.3.2 'Profession'	9
		1.3.3 Academic Work and the Functions of Higher Education	11
		1.3.4 The Issue of 'Academic Freedom'	12
		1.3.5 Specific Models of the University and Global Trends	13
		1.3.6 Academic Careers	15
	1.4 Recent Major Changes Affecting the Academic Profession		16
		1.4.1 Relevance	16
		1.4.2 Internationalisation	16
		1.4.3 Management	17
	1.5 The Second Comparative Survey of the Academic Profession		18
	1.6 This Volume		20
	References		20
2	**The Design and Methods of the Comparative Study**		25
	2.1 Introduction		25
	2.2 The Target Group		26
		2.2.1 Countries	26
		2.2.2 Institutions	27
		2.2.3 The Academic Profession	27
	2.3 Conceptual Framework and Themes Addressed		28

	2.4	Sampling Design and Number of Respondents	30
		2.4.1 Analytic Goals	30
		2.4.2 Design Effect (Deff Coefficient)	30
		2.4.3 Structure of Higher Education	31
	2.5	Data Coding and Analysis	33
	2.6	Utilisation of Data	35
3	**The Variety of Countries Participating in the Comparative Study**		**37**
	3.1	Introduction	37
	3.2	Indicators on Economy, Labour Market and Technology	39
	3.3	Indicators on Educational and Research Expenditures	41
	3.4	Enrolment	42
	3.5	Academic Productivity	42
	3.6	Basic Information on Higher Education Systems	43
		3.6.1 Canada	43
		3.6.2 United States of America	45
		3.6.3 Finland	46
		3.6.4 Germany	48
		3.6.5 Italy	49
		3.6.6 The Netherlands	50
		3.6.7 Norway	52
		3.6.8 Portugal	53
		3.6.9 United Kingdom	54
		3.6.10 Australia	56
		3.6.11 Japan	58
		3.6.12 Korea	59
		3.6.13 Hong Kong	61
		3.6.14 Argentina	62
		3.6.15 Brazil	63
		3.6.16 Mexico	65
		3.6.17 South Africa	66
		3.6.18 China	67
		3.6.19 Malaysia	68
	References		70
4	**The Academic Career**		**75**
	4.1	Introduction	75
	4.2	Biography and Career	78
		4.2.1 Gender Distribution	78
		4.2.2 Qualifications	80
		4.2.3 Professional and Institutional Mobility	81
		4.2.4 International Mobility	84

	4.3	Employment Conditions	88
		4.3.1 Part-Time and Short-Term Employment	88
		4.3.2 Income	91
	4.4	Work Situation	94
		4.4.1 Quality of Facilities and Resources	94
		4.4.2 Perceived Change of Working Conditions	97
	4.5	Time Budget	98
		4.5.1 Time Committed to Work and Time Distribution Across Work Tasks	98
		4.5.2 Weekly Working Hours	99
		4.5.3 Work Time Spent on Teaching and Research	102
		4.5.4 Work Time Spent on Other Assignments	105
	4.6	Assessment of the Professional Situation	106
		4.6.1 Reflection of the Professional Situation	106
	4.7	Commitment to the Discipline, Department and Institution	109
	4.8	Job Satisfaction	111
	4.9	Summary of Major Findings	113
	References		116
5	**Research and Teaching: The Changing Views and Activities of the Academic Profession**		**117**
	5.1	Conceptual Framework	117
	5.2	Preferences for Research and Teaching	119
	5.3	Factors Underlying Research and Teaching Orientation	124
	5.4	Allocation of Working Time to Research and Teaching	126
	5.5	Perceived Links Between Research and Teaching Orientation	127
	5.6	Factors Affecting Compatibility Between Research and Teaching	130
	5.7	Teaching Approaches	131
	5.8	Teaching Modes	135
	5.9	Notions and Approaches to Research and Scholarship	137
	5.10	Research Activities	140
	5.11	Research Output	146
	5.12	Concluding Observations	151
	Appendix		153
	References		162
6	**Faculty Perceptions of the Efficacy of Higher Educational Governance and Management**		**165**
	6.1	Introduction	165
	6.2	The CAP Approach	166
	6.3	A Framework for Analysis	166
	6.4	Decision-Making and the Academic's Perception of Their Participation	167
	6.5	The Evaluation of Teaching and Research	171
	6.6	Influence	173

6.7	Perceptions of Teaching and Research Strategies	175
6.8	Communication-Oriented Management	176
6.9	Operationally Oriented Management Style	180
6.10	Protection of Academic Freedom	185
6.11	Institutional Affiliation and Engagement	185
6.12	Conclusion: Variations in the Model's Applicability	190
	Appendix	192
	References	211

Appendix 213
   The Changing Academic Profession: Questionnaire 213

Bibliography 231
   Publications of the Project "The Changing Academic
   Profession" (CAP) 231

About the Authors

Ulrich Teichler is professor since 1978 and former director of the International Centre for Higher Education Research, University of Kassel (INCHER-Kassel), Germany; he also was dean and vice-president for some period at his university. Born in 1942, he was a student of sociology at the Free University of Berlin and a researcher at the Max Planck Institute for Educational Research, Berlin. His doctoral dissertation was on higher education in Japan. He has had extended research periods in Japan, the Netherlands and the USA. For a period each, he was professor on part-time/short-term basis at the Northwestern University (USA), College of Europe, Bruges (Belgium), Hiroshima University (Japan), and Open University (UK) and had other teaching assignments in Argentina, Austria, Germany and Norway. Key research areas include higher education and the world of work, comparison of higher education systems, international mobility in higher education and the academic profession. Ulrich has more than 1,000 publications to his name; he is (co-)author and (co-)editor of about 50 books each; publications are translated into 20 languages. He is a member of the International Academy of Education (IAE) and the Academia Europaea (AE), and he served key functions in both academics; he is former chairman of the Consortium of Higher Education Researchers (CHER), former president and distinguished member of EAIR, vice-president of the Society for Research into Higher Education (SRHE) and honorary member of the Gesellschaft für Hochschulforschung (GfHf)—the association for higher education research in the German-speaking countries. He was honoured with the Comenius Prize of UNESCO, the Dr. h.c. of the University of Turku (Finland) and a Festschrift each in the English and the German language. He is sponsor of the Ulrich Teichler Prize for the best doctoral and master theses on higher education submitted to universities in German-speaking countries.

Akira Arimoto is the president and trustee of Kurashiki Sakuyo University (KSU) in Japan and professor and director at Research Institute for Higher Education (RIHE) at KSU. Prof. Arimoto was professor and director of RIHE at Hiroshima University and also at Hijiyama University. Dr. Arimoto is professor emeritus of Hiroshima University, associate member of the Japan Council of Science and president of the National Association of RIHEs. He is a member of editorial board of the book series 'Higher Education Dynamics' and a series editor of the book series 'The Changing Academy'. He served as chair of UNESCO's Global Scientific Committee for the Asian and Pacific region, president of the Japanese Association of Higher Education Research (JAHER) and president of the Japan Society of Educational Sociology (JSES). He was a visiting fellow, as the first Nitobe Fellow at the International House of Japan, to Yale University, Max Planck Institute and Lancaster University. His recent books include the following: *The Changing Academic Profession in Japan* (editor, Tamagawa Univ. Press, 2008), *The Changing Academic Profession in the World* (editor, Ibid., 2011) and *National Innovation and the Academic Research Enterprise* (chapter, ed. by D. Dill and F. Van Vught, The Johns Hopkins Univ. Press, 2010); *Changing Governance and Management in Higher Education* (chapter, ed. by W. Locke, W. K. Cummings and D. Fisher, Springer, 2011); *University Rankings* (chapter, ed. by J. C. Shin, R. K. Toutkoushian, U. Teichler, Springer, 2011); and *The Emergent Knowledge Society and the Future of Higher Education* (chapter, ed. by D. E. Neubauer, Routledge, 2012).

William Cummings is professor of international education at the George Washington University, Washington, D.C., USA. He received his PhD in sociology from Harvard University in 1972. Since then, he has taught at the University of Chicago, the National University of Singapore, Harvard University and the State University of New York at Buffalo. He has directed the Office of International Education at Harvard University and served as associate dean for research at the George Washington University. He has directed projects at the National Science Foundation, the East-west Center, University of Hawaii and the Ford Foundation and served as an advisor to the Ministry of Education in Ethiopia. He is the author of *Education and Equality in Japan* (Princeton, N.J.: Princeton University Press, 1980), *Profiting from Education* (New York: Institute of International Education, 1990) (with Gail Chambers), *The Japanese Academic Marketplace and University Reform* (New York: Garland Publishing Inc., 1990) and *The Institutions of Education* (Oxford: Symposium Books, 2003) as well as numerous journals articles. Most recently, he coedited *Scholars in the Changing American Academy* (with M. J. Finkelstein, 2012, Springer) and *Crossing Borders in East Asian Higher Education* (with G. Postiglione and D. Chapman). Together with Akira Arimoto, Hiroshima University, and Ulrich Teichler, Kassel University, he conceived and co-led the Changing Academic Profession Project as well as coordinated the US study with Martin Finkelstein.

Chapter 1
Introduction

1.1 The Scope of the Study

More than 100 scholars from 19 countries all over the world have cooperated over a period of 8 years (from 2004 to 2012) in portraying 'The Changing Academic Profession (CAP)' in comparative perspective. To launch this ambitious endeavour, they examined the state of knowledge about the academic profession and made strategic decisions about the directions they would choose for enhancing the state of knowledge. From the outset four thoughts were on their minds:

First, this project is the second major effort in the history of higher education research to undertake a major comparative survey of the academic profession. Therefore, a look back to the first project of this type was natural in order to understand the typical potentials and problems of such an undertaking with the help of prior experience, to take this as an opportunity to examine changes over time and to identify challenges for the improvement of research on the academic profession.

Second, the CAP project team, in reviewing the public discourses as well as the state of knowledge of higher education research and science research, noted that the academic profession has not been among the top priority areas in recent decades. Rather themes such as the expansion of higher education and its consequences; the relationship between academic knowledge and innovation; the extent of homogeneity versus diversity of higher education systems; teaching, learning, curricula and competences; the education and training function of higher education; the coexistence of teaching and research; research productivity; teaching, research and possibly other functions of higher education; higher education and graduate employment; and finally governance and management of higher education were in the 'limelight'. Therefore this project was bound to underscore the argument that more attention needs to be paid to the core 'workers' within higher education and their perceptions of changes in their work and workplace.

Third, even though the academic profession has not been a priority in the public debates and the respective research, the project team from the outset was aware of the fact that the academic profession could be an interesting multifaceted theme in the intellectual discourse and in the research activities on higher education and science. The need was felt to identify the major lines of such analysis both for the purposes of choosing thematic priorities in the questionnaire surveys and of interpreting the findings in the light of the major conceptual frameworks at hand.

Fourth, the recent developments in higher education and science are often said to be extraordinarily dynamic. Therefore, the scholars collaborating in the CAP project decided to address 'change' not only in terms of changes in the views and activities of the academic profession in the most recent two decades but also in terms of paying attention to recent salient changes in the challenges to the academic profession in their external and internal environment. Three thematic areas were eventually pinpointed which ought to be taken into consideration in the new comparative study: the growing expectation that academic work should be relevant, the spreading internationalisation of higher education and academic work and the increasing power of managers in higher education.

1.2 The Predecessor Survey of the Early 1990s

1.2.1 The Carnegie Initiative and the Design of the Study

Entry rates to higher education beyond 10%, some years later beyond 20% and eventually beyond 30% were a reality in the United States of America long before they were realised in other parts of the world. Moreover, the systematic analysis of developments in higher education—that is, higher education research—emerged in the USA earlier on a substantial scale than in other countries. Already in 1969, the Carnegie Foundation for the Advancement of Teaching initiated the first survey of the academic profession that addressed the attitudes, values and professional orientations of the professoriate, reviewed the working and employment situation and chronicled its changing demographic profile. In the 1980s, various literature studies, surveys and expert analyses of the Carnegie Foundation, guided by its President Ernest L. Boyer, stirred up enormous debates in the USA about the state of higher education—notably, as these studies made clear, that the public debate often had focused too much on the prestigious research universities and had overlooked the changes of the overall system related to rapid expansion and the changing social functions of higher education.

Underlying the surveys of the academic profession initiated by the Carnegie Foundation was a growing sense of crisis in the academic profession: The expansion of the higher education and research and their growing relevance was neither matched by improving conditions for academic work nor by a status uplift for the academic profession (see Clark 1987; various articles in European Journal of Education 18/1983/3; Finkelstein 1984; Bowen and Schuster 1986; Altbach 1991).

Ernest L. Boyer began the first steps for the preparation of a comparative study in 1990. He was convinced that the US audience would benefit from knowing whether issues of the academic profession were similar across the globe. Some of the major changes in the academy and the issues it faced were perceived to be worldwide, while in other respects, different traditions and different policies were evident. Thus, an international comparison seemed to be of interest. Moreover, the professoriate had developed more and more international communication and collaboration. Colleagues across the countries seemed to benefit from the international exchanges, and these exchanges seemed to enrich the world's reservoir of knowledge.

The Carnegie Foundation explored possible research partners in different countries of the world, provided funds for partners from middle-income countries to undertake national surveys and volunteered to take the lead for the joint data processing and for the analysis of results. Preparatory meetings were held in 1990 and 1991 in order to develop a conceptual framework and a questionnaire drawing from the most recent US predecessor survey (Carnegie Foundation for the Advancement of Teaching 1989; see Boyer 1990) while at the same time covering the key issues and the key conditions faced by a large number of countries.

Thus, in this first international survey of the academic profession, commonly called the Carnegie Survey of the Academic Profession, information was collected about the demographic facts of the profession, the employment and work situation, time spent on various activities, attitudes towards teaching and learning and actual activities in these areas, the governance of academic institutions, and morale. The survey was carried out in 15 countries (more precisely 14 countries and a 'territory') from all continents. The questionnaire was mailed in 1992 and 1993 to altogether more than 40,000 persons. Response rates varied from about 70% to less than 30%, and 19,161 respondents provided the information for the comparative analysis (see Altbach and Lewis 1996; Enders and Teichler 1995b, pp. 5–8; cf. the slight variation in the report by Whitelaw 1996).

1.2.2 The Synthesis of Results

A relatively short overview of the results of this first comparative study was published by the Carnegie Foundation in 1994 (Boyer et al. 1994). The major publication, made available 2 years later (Altbach 1996), was a collection of country reports supplemented by a comparative analysis on the part of two US scholars who had not been involved in the comparative project at the time the joint questionnaire had been developed. Scholars involved in the project published various national and comparative data analyses, among them substantial reports on Japan (Arimoto and Ehara 1996) and Germany (Enders and Teichler 1995a, b). Finally, several reports on the project contributed to a major conference of the Academia Europaea held in

1996, and the proceedings were published in the same year (Maassen and van Vught 1996). Also articles were published in a special issue of the journal 'Higher Education' in 1997 (Welch 1997).

The 1994 comparative report highlighted a broad range of findings (cf. the summary in Höhle and Teichler 2013). In most countries, the academic profession has remained more strongly male dominated than the USA, and the proportion of youth viewed as well equipped for study in higher education is rated smaller than in the USA. Across countries, scholars feel most closely affiliated to their discipline, but their sense of affiliation to their university varies widely. The role they attribute to research in their overall activities also varies. Across countries, the authors observed a relatively low degree of satisfaction with the prevailing modes of evaluating academic work. Salaries in most countries were viewed as high or acceptable. Overall satisfaction seemed to be high, and the overall academic climate was rated positively. Views varied significantly across countries as regards the assessment of working conditions, and in some countries, many academics considered their work to be a source of personal strain. Across all countries, academics expressed dissatisfaction with the prevailing conditions of governance. In most countries, academics felt academic freedom was sufficiently protected, while the views varied concerning the extent to which academics should play an active role in society. Finally, the majority of academics all over the world believe that international ties are highly important for the academic profession, though the actual incidence of international collaboration and mobility seem to differ strikingly by country. The analysis concludes 'Scholars everywhere, while maintaining national distinctions, acknowledge common concerns – not just intellectually but professionally as well. And in the century ahead, three critical issues will influence profoundly the shape and vitality of higher learning around the world' (Boyer et al. 1994, p. 21): student access and the balance of access and excellence, governance ('How can the university reorganize itself to achieve both efficiency and collegiality?') as well as the relationships between teaching, research and services (rewards and increased contribution to public good).

In the major publication of the Carnegie study, Altbach and Lewis (1996, pp. 47–48) summarise the findings of the country reports of as follows: 'One cannot but be struck by the many similarities among the scholars and scientists in the diverse countries. It is with regard to those working conditions most affected by local political and cultural customs and policies that international differences are most apparent.

The professoriate worldwide is committed to teaching and research, and in varying degree to service. While there is a feeling that higher education faces many difficulties and that conditions have deteriorated in recent years, most academics are committed to the profession and to its traditional values of autonomy, academic freedom, and the importance of scholarship, both for its own sake and for societal advancement. Academics are not especially supportive of senior administrators, yet they express remarkable loyalty to the profession and to other academics. They seem prepared to respond to the call that higher education contribute more tangibly to economic development and social well-being. They believe that they have an obligation to apply their knowledge to society's problems'.

After naming some differences between countries, the authors continue: 'Resiliency, determination, and a focus on the core functions of higher education characterize the academic profession in these fourteen countries. While the vicissitudes experienced by the profession in recent years have been considerable, the professoriate is by no means demoralized. In all but three countries, 60% or more agree that this is an especially creative and productive time in their fields. Professors are generally satisfied with the courses they teach, and with few exceptions are pleased with the opportunity they have to pursue their own ideas. The intellectual atmosphere is good; faculty do not regret their career choices and are generally happy with their relationships with colleagues.

This portrait of the professoriate depicts a strong, but somewhat unsettled profession. Academics around the world are inspired by the intellectual ferment of the times. The intrinsic pleasures of academic life obviously endure. Academe is facing the future with concern but with surprising optimism' (ibid, p. 48).

1.2.3 An Additional Interpretation

Some additional aspects are put forward in the overview of the major results presented by Teichler (1996), where he concentrates the analysis on six economically advanced countries and stresses the merits of a breakdown of responses into three groups: university professors, junior academic staff at universities and academics at other institutions of higher education. In summarising the findings of the Carnegie Survey, Teichler (ibid., p. 59) points out, first, that the academic profession 'is more satisfied with their profession than the prior public debate suggested'. He underscores, though, that satisfaction is higher among university professors than the other two groups, and the areas for which dissatisfaction is expressed vary substantially by country. Second, a clear link between teaching and research has persisted for university professors. 'Neither is research endangered because of teaching and administrative loads nor is teaching put aside to research-oriented motives and research-oriented assessment' (ibid, p. 60). However, individual options vary strikingly among university professors, and the link between teaching and research is less obvious for large proportions of junior staff as well as for academics at other higher education institutions.

Third, the author notes surprising commonalities among university professors across disciplines, notably 'in their value judgments about the university administration, about the role higher education is expected to play and about the views on how higher education is perceived and estimated in the public' (ibid.). In contrast, the author notes substantial differences on many issues between senior and junior academics at universities as well as between academics at universities and other institutions of higher education.

Fourth, Teichler places a greater emphasis on differences between countries than the other authors. Among others, 'the English senior academics at universities consider themselves more strongly a profession under pressure than their colleagues in other European countries' (ibid, p. 61). According to the author, the country differences are striking 'as regards the role foreign languages and international relationships play for their academic life. Sweden belongs to those countries, where a view prevails which I would call 'internationalise or perish'. Germany belongs, as also Japan, to those countries which I would call 'two-arena countries': scholars might opt whether they more strongly prefer national or international involvement and visibility. Actually, the Dutch scholars seemed to be closer on average to their Swedish than to their German colleagues in this respect. Finally, many English scholars, though to a lesser extent than their US-American colleagues, seem to take 'internationalisation through import' for granted' (ibid.).

Fifth, junior academics at universities are more a heterogeneous groups than professors as far as priorities and actual time spent for various functions are concerned. On average, they assess the working conditions favourably but are clearly less satisfied than university professors, though they are similar to them with respect to academic values.

Sixth, not surprisingly, the views and activities of academics at other institutions of higher education are clearly shaped by the dominance of teaching. They tend to be less satisfied with their overall professional situation than academics at universities.

Seventh, the administration is assessed by academics on average neither positively nor negatively. Most academics do not see any significant infringement as regards their academic work though some point out visible restrictions. Eighth and finally, Teichler points out that academics, though in the majority clearly defending the right to pursue research for its own sake, do not think of themselves as an 'ivory tower profession'. Rather they expect research and teaching will help resolve basic social problems.

Altogether, according to this analysis, the international comparative study undertaken in the early 1990s does not depict the academic profession as suffering from status loss, resource restrictions or adverse administrative conditions. Criticism of the conditions for academic work is by no means infrequent, but the academic profession seems to be in the position to stress activities they favour and to shape their job role themselves in a predominantly satisfactory way.

1.2.4 Follow-Up Thoughts

This does not mean, however, that the Carnegie study was successful in changing the perception of the situation of the academic profession substantially. In depicting the public debate a few years afterwards, Enders—actually a team member of the Carnegie study and thus knowing its results very well—points out that the academic profession continues to be under pressure: rapid loss of status, tighter resources, reduced power of the academic guild and blamed for not providing the services expected. 'Furthermore, one fears a decline in the faculty morale, disillusionment of their mission, seeing themselves as academic workers who are merely doing routine jobs and who are no longer strongly committed to the traditional norms and values of the profession' (Enders 2001b, p. 2). Similarly, Altbach (2000b, p. 1) notes a 'deterioration of the academic estate'. An even wider range of challenges is identified by Welch (2005a, p. 1) for the academic profession 'in uncertain times'.

Some subsequent analyses have paid more attention to the situation of junior academics. Notably in European countries, the long process of concurrent learning and productive work and the high selectivity of the profession result in a long period of unsecure employment with reduced access to resources (see Altbach 2000a; Enders 2001a; Enders and De Weert 2004; Teichler 2006); apparently, junior academics in other countries such as the USA face similar problems (cf. Schuster and Finkelstein 2006).

In reviewing the state of research and public discourse on the academic profession about a decade after the Carnegie study, Enders (2006, p. 19) ends his overview article for a handbook with the following cryptic sentence: 'Overall, the fate of the academic profession may lie solely in how it responds to changes that impact on universities and higher education systems worldwide in the coming years'.

The comparative studies on the academic profession thus lead to the following conclusions: The academic profession—possibly more so than in the past—is exposed to substantial expectations and pressures, but these expectations and pressures are not forcing scholars to develop a common view of their situation or of how they should act. Rather while academics believe they have to respond, they feel they have leeway for interpretation and for the selection of various directions of action.

1.3 Diverse Issues to Be Addressed in the Analysis of the Academic Profession

Though the academic profession, as already pointed out, seldom has been in the limelight of the public discourse on higher education as well as of research on higher education and science, we note that a broad range of themes could be on the agenda, if the academic profession was the focus of consideration (cf. the overviews in major handbooks by Altbach 1991; Morey 1992; Enders 2006; cf. also The academic profession (1983); Welch 2005b).

In laying the conceptual foundation for the questionnaire survey, six themes were identified to receive special attention both in the development of the survey questionnaire and for the subsequent analyses.

1.3.1 *'Academic'*

In employing the terms 'academy' and 'academic', we draw from a long historical tradition. One type of academy was as a formal organisation focused on education beginning with Plato's school in ancient Athens. The other type of academy was an association for the protection and advancement of knowledge such as the

Museum founded by Ptolemy I in the third century BC. From these early origins, academies of both types have been founded first in Western Europe and subsequently around the world; for example, the Arabs established academies in Cordoba and Samarkand.

The popularity of academies seemed to wane in the late medieval ages but again was resurrected in the Renaissance. For example, the Academie Francaise was established in Paris in 1635 and the Royal Society was established in London in 1660. These academies held meetings to discuss new developments in knowledge, published journals and sponsored selected projects.

Many who were welcomed as members in these early academies were independent intellectuals, but over time an increasing proportion had their primary association with a university or college or institute. So on the one hand, those associated with intellectual work looked to the academy as a locus for the validation of their intellectual achievements, and on the other hand, they looked to the formal organisations of higher learning for a worksite and a salary. Over the years, the concept of the academic came to be more firmly associated with those employed in the formal organisations and less associated with the academies. In recent decades, numerous academies have been established as major research centres, notably in the Soviet Union and some of the successor countries as well as in China, while in many other countries, the term academy was predominantly linked to associations of intellectuals.

Moreover, the term 'academic' is often employed for characterising the character of intellectual endeavours: 'academic' versus general in characterising college-preparatory schools in contrast to other secondary schools and 'academic' versus professional study programmes in characterising those programmes closely linked to academic disciplines without an explicit preparatory task for a certain professional area.

In the framework of this study, the term 'academic profession' is being employed as one of the most neutral terms (similarly scholar or scientist) or as the most neutral term in the English language to cover persons employed at institutions of higher education for the purpose of teaching and/or research. It should be noted, however, that such a comparative study enforces the participants to free themselves from the specific historical connotations within individual countries in order to recognise the smallest common denominators. This might be illustrated for Japan and Germany—two countries represented by the authors of this publication. The book *Henbô suru nihon no daigakukyôjushoku* (Arimoto 2008) might be literally translated as 'Transformation of the profession of the Japanese university professor', but it is translated on the book cover into English as 'The Changing Academic Profession in Japan'. And the German authors created a specific term 'Hochschullehrerberuf' (literally translated 'The profession of the higher education teacher'), because there are formally separate terms in Germany for professors and junior academics and because the most suitable term in the German language, that is, 'Wissenschaftler', covers both scholars active at higher education institutions and at institutions or units in charge of research.

The third and fourth themes touch upon the work of the academic profession: What are the core functions of higher education and the core tasks of academics and the interrelationships of these tasks? And how are the configuration of these tasks and actual activities determined?

Across those specific themes, a cross-cutting theme is how similar and varied is the academic profession, and what have been the drivers for similarities in certain aspects across countries? Finally, it is important to address various issues of academic careers.

1.3.2 'Profession'

The term 'profession' is appropriate in the framework of this study, because the persons surveyed make their living with academic work and as a rule are 'employed' with a contract that guarantees money in exchange for regular work under specified work and employment conditions. A comparative project, however, faces the problem that the terms chosen in the individual countries have different connotations and the use of English as a lingua franca in an international project often creates the misunderstanding that the specific connotations of the term 'profession' in the United States and the United Kingdom also apply to other countries in the project.

In the United Kingdom and United States, we note—in contrast to many other countries participating in this project—a polarised terminology. The word 'profession' is employed only for a minority of occupations, which are characterised by specialised knowledge and training, by a certain degree of self-control, and possibly by strict rules of admission to this occupational group. In other countries, the terms might have completely different connotations: For example, the German 'Beruf' comprises all occupations, the university professor and the cleaning personnel, and can be literally translated as a 'calling'.

In the framework of a study on the academic profession, it is certainly important to understand the extent to which scholars employed at institutions of higher education consider themselves jointly belonging to an occupation characterised both by a specific institutional home and the functions of these institutions. Four issues are frequently discussed suggesting that such a common understanding of an academic profession cannot be taken for granted.

First, many academics consider themselves to be affiliated more clearly to an academic discipline than to any institutional type. The relevance of disciplines is visible in higher education by the fact that some institutions concentrate on certain disciplines or disciplinary groups (e.g. colleges of fine arts) and that many universities have established organisational subunits (faculties, schools, departments, etc.) along disciplinary lines. Moreover, a mathematician might consider any other scholar specialised in mathematics as a 'colleague'—irrespective of whether the other mathematician works at his institution of higher education, another institution of education, a research institute or possibly an R&D unit of the company. There might be multiple senses of affiliation, but an institution of higher education cannot take for granted that the professional loyalty of their academic employee rests primarily with their institution.

Second, the professor can be viewed as being at the apex of a ladder in a certain professional area. University professors can be understood as exemplars of the 'key profession' (Perkins 1969), that is, as having the highest expertise in particular professional areas which are instrumental in enhancing the professional competence in these areas beyond academia. The university professor of engineering is not only at the top of his academic discipline within engineering, but she or he is also the top knowledgeable expert of his or her engineering profession. The element of the key profession, in reverse, plays a role in Latin American countries, where many regular university professors are primarily professionals in their respective areas of practice (e.g. lawyers), yet they spend a substantial proportion of their overall work time as university professors, thus in their double role being permanent two-way transmitters of knowledge.

Third, the conditions for the different status groups of persons undertaking teaching and research activities might be so distinct that no common affiliation to a single occupational category is likely. The strong emphasis placed on titles, for example, 'professor', points in this direction. In Germany, for example, the Federal Constitutional Court has ruled that academic freedom in the strict sense applies only to university professors, and, as already pointed out, different occupational terms are employed for professors and other academic staff.

Fourth, diversity in higher education is so pervasive in some countries that those employed in certain sectors of the higher education system do not feel they are part of the same occupational category as their counterparts in other sectors. It might be questionable, whether the 'Harvard' scholar has as much institutional loyalty as the 'Mitsubishi' employee. However, institutional types can be interpreted in some countries certainly as a 'watershed'. A senior academic at another higher education institution in the Netherlands or in Finland—countries where a doctorate is not viewed as being the normally required entry qualification for senior academic positions at those institutions—might be viewed as having hardly anything in common with a university professor.

The relevance of those segmentations, possibly pointed out on the basis of conceptual frameworks, is by no means trivial for a comparative study. In some countries, the average number of publications produced by a person defined in this project as belonging to the academic profession might be considered to be an interesting piece of information. In other countries, this information might be considered as irrelevant as the average temperature across days and night across the whole year, while information about average summer temperature or average winter temperature might be viewed as relevant. For example, the German study on the findings of the Carnegie study (Enders and Teichler 1995b, pp. 50–51) reports that university professors had 19 publications on average in the most recent 3 years, junior staff at universities 9 publications and academics at other institutions 6 publications, but it does not provide an aggregation of the number of publication of the average academic (employed at any higher education institution) in Germany.

1.3.3 Academic Work and the Functions of Higher Education

Higher education is generally viewed to be responsible for the generation, preservation and dissemination of systematic knowledge. In transferring functions into the tasks of the core personnel of higher education institutions, teaching and research are generally named, while terms and concepts vary regarding other functions of higher education and other tasks of the academic profession, for example, 'service' being often named in recent years.

Historical accounts of higher education point out that teaching and research have not always been named as the key functions. Nevertheless experts agree that most higher education institutions at the apex of the national higher education systems all over the world have been influenced by the 'idee' of the university formulated in the early nineteenth century by Wilhelm von Humboldt, that is, the 'unity of research and teaching'. High-quality universities all over the world are based on the belief that the close interaction of research and teaching within a higher education institution is mutually beneficial for both functions. Academics' involvement in research can ensure that teaching is based on the cutting edge of new knowledge, and academics' involvement in teaching can turn out to be creative for generating new ideas for research as well as for including the next generation of scholars early on in creative research activities.

However, the linkages between research and teaching are not always as close as the widely shared view about the pervasive influence of the idea the 'unity of research and teaching' suggests. First, a close link between research and teaching seems to apply only for parts of the overall higher education and research system. On the one hand, statistics on funding of higher education and research as well as on higher education and research staff show that only the minority of the research activities in all major economically advanced countries are accommodated within higher education; the major bulk of research takes place within industry (often called 'research and development') or in research institutes outside higher education—though to a varying degree by country. Only 'basic research' seems to be predominantly located within universities, but this privilege seems to be losing its momentum in recent decades with the increasing societal expectation for research to be visibly relevant, as often underscored in recent years with terms such as the 'knowledge society', the 'knowledge economy', 'targeted research' and 'mode 2 research'. On the other hand, the growth of enrolment in higher education has led to an increasing diversification of higher education institutions, whereby sizeable proportions of the institutions of higher education systems are expected to concentrate exclusively or predominantly on teaching. While in some countries, a clear divide of institutional types has been established, the mix of functions varies from one institution to the next in other countries. In Europe, the term 'university' is reserved in most countries for those institutions that strive for a balance of research and teaching; in the United States and some other countries, terms such as the 'research university' are employed in order to underscore that not all of the institutions of higher education that call themselves 'universities' pursue the ideal of a balance of research and teaching.

Second, the 'unity of research and teaching' often is not consistently reinforced even in those institutions striving for a balance of research and teaching. At some institutions, the teaching load or expected contact hours with students might be more or less the same for all professors, while at other institutions, the teaching assignment might differ widely between professors. At some institutions, junior academics are expected to teach and to undertake loads similar to senior academics, while at other institutions, they may have lower teaching loads than senior staff. At some institutions again, some of the junior staff have predominantly research tasks, while at others they may largely have teaching tasks. Institutions of higher education might vary in the extent to which they evidence concern for the proper training for teaching as well as for proper research training or the extent to which they leave this to the academics themselves. Also they may vary on the extent to which competences in these various tasks are taken into consideration in personnel policies. As a rule, teaching tasks are more highly regulated and supervised within higher education institutions than are research tasks, while research tasks are often strongly affected by external grants, reputations built up for the external world, etc. Moreover, higher education policies and the general public climate change over time in putting the emphasis for some period on accommodating large numbers of student, in raising the quality or raising the relevance on teaching, in increasing resources for research, in underscoring the quality of research, in emphasising the relevance of research, etc.

Third, even under these changing conditions favouring a balance or putting more emphasis on one of these two major tasks, the situation is vulnerable as regards the efforts of the individual academics to strike a balance between teaching and research. The enormous freedom of shaping the schedules of academic work for the academics themselves does not only imply a chance for them to find individually a suitable linkage between research and teaching, but they might be overwhelmed by the acute regulations and pressures for taking care of teaching so much that they do not find time and energy to protect the less regulated research tasks or they might be driven so much by the resources, incentives and conditions for achieving a reputation in the area of research that the teaching tasks are not paid appropriate attention.

1.3.4 The Issue of 'Academic Freedom'

The academic profession generally is viewed as a profession with enormous leeway for the individual academics to shape their work by themselves. This highly appreciated opportunity is often called 'academic freedom'.

'Academic freedom' can be defined as 'a situation in which individual academics might act without consequences that can do damage to their status, their tenure as members of academic institutions, or their civil conditions' (Shils 1991, p. 5). It might be specified further: 'Academic freedom is a situation in which academics might choose what they assert in their teaching, in their choice of subjects for research, and in their publications. Academic freedom is a situation in which the individual academic chooses a particular path or position of intellectual action. Academic freedom arises from a situation in which authority ... cannot prevent the academic from following the academic path that his intellectual interest and capacity proposes' (ibid., pp. 5–6).

Academic freedom is advocated—not merely by the academics themselves for serving their interest—in order to ensure that academic activities are not limited by conventional wisdom. Research is more likely to be innovative and creative, and graduates from higher education are more likely to cope with unforeseen and indeterminate work tasks and undertake superior problem-solving on the job. Critical thinking may also challenge the status quo of knowledge in its search for completely new insights.

Two different discourses on academic freedom should be identified. First, the extent of the right and opportunity of academics to decide about the nature or organisation of academic work is at stake: Do those in power—laws and orders, governments, boards, university and faculty managers and administrator, etc.—instruct the academics what to do and not to do? To which extent do they control and supervise academic work? Moreover, do incentives and sanctions, resources, etc. restrict the opportunities of following the academic paths the academics might choose?

Views vary whether the second issue should be considered to be in the domain of 'academic freedom' or not: the extent to which academics can choose their academic activities freely according to the rationales of the knowledge system and the extent to which they 'pursue knowledge for its own sake' or, in reverse, the extent to which they are expected—or even held accountable—to take into consideration in their academic work the practical value of their academic work for culture, society, economy and technology.

It is generally assumed that academic freedom cannot be unlimited in terms of the right of proclaiming any 'knowledge' which cannot be viewed as 'true' according the minimum consensus of academic endeavour or in terms of a right to refuse any cooperation necessary to shape jointly a study programme. But beyond these generally accepted views about misuse, we note an extraordinarily broad range of views about acceptable instruction, controls, incentives and pressures to conform to the presumed standards of quality, to do academic work effectively and to undertake presumably relevant academic work.

As will be discussed below, the CAP team has decided in the initial phase to pay attention notably to three issues where most experts assume substantial change in recent years, whereby two are closely linked to the issue of 'academic freedom': the increasing power of university management as well as the increasing expectations to undertake visibly relevant academic work.

1.3.5 Specific Models of the University and Global Trends

Higher education systems in the various countries of the world are influenced both by worldwide common challenges and approaches as well as by specific characteristics typical of particular regions, countries and institutions. On the one hand, higher education undoubtedly is shaped by the universalistic elements of the various disciplines, by worldwide discourses about the best possible solutions, by international cooperation and by global competition for academic success. On the other hand, we note striking differences between higher education systems all over the world. Variations between countries might reflect the different extent to which certain 'models' of higher education have taken root within the respective countries; they might be the results of national traditions and rules, for example, regarding the occupational system for which study programmes prepare students, and they might mirror the political approaches currently prevailing in the respective countries.

As regards 'models', many historians point out that the concepts of the modern university, which became dominant at the beginning of the nineteenth century, remained highly relevant up to today (see, e.g. Perkins 1991). For example, the Humboldtian model emerging in Germany seem to have had on the one hand a worldwide influence in terms of an appreciation of a close link between teaching and research but on the other hand served as a specific model in seeing the university professor as a person primarily devoted to research, whereby the research-related knowledge transmission and the academic discourse between the scholars and the students ensure the students' intellectual enhancements without any strong emphasis on professional skills of teaching and the logic of the teaching and learning process. In contrast, efforts to foster deliberate mechanisms of teaching and learning and to qualify the scholars explicitly for teaching played a strong role in the English tradition, whereby education was viewed as playing a substantial role in the cultural enhancement and personality development of the learners. Over the years, research began to play an increasing role but not in the Humboldtian tradition of subordinating the logic of teaching and learning to the rational of research-type inquiry. Finally, the Napoleonic model spread from France to many countries of the world, with its strong emphasis on an intellectually demanding professional training.

Experts agree that higher education in the United States has absorbed various components of the German and the English 'model' and eventually developed various indigenous characteristics which had a strong impact on higher education worldwide in the twentieth century (see Ben-David 1977). Three elements are most frequently noted in this respect: first, the establishment of graduate schools to synthesise learning through research and deliberate educational efforts at competence enhancement; second, the strong power of university management as a mechanism of striking a balance between the need for 'academic freedom' and the quest for societal relevance through close communication between those in power and the academic profession; and third, the enabling of an early and pervasive process of expansion of higher education and research through a flexible system of vertical and horizontal diversity (see Trow 1974, 2006). These features turned out to be highly influential all over the world after World War II (see Ben-David 1977; Rüegg 2011).

Many experts point out that pressures have increased in recent years to follow a global model of successful higher education, and the room for diverse models or national patterns of higher education is clearly on the decline. Recommendations originating from the World Bank to middle-income and low-income countries as well as the normative components underlying the most popular international 'rankings' of 'world-class universities' are widely viewed as incarnations of the new 'global' model (cf. the debates on ranking and world-class universities in Sadlak and Liu 2007; Shin et al. 2011).

1.3.6 Academic Careers

Academic careers are characterised—in comparison to other occupations held by university graduates—by a relatively late start, by a very long initial phase and, correspondingly, by a late consolidation.

- While entry to the legal, medical or engineering occupations, for example, is in most countries largely predetermined by the choice of the field at entry to higher education or soon afterwards, entry to the academic profession remains open in most cases up to the award of a master or equivalent degree. This is due to the fact discussed above that the academic profession is not a professional specialisation along others but rather is the key profession, that is, the intellectual apex for all professions.
- The period of learning and maturation for eventually being considered a fully fledged member of the academic profession is enormously long. While in other occupational areas university graduates might be considered to be fully competent professionals 1–3 years after graduation, the 'formative years' of academics (Teichler 2006) might comprise a period of 10–15 years after graduation in which they are assumed both to do productive academic work and enhance the competences considered necessary to be a full-fledged member of the academic community.
- In many countries of the world, academics eventually reach a consolidated professional status and position at a comparatively advanced age. Often, the transition from a provisional and partial learner status to a full-fledged member of the academic professional with all the academics right and a solid employment situation takes place at the age of about 40 years on average.

Additionally, the formative career stage of the academic profession is highly selective in many countries. While in most other profession the majority of those entering the profession will persist, unless they want to change or the profession experiences an overall shrinkage, only a minority—in some countries as low as one tenth—of those opting for the initial steps of academic work will end up in a consolidated position within the higher education and research system.

Moreover, the academic career might be characterised by a discrepancy of reputation and remuneration. Academic employment and work is viewed in most countries as highly prestigious and respected. And academics tend to have strong intrinsic motivation and a strong affiliation with their academic role. Yet, remuneration does not match in most countries the degree of selectivity and reputation; in various countries, remuneration of academics does not surpass substantially the average income of university-trained persons.

1.4 Recent Major Changes Affecting the Academic Profession

An analysis of the academic profession cannot merely address those features of the academic environment, the academic work and the academic careers that have persisted for decades. Rather, the academics' situation and activities are in constant flux. Therefore, special attention has to be paid to recent changes. In the starting phase of the project 'The Changing Academic Profession' (CAP), the scholars initiating the new project were convinced that three 'key challenges' have gained prominence recently: a higher expectation of relevance, a growing internationalisation and a substantially increased managerial power in higher education (see Kogan and Teichler 2007b; Research Institute for Higher Education, Hiroshima University 2006; cf. the more detailed explanations in Cummings 2006; Brennan 2007). To quote Kogan and Teichler extensively:

1.4.1 Relevance

'Whereas the highest goal of the traditional academy was to create fundamental knowledge, what has been described as the 'scholarship of discovery', the new emphasis of the knowledge society is on useful knowledge or the 'scholarship of application'. This scholarship often involves the pooling and melding of insights from several disciplines and tends to focus on outcomes that have a direct impact on everyday life. One consequence is that many future scholars, though trained in the disciplines, will work in applied fields and may have options of employment in these fields outside of the academy. This provides new opportunities for more boundaryless forms of academic career and knowledge transfer while it may also create recruitment difficulties in some places, and especially in fields such as science, technology and engineering.

There are strong interdependencies between the goals of higher education, the rules for distributing resources, and the nature of academic work. The changes associated with movement from the 'traditional academy' with its stress on basic research and disciplinary teaching to the 'relevant academy' are largely uncharted and are likely to have unanticipated consequences. The task of the project is therefore to understand how these changes influence academic value systems and work practices and affect the nature and locus of control and power in academe' (ibid., p. 10).

1.4.2 Internationalisation

'National traditions and socio-economic circumstances continue to play an important role in shaping academic life and have a major impact on the attractiveness of jobs in the profession. Yet today's global trends, with their emphasis on knowledge production and information flow, play an increasingly important role in the push towards the internationalisation of higher education. The international mobility of students and staff has grown, new technologies connect scholarly communities around the world, and English has become the new lingua franca of the international community.

The economic and political power of a country, its size and geographic location, its dominant culture, the quality of its higher education system and the language it uses for academic discourse and publications are factors that bring with them different approaches to internationalisation. Local and regional differences in approach are also to be found. Therefore, questions are raised about the functions of international networks, the implications of differential access to them and the role of new communication technologies in internationalising the profession' (ibid., pp. 10–11).

1.4.3 Management

'In academic teaching and research, where professional values are traditionally firmly woven into the very fabric of knowledge production and dissemination, attempts to introduce change are sometimes received with scepticism and opposition. At the same time, a greater professionalization of higher education management is regarded as necessary to enable higher education to respond effectively to a rapidly changing external environment. The control and management of academic work will help to define the nature of academic roles—including the division of labour in the academy, with a growth of newly professionalised 'support' roles and a possible breakdown of the traditional teaching/research nexus. New systemic and institutional processes such as quality assurance have been introduced which also change traditional distributions of power and values within academe and may be a force for change in academic practice. The project will examine both the rhetoric and the realities of academics' responses to such managerial practices in higher education.

A number of views can be discerned about recent attempts at the management of change in higher education and the responses of academics to such changes. One view would see a victory of managerial values over professional ones with academics losing control over both the overall goals of their work practices and their technical tasks. Another view would see the survival of traditional academic values against the managerial approach. This does not imply that academic roles fail to change, but that change does not automatically mean that interests and values are weakened. A third view would see a 'marriage' between professionalism and managerialism with academics losing some control over the goals and social purposes of their work but retaining considerable autonomy over their practical and technical tasks. The desirability of these three different positions is also subject to a range of different views' (ibid., p. 11).

1.5 The Second Comparative Survey of the Academic Profession

In 2004, William Cummings, professor at George Washington University (Washington DC, USA), invited higher education researchers from various countries to collaborate in a new comparative study on the academic profession and to raise funds from their respective national sources. In the framework of five meetings held from 2004 to 2006 in Paris (France), London (United Kingdom), Stockholm (Sweden), Hiroshima (Japan) and Kassel (Germany), the state of research on the academic profession was carefully analysed, the conceptual base of the new project was developed, the methodological approach was specified and the questionnaire was formulated (see the documentation of the key contributions to the preparatory workshops in Research Institute for Higher Education, Hiroshima University 2006; Kogan and Teichler 2007a; Locke and Teichler 2007).

Scholars from 19 countries (more precisely, 18 countries and 1 territory) succeeded in raising funds to participate in the survey predominantly in the years 2007 and 2008. About half of them had participated in the Carnegie study and thus provided the basis for a sub-analysis of the extent to which the situation and the views of the academic profession had changed over time.

The major financial supporters for the CAP study have been in Argentina, Agencia National de Promoción de la Ciencia y la Tecnología (ANPYCT), Ministerio de la Ciencia y la Tecnología de la Nación as well as Programa de Promoción de la Universidad Argentina (PPUA), Secretaria de Políticas Universitarias, Ministerio de Educación; in Australia, Centre for Higher Education Management and Policy (CHEMP), University of New England as well as LH Martin Institute, University of Melbourne; in Brazil, Fundação de Amparo à Pesquisa do Estado de São Paulo (FAPESP); in Canada, Centre for Policy Studies in Higher Education and Training (CHET) and Faculty of Education, University of British Columbia as well as Ontario Research Chair in Postsecondary Education Policy and Measurement, University of Toronto; in China, Ford Foundation—China Office; in Finland: Ministry of Education and Culture; in Germany, Bundesministerium für Bildung und Forschung as well as International Centre for Higher Education Research, University of Kassel (INCHER-Kassel); in Hong Kong, Research Grants Council of the University Grants Committee, Hong Kong Special Administrative Region of the People's Republic of China; in Italy, Compagnia di San Paolo; in Japan, Japan Society for the Promotion of Science (JSPS); in Korea, National Research Foundation of Korea; in Malaysia, Department of Higher Education, Ministry of Higher Education Malaysia as well as Universiti Sains Malaysia; in Mexico, Universidad Autónoma de Baja California, Universidad Autónoma de Sinaloa, Fondo para la Consolidación de Universidades Públicas Estatales y con Apoya Solidario, Dirección General de Educación Superior, Secretaría de Educación Pública as well as Programa Intergral de Fortalecimiento Institucional; in the Netherlands, Dutch Ministry of Education, Culture and Science (Min. OC&W); in Norway: Research Council of Norway as well as Committee for Mainstreaming—Women in Science; in Portugal, Centro de

1.5 The Second Comparative Survey of the Academic Profession

Investigação de Políticas do Ensino Superior (CIPES); in South Africa, Ford Foundation; in the United Kingdom, Higher Education Funding Council for England (HEFCE), Universities UK, GuildHE, the Higher Education Academy as well as University and College Union; and in the United States of America, George Washington University and Seton Hall University.

The project 'The Changing Academic Profession (CAP)' has been coordinated by William Cummings. Major decisions were taken by a concepts commission chaired by John Brennan (Centre for Higher Education Research and Information of the Open University, located in London, United Kingdom) and by a methods commission chaired by Martin J. Finkelstein (Seton Hall University, South Orange, NJ, USA). The data coordination was undertaken by Ulrich Teichler (International Centre for Higher Education Research, University of Kassel, Kassel, Germany).

Team members wrote analyses on select themes on the occasion of about a dozen joint conferences held from 2007 to 2012 in Argentina, Australia, Canada, China, Finland, Germany, Italy, Japan, Mexico, Norway and the United States. Some results were published in conference proceedings (Research Institute for Higher Education, Hiroshima University 2008, 2009, 2010; Diversification of Higher Education and the Academic Profession 2010; Fernández Lamarra and Marquina 2012), and national studies of the academic profession in comparative perspective were published in some countries (Coates et al. 2009; Aarrevaara and Pekkola 2010; Bentley et al. 2010; Jacob and Teichler 2011; Rostan 2011; Cummings and Finkelstein 2012). The major results of the study, however, are expected to be published in comparative perspective from 2011 to 2013 in the book series 'The Changing Academy—The Changing Academic Profession in Comparative Perspective' published by Springer. The first two volumes of this type were published in 2011 and 2102 (Locke et al. 2011; Bentley et al. 2013). In addition to a general overview in this book, further volumes are envisaged on academic biographies and careers, job satisfaction and its determinants, the internationalisation of the academic profession, teaching and research as well as on the academic profession in emerging countries.

It might be added finally that the CAP study triggered two subsequent comparative studies on the academic profession. First, the coordinator of the German CAP study initiated a research consortium comprising a larger number of European countries. In the study 'The Academic Profession in Europe: Responses to Societal Change' (EUROAC), funded by the European Science Foundation (ESF) and national research promotion agencies, scholars from six additional European countries (Austria, Croatia, Ireland, Poland, Romania and Switzerland) undertook a questionnaire survey in 2010 which in most parts is identical to the CAP questionnaire. Through a merger of these data with those of the European countries of the CAP survey, a comparison can be undertaken of 12 European countries (cf. Kehm and Teichler 2013; Teichler and Höhle 2013). Second, the Japanese researchers involved in the CAP project invited scholars from other Asian countries in 2011 to join a new project on the academic profession in Asia.

The emergence of these new studies suggests that the comparative analysis of the academic profession does not remain anymore an only occasionally addressed theme of higher education research. Also, as the number of countries grows, the quality of systematic information on the academic professions tends to increase.

1.6 This Volume

This volume intends to provide an overview on the major findings of the CAP project. It covers more or less all themes addressed in the common questionnaire. Thus, a comprehensive presentation is put forward without in-depth discussion of the prior state of knowledge and without a detailed interpretation of the findings—tasks to be left to the thematic volumes.

Three authors have contributed to this volume—actually those members of the international research team who played major coordination roles: Akira Arimoto, William K. Cumming and Ulrich Teichler. Chapter 1 was written by all three authors, Chaps. 2 and 3 by William K. Cummings and Ulrich Teichler, Chap. 4 by Ulrich Teichler, Chap. 5 by Akira Arimoto and Chap. 6 by William K. Cummings.

The authors wish to express their gratitude for substantial editorial support to Ester Ava Höhle, Christiane Rittgerott and Dagmar Mann (all staff members of the International Centre for Higher Education Research, University of Kassel, Germany).

References

Aarrevaara, T., & Pekkola, E. (2010). *Muuttuva akateeminen profession suomessa – maaraportti* [The changing academic profession in Finland – national report]. Tampere: Tampere University Press.

Altbach, P. G. (1991). The academic profession. In P. G. Altbach (Ed.), *International higher education: An encyclopedia* (pp. 23–45). New York: Garland Publishing.

Altbach, P. G. (Ed.). (1996). *The international academic profession: Portraits of fourteen countries*. Princeton: Carnegie Foundation.

Altbach, P. G. (Ed.). (2000a). *The changing academic workplace: Comparative perspectives*. Boston: Boston College, Center for International Higher Education.

Altbach, P. G. (2000b). The deterioration of the academic estate: International patterns of academic work. In P. G. Altbach (Ed.), *The changing academic workplace: Comparative perspectives* (pp. 1–23). Boston: Boston College, Center for International Higher Education.

Altbach, P. G., & Lewis, L. S. (1996). The academic profession in international perspective. In P. G. Altbach (Ed.), *The international academic profession: Portraits of fourteen countries* (pp. 3–48). Princeton: Carnegie Foundation.

Arimoto, A. (Ed.). (2008). *Henbô suru nihon no daigakukyôjushoku* [The changing academic profession in Japan]. Tamagawa: Tamagawa University Press.

Arimoto, A., & Ehara, T. (Eds.). (1996). *Daigaku kyôjushoku no kokusai hikaku* [International comparison of the academic profession]. Tokyo: Tamagawa University Press.

Ben-David, J. (1977). *Centers of learning: Britain, France, Germany, United States*. New York: McGraw-Hill.

References

Bentley, P. J., Coates, H., Dobson, I. R., Goedegebuure, L., & Meek, V. L. (Eds.). (2013). *Job satisfaction of the academic profession*. Dordrecht: Springer.

Bentley, P., Kyvik, S., Vaboe, A., & Waagene, E. (2010). *Forskningsvilkar ved norske universiteter I et internasjonalt perspektiv* [Research conditions at Norwegian universities from a comparative perspective] (Rapport, 8/2010). Oslo: NIFU STEP.

Bowen, H., & Schuster, J. (1986). *American professors: A national resource imperiled*. New York: Oxford University Press.

Boyer, E. L. (1990). *Scholarship reconsidered: Priorities of the professoriate*. Princeton: Carnegie Foundation.

Boyer, E. L., Altbach, P. G., & Whitelaw, M. J. (1994). *The academic profession: An international perspective*. Princeton: Carnegie Foundation.

Brennan, J. (2007). The academic profession and increasing expectations of relevance. In M. Kogan & U. Teichler (Eds.), *Key challenges to the academic profession* (pp. 19–28). Kassel: International Centre for Higher Education Research Kassel.

Carnegie Foundation for the Advancement of Teaching. (1989). *The condition of the professoriate: Attitudes and trends: A technical report*. Princeton: Carnegie Foundation.

Clark, B. R. (Ed.). (1987). *The academic profession: National, disciplinary and institutional settings*. Berkeley/Los Angeles: University of California Press.

Coates, H. B., Dobson, I., Edwards, D., Friedman, T., Goedegebuure, L., & Meek, L. V. (2009). *The attractiveness of the Australian academic profession: A comparative analysis*. Melbourne: LH Martin Institute for Higher Education Leadership and Management, Educational Policy Institute & Australian Council for Educational Research.

Cummings, W. K. (2006). The third revolution of higher education: Becoming more relevant. In Research Institute for Higher Education, Hiroshima University (Ed.), *Reports of changing academic profession project workshop on quality, relevance and governance in the changing academia: International perspectives* (pp. 209–222). Hiroshima: RIHE.

Cummings, W. K., & Finkelstein, M. J. (2012). *Scholars in the changing American academy: New contexts, new rules and new roles*. Dordrecht: Springer.

Diversification of higher education and the academic profession (special issue). (2010). *European Review, 18* (Suppl. 1).

Enders, J. (Ed.). (2001a). *Academic staff in Europe: Changing contexts and conditions*. Westport/London: Greenwood Press.

Enders, J. (2001b). Between state control and academic capitalism: A comparative perspective on academic staff in Europe. In J. Enders (Ed.), *Academic staff in Europe: Changing contexts and conditions* (pp. 1–23). Westport/London: Greenwood Press.

Enders, J. (2006). The academic profession. In J. F. Forest & P. G. Altbach (Eds.), *International handbook of higher education* (pp. 1–21). Dordrecht: Springer.

Enders, J., & De Weert, E. (Eds.). (2004). *The international attractiveness of the academic workplace in Europe*. Frankfurt a.M: Gewerkschaft Erziehung und Wissenschaft.

Enders, J., & Teichler, U. (1995a). *Berufsbild der Lehrenden und Forschenden an Hochschulen* [The professional image of those teaching and undertaking research at institutions of higher education]. Bonn: Bundesministerium für Bildung, Wissenschaft, Forschung und Technologie.

Enders, J., & Teichler, U. (1995b). *Der Hochschullehrerberuf im internationalen Vergleich* [The academic profession in international comparison]. Bonn: Bundesministerium für Bildung, Wissenschaft, Forschung und Technologie.

Fernández Lamarra, N., & Marquina, M. (Eds.). (2012). *El futuro de la profesión académica* [The future of the academic profession]. Sáenz Pena: EDUNTREF.

Finkelstein, M. J. (1984). *The American academic profession: A synthesis of social scientific inquiry since World War II*. Columbus: Ohio State University Press.

Höhle, E. A., & Teichler, U. (2013). The academic profession in the light of comparative surveys. In B. M. Kehm & U. Teichler (Eds.), *The academic profession in Europe: New tasks and new challenges* (pp. 23–38). Dordrecht: Springer.

Jacob, A. K., & Teichler, U. (2011). *Der Wandel des Hochschullehrerberufs im internationalen Vergleich: Ergebnisse einer Befragung in den Jahren 2007/08* [Change of the academic profession in international comparison: Results of the survey of the years 2007-08]. Bonn/Berlin: Bundesministerium für Bildung und Forschung.

Kehm, B. M., & Teichler, U. (Eds.). (2013). *The academic profession in Europe: New tasks and new challenges*. Dordrecht: Springer.

Kogan, M., & Teichler, U. (Eds.). (2007a). *Key challenges to the academic profession* (Werkstattberichte, Vol. 65). Kassel: International Centre for Higher Education Research Kassel.

Kogan, M., & Teichler, U. (2007b). Key challenges of the academic profession and its interface with management: Some introductory thoughts. In M. Kogan & U. Teichler (Eds.), *Key challenges to the academic profession* (Werkstattberichte, Vol. 65, pp. 9–15). Kassel: International Centre for Higher Education Research Kassel.

Locke, W., & Teichler, U. (Eds.). (2007). *The changing conditions for academic work and careers in select countries* (Werkstattberichte, Vol. 66). Kassel: International Centre for Higher Education Research Kassel.

Locke, W., Cummings, W. K., & Fisher, D. (Eds.). (2011). *Changing governance and management in higher education*. Dordrecht: Springer.

Maassen, F. A. M., & van Vught, F. A. (Eds.). (1996). *Inside academia: New challenges of the academic profession*. Utrecht: De Tijdstroom.

Morey, A. (1992). Introduction: Faculty and students: teaching, learning and research. In B. R. Clark & G. Neave (Eds.), *The encyclopedia of higher education* (pp. 1515–1535). Oxford: Pergamon Press.

Perkin, H. (1969). *Key profession: A history of the Association of University Teachers*. London: Routledge/Palmer.

Perkin, H. (1991). History of universities. In P. G. Altbach (Ed.), *International higher education: An encyclopedia* (pp. 169–204). New York: Garland Publishing.

Research Institute for Higher Education, Hiroshima University (Ed.). (2006). *Reports of changing academic profession project workshop on quality, relevance and governance in the changing academia: International perspectives* (COE Publication Series, Vol. 20). Hiroshima: RIHE.

Research Institute for Higher Education, Hiroshima University (Ed.). (2008). *The changing academic profession in international comparative and quantitative perspectives* (RIHE International Seminar Reports, Vol. 12). Hiroshima: RIHE.

Research Institute for Higher Education, Hiroshima University (Ed.). (2009). *The changing academic profession over 1992–2007: International, comparative and quantitative perspectives* (RIHE International Seminar Reports, Vol. 13). Hiroshima: RIHE.

Research Institute for Higher Education, Hiroshima University (Ed.). (2010). *The changing academic profession in international comparative and quantitative perspectives: A focus on teaching & research activities* (RIHE International Seminar Reports, Vol. 15). Hiroshima: RIHE.

Rostan, M. (Ed.). (2011). *La professione academica in Italia: Aspetti, problemi e confronti nel contesto europeo* [The academic profession in Italy: Aspects, problems and comparisons within the European context]. Milano: Edizione Universitarie di Lettere Economia Diritto.

Rüegg, W. (Ed.). (2011). *A history of the university in Europe. Vol. IV: Universities since 1945*. Cambridge: Cambridge University Press.

Sadlak, J., & Liu, N. C. (Eds.). (2007). *The world-class university and rankings: Aiming beyond status*. Bucharest/Cluj-Napoca: UNESCO-CEPES/Presa Universitara Clujeana.

Schuster, J., & Finkelstein, M. (2006). *The American faculty: The restructuring of academic work and careers*. Baltimore: John Hopkins University Press.

Shils, E. (1991). Academic freedom. In P. G. Altbach (Ed.), *International higher education: An encyclopedia* (pp. 1–22). New York: Garland Publishing.

Shin, J. C., Toutkoushian, R. K., & Teichler, U. (Eds.). (2011). *University rankings: Theoretical basis, methodology and impacts on global higher education*. Dordrecht: Springer.

Teichler, U. (1996). The conditions of the academic profession: An international, comparative analysis of the academic profession in Western Europe, Japan and the USA. In P. A. M. Maassen

& F. A. van Vught (Eds.), *Inside academia: New challenges of the academic profession* (pp. 15–65). Utrecht: De Tijdstroom.

Teichler, U. (Ed.). (2006). *The formative years of scholars*. London: Portland Press.

Teichler, U., & Höhle, E. A. (Eds.). (2013). *The work situation, views and activities of the academic profession: Findings of a survey in twelve European countries*. Dordrecht: Springer.

The academic profession (special issue). (1983). *European Journal of Education, 18*(3).

Trow, M. (1974). Problems in the transition from elite to mass higher education. In OECD (Ed.), *Policies for higher education* (pp. 51–101). Paris: OECD.

Trow, M. (2006). Reflections on the transition from elite to mass to universal access. Forms and phases of higher education in modern societies since WW II. In J.J.F. Forest & P. G. Altbach (Eds.), *International Handbook on Higher Education* (pp. 243–280). Dordrecht: Springer.

Welch, A. R. (Ed.). (1997). Special issue on the academic profession. *Higher Education, 34*(1), 299–419.

Welch, A. R. (2005a). Challenge and change: The academic profession in uncertain times. In A. R. Welch (Ed.), *The professoriate: Profile of a profession* (pp. 1–19). Dordrecht: Springer.

Welch, A. R. (Ed.). (2005b). *The professoriate: Profile of a profession*. Dordrecht: Springer.

Whitelaw, M. J. (1996). The international survey of the academic profession 1991–1993: Methodological notes. In P. G. Altbach (Ed.), *The international academic profession: Portraits of fourteen countries* (pp. 669–677). Princeton: Carnegie Foundation.

Chapter 2
The Design and Methods of the Comparative Study

2.1 Introduction

The research project 'The Changing Academic Profession' was a collective effort of scholars from 19 countries (or more precisely from 18 countries and the 'special administrative region' of Hong Kong; for reason of simplification, we will refer to 'countries' in the subsequent text). The participating scholars had to cope with a conflicting situation. On the one hand, they intended to undertake a joint questionnaire that required a high degree of consensus or at least a readiness for compromise in order to develop a largely identical questionnaire for all countries. On the other hand, they wanted to reflect the specific issues of the academic profession in their own country, and they had to do this among others, because they had to raise the necessary funds for the national component of the project within their own country. Therefore, this project required a substantial period of careful preparation where choices had to be made as regards the target group, the conceptual framework and the themes of the questionnaire as well as many operational issues, and additionally many decisions in these domains had to be added in the course of the project work.

The conceptual and thematic choices have been discussed thoroughly in the introductory chapter. Therefore, only the key conceptual and thematic choices will be outlined in this chapter.

It should be pointed out that an international project with decentralised responsibilities requires central coordination as regards the formulation of the joint questionnaire, the sampling and surveying approaches and eventually the creation of a joint data set. Therefore, the scholars involved in the CAP project established a methods commission chaired by Martin J. Finkelstein (Seton Hall University, South Orange, NJ, USA) and including Elizabeth Balbechevsky (University of Sao Paulo, Brazil), Hamish Coates (Australian Council for Educational Research, Australia), Tsukasa Daizen (Hiroshima University, Japan), Jesus Galaz-Fontez (Autonomous University of Baja-California, Mexico), Amy Metcalfe (University of British Columbia, Canada) and Michele Rostan (University of Pavia, Italy). The methods commission consulted all national teams repeatedly and eventually took the final decisions as regards all key issues of the formulation of the international master questionnaire, the setting for standards for the survey process and the rules for the establishment of the international data set. The establishment of the international data set was undertaken by a data team coordinated by Ulrich Teichler (International Centre for Higher Education Research, University of Kassel—INCHER-Kassel—in Germany).

2.2 The Target Group

2.2.1 *Countries*

The initiators of the CAP project aimed similarly as those of the first comparative survey on the academic profession, that is, the Carnegie study, to include countries from all over the world; they wanted to include countries where concepts of higher education had emerged in the past which had been internationally influential; they wanted also to include all of the very large countries in the world. Last but not least, they intended to include as many countries as possible that had participated in the Carnegie survey in order to measure change over time by comparing the results of the two studies. Efforts were made to identify scholars willing and suitable to be active in such a comparative study, and the final number of countries eventually depended on these scholars' success in raising the necessary funds within their respective countries.

Eventually, ten countries were represented in the CAP which had been covered already in the Carnegie survey (in alphabetical order): Australia, Brazil, Germany, Hong Kong, Japan, the Republic of Korea, Mexico, the Netherlands, the United Kingdom and the United States of America. While four countries participating in the Carnegie study eventually are not represented in the CAP study (Chile, Israel, Russia and Sweden), nine countries were newly incorporated into the CAP study: Argentina, Canada, China, Finland, Italy, Malaysia, Norway, Portugal and South Africa. Thus, the CAP study comprised altogether 19 higher education systems: 18 countries and the special administrative region of Hong Kong.

It should be added that scholars from some additional countries were involved in the preparation of the CAP project but eventually did not get the necessary financial means for participation, for example, France, India and Russia.

The 19 higher education systems might be grouped according to various dimensions, for example, continent, higher education philosophy or extent of expansion of higher education (e.g. enrolment rate). In various analyses of the data, the authors of the CAP teams, in fact, chose different classifications. However, the CAP team recommended differentiating at least between the 13 'mature higher education systems' (sometimes also called 'advanced' in the various publications of the project) and the 6 'emerging higher education systems', the latter being Argentina, Brazil, China, Malaysia, Mexico and South Africa. The distinction was primarily made between the former being high-income countries and being in principle self-sustainable in research training and the latter being middle-income countries where large numbers of scholars are trained for the academic career abroad.

2.2.2 Institutions

As academics' addresses had to be collected in most countries with the help of institutions of higher education, an institutional target group (rather than a programme target group or a functional target group) had to be defined. Academics who are professionally active at higher education institutions that offer a baccalaureate degree (Tertiary Type A according to the OECD classification or Level 5A of the UNESCO ISCED-97 classification) or any higher credential became the target population. Thus, the CAP survey, in contacting potential respondents through institutions, might include some institutions that provide both bachelor programmes and other shorter or vocationally tertiary education programmes, but those tertiary education institutions were excluded that only offered short or vocationally oriented tertiary education (Tertiary Type B or ISCED Level 5b) programmes, for example, junior and community colleges in various countries and kôtô senmon gakkô in Japan. Excluded as well were public research institutes without a teaching function (e.g. Max Planck institutes in Germany). Some countries (e.g. Argentina) excluded private institutions of higher education, if overall they played a marginal role within the system.

Some countries, indeed, included junior colleges, and others included public research institutes. In those cases, the respondents from these institutions were not incorporated into the international CAP data set.

2.2.3 The Academic Profession

The target population of the CAP study are persons employed full-time or at least a substantial part of their work time at an institution of higher education for teaching and/or research purposes. Through this definition, two types of persons were excluded in principle that might not be consistently distinguished: auxiliary staff (e.g. teaching assistants in US terms, *wissenschaftliche Hilfskräfte* in German terms) and staff primarily active in management and service functions.

The practices varied as regards addressing persons not employed full-time. In the beginning, the researchers of the various countries agreed to include full-time employed academics as well as part-time employed academics if they are regular employees and are paid to serve at least half of the regular work time. In practice, however, two countries included only full-time academics. Various others aimed to address full-time academics but did not exclude a minority from the data set who happened to be employed part-time. Other countries deliberately targeted part-time employed academics as well as full-time as long as the part-timers were employed at least half-time. Finally, two Latin American countries included also academics employed or working on honorarium basis for less than half-time, if they were obvious members of the academic profession, for example, professionals in law or medicine who were hired to serve a regular professorship.

In the analysis of the data, three *subgroups of respondents* played an important role. First, as already pointed out, countries were grouped into *mature versus emerging higher education systems*.

Second, academics were divided according to type of *higher education institutions*. The term 'university' in this comparative study refers to institutions that are more or less equally in charge of teaching and research, while 'other higher education institutions' are those with a dominant teaching function. These terms were viewed as the most suitable brief formulations to underscore the different functional portfolios of the varying institutions which are often similarly reflected in the tasks of their academic staff, even though some institutions with a clearly dominant teaching function might also be called 'university' in some countries (e.g. in China, Japan and Korea) and even though some institutions with both major teaching and research tasks might not be named 'university' (e.g. institute of technology, *Technische Hochschule*).

Third, the respondents were classified as *senior versus junior academics*. Senior academics were named those respondents who were employed in staff categories equivalent to full professors and associate professors in the United States of America. All other academics were classified as junior academics. Actually, the borderline between senior academics and junior academics cannot be drawn clearly in all of the countries participating in the CAP project.

2.3 Conceptual Framework and Themes Addressed

The underlying concepts and thematic areas have been already discussed in the introductory chapters. Therefore, some issues can be briefly sketched here, while others need further explanations. The scholars involved in the preparation of the comparative study agreed to raise six major research questions:

1. To what extent are the nature of academic work and the trajectory of academic careers *changing*?
2. What are the external and internal *drivers* of these changes?
3. To what extent do changes *differ between countries and types of higher education institutions*?
4. How have the *academic professions responded*—attitudinally and behaviourally—to changes in their external and internal environment?
5. What are the *consequences* of the changes and faculty responses to them *for the attractiveness of an academic career*?
6. What are the *consequences for the capacity of academics*—and their universities—to contribute *to the further development of knowledge societies and the attainment of national goals*?

2.3 Conceptual Framework and Themes Addressed

The choice of themes has been influenced by the preceding Carnegie study undertaken in the early 1990s. Notably questions regarding career and employment as well as a few regarding teaching were repeated to provide the opportunity to measure change over time. However, most of the questions of the CAP questionnaire were newly formulated—in part in order to improve the formulations but mostly in order to take up new themes considered important in the light of the priorities of the project and the changing situation of the academic profession.

The emphasis on 'change' in the title of the CAP project affected the formulation of the questionnaire and the analysis and interpretation of findings in different ways. First, *three thematic areas* were chosen *that have become more prominent and pervasive in recent years* in setting conditions for academic work and possibly characterising academic work itself:

- The growing expectation or pressure to demonstrate the visible *relevance* of academic work
- The increasing *internationalisation* (and possibly globalisation or regionalization) of the context and possibly the essence of academic work
- The growing *managerial power* and steering in higher education

Second, ways were chosen of measuring change over time with the help of *identical or similar questions to those posed in the predecessor questionnaire*. This can be interpreted clearly historically; for example, one could try to establish whether young researchers have more responsible roles in research vis-à-vis professors these days than the previous generation of young researchers. Or this can be interpreted as biographic and historical interaction: Did the proportion of women being junior academics of the early 1990s succeed to be promoted to senior academics in about the same proportion today, or is the proportion of senior academics today clearly lower than that of junior academics a generation ago, thus confirming concepts such as the 'glass ceiling'?

Third, *perceptions of change* were explicitly addressed. Respondents were asked whether they have observed change in some respect—since a few years, since the start of their academic career, etc.: Actually only a few questions of this kind were posed because such views might be biased retrospective judgments. Moreover, even if not retrospectively biased, a report about increased resources for academic work might only mirror the increasing success of an individual in the course of his or her career possibly effected by seniority but might not be valid for indicating whether resources for academic work have grown on average in the respective country.

As a rule, identical questions for all countries were preferred. Specific questions were posed in the individual country questionnaires for two reasons:

- First, national specifications are needed in various cases, for example, types of educational institutions and staff categories.
- Second, some of the individual country questionnaires were supplemented by themes to be of special interest within the conceptual framework of the respective scholars or as specific higher education issues within the respective countries.

In principle, the teams of the individual countries participating in the CAP were *free to delete some questions or items in the national questionnaires*, if they were viewed as irrelevant, regulated for everybody, sensitive or otherwise disturbing. Actually, very few of the common questions and items were deleted in national versions of the master questionnaire. Thus, the international CAP project team succeeded in agreeing to a highly standardised questionnaire with 53 identical or similar questions—mostly with response categories provided—with about 400 variables. The time needed to respond was estimated to be about 40–50 min. at the outset, whereby the actual time certainly was spread more widely.

2.4 Sampling Design and Number of Respondents

The sampling design for the respective national CAP surveys was recommended by the CAP Methods Group based on a proposal prepared by the CAP project coordinator William K. Cummings. Actually, the sampling design was shaped by three factors: the analytic goals of the project, the design effect of the sampling design selected by each country and the structure of higher education in each country.

2.4.1 Analytic Goals

Early on, the project decided on an *effective completed sample of 800 for each participating country*. For inferring population characteristics from sample data, a certain minimum completed sample size is necessary to attain respectable confidence intervals. To obtain decent confidence intervals for a descriptive proportion such as the proportion of a population that agree on some issue, a completed sample size of circa 300 is helpful. To cross-tabulate the first variable with a second and get good confidence intervals, we need to nearly double the sample size. To bring in a third level of analysis, further expansion is required. It was in this manner that the project decided on an effective completed sample size of 800—it will easily enable statistically significant analysis up to the third level of analysis. The figure 800 is for the actual number who respond and not for the number sampled.

Our expectation was that respondents in each nation would be representative of the population of academic staff. Thus, the goal in CAP sampling was to obtain a completed effective sample of 800.

2.4.2 Design Effect (Deff Coefficient)

The project explored a number of sampling designs, including *simple random sampling*, where each respondent in the population has an equal probability of being included; *stratified sampling,* wherein the population is broken into subgroups, but

2.4 Sampling Design and Number of Respondents   31

the sampling ratios in the subgroups are equal; *stratification with unequal sampling ratios between groups* to oversample small subgroups who might be marginalised if sampling ratios were equal; and *cluster sampling* wherein several units (A) from the population of units are first selected, and then within each unit, a certain number of individuals are selected (B).

2.4.3 Structure of Higher Education

The overall project sought to adjust sampling design to the structure of the individual national systems of higher education, ranging from small and relatively homogeneous systems to those which are larger and more diverse in terms of institutional types. It adopted the following basic sampling principles:

In countries, where there are relatively few institutions (50 or less) and they are somewhat similar, the best approach was seen to develop a list of all academics in the institutions and randomly sample the target sample of 1,800 academics (600 * 1/.33 or the response rate ratio).

Where there are *many institutions* and they are similar, a one- or two-stage cluster sample was recommended: In the one-stage sample, a moderate number of institutions were to be selected (perhaps 20), and then all of the academics in those institutions were selected. Because of the cluster sample design, a multiple of 600 academics would need to be selected (Deff (=3 plus) * 600) or somewhere upwards of 1,800 academics. In the two-stage sample, a larger number of institutions were randomly selected (A = 50 plus), and then within each of these, a relatively small samples of academics (B = circa 12–15) are randomly selected so that A * B = Deff * 600 or approximately 1,800. Further steps had to be taken into consideration if the higher education system of a particular country was considered to be more heterogeneous.

As already pointed out in the first case, the sample had to be based on an estimate of the response rate. For example, if 800 responses are desirable and a response rate of one-third could be expected, one had to sample at least 2,400, or similarly, if 1,800 responses were strived for and if a *response rate* of one quarter could be expected, one had to sample at least 7,200.

The scholars in the individual countries opted for *different strategies in sending the questionnaires*. Some mailed questionnaires only, and some sent the questionnaires through mail and online. In three countries (Canada, Korea and the USA), the questionnaires were available only online. In South Africa, student assistants at each participating universities distributed the questionnaires to the individual academics' offices; also in Mexico, the questionnaires were 'delivered by hand'.

The questionnaires were sent to some 100,000 academics selected in the various countries in 2007–2008 and only in the Netherlands in 2010. The number of *reminder actions* varied by country (e.g. two in Germany, three in Canada and five in the USA). Eventually, 25,819 valid responses were received, that is, from respondents fitting to the target groups, whereby the questionnaire was sufficiently complete to be used in the subsequent analysis.

Table 2.1 Survey 'The Changing Academic Profession': number of respondents (weighted cases) by status and institutional type

	Universities		Other HEIs		
	Seniors	Juniors	Seniors	Juniors	Total
Argentina	105	810	–	–	915
Australia	200	669	76	286	1,377
Brazil	364	186	311	274	1,147
Canada	743	416	–	–	1,159
China	1,309	1,697	204	375	3,640
Finland	208	810	74	232	1,374
Germany	152	888	91	41	1,215
Hong Kong	191	377	–	–	586
Italy	1,061	645	–	–	1,711
Japan	189	45	701	187	1,126
Korea, Republic of	127	37	503	243	909
Malaysia	262	650	45	176	1,219
Mexico	556	121	861	310	1,973
Netherlands	208	208	394	400	1,209
Norway	391	509	31	34	986
Portugal	102	431	51	766	1,510
South Africa	421	176	3	3	749
United Kingdom	288	612	7	32	1,369
United States	424	420	144	121	1,109
Total	7,301	9,707	3,496	3,480	25,282

After a *process of weighting* the respondents by institutional type, and academics' rank and gender in order to counterbalance biases in the composition of the data as compared to the composition of the academic staff in the respective countries, a final data set with 25,282 weighted cases was created. Table 2.1 provides an overview regarding the number of responses according to the final data set.

In almost all countries, the desired minimum number of 800 respondents has been reached. In a few countries, in contrast, the number of the responses surpassed clearly the approximate number strived for. Notably, more academics than anticipated responded in China.

The *response rates* cannot be established precisely for all countries as a consequence of complex procedures of contacting potential respondents. In some cases, the questionnaires were sent out by the individual institutions of higher education, and no detailed respective information was provided. In some countries, it is not clear whether the number of responses refer to all responses or to those responding to major parts of the questionnaire. Actually:

– Extremely high response rates are reported for China (86%) and Mexico (70%) and possibly a non-reported high rate in South Africa where questionnaires have been carried from office to office.
– Response rates above 30% are stated for Norway (36%), Italy (35%), Argentina (34%) and Germany (32%).

- Response rates between 20 and 30% are most frequent: Finland and Malaysia (28% each), Netherlands (26%), Brazil (25%), Australia (24%), Japan (23%) and USA (21%).
- Response rates below 20% (in several cases online survey only): Canada (17%), United Kingdom (15%), Hong Kong and Korea (13%) and Portugal (4%).

It should be noted that the response rates have been about 40% on average in the Carnegie survey, thereby varying between 70% and almost 30%. In the CAP survey, the response rates have been around 30% on average, and they are lower in almost all countries that already participated in the Carnegie study. The only exception is Germany, where the response rate was exceptionally low in 1992 (28%) and a moderate increase can be observed in 2007 (32%). Altogether, increasing survey fatigue, lower participation rates in online surveys as well as incomplete response in online surveys have contributed to an overall decline of the response rates. However, there are no indications that the decline of the response rate has led to an enlarged sample bias, and as pointed out below, major biases according to various criteria can be counterbalanced by a weighing of responses.

2.5 Data Coding and Analysis

The project teams of the individual countries were responsible for the data entry and for the first step of data cleaning. Subsequently, the data were transferred to a central team of CAP data coordinators—Oliver Bracht, René Kooij and Florian Löwenstein, with advisory support by Harald Schomburg und Ulrich Teichler—at the International Centre for Higher Education Research (INCHER-Kassel) of the University of Kassel in Germany.

In order to have an information basis for a compatible handling of the data gathering of the various countries, the Methods Group and the central data coordinators—under the leadership of Hamish Coates—developed a '*national survey audit schedule*' asking the individual country teams to provide detailed information on various procedural steps they had undertaken, notably:

- Whether more than a single version of a questionnaire was employed and, if so, how they varied
- In which respects the national questionnaire differs from the international CAP master questionnaire
- What procedure had been undertaken in the translation of the questionnaire from the English master version to other versions and whether any problems occurred which affected the international comparability of results
- Whether they had employed paper and/or online surveying
- How the academic profession as well as the higher education institutions were defined for inclusion into the survey (respectively, what was excluded)
- How the sampling design and the actual sampling procedure compared
- When the survey has been undertaken

- How the potential respondents have been approached
- How many follow-ups have been undertaken
- How many persons have been addressed and actually have responded
- What procedures have been undertaken and what decisions have been made regarding completeness of answers, unexpected data errors, etc.
- What the characteristics of the national data set are that might have to be taken into consideration in the production of a central data set

Initially, the central data team established an *international codebook*. This was necessary to ensure the compatibility of data entry in the individual countries. Moreover, it served the accommodation of the country-specific categories (e.g. ranks of academic staff and types of higher institutions) in the international data set. In order to ensure comparability of the various data files, a number of further coding modifications had to be undertaken, because some countries have opted for additions, modifications or deletions of individual questions and items.

Subsequently, the central data team at INCHER-Kassel undertook—with advice of the CAP Methods Group—various steps of further *data cleaning*. In the first stage, it developed a detailed list of questions according to which the individual country teams were asked to prepare reports about the survey procedures as well as about the data quality. In subsequent steps, the country teams were asked to answer specific questions as regards visible problems of the national data set, for example, perceived incongruities or large amounts of apparently missing data. In this process, new questions and incongruities surfaced, and various steps of inquiries, new definitions of codes, new productions of data sets, etc. turned out to be necessary. Moreover, a set of decisions had to be taken as regards the handling of missing data. Finally, a country was incorporated in the data set where the survey could be undertaken only 3 years later. As a consequence, the whole process from the first steps of data entry towards the final data set stretched from spring 2008 to the release of the final data set in September 2011.

As part of the overall process of international data coordination, *sample weights* were made. The central data team at INCHER-Kassel team solicited basic population data from the individual countries on the national distribution of the academic profession by institutional type, academic field, gender and academic rank (professor, etc.). These were used to weight the actual sample values to reflect the basic population parameters across all participating countries.

All CAP country teams were given access to the international data set, and—in order to facilitate the further analytical work—sets of standard frequency tables were provided. Thus, each team could undertake comparative analyses from the outset. The process of writing analyses, presenting them at conferences and publishing the results already started in 2008. Readers of the publications have to bear in mind that the early reports still might be based on data sets that slightly deviate from the final data set made available in September 2011.

In the course of the project, various new indices and other scores were created by the members of the CAP team. In some instances, they were provided as part of the central data set, for example, 'international activities', 'international mobility status', 'varied teaching activities' and 'publication index'. In other instances, they were produced and used by individual national CAP teams.

2.6 Utilisation of Data

The project 'The Changing Academic Profession' is a federated project. The various national teams, in principle, are the 'owners' of the national data. They volunteered to make the data available to their colleagues of the CAP teams in the other countries in order to produce an international data set. This enables the national team from the outset to analyse their national data in comparative perspective. Moreover, this provided the basis to undertake comparative analyses jointly.

In the same spirit, the team members have been responsible themselves for the use of data within the publications and other reports. A glance at the first more than 100 articles published based on the CAP data suggests, first, that the use of provisional data sets in the first few years, before the final data has been produced in September 2011, has led to some, though altogether moderate, inconsistencies between the publications. Second, analyses vary substantially to the extent they provide information only on all respondents of each country participating or they differentiate between status groups, types of higher education institutions and possibly other characteristics.

Finally, it is worth noting that the first analyses are rich in demonstrating similarities across countries and differences between countries but often do not succeed in discussing the national contexts and characteristics of higher education which might explain the findings. In sum, we might argue that collaboration in the CAP project succeeded well for creating a good quality of a data set. It turns out to be more difficult to cover the issues of the academic profession in the individual countries well with the help of a common international questionnaire and to provide sufficient information about each country in order to interpret the findings comparatively in a well-informed way.

Chapter 3
The Variety of Countries Participating in the Comparative Study

3.1 Introduction

In talking about 'higher education systems', we tend to refer to macro-societal entities of higher education that are embedded in nations. Higher education is viewed as being both global and international as well as national and even local (see Kerr 1990). On the one hand, higher education is international or global in many respects, such as in the belief that there are more or less common standards of truth, ways of academic reasoning, appropriateness of methodology and quality of academic work. Systematic knowledge is considered to be universal and valuable across borders, even if it is not universal. Maturation to a high level of academic work is generally viewed as a long process which requires many formative years characterised by concurrent learning and productive work. Teaching in academia is expected to lay the foundation for the subsequent productive work of graduates by both enhancing generic competencies of academic knowledge and reasoning and fostering scepticism and critical thinking. A certain degree of 'academic freedom' and loose coordination is viewed as essential for the stimulation of creative academic work.

On the other hand, curricula and examinations, careers of academics and modes of governance vary across countries. In many countries, these issues are nationally determined through regulatory and funding powers, but even if those powers are decentralised within countries, as is the case in Brazil, Canada, Mexico, Germany, the USA and to a certain extent as well in Australia (see Martinez Cortés and Teichler 2010) among the countries participating in this study, they have so many common elements that it seems justified to consider higher education as a 'system' for the whole country. Therefore, the CAP study only comprises the special administrative

---

With contributions by Timo Aarrevaara, Norzaini Azman, Elizabeth Balbachevsky, John Brennan, Egbert De Weert, Ian Dobson, Futao Huang, Mónica Marquina, Amy S. Metcalfe, Gerald Postiglione, Michele Rostan, Rui Santiago, Hong Shen, Jung Sheol Shin, and Agnete Vabø

unit of Hong Kong along 18 countries as a single exception—a 'system' which is legally not an independent country but has characteristics which are clearly apart from those in most of the areas of the respective country (i.e. China).

A comparison of the academic profession across many countries, first, helps to highlight the common characteristics across countries. We note the extent to which there is a single academic profession worldwide. Second, an account of international variety is a 'gold mine' for understanding the academic profession in various respects: Differences suggest us not to overestimate but rather to relativise common conditions and features thus to see the specific features of each case, but it also shows that there are opportunities for different options and thus broaden understanding for potential directions of reform in each country (see the discussion of comparative higher education research in Teichler 1996).

The study 'The Changing Academic Profession' comprises an enormous variety of countries. While it cannot be viewed as representative of the 200 countries in the world, the initiators of the study tried to get as many countries involved as possible and especially to include those countries that participated in the predecessor study, the Carnegie study. Thus, it took up the rationales of the previous study to have many large countries involved and countries which had an international influence as roles models. On the other hand, low-income countries were not able to join. Finally, particular factors have come into play, namely, the competence and readiness of researchers to participate and funds made available for undertaking the study. This notwithstanding, a remarkably broad range of characteristics of national higher education all over the world are represented in the CAP study.

In order to ensure that the variety of cases is really helpful for understanding common features and potential challenges faced by the participating systems, background information is required about the academic profession, the higher education systems and possibly their cultural and socio-economic context. Therefore, efforts have been made to provide such information to the colleagues in the countries participating in the CAP study as well as for the readers of the results. Notably, preparatory conferences have played a major role in information gathering and reasoning. Also, scholars from different countries collaborated in the analysis of findings and, thus, made their colleagues constantly aware of the need to enhance the comparative understanding of the individual countries.

First, the national higher education systems will be described with the help of *quantitative indicators*. This overview draws from a previous publication where the concepts and the methods are explained (Cummings 2008). Such an overview is important, because it shows the enormous variety of the countries involved and indicates the conditions under which the academic profession in each country operates. As will be shown, for example, the enrolment rates of students of the respective age group in tertiary education varied in 2005 between more than three-quarters on the one hand and less than one-quarter on the other hand. Or to take another example, the expenditures for research and development as a per cent of the gross domestic product (GDP) in 2002 ranged from more than 3 percent to less than half a per cent.

Second, participants in the CAP project are convinced that major parts of the information needed for the comparative analysis are not available and cannot be appropriately presented in the form of such indicators. If the comparison relied only on quantitative indicators, one would miss many features salient to understanding the characteristics of individual countries. Therefore, the introductory sections to thematic national reports on the academic profession (see e.g. RIHE 2006) as well as national reports based on survey findings tend to focus on the context (see e.g. Locke et al. 2011).

This chapter does not intend to describe the higher education systems of the countries participating in the CAP study according to a common thematic framework; rather, it documents specific highlights which the team members of each country have underscored in these respective texts or have contributed directly to the subsequent text.

3.2 Indicators on Economy, Labour Market and Technology

Indicators on the economy, labour market and technology of countries tend to be viewed as important for higher education on the one hand in order to illustrate the potentials of countries to contribute to a well-funded and possibly high-quality higher education system. On the other hand, higher education is generally seen as an area of investment to stimulate economic growth, societal well-being and technological development.

Table 3.1 provides an overview on the *gross domestic product (GDP) per capita*, that is, the most widely used measure of economic wealth. Data are provided on the years 1980 and 2005 as well as the average annual growth during this period.

Table 3.1 GDP per capita in selected countries, 1980 and 2005 (US $, price level of 2000)

Country	1980	2005	Annual growth (%)
Argentina	7,550	8,094	0.3
Australia	14,194	23,039	2.0
Brazil	3,256	3,596	0.4
Canada	16,598	25,064	1.7
China	186	1,448	8.5
Hong Kong, China	11,522	29,944	3.9
Finland	15,566	25,712	2.0
Germany	15,701	23,905	1.7
Italy	13,094	19,329	1.6
Japan	23,916	39,075	2.0
Korea[a]	3,358	13,801	5.8
Malaysia	1,848	4,436	3.6
Mexico	5,114	6,172	0.8
Netherlands	16,436	24,696	1.6
Norway	22,257	39,968	2.4
Portugal	6,300	11,023	2.3
South Africa	3,463	3,405	−0.1
United Kingdom	15,482	26,890	2.2
United States	22,567	37,267	2.0

Source: Adapted from Cummings (2008)
[a]1985

Table 3.2 Employment in agriculture and service sectors in selected countries, 1980 and 2005 (per cent of total employment)

Country	Agriculture		Service	
	1980	2005	1980	2005
Argentina	.	1.1	.	75.1
Australia	6.5	3.6	62.4	75.0
Brazil	.	.	.	57.9
Canada	5.4	2.7	66.0	75.3
China	68.7	.	11.7	.
Hong Kong, China	1.4	0.3	48.4	84.6
Finland	13.3	4.8	52.2	69.4
Germany	.	2.4	.	67.8
Italy	14.0	4.2	48.7	65.1
Japan	10.4	4.4	54.0	66.4
Korea[a]	16.2	3.3	47.3	59.0
Malaysia	37.2	.	38.7	71.0
Mexico	26.0	15.1	24.1	58.6
Netherlands	.	3.0	.	72.9
Norway	8.3	3.3	62.3	75.9
Portugal	27.3	.	36.1	.
South Africa	.	.	.	.
United Kingdom	2.6	1.4	58.9	76.3
United States	3.6	1.6	65.7	77.8

Source: Adapted from Cummings (2008)
[a]1985
· No information available

In 2005, the highest GDP per capita is reported for Norway, Japan and the United States—close to 40,000 US$ each. On the other hand, the GDP per capita was below 5,000 US$ in South Africa, Brazil and Malaysia at that time and below 2,000 US$ in China. As the growth rate of most of the CAP countries with below average GDP per capita has been relatively high in recent years, one might expect a trend towards a smaller variation in economic wealth.

Along with economic growth, *employment in agriculture* has declined and *employment in services* has grown. Table 3.2 shows the proportion of total employment being active in agriculture as well as in services both in 1980 and in 2005.

Accordingly, more than 70% of all persons employed work in the service sector in about half of the economically advanced countries participating in the CAP study. The same holds true for Argentina and Malaysia among the emerging countries. Data presented in Table 3.2 is not complete on 1980. As far as information is available on both points in time, growth in the service sector has been most pronounced in Mexico.

Higher education is expected to contribute to technological innovation. Table 3.3 shows the *proportion of all manufacturing sales* in 1995 and 2003 of the countries included here that are *high technology*. It was highest in the United States and in Finland in 2003 among the advanced countries participating in the CAP study and in Malaysia among the emerging countries. Whereas in some countries this proportion hardly changed during the period observed, we note more than a doubling in the United States, China and Finland.

Table 3.3 Percentage of all manufacturing sales that are high technology in selected countries, 1995 and 2003

Country	1995	2003
Argentina	4.1	5.1
Brazil	18.8	17.7
Canada	10.3	9.8
China	7.1	19.0
Hong Kong, China	22.7	19.8
Finland	11.8	29.0
Germany	9.4	11.7
Italy	8.7	9.0
Japan	15.6	15.7
Malaysia	26.7	32.2
Mexico	9.3	12.7
Netherlands	9.1	6.6
Portugal	7.0	8.9
South Africa	4.2	3.3
United Kingdom	14.6	16.3
United States	12.7	34.2

Source: Adapted from Cummings (2008)

3.3 Indicators on Educational and Research Expenditures

International statistics on education expenditures are not viewed as highly reliable because national definitions and modes of gathering vary substantially. Yet, Table 3.4 might be useful to provide some approximations.

Public and private expenditures on education make up almost 6% of gross national product on average in the countries participating in the CAP study for which respective information is available, whereby the figures vary substantially by country. A rate of about 8% is reported for Malaysia and of about 7% for the United States and Norway. In contrast, rates below 5% hold true for about one-quarter of the countries for which information is provided.

The average rate of *expenditures for R&D* (including varying proportions for research at higher education institutions) reported in Table 3.4 is 1.7% of GDP. Striking differences can be observed between Finland (3.5%) as well as the United States (2.7%) and Germany (2.5%) on the one hand and Argentina and Mexico (0.4% each) on the other hand.

Finally, Table 3.4 informs about the *expenditures per student in tertiary education*—US$ adjusted for purchasing power. These data are often challenged as being based on quite varied national calculations. According to the data available, the expenditures per student are by far the highest in the United States (more than 20,000 US$). They are about two-thirds of that level in Malaysia, Norway and the Netherlands. In contrast, they are only moderately above 3,000 US$ in Argentina, about 6,000 US$ in Mexico and about 7,000 US$ in Portugal. On average, economically more affluent countries spend a higher proportion of their GDP on

Table 3.4 Public and private expenditures on education and on R&D in selected countries 2002

Country	Public and private exp. on Edu/GNP 2002 (%)	R&D expenditures % of GDP ca. 2002	Expenditures per tertiary student 2002 (US$ PPPS)
Argentina	.	0.4	3,235
Australia	5.6	1.5	12,416
Brazil	.	1.0	10,361
Canada	4.4	1.9	.
China	.	1.2	.
Finland	6.0	3.5	11,768
Germany	5.3	2.5	10,999
Italy	4.9	1.1	8,636
Japan	4.7	3.1	11,716
Malaysia	8.1	.	14,405
Mexico	6.2	0.4	6,074
Netherlands	5.1	1.9	13,101
Norway	7.0	1.7	13,719
Portugal	5.8	0.9	6,960
United Kingdom	5.9	1.9	11,822
United States	7.2	2.7	20,545

Source: Adapted from Cummings (2008)
· No information available

R&D. However, the highest rates are three times or even higher than the lowest rates both among advanced countries (ranging from 0.9 to 3.5%) and among emerging countries (ranging from 0.4 to 1.2%)

3.4 Enrolment

The percentage of *tertiary education students enrolled of the respective age group* has risen substantially in recent years. Table 3.5 reports that the average rate in CAP countries was 24% in 1980 and more than doubled to 54% by 2005. In 1980, the highest rates were in Canada and the United States, while Finland and Norway had comparatively high rates as well in subsequent years. China (2% in 1980 and 20% in 2005) and Malaysia (from 4 to 32%) started with a very low level but experienced enormous growth rates over the years.

3.5 Academic Productivity

Cummings (2008) provides figures on *science and engineering articles* as indicators of academic productivity. Actually, the number of articles in science and engineering per one million persons was around the year 2000:

– More than 900 in Finland (960)
– Around 800 in the United Kingdom (822), the Netherlands (800) and Australia (794)

Table 3.5 Percentage of tertiary education enrolment among the respective age group in selected countries from 1980 to 2005

Country	1980	1995	2000	2005
Argentina	22	38	53	65
Australia	25	72	65	72
Brazil	11	11	16	24
Canada	57	103	59	62
China	2	5	8	20
Hong Kong, China	10	.	.	31
Finland	32	67	83	92
Germany	34	43	.	.
Italy	27	41	49	66
Japan	31	40	47	55
Korea	13	45	79	96
Malaysia	4	11	26	32
Mexico	14	14	19	24
Netherlands	29	49	53	61
Norway	26	55	70	80
Portugal	11	34	48	56
South Africa	.	17	14	15
United Kingdom	19	48	58	60
United States	56	81	69	83

Source: Adapted from Cummings (2008)
·No information available

- Somewhat more than 700 in the United States (722) and Norway (720)
- Substantially lower in other advanced countries for which information is available: Canada (666), Germany (530), Japan (446), Italy (371), Korea (207) and Portugal (191).

The respective figures are clearly lower in emerging countries: Argentina (78), South Africa (56), Brazil (39), Mexico (32), Malaysia (22) and China (15). It should be noted that these figures have increased substantially thereafter in selected emerging countries and also in some advanced countries.

3.6 Basic Information on Higher Education Systems

3.6.1 Canada

Higher education in Canada has been shaped by strong influences from the United Kingdom, France and the United States. The British North America Act of 1867, later renamed the Constitution Act, bestowed the fiscal and governance responsibilities for education to the provinces. As a federation of ten provinces and three territories, Canada thus has a distributed higher education system, with each province and territory having the ability to create uniquely designed systems with minimal federal or interprovincial coordination (see Metcalfe et al. 2011). With the exceptions of providing educational opportunities for Aboriginal learners and for military education, the federal government is not involved directly in the provision of postsecondary education. However, the federal government has exercised considerable influence over the research universities, as the economic contributions of research and the development of a highly skilled workforce are federal concerns. Yet, there is no federal-level ministry for education or higher education in Canada, and there are limited official surveys of postsecondary education conducted at the national level.

In the absence of federal oversight, membership-oriented academic bodies have influenced the development and the coordination of provincial systems to some extent. For example, the Association of Universities and Colleges of Canada (AUCC), with 95 member institutions, is a powerful advocate for higher education in the country and has strict rules for affiliation. Without an official federal definition of what it means to be a 'university' in Canada, membership in the AUCC has become a defining characteristic with meaning across the provinces. Member institutions of the AUCC are degree-granting, autonomous and not-for-profit entities. While there are some private universities in Canada, these are mostly non-profit. Unlike the neighbouring United States, Canada's highest-profile research universities are public institutions rather than private.

Most provinces in Canada have differentiated institutional types that form a provincial system within the larger Canadian postsecondary context. Universities are degree-granting institutions, with coursework leading to bachelor's, master's and doctoral degrees. Colleges usually do not grant degrees but instead offer coursework leading to diplomas, although some colleges now grant bachelor's degrees in limited fields. In many ways the 'colleges' of Canada are like the 'community colleges' of the United States. Quebec has a unique system relative to the other provinces in that it offers preuniversity courses through public institutions called *College d'enseignement generale et professionnel* (CEGEP), which are mandatory for university entry. The CEGEPs also offer vocational coursework for students not planning to enter university studies.

In addition to their degree-granting status, universities in Canada are characterised by their research activities, along a spectrum of minimal research in the teaching universities to extensive research activity at the institutions with medical schools. The leading research universities have formed a group known as U15, with the intent of sharing strategies for further developing Canada's research and scientific infrastructure. Enhancing doctoral education, which is tied to both the research and teaching performance of universities at both the undergraduate and graduate levels, is a primary concern of U15 member institutions.

The academic profession in Canada is very similar to that in the United States in that it is organised into three phases: assistant professor, associate professor and full professor (Metcalfe 2008). Traditionally faculty have entered into the academic profession through a 'tenure-track' appointment at the assistant professor level, and after a period of probationary time, they are eligible for review to be promoted and granted tenure at the associate professor level. Many professors live out the rest of their careers at this level. Some professors choose to stand for review later in their careers to be promoted to full professor, a status that affords one the highest academic accolades and responsibilities. While all faculty can be involved in academic governance in Canada, where there is a strong value placed on labour unions and collective bargaining, full professors have traditionally held most of the peer-elected positions in academic senates and faculty associations. While there is little data to understand the trend nationally, there has likely been an increase in the number of limited-contract, non-tenure-track faculty in Canada, which has implications for academic governance and development of the profession.

3.6.2 United States of America

Higher education in the United States of America is often viewed as having served in the twentieth century more than any other higher education system as a role model for other countries in the world. Notably, the outstanding research quality of some top institutions, the separate institutionalisation of doctoral training and other advanced training in graduate schools and the strong power of university leadership are widely perceived as distinctive features of the American system.

Finkelstein and Frances (2006) describe the early history of US higher education as the coexistence of private and public higher education, the latter predominantly supervised and funded by the individual states, but with a strong internal power from early on. The model of the research university had already developed in the late nineteenth and early twentieth century. Massification is seen as a major feature soon after World War II, and in this context, equality of opportunity became a major priority of higher education in the USA alongside the quality of the research university. The reputation of the research university created an incentive for students and scholars all over the world to move to the USA notably for graduate education and academic work. We possibly might add that there is a more pronounced view in the USA than anywhere else as regards a divide of character between academic disciplines (some of them called 'liberal arts') and professional disciplines.

Although the private sector of higher education in the USA is relatively much smaller (25% of students) than in countries such as Japan and Korea, it has had a stronger impact on the public sector than in many other countries. It lead to a 'marketisation' in terms of funding of the higher education institutions through students 'voting with their feet' and strong reliance on other 'competitive' funds, for example, research promotion funds.

Institutions of higher education in the USA are often described notably as research universities, characterised by the important role of research and doctoral training in all or most fields; comprehensive universities with substantial research activities and doctoral training in selected fields; 4-year colleges, offering predominantly bachelor's programmes; and community colleges with mostly 2-year programmes. There are other institutional types as well, and many descriptions focus on differences of reputation rather than formal institutional types. Study programmes are often described according to stages: 2-year programmes (notably those at community colleges) leading often to associate degrees, 4-year programmes leading to bachelor's degrees and graduate programmes leading to master's degrees or professional degrees and eventually doctoral degrees. At many universities and colleges, 4-year students select courses from a variety of disciplines during the first 2 years, before they make a choice or are allocated to a specific field of study from the third year on.

The typical academic career in USA starts with doctoral study whereby some graduate students might serve auxiliary functions as research assistants and teaching assistant. Upon the doctoral award, some will be postdoctoral fellows for a while and others lecturers, while an assistant professorship for 6 years is the most desirable next step after the doctoral award. The typical career steps for senior academics are those of an associate and a full professor. Assistant professors, as a rule, are not permanently employed, and the same might be true for the early years of associate professors, but risks are kept in bound by 'tenure-track' models which envisage permanent employment and career progression within the same institution for the successful ones.

The character of the academic profession in the USA is often misunderstood by looking only at the research universities. The career patterns and the composition of the academic profession, however, is substantially more diverse (see Finkelstein 2010). Finkelstein and Frances point out that the proportion of academics employed in research universities among all tertiary education has declined from about 45% in 1970 to about 33% in recent years. Concurrently, the proportion of women, foreign-born, ethnic minority and part-time employed has substantially grown. Concurrently the career paths of academics have become more diverse, the number of those in charge of specialised functions has increased and the role of academics in campus governance has been shrinking. The authors conclude: 'While we can continue to use the knowledge we have learned about traditional academic careers in the liberal arts and sciences, a new map of academic careers must be drawn on the basis of the new and discontinuous realities of American higher education in a global, market-driven, knowledge-based age' (ibid., p. 253).

3.6.3 *Finland*

Higher education in Finland is provided via a binary system of universities (research universities) and polytechnics (universities of applied sciences, *AMK*). Universities were based on European models, and the first was established in the seventeenth century. Other institutions acquired university status in the early years of the twentieth century, with the establishment of regional universities in the 1950s and 1960s in line with contemporary regional development policies. Research is a major focus for universities, and their teaching provides a more theoretical education than that provided by polytechnics. Universities provide first, second and third cycle degrees.

Polytechnics were formed via the amalgamation of myriad small trades and vocational colleges, in order to raise the standard of vocational education and to rationalise the structure of the education system (to paraphrase the Ministry of Education). Polytechnics offer 3- or 4-year programmes and are meant to have a close working relationship with working life and to foster regional development. There is a preference for practical skills in teaching and learning, and polytechnic research also tends to have a practical focus. These institutions took their first students in 1991. In line with practice in other parts of Europe, polytechnics now refer to themselves as 'universities of applied sciences'(Aarrevaara et al. 2011).

Until the Universities Act 2009 took effect from 1 January, 2010, universities were part of state administration and university employees were civil servants. Universities, therefore, are now independent of the government in one sense, even if they remain financially dependent on the government as the main source of funds. In the new environment, a dual-governance model has replaced the single prereform system (Aarrevaara et al. 2009). The universities' new status enables them to seek funds from sources other than the government, via fees levied on students from outside the EU and EEA, and through private bequests and donations. However, restrictions remain on both of these activities, but over time, a more market-oriented situation is likely to develop. Eventually, there may be a closer examination of the levying of tuition fees on domestic students under certain circumstances, but this radical step is not part of the current reform agenda.

Universities can now be institutions subject to public law or foundations subject to private law, the latter subject to raising large sums of private capital. Two universities opted for the second, more 'private' track. One of those two is the product of a set of institutional mergers, but there have been other institutional mergers, and more are planned. Currently there are 16 universities funded via the Ministry of Education and Culture, but three small creative and performing arts universities will merge from 2013, reducing the number to 14.

Governance arrangements are different in the polytechnic sector. Although sectoral reform is planned for 2014, most of the 26 polytechnics are administered through licence holders, most of which are municipal councils. Anticipated reform will see polytechnic governance structures moving closer to those of the universities.

Finnish students attending both sectors are relatively well off in terms of student welfare, a mixture of non-refundable grants and low-interest loans that can be repaid after the completion of studies. The national government provides financial aid intended to cover living costs, and Finnish legislation does not permit tuition fees to be charged to domestic degree students. This is due to principles of the welfare state which are written into the Finnish constitution, including regulations relating to the provision of free education to all students studying for a degree. However, welfare payments have not kept up with inflation in the cost of rental housing, particularly in the capital region. This means that most students are also members of the casual workforce, and many delay the completion of their studies, leading to Finland having the oldest university graduates in Europe.

3.6.4 Germany

The concept formulated by Wilhelm von Humboldt for the establishment of the University of Berlin in 1980 is widely viewed as the most influential vision for the modern university worldwide. The 'idea of the university' is characterised by a strong link between research and teaching, academic freedom which comprises the pursuit of knowledge for its own sake and a strong community of scholars and students where students' learning is facilitated by academic, research-oriented discourse.

The Humboldtian concept of the university is not characterised by a balance between teaching and research but rather by the dominance of research over teaching and learning. The link between research and teaching has a long-lasting effect, according to which university professors are more or less equally in charge of teaching and research and the teaching load is more or less the same for all professors (see Teichler and Bracht 2006; cf. also Kehm 2006). The professors in Germany are traditionally powerful decision-makers within universities, while the government is powerful in many general administrative matters as well as some academic matters such as the selection of professors from a list of three candidates suggested by the university and the protection of academic freedom. Academic freedom is not understood to serve an 'ivory tower' but rather as the essential precondition for creative thinking which eventually should yield the most valuable results for society.

Traditionally, universities were established and funded by the rulers of the various territories. Nowadays, the legislative power and the funding responsibility rest with the governments of the 16 *Länder* of the Federal Republic of Germany. The national government plays a role in the funding of research and in some higher education tasks; for example, from the late 1960s until recently, it shared some coordinating functions with the individual states. It is often argued that the decentralised steering has reinforced in Germany under specific conditions the notion that universities ideally should be equally strong in academic quality: This ensures that students can be inter-institutionally mobile at any time during the course of study and that there is a system of mandatory academic mobility; university professors always should be appointed who previously had been active at another institution.

When enrolment in higher education expanded in the 1960s, a decision was taken to establish *Fachhochschulen* as a second major type of higher education with a dominant teaching function. The teaching load of *Fachhochschule* professors is more than twice as high as that of university professors.

In the early twentieth century, a study structure prevailed where university students were awarded a first degree after about 4–5 years, which was called a *Diplom*, *Magister* or *Staatsexamen* and was considered equivalent internationally to a master's degree. Doctoral candidates predominantly were supervised by individual professors and were not required to pursue any taught programme. But many reforms started in the 1990s and continued into the early years of the twentieth century; among them was a stronger university management at the expense of the historically strong influence of the professors, a new cycle system of bachelor's and master's programmes and degrees as well as the establishment of doctoral programmes along the traditional system of individual supervision. In this framework, *Fachhochschulen*, now as rule translated into English as universities of applied sciences, could establish both bachelor's and master's programmes but were not granted the right to award doctoral degrees.

At German universities, large numbers of junior staff both without and with a doctoral degree are employed mostly for a period of only a few years. Most of those paid through a university position are in charge of research and teaching, while most of those paid by external grants solely are in charge of research. Traditionally, the entry qualification for a professorship was a *habilitation*, that is, a second-level doctorate based on about 5 years of academic work beyond the doctorate. The professorate is divided into the highest level (W3), traditionally called *Ordinarius*, and a lower-ranking professor position (W2), where candidates were recruited from outside and no internal promotion system exists between the two levels. Recently, a junior professor position has been established which in many respects resembles that of a US assistant professor position. The entry qualification for a professorship at *Fachhochschulen* is a doctoral degree and a subsequent 5 years of professional work, among them at least 3 years in the professional area targeted by the study programmes the professor will be in charge of. There are only small numbers of junior staff positions at *Fachhochschulen*.

3.6.5 Italy

The Italian higher education system was established in 1859 on the eve of the political unification of the country. Higher education in the Kingdom of Piedmont was shaped after the French and the Prussian models. It provided the basis for the system of the new unified country, modelling its main traits for more than one century. Italian higher education has largely coincided and still coincides with the university system. There has been little room for functional diversification and competition between institutions. Universities have always provided teaching, research and service. Starting with the establishment of the Kingdom of Italy, higher education has developed under a strong state monopoly, and the private sector has always been small. The relationships between the state, universities and the academy might be described as characterised by a strong tension between centralisation and autonomy (Rostan 2008).

After the end of World War II, when the Kingdom collapsed following Italy's defeat in war, fascism ended, and the Italian Republic was founded, both the country and higher education slowly recovered. The shift from an elite to a mass system occurred between the 1950s and the 1970s following the so-called economic miracle and the slow establishment of a modern welfare state. Depending on the measures, in the last half-a-century Italian higher education has grown by six to eight times (Rostan 2011).

Following the Bologna process, the old national frame of study programmes mainly based on one single long cycle of study and one degree (the *laurea*) has been entirely replaced by a European frame based on the bachelor's/master's scheme leading to two degrees (the new *laurea* and the new *laurea specialistica*, later renamed as *laurea magistrale*). Only doctoral programmes—introduced in 1980—and study programmes regulated by European directives have been left untouched.

The Italian academic profession has always been strictly regulated. Academics were, and are, civil servants whose rights, duties and salaries are determined by law. Since 1980, a three-layered structure of the profession has been established. The professoriate consists of two positions, *professore ordinario* (full professor) and *professore associato* (associate professor), while a third position is that of *ricercatore* (researcher). These are all permanent or 'tenured' positions differentiated according to scientific expertise and job tasks. Academics are mainly recruited by *concorso* (public competition). Since 1998, academics are no longer considered to be employed centrally by the Ministry of Universities but rather are employees of their institution. In the last thirty years, the Italian academic career has consisted of five main steps: (a) obtaining a doctoral degree; (b) experiencing a more or less long period of training characterised by temporary appointments, sometimes even unpaid; (c) becoming *ricercatore*; (d) entering the professoriate as associate professor; and (e) being promoted to full professorship (Rostan 2010).

The size of the academic profession has increased with the expansion of the system. At the time when the CAP survey was carried out, there were about 62,000 academics (Rostan 2011). Their number dropped by 8% in the following years due to budgetary constraints imposed on higher education.

Recently, Parliament has passed a substantial reform (see Law n. 240/2010) which will profoundly change the governance and the organisation of higher education institutions and reshape both the status and the recruitment of Italian academics. The law dismisses the tenured position of *ricercatore*, substituting it with temporary positions. It also introduces a two-step recruitment procedure for the professoriate based on an *abilitazione scientifica nazionale*—that is, a national qualification—and competitions at the local level.

3.6.6 The Netherlands

In the international literature, the Netherlands are sided with the countries with a strong research tradition. The quality and quantity of research in the research-intensive universities is testified by international comparisons across all broad discipline groups, and several Dutch universities enjoy an international reputation and are well represented in global rankings. There are 13 research-intensive universities, nine of which are covering a wide range of academic disciplines, three mainly in science and engineering and another in agricultural science. In addition there is the Open University (De Weert 2006).

Alongside these universities, the higher professional institutions have been developed, currently absorbing more than 65% of the total higher education student population. There are about 40 institutions (*Hoger Beroepsonderwijs—HBO*) that have the task of providing theoretical and practical training for various professional fields as well as of transferring and developing knowledge for the benefit of both the industrial and service sectors. Since the last decade, they have been assigned a research role too, focusing on practice-oriented research for business and for the advancement of professional practice. In the context of internationalisation, the institutions have adopted the name 'universities of applied sciences'.

Current government policies focus on the increase of R&D investment which is quite low compared to the OECD average. An example is the selection of high priority areas of research, where higher education institutions are expected to collaborate with business and industry and to engage in public-private partnerships. Accountability requirements are underscored through performance agreements between individual institutions and the government. These agreements comprise measurable outcome target as regards progress in studies and success rates as well as research profiles and the assessment of research outcomes.

The standard model for university academics to allocate a fixed percentage of time for teaching, research and administration (40, 40 and 20%, respectively) has been replaced by a staffing model that allows more freedom for a differentiated work role regarding teaching and research. Accordingly, these tasks may be allocated in different proportions of workload of individual faculty members, thus taking into account the full range of facets of academic work to be expected from researchers and teachers as well as the different aspirations and competences of faculty. However, climbing the academic ladder on the basis of either research or teaching performance is difficult as these tasks have equal weight in decisions on promotion and tenure.

In the *HBO* sector, a new staff category has been established recently. As the sector is primarily in charge of teaching, but research plays an increasing role, the position of a lector has been created: that of a senior academic who has a leading role in a research group. Traditionally, the Dutch academic career is a relatively simple hop, step and jump movement: After obtaining the doctoral degree and a fixed-term postdoc position, a candidate is eligible for a (mostly) tenured position of university docent (assistant professor) and may proceed to university main docent (associate professor) and finally full professor. This career system has been based on the formation principle: Promotion occurs when a (higher) position becomes available. According to current legislation, fixed-term appointments can be renewed up to a maximum of 6 years. The move from nontenured to a tenured position is a crucial step in a career.

This formation principle is gradually being overhauled by a career system based on tenure tracks. Dutch universities adopted this system as a way of attracting and retaining young promising academics and to provide the opportunity for promotion them to a professorial position. A related concern has been to attract academics from other countries. Candidates have to succeed according to individual performance agreements for a period of 5–6 years or otherwise will be discharged.

3.6.7 Norway

To understand Norwegian higher education, it is important to note that it is shaped within the context of a young nation (the oldest university has been established in the capital Oslo in 1811), a small country (app. 4.5 million inhabitants), and within the context of an oil-producing economy with good conditions to realise the welfare state policy objectives in a social democratic regime placing great emphasis on higher education as a strategy to reduce social inequality (Vabø and Aamodt 2008).

With large differences between fields of science, however, the university system has been significantly influenced by the German Humboldt tradition. Partly this has resulted in a strong emphasis on and justification for research-based instruction (Kehm et al. 2010).

Among its public accredited institutions of higher education, Norway has seven universities, nine specialist universities, 22 university colleges and two national colleges of art. With the exception of a relatively small private sector, all higher education institutions are state funded. Approximately 86% of the students are enrolled in public institutions. Apart from the Norwegian School of Management (BI), most private institutions are quite small. All institutions, first and foremost the universities, are responsible for conducting basic research and researcher training.

Although Norway in principle operates with a binary structure, universities and colleges do not function as separate qualification pillars, rather as an integrated sector where undergraduate studies at a college are basically approved by the universities. Colleges are also required to conduct research, and many also offer graduate degree programmes.

In the wake of the Bologna process in 2003, Norway introduced the bachelor's-master's degree structure which applies to the whole sector. The number of students spreads relatively evenly between universities and colleges, but the universities have the highest number at master's and Ph.D. level as well as a much wider variety of study programmes. As regards Ph.D. level, Norway has had a significant expansion in the recent decade—with 242 annual dissertations per million capita—although Norway in Nordic comparison still lags behind Finland and Sweden.

The state is an important factor in funding, regulating and steering the system. In line with international trends, however, more market-oriented modes of governance have been introduced in higher education characterised by more autonomous governing bodies at the institutional level, relying upon strategic management methods and incentive-based funding. Institutions of higher education have achieved a relatively high degree of freedom of choice of management models, that is, whether to appoint or elect senior management. So far, most universities have preferred the latter model.

The academic profession in Norway is dominated by two categories: full professors and associate professors, while a teaching-oriented category—lecturers—is most prominent in the state college sector. Furthermore, there are a number of smaller categories, such as postdocs, researchers, teachers as well as adjunct positions.

In international comparison, the positional hierarchy is relatively egalitarian with small differences in duties and pay between professors and other academic staff. Nevertheless, universities and colleges in Norway as well have been criticised for the apparent assumed heavy use of temporary staff.

As both universities and colleges are required to ensure quality through research-based teaching, the vast majority of academic staff has the opportunity of conducting their own research. Ph.D. students are considered to be academic staff; therefore, they have higher salaries and better working conditions than their colleagues in other European countries.

The number of foreign academics is constantly rising: Their proportion in the higher education sector in Norway increased from 18% in 2001 to 25% in 2009.

3.6.8 Portugal

The Humboldtian 'model' was officially the basis for structuring the Portuguese higher education system throughout the twentieth century. However, between the beginning of 1930s and the 1974 democratic revolution, this model was more of a symbolic reference to nonconformists' academics than a factual framework for the organisation of the academic life of universities. Subsequent to 1974, the Humboldtian logic shaped the organisation of academic work and notably the relationship between teaching and research.

Up to the 1990s, the influence of new public management (NPM) over higher education was more rhetorical—naming such issues as efficiency, quality, excellence and accountability—rather than practical. Also, direct state supervision was only gradually removed by steering at a distance and increased institutional autonomy.

The NPM concepts and practices spread along strong criticism vis-à-vis the corporatist nature of collegiality and the social inefficiency of curricula and knowledge production. In 2007, a new higher education law was enacted in Portugal which brought about in-depth transformations in the power architecture of the system and its institutions. The political and strategic power was concentrated at the top of higher education institutions. A general board with many external stakeholders took over the functions of the academic senate and the polytechnic assembly, respectively. University rectors and polytechnic presidents became top executives along the implementation of a line management structure. National accreditation and evaluation systems were established. A business-oriented 'philosophy' spread in higher education; academics were assessed according to students' opinions and indicators of teaching and research productivity. Competitive research funding should not only reward the more successful academics but also was aimed at promoting the stratification of the system, that is, a divide between research universities and teaching universities. Finally, science and technology policies were aimed at creating close ties between knowledge, economy and the entrepreneurial tissue.

The new steering system in higher education had important consequences for the academic profession in Portugal. The self-determining professional logic was substituted by a managerial logic. The emphasis on new organisational procedures and instruments certainly has to be viewed as an attempt to transform the academics identities, cultures and professional behaviours. In this context, organisational rationalism might weaken the academic professionalism. However, in spite of increasing controls and the deterioration of the conditions for academic work, the 'traditional' beliefs and values of the bureaucratic-collegial and academic knowledge logics seem to persist.

3.6.9 United Kingdom

Higher education in the *United Kingdom* is widely held up as a specific prototype of higher education where a strong emphasis on teaching and learning is well compatible with a high quality for research. Historical references to universities in the UK often underscore the important and influential roles of the universities in Oxford and Cambridge which were aimed to develop an academically and otherwise well-rounded personality through close communication between scholars and students.

Description of the system tend to point at the historical sequence of being founded or officially recognised as universities: The medieval universities (notably Oxford and Cambridge), the various member institutions of the University of London and the Universities of Wales, the 'civic universities' founded around 1890, the colleges founded after the World War II that later were upgraded to universities and finally the former 'polytechnics' are called frequently now 'post-1992' or 'new' universities. It is worth noting that the vast majority of UK universities had past 'lives' as other types of higher education institutions—colleges, institutes, polytechnics, etc.—and often had to play an apprenticeship relationship to an established university before being granted university status in their own right. This is as true of the nineteenth century 'civics' as it was of the late twentieth polytechnics. Additionally, one has also to bear in mind that many accounts refer to England only or to England, Wales and Northern Ireland, while separate policies and traditions have played a substantial role in Scotland (see Naidoo and Brennan 2006).

British universities 'are legally independent corporate institutions with charitable status and accountable to the Government through a governing body which carries ultimate responsibility for all aspects of the institution' (ibid., p. 46). They tend to be described as having an exceptionally high degree of autonomy from government and having 'robust governance mechanisms' with a strong role of academics in decision-making. However, higher education policies of funding and quality management have now prevailed for more than two decades which strongly underscore the public expectations to be accountable financially and to make visible the contribution of higher education institutions to the knowledge society and knowledge economy. Although almost all are 'public' institutions, they differ substantially in their sources of funding with the more elite research institutions receiving only a minority of their funding as basic subsidy from the state.

Since the upgrading of former polytechnics in 1992, the sector of other 'higher education institutions' is small, even if it comprises almost one-third of the number of institutions, many of which combine 'higher education' provision with provision at 'lower' and more vocational levels of post-school education. More recently, the government's requirement for the granting of degree-awarding and university status has been relaxed (in terms of numbers of students and in terms of postgraduate and research functions), partly in order to encourage the growth of private providers. Altogether, UK higher education is often characterised as comprising a relative small elite sector of internationally recognised research universities in a system marked by vertical differences in institutional reputations which are relatively steep in comparison to other European countries. Unlike many other European countries, the UK tradition (though more particularly the English tradition) has been for students to 'go away' to university rather than attend a local institution, something which is assisted in creating a strong—and social-class-related—reputational hierarchy of institutions. In the English part of the UK system in particular, it is often difficult to distinguish between 'academic' and 'social' elitism in the reputational differences between institutions.

Though the United Kingdom often has been considered to be prototype for a bachelor's-master's structure recently spreading across continental Europe as well, actually a very complex system of 'qualifications' exists. The traditional 3-year (occasionally four when some kind of work experience element is included) bachelor's degree was the key qualification with awards to students graduated in terms of an 'honours' classification. Generally, 1-year 'taught' master's degrees played a mixture of functions, sometimes offering a vocational preparation to a particular professional field. In the second half of the twentieth century, there was also a growth in master's courses as a mid-career experience with generally part-time courses taken as a means of either changing career direction or speeding career advancement. There has also been a growth of various 'certificates' upon completion of mostly 1-year programmes, 'foundation degrees', 'diplomas', etc., after mostly two years, with part-time provision of courses increasingly common. (Compared with many countries, the UK has maintained quite a hard distinction between full-time and part-time courses, with little opportunity for students to 'stretch' the duration of the former.) Finally, there are doctoral degrees, increasingly with both 'academic' and 'professional' provision and again both full-time and part-time. On the whole, the various postgraduate programmes are mostly not viewed as integrated into a separate 'graduate school'.

Entry to the academic profession in the UK has always had a flexibility not always to be found in other systems. In particular, possession of a doctorate has not been an essential requirement, though increasingly competition in the academic labour market has been making it so. The traditional academic career would typically begin with a research position, on a fixed-term contract and frequently part of a 'team' of researchers. For some researchers, a succession of different fixed-term contracts could follow over many years, while others could move quite quickly to a permanent 'tenured' lectureship which combined both teaching and research functions. However, patterns vary between subject fields where opportunities for funded research positions differ considerably. Performance-related promotion for permanent staff could then take academics through statuses of 'senior lecturer', 'reader' and finally to 'professor'. Especially in the more professional/vocational fields, there could also be mid-career entry into the academic profession as people moved across from 'practice' to 'research and professional formation' functions within their chosen field.

In recent years, progression through and relationships within the academic profession have become more competitive with all kinds of performance measures introduced by institutions as a reflection of their own competitive positioning within an increasingly market-driven system. As competition is most typically about outputs and performance in research and publications, there have been concerns expressed in some institutions that this is damaging the traditionally strong UK emphasis on learning and teaching and, more broadly, the relationships between academics and their students.

3.6.10 Australia

In 2012, Australia had 37 public universities, two private universities, one private 'specialist university' and two other public higher education institutions with self-accrediting status. Additionally, there were 68 non-self-accrediting higher education providers (11 public, 57 private) (Wheelahan et al. 2011). Universities are distinguished from other providers of postsecondary education based on their ability to award their own degrees (self-accreditation), commitment to research (in particular basic research), comprehensiveness (in range of academic fields and qualifications awarded), academic freedom, self-government, broad social responsibilities and multiple missions (Norton 2012b).

Australian universities offer bachelor's degrees of typically 3 years in arts, science, commerce and economics, four years in engineering and law, and four to six years in dentistry and medicine. Notable exceptions are the University of Melbourne and the University of Western Australia who offer a limited range of generalist undergraduate degrees, with postgraduate entry into professional degrees (e.g. engineering, law, medicine). At the postgraduate level, coursework-based degrees include graduate certificate (1/2 year), graduate diploma (1/2–1 year) and coursework-based master's (1–2 years). Postgraduate research-based degrees include master's by research (2 years), Ph.D. and professional doctorates (3 years). Entry into doctoral-level programmes generally requires a bachelor's degree with honours (or equivalent), an additional undergraduate year of research training and specialised coursework.

Australia's 39 universities are represented by Universities Australia, the higher education industry's peak consultative and advisory body. Despite uniform status, universities vary considerably in their research and teaching profile. Many Australian universities are also members of subgroup associations which negotiate policy positions based on the specific needs of their members. For example, the Group of

3.6 Basic Information on Higher Education Systems

Eight (Go8) is a lobby group of the oldest and most prestigious research-intensive universities. The Go8 universities dominate competitive research funding grants, research publishing and the training of Ph.D. candidates.

Over the past three decades, Australian universities have expanded rapidly due to the transition from an elite to a mass higher education system. According to Norton (2012b, p. 5), the proportion of the adult working population with higher education qualifications increased from 3% in the 1970s to almost 25% by 2011. Since 1991, the number of persons enrolled in higher education has more than doubled, from 530,000 in 1991 to 1.22 million by 2011. In 2011, domestic students (Australians, New Zealanders and permanent residents) accounted for the majority of enrolments (73%). However, international enrolments increased dramatically from less than 6% of total enrolments in 1991 to 27% in 2011 (DIISRTE Various years). Importantly, the impact of international students has been uneven, with the majority enrolled in management and commerce (51% in 2011) and coming from Asian countries (81% in 2011).

Higher education providers, both public and private, receive public funding for teaching domestic students through the Commonwealth Grants Scheme (CGS). In real terms, CGS funding declined sharply on a per student basis during the 1990s, before recovering somewhat since 2003 (Lomax-Smith et al. 2011). Much of the shortfall in CGS funding has been counteracted by the progressive increase in tuition fees. Domestic students contribute roughly 40% of the cost of their tuition through tuition fees (Norton 2012a). The growth in international student enrolment has also increased the income of Australian universities, which accounted for 17.5% of university income in 2010. Tuition fees for international students may be set by the market to cover the full cost of their education, whereas tuition fees for most domestic students are restricted by law (Norton 2012b). Overall, these changes have meant that the Australian government is no longer the primary funder of tertiary education. In 2008, private individuals contributed the majority of funding (55%), the sixth highest proportion of private funding among OECD countries (OECD 2011, p. 238).

Staff numbers have not kept pace with the growth in student enrolments. Using national staff and student statistics, Coates and colleagues (2009) reported that between 1989 and 2007, the number of academic teaching staff ('teaching-only' and 'teaching and research' positions) increased by 28%. This is despite a doubling of student enrolments. They estimate that the student to academic teaching staff ratio increased from 13 to 22 over the 1989–2007 period. A second dramatic change was the dramatic increase in the proportion of staff employed on casual contracts. Over this same period, casual employment of teaching staff (in full-time equivalent terms) increased to 22% of the total academic teaching workforce. This compared with a 14% increase in continuing and fixed-term contract employment. Unfortunately there are no accurate national statistics on the number of casual teaching staff. One full-time-equivalent casual employee may equate to two staff members each working half of a full-time load or five casuals each working one day per week. However, using academic staff superannuation data from 2010, May (2011) estimated that casuals comprised 61% of all academic employees.

Unlike countries with teaching-focused institutions and polytechnics, Australian universities have needed to teach more students while maintaining a formal commitment to research and recruitment of research qualified staff. The extraordinary increase in number of students, particularly from non-English-speaking countries, combined with declining public funding and casualisation of employment, raises many challenges for how universities will teach an increasingly diverse student population. By international comparison, Australian academics show some of the lowest levels of interest in teaching (relative to research) and are among the least satisfied (Coates et al. 2009). Although some universities are creating teaching-focused career paths, the commitment to research remains a key feature that distinguishes universities from other higher education institutions. It will also likely remain the key motivator for those aspiring to enter academic careers.

3.6.11 Japan

Higher education in Japan has been paid attention internationally as a potential model because Japan has succeeded more than other countries in catching up—being a latecomer of industrialisation and modernisation in the nineteenth century—to one of the economically most successful societies, whereby conventional wisdom suggests that education and research have been foundations of this success story. However, descriptions vary substantially of the higher education system and of the academic profession in Japan.

The establishment of a modern system of higher education is often described as having started with the foundation of the University of Tokyo in 1877 (see the overview in Huang 2007). Many scholars from abroad were hired, and many Japanese scholars were sent abroad to create the basis for universities, whereby the German research university is viewed as a very important model, but not the only model considered. Public investment concentrated to a high degree on science and engineering, while private universities already early on became the largest sector with a large proportion of students in the humanities and social sciences. From early on, Japanese higher education was highly stratified, whereby most nonelite institutions took the elite universities as their role models.

After World War II, higher education in Japan, influenced by the United States, was fundamentally reorganised. Four-year bachelor's programmes, 2-year master's programmes and 3-year doctoral programmes were introduced. Japan became also one of the first countries experiencing a massification of higher education. Japanese higher education, however, remained different from US higher education as far as governance is concerned: The strong role of the ministry of education remained, presidents remained representatives of the academic profession in publicly funded universities, professors had a substantial say in internal administration and graduate schools did not become entities clearly separate from 'faculties'. Moves towards what is internationally often called a 'managerial university' started only at the beginning of the twenty-first century.

Huang (2006), in reviewing the respective literature, names three striking characteristics of the Japanese higher education system. First, there is a large proportion of private higher education with more than three-quarters of the students enrolled. Second, there is a divide in the coordination and resources between a strongly government-coordinated public sector on the one hand and a market-oriented private sector on the other hand. Third, there is a steep hierarchical pattern of the higher education system, notably in resources for research and in the entry level of students as well the career chances of graduates. As a consequence, competition for entry to higher education is often characterised as extreme, while the four years of study tend to be described as less demanding than in many countries with less rigorous sorting at entry.

The academic career ladder in Japan looks similar to that of the USA at first glance with positions of assistants, assistant professors, associate professors and professors. But many features are different: a chair system rather than a department system at the majority of publicly funded universities, little inter-institutional mobility at the prestigious universities, few junior academic positions, early permanent employment and a 'seniority system', and an enormous emphasis on research in academic careers even at less prestigious universities. Arimoto (2006), among others, adds two characteristics which the Carnegie Study of the 1990s has pointed out: A low proportion of women among academics and 'high psychological stress'.

3.6.12 Korea

The tradition of a higher learning institution has 1,600 years of long tradition in Korea. The first higher learning institution *Taehak* (great learning institution) was established in the *Goguryeo* Dynasty in AD 394. The main goal of the higher learning institution was to educate officials based on Confucianism. The higher learning institution was *Gukhak* (national higher learning institute) (AD 682) during the consolidated *Silla* Dynasty. The higher learning institution changed its name to *Gukzagam* (AD 992) in the Korea Dynasty, then *Sungkyunkwan* (AD 1289) in the end of the Korea Dynasty and in the *Chosun* Dynasty (Lee 2002). Currently *Sungkyunkwan* University is in the same place with buildings, lecture halls, residence building and libraries. The higher learning institution was well linked to the examination systems to hire officials. Through the combination of higher learning and official hiring exam systems, higher learning institutions were institutionalised as a core social system through their long history in Korea.

Modern higher education was introduced in the mid-1890s. National higher learning institutions for teacher training and foreign language institution were established in 1895 and a medical institution in 1899. Agricultural, business and engineering institutions were also established in 1899. In addition to the national institutions of higher learning, western missionaries, especially US missionaries, were actively involved in establishing higher learning institutes as a means for their missionary work. The missionaries tried to enlighten Koreans through the modern thoughts and knowledge. Some well-known Korean universities, for example, Korea University, Yonsei University and Ewha Womans University were established in that period. During the colonial period (1910–1945), the German university model was implanted by establishing Kyungsung Imperial University in 1926, modelled after Tokyo Imperial University, and technical training institutions were established as well (Lee 1989).

After the independence from colonial control, Korean higher education has rapidly grown. Enrolment notably grew in the 1980s and 1990s (Shin 2012). The tertiary enrolment in Korea now has reached 99% and thus is higher than in any other OECD country. In addition, the per capita research productivity of Korean academics is also remarkably high. More than 95% of the professors hold Ph.D.s, and among them more than 40% were awarded by a foreign university.

The enrolment growth was facilitated by the private sector which serves more than 80% of the students. The growth of research productivity is accomplished through aggressive investment in research and development since the late 1990s with R&D expenditures comprising 3.5% of the GDP (Shin 2012). These accomplishments are supported by strong desire for education and economic development that Korea has accomplished during a short time frame.

This notwithstanding, Korean higher education is confronted with complicated challenges in the rapid growth period. Overeducation is always a controversial issue among academics and policymakers, and graduate unemployment has become a hot issue. The rapid increase of student tuition caused serious social controversies. In addition, global rankings and world-class universities led many Korean universities to encounter fierce research competition. Korea is at the forefront of the challenges caused by massification and global rankings (Shin and Jang 2013). Korean higher education is at the crossroads. As a response, the Korean government pushes universities to transform into corporate entities; it upgrades quality assurance schemes and adopts teaching support programmes. It remains to be seen whether the issues at stake will deteriorate and whether Korean higher education can overcome these challenges and eventually will be a model for future development in other countries.

The academic ranks of Korean professors were full-time lecturer, assistant professor, associate professor and full professor. Recently, Korean government eliminates full-time lecturer position so that current ladders are three levels—assistant professor, associate professor and professor. Tenure status is given to associate professors in most universities. They are required to publish certain number of publications to be hired and promoted; their academic performance is evaluated by committee. Faculty hiring and promotion are becoming more rigorous in recent days because many universities require publication in international journals. Postdoctoral training used to be a requirement in natural sciences and engineering, and it is not unusual in many social sciences areas (Shin and Cummings 2010). Female academics are growing fast (18%) and academic inbreed (25% nationwide in 2010) is lessened by aggressive government policies since the early 2000s. In addition, universities began to open their job markets to international scholars. Through the changes, meritocracy is institutionalising in Korean universities.

3.6.13 Hong Kong

Hong Kong, with a population of only about seven million, has a higher education system that places a major emphasis on quality assurance and efficient management. While the Hong Kong Special Administrative Region (SAR) is part of the People's Republic of China, its universities have played a role in bridging minds between the Chinese mainland and the rest of the world (Postiglione 2010).

The University of Hong Kong, Hong Kong's first university, was established in 1911 and stood alone for over 50 years. Mass schooling led to the establishment of a Chinese medium university in 1963. The two universities became elite training grounds for civil servants, professionals and urban elites. Currently, Hong Kong has eight institutions funded by the public through the University Grants Committee (UGC), eight self-financed institutions mainly focused on teaching programmes and a publicly funded Academy of Performing Arts. The eight publicly funded universities play the key role in driving research, and the UGC, which directs government funding to universities, conducts periodic research assessment exercises to investigate the research publication outputs of individual departments.

Research productivity is on the rise in Asia, and Hong Kong often leads the region in the rate of increase in the publication of refereed journal articles. According to ISI Web of Science data, the number of articles published in Hong Kong was 999 in 1999 and 10,533 in 2011. Also according to other indicators, research productivity is significantly higher than elsewhere. Various universities of Hong Kong are in top positions of Asian universities rankings and among top 100 in world rankings; these results suggest that higher education in Hong Kong has a vibrant research climate, with a decrease in the percentages of non-productive academics (Postiglione 2011). However, enrolment in tertiary education is relatively lower than in Japan and Korea.

Several factors drive Hong Kong's universities (Postiglione and Jung 2012). The first is *governance*. The Research Grants Council and the University Grants Committee steer the higher education sector by prioritising funding and setting broad guidelines on performance. Beyond this, the universities are virtually autonomous in other respects and manage their affairs as they see fit. A second key factor is *internationalism*. Hong Kong's internationalism has shifted slowly away from a total focus on the United Kingdom, Australia and North America, to include more academics from the Chinese mainland and a small but increasing number of top academics from other continents. Most of the top academics at research universities have overseas doctorates, and many remain mobile and move to academic and administrative posts in overseas universities. A third factor is *academic leadership*. Leaders in academic fields play a role in the external assessment of research grant applications and in the external assessment of all teaching programmes and doctoral dissertations. Academic recruitment is done internationally, and promotion and tenure are performance based and quite competitive. Finally, there is also a high degree of *academic freedom*.

In 2012, the traditional British 3 + 4 + 3 education system was changed to a 3 + 3 + 4 structure (three years of junior and three years of senior secondary education followed by a 4-year university system). With the launch of its new higher education system, Hong Kong has been moving forward as a higher education hub not only in Asia but also internationally, based on established traditions and strengths.

3.6.14 Argentina

The Argentine higher education system manifests a highly complex historical evolution characterised by the absence of long-term agreed policies, an emphasis on teaching and professional training (but not on research), a reliance on part-time faculty and massification concentrated in the public university sector.

The University Reform of 1918, stimulated by a strong student movement throughout with impact towards Latin America, gave Argentine universities several specific characteristics that were common to creating a regional model. The concept of autonomy with self-governance by the participation of students, alumni and professors set as the distinguishing features (Fernández Lamarra et al. 2011). Following the 1918 reform, higher education had a relatively sustained development in this framework during the twentieth century, with expansion produced almost exclusively by the growth of the public university sector, which constitutes today more than 85% of the university enrolment, thus far exceeding the Latin American average of less than 50%.

Separate from the university sector, the nonuniversity sector of higher education is dedicated to the training of teachers and technicians. These institutions constitute less than one-third of the total higher education enrolment, and they are perceived as devalued options when compared to the possibilities offered by the university.

The expansion in the Argentine university enrolment began around the middle of the 20th century, with peaks that coincide with periods of political democracy and respect for autonomy and times of retrogression during the periods of rule by military governments. Between 1955 and 1966, the system grew by 75%. The 1960s were years of splendour and growth, since national policies focused on research and development based on science and technology. The 1960s are considered the golden age of the public university due to the quality of its professors and curricula. Nonetheless, not until the 1970s did the university panorama truly diversify, thanks to the creation of twelve nationally run universities, for a total of twenty-five up from ten in the early 1970s. The number of students tripled from 1955 to 1973 (Marquina and Fernández Lamarra 2008).

The military coup in 1976 initially led to stagnation and then a fall in university enrolment. This was reverted with the return to democracy and the principles of joint student governance and open competition among candidates for senior teaching positions. From 1984 to 1990, the number of students enrolled in universities grew sharply from 443,400 students in 1984 by 65% to 679,400 in 1990.

The unplanned expansion stemming from larger enrolment was accompanied by an increased reliance on part-time professors. Today most teachers (62%) are part-timers (10 h per week), while a very low percentage of teachers (14%) are full-time (40 h per week). There is an intermediate group (24%) with about 24 h per week. Recently, part-time faculty tends to decrease slightly.

The most recent law on higher education, Law 24,521, was passed in 1995. This is the first attempt to regulate universities and other nonuniversity institutions of higher education, mostly teacher training institutes, thus giving shape to the overall system of higher education The new regulations favour the creation of new universities, especially in the outskirts of Buenos Aires, some of which attempted to expand professional options and to modify the organisational structures of traditional universities (Marquina 2011).

The political agenda for universities during the 1990s was clearly set within the international trends of the era, placing emphasis on the efficiency of institutional administration and improvement in educational quality. New options of funding research and of developing specific programmes, assigned competitively to institutions or research teams, fit into place with similar practices already carried out for the sector by the Ministry of Education.

The current map of higher education in Argentina is characterised by a strong institutional diversification, with a dominance of the public sector covering 74% of enrolment in higher education and with a dominance of universities (81%), whereby enrolment at private universities is growing in recent years. Yet, public institutions continue to enrol most of the students as the consequence of open access and free tuition.

According to international statistics, Argentina has the highest enrolment rate in Latin America (65% of the 20–24 years old in 2007). Even though access is uneven according to region and social background, students at universities are heterogeneous according to their social backgrounds and cultural capital, prior academic training and skills, expectations, behaviours and interests. As this is not properly addressed by the universities, high dropout rates are evident in the first year of study thus putting in question the social benefits provided by the open access. According to the Secretariat of University Policies, the early dropout rate in 2007 reached 60%, and the graduation rate was only around 20% (Chiroleu and Marquina 2010).

3.6.15 Brazil

Brazilian higher education is a known case of extreme diversity, both in terms of institutional settings and in terms of ownership. Among its more than 2,300 institutions, one can find examples of almost everything: from small, family-owned, isolated professional schools to huge research universities with budgets of more than two billion dollars a year. Brazilian higher education comprised 2,378 institutions in 2010, of which 190 were universities. Only 12% of the institutions are public. Public institutions may be owned by the Federal Government or by state (provincial) governments or by municipalities (local government). On average, public institutions are bigger and more established than the private ones: They represent 53% of all Brazilian universities and respond for most of the country's graduate education. The private sector includes 2,100 institutions and answers for 73% of all undergraduate enrolments. Inside the huge private sector (89% of all institutions), there are family-owned institutions, community-owned institutions, denominational institutions, institutions belonging to enterprises' associations and for-profit institutions with shares at the stock market.

One of the most salient features of Brazilian higher education is the presence of strong lines of differentiation that cuts across the standard classifications that oppose private to public or even university to nonuniversity institutions. Inside the public sector, the most important line of differentiation is the size of graduate education, in particular doctoral programmes, that is usually linked to an active research profile (Balbachevsky and Schwartzman 2010). These are also the institutions that are able to draw in the majority of the country's public resources for science support and, by providing a good up-to-date infrastructure for research, succeed in attracting the most talented and competitive scholars in the country. Together they awarded more than 80% of the doctorates granted in the country in 2010. The other public institutions, even when holding university status, are undergraduate-oriented institutions with opportunities for access to research support (Schwartzman and Balbachevsky 2009).

The last two decades witnessed strong processes of differentiation and stratification inside the private sector, with the growth of a segment of prestigious elite institutions catering for children from affluent families. Some of these institutions are modernised Catholic universities or other denominational institutions, but many are lay institutions offering programmes well regarded in the labour market. Though being mainly undergraduate-oriented institutions, they value their academic staff degree and research reputation because these are signs of quality in the market they operate.

Notwithstanding these recent developments, the vast majority of institutions in the private sector in Brazil are still confined to a mass education market, where the lower price charged for education is the main differential. In this segment, small isolated professional schools prevail, offering few undergraduate programmes. In the last ten years, various huge for-profit universities emerged, offering dozens of different undergraduate programmes. Irrespective of their size and the entrepreneurial initiatives launched by the institutions' top management, they are still confined to a kind of 'commodity-like' market, where the gains are mainly sought in improving the institution's operational scale. As such, they have an academic environment almost as poor as the one found in the small family-owned isolated professional schools.

In spite of the institutional maze described above, the provisions for degrees are unusually simple: Traditionally, all higher education institutions in Brazil are allowed to grant the same first degree, the bachelor's degree. Following the old Napoleonic tradition, the bachelor's degree in Brazil is both a professional certification and an academic credential entitling the holder to advance his/her studies into postgraduate studies. In order to be assured that the certifications are of legal equal value, an elaborate system of formal regulations has been developed since the 1930s, when the first university law was enacted. The entire system is controlled by a Federal Council of Education and the bureaucracy of the Ministry of Education's powerful

Secretary of Higher Education. It is the clash between the diverse environment with the rigid and the uniform model imposed by the regulatory bodies that creates some of the most interesting features and dynamics of Brazilian higher education (Balbachevsky and Schwartzman 2011).

3.6.16 Mexico

With a history that dates back to the sixteenth century, Mexican higher education, in parallel with the country as a whole, has grown and developed in important ways during the last 40 years. At a quantitative level, the Mexican higher education system has increased its size. Institutions, students, faculty, academic programmes, research and allocated budget, all of these indicators have increased substantially (Rubio Oca 2006). So, for example, while in the early 1970s a little more than a quarter of a million students attended higher education, representing a gross enrolment rate of about 6%, in 2011 there were more than three million students enrolled, for a gross enrolment rate of approximately 33%. However, if net enrolment rates are calculated, then figures are considerably smaller (Gil-Antón et al. 2009).

At the same time, there have been major qualitative changes in Mexican higher education. In a context of a strong public-funding tradition, private enrolment of students has increased and now reaches around one-third of all students, global female participation has reached a parity level with that of males, academics with a full-time appointment are now a larger percentage of all academics (from almost non-existing in 1970 to almost a third of about three hundred thousand) and their profile (mainly highest degree) and productivity have improved significantly (Galaz-Fontes et al. 2009). Notwithstanding such changes, Mexican academics can be said to be centred in teaching, despite the push towards research of several very important public policies.

Additionally, the relationship between public higher education and the Mexican state has changed in various important ways. Coming from a position in which the state funded public higher education in a more or less generous and benevolent way based largely on political considerations, performance-based funding is now accepted as the way by which higher education institutions are able to secure public funds beyond a level that many consider barely enough to keep matters functioning at the current state of affairs. This evaluation approach, coupled with a discourse centred on quality and social pertinence, understood mainly in terms of building links to business and industry, has been applied to institutions as a whole, academic programmes, students, faculty and research activities. The situation is such that many observers consider that Mexican higher education is currently 'over-evaluated' and claim that merit-pay systems, whether at the individual or institutional level, have promoted strategies to satisfy the need for appropriate indexes while maintaining the old state of affairs.

In the particular case of academics, the conditional monetary transfer approach (Villatoro 2005) has led to a situation in which academics' incomes depend largely (up to 60% for research-oriented faculty) upon their performance in merit-pay systems, which is pushing academics to pay more attention to fulfilling the requirements of the programmes by which they make their living than to their work in itself, including their teaching—a situation that has made academics to be described as a managed profession (Galaz Fontes et al. 2011). Situations such as these have led the National Association of Universities and Higher Education Institutions (ANUIES 2012) to propose the construction of a new generation of public policies in which more funding should be secured for long-term plans, and evaluation itself and the performance-based approach should be seriously evaluated in order to retain that which has shown to work and, at the same time, avoid the danger of working to meet the formal requirements of a larger than necessary number of programmes, losing sight of what is really taking place in higher education.

3.6.17 South Africa

South Africa's university sector is the strongest and most diverse in Africa. In the new landscape, there are nearly double the number of students of all races—three-quarter of a million in all—enrolled in the fewer, but larger, public universities, and nearly one in five young South Africans enter higher education. More than half of all students are women, and some 8% are international students, most of them from other African countries but also thousands from Europe, Asia and the Americas.

There are three types of universities, and together they offer a full range of courses leading internationally recognised qualifications. All public universities conduct research, which supports teaching and is frequently aimed at tackling the challenges that South Africa and the developing world face. Public funding of higher education has increased in recent years, and universities have received a major funding boost from government to refurbish buildings, construct new facilities, upgrade equipment and libraries, improve outputs and produce more science, engineering and technology graduates.

South Africa's apartheid legacy was a higher education sector that was racially divided, of uneven quality, and beset by duplications and inefficiencies. Under apartheid there were separate institutions for different race groups; historically, 'white' institutions were most favourably located and resourced and conducted almost all research, and there was a binary system featuring academic universities and vocational technikons. Higher education in a democratic South Africa faced huge challenges—primarily the need to achieve greater equity, efficiency and effectiveness within institutions and the system. Universities had to open their doors to students of all races, transform curricula to become more locally relevant but also geared to a knowledge-driven world, train growing numbers of different types of graduates essential to economic growth and development and produce scholars able to tackle South Africa's problems through research responsive to all society's needs.

The present government drove a radical restructuring of higher education aimed at making it stronger and more focused and efficient, within a framework of policies and regulations including the 1996 National Commission on Higher Education, 1997 Education Act and the 2001 National Plan for Higher Education. The binary divide in higher education was dismantled, and the number of institutions was cut from 36 to 23 through mergers and campus incorporations involving most institutions. No campuses were closed, so there remains as much higher education provision as there was before.

The new landscape in South Africa comprises three types of institutions: 'traditional' research-focused universities, universities of technology and 'comprehensive' universities that combine academic and vocationally orientated education. Currently the system has eleven universities, 'traditional' universities that offer bachelor's degrees and have a strong research capacity and high proportions of postgraduate students; six universities of technology, vocationally orientated institutions that award higher certificates, diplomas and degrees in technology and have some postgraduate and research capacity; and six comprehensive universities, offering both bachelor and technology qualifications and focusing on teaching but also conducting research and postgraduate study.

3.6.18 *China*

Chinese higher education has been a long history; however, when we talk about the modern higher education of China, we usually mean the six decades since 1949, when the People's Republic of China was established. The central government changed some private universities and colleges to public ones and also recognised most public institutions that had been supported by the *Kuomintang* government. Thus, the higher education system of PRC consisted of 205 universities and colleges in 1949.

The '17-year' period from 1949 to 1966 tends to be considered the best time for higher education development in China, sandwiched in between the 'inner war' and the 'cultural revolution'. Most institutions followed the Russian model with a prime emphasis on teaching and training. Chinese universities had only a few research projects, while research was concentrated in the Chinese Academy of Sciences system. The universities had no doctoral education programmes and few master's programmes. Ambitious scholars could either submit dissertations for evaluation towards a doctorate or pursue a foreign (many Russians) Ph.D. Also, curricula often followed Russian samples, and the Russian language was the major foreign language taught in schools. However, the higher education system provided a large number of intelligent graduates for meeting the country's demand in the '17-year' period.

The well-known Cultural Revolution stopped the stable successive progress of higher education system, as campus doors were shut. Near the end of Cultural Revolution, the doors were opened narrowly, and some youths who had been from workers, peasants and soldiers were admitted upon recommendation without a test of their academic abilities.

The reform began at 1976, when the campus doors were opened widely, though from 1997 onwards came to be based on performance in the National College Entrance Examination. However, neither graduate education nor faculty promotion based on performance was revived initially. Also research remained the domain of the Academies of Sciences. A few non-profit private nondegree award colleges were established in the late 1970s, and graduate education as well as faculty promotion recovered in the early 1980s. The whole process of readjustment after the Cultural Revolution lasted 20 years—until the mid-1990s. During these years, master's and doctoral programmes were established as well, and an academic career ladder was established with full professors, associate professors, lecturers and assistant teachers.

The year 1999 was a major turning point in the history of Chinese higher education. First, the central government implemented a loan scheme for filling the financial gap of the needy students who could not pay the tuition fees introduced in 1997. The second was to encourage private investment in higher education in order to facilitate the transition from the elite stage to the mass stage of higher education. Already a year earlier, the central government announced a '985 Project' of promoting the emergence of elite universities. In 2001, a further '211 Project' was promulgated aiming to support 100 good universities in the twenty-first century. So far, there are 38 '985 universities' affiliated to State Ministry of Education, and 100 '211 universities' are affiliated to State Ministry of Education, other state ministries or local government affiliations—each in charge of funding. The financial situation of the individual higher education institutions actually varies substantially. Between the top universities and the 3-year colleges, there is a vast number of about 2,000 institutions, often—public or private—4-year colleges, colleges linked to ministries and the party, as well as 'independent colleges' which work in close cooperation with well-established universities.

As a consequence, the level of research, teaching and service has substantially increased in the recent two decades. Diversity has increased between '985 universities' and 3-year colleges. The gross participation rate of higher education grew from 10% in 1998 to 27% in 2011. Yet, higher education in China is criticised being short of qualified faculty, lacking funds and being overburdened by administrative control and evaluation and being apart from society. Moreover, critique is voiced that increased emphasis on research undermines teaching, that rankings replace evaluation, that corruption increases and undermines academic credibility, etc. In sum, there are major debates on salient issues of the future of higher education which address both the character and quality of higher education as well as the system of governance and control.

3.6.19 Malaysia

The relatively young institutional history of Malaysian higher education is a part of the process of the creation of human resource development and knowledge generation for the economic growth of the country. The Malaysian system of higher education is a binary system that consists of a university and a nonuniversity sector. Prior to the 1990s, the university system consisted of primarily public universities which were regulated by the Department of Higher Education and funded from the national budget. The nonuniversity system then consisted of polytechnics and colleges established and funded by various government ministries.

The first university (Universiti Malaya) was founded in the 1950s, and between 1957 to 1980s, the public university sector expanded with the establishment of new public universities offering a diverse array of academic and technical disciplines relevant to national development. The University and University College Act, 1971, was the legislative framework that governed the public universities. During this period, university education was primarily provided by the public sector. There were 20 public universities while the nonuniversity sector included university colleges, polytechnics and colleges offered technically and vocationally oriented courses that prepared students for the labour market.

Beginning in the 1980s, the trend towards diversification in the provision of higher education became evident with the establishment of both public and private universities and university colleges as well as colleges. In particular, there was a rapid growth of private higher education providers. By the mid-1990s, with the intensification of the globalisation process and the internationalisation of higher education, educational reforms began to take place. The Private Higher Education Act 1996, the National Council on Higher Education Act 1996, the National Accreditation Board Act 1996 and the University and University College (Amendment) Act 1996 were enacted to liberalise, regulate and privatise higher education to meet the national development objectives. The establishment of the Ministry of Higher Education and the Malaysian Qualifications Agency was the beginning of state active involvement in regulating the quality and diversity of higher education system in Malaysia (Azman et al. 2011). These developments were timely as higher education was seen as vital to Malaysia's economic growth, and these reforms provide the necessary regulatory framework for the liberalisation and privatisation of higher education on a larger scale to meet Malaysia's national development objectives (Azman et al. 2010).

The added capacity of the private institutions in particular tripled student enrolment within a decade. The higher education institutions expanded just enough to accommodate demographic growth, but overall, the system accommodated Malaysian demographic expansion and increased the opportunity for higher education. The launching of the National Higher Education Strategic Plan (2006–2015) in 2006 marked the beginning of serious transformation in the higher education system and institutions in Malaysia, while recent key government policies such as the New Economic Model and the Tenth Malaysia Plan, 2011–2015, underscored the need to spearhead human capital formation through the development of 'world-class' higher education institutions (Ministry of Higher Education 2007).

The stratification of public universities into several distinct categories based on their ascribed mission and vision was clear indicative statements of planned development of institutions and the system as a whole. *Universiti Sains Malaysia* was chosen as the only university for the Accelerated Programme for Excellence (APEX), aimed at initiating transformations in the Malaysian higher education system through sharing of best practices and innovative (and creative) ideas. Below this APEX status university are the research universities which are deemed relevant and critical in Malaysia's drive towards achieving world-class institutions. The next level is 11 comprehensive/focus universities. At the base of the Malaysian public higher education system hierarchy are the four technical universities, which were established to supply the nation with a technically trained workforce. The realignment of the role and mission of technical universities, polytechnics and community colleges which are mostly located outside the core region (Klang Valley) through the higher education transformation plan reflects the government's effort to use higher education as an instrument to redress inequity and regional imbalances in the less developed regions.

The academic rank system in Malaysia is generally composed of four career rungs: lecturer, senior lecturer, associate professor and professor. In well-established universities such as the research universities, only people with doctorates can be hired directly as a lecturer. The academic rank is divided into several grades—each grade being defined by a common or prescribed salary scale. Academic grades range from DS45 (lecturer) to DS51/52 (senior lecturer), DS53/54 (associate professor) and VK7 (professor). The formal description of the professoriate is uniform, but in practice, professors in Malaysia are further divided into three salary categories referred to as professor (special grade) C, B, A and distinguished professor. There is a hierarchy of income and prestige among the various levels.

References

Aarrevaara, T., Dobson, I. R., & Elander, C. (2009). Brave new world? Higher education reform in Finland. *Higher Education Management and Policy, 21*(2), 41–58.

Aarrevaara, T., Dobson, I. R., & Pekkola, E. (2011). CAPtive academics: An examination of the binary divide in Finland. In W. Locke, W. Cummings, & D. Fisher (Eds.), *Changing governance and management in higher education: The perspectives of the academy* (pp. 243–262). Dordrecht: Springer.

Arimoto, A. (2006). The changing academic profession in Japan: Its origins, heritage and current situation. In RIHE (Ed.), *Reports of changing academic profession project workshop on quality, relevance and governance in the changing academia: International perspectives* (COE Publication Series, Vol. 20, pp. 183–194). Hiroshima: Hiroshima University.

Asociación Nacional de Universidades e Instituciones de Educación Superior. (2012). *Inclusión con responsabilidad social: Una nueva generación de políticas de educación superior* [Inclusion with social responsibility: A new generation of policies in higher education]. México: Autor.

Azman, N., Sirat, M., & Karim, M. E. (2010). Building future scenarios for Malaysian universities. *Journal of Asia Public Policy, 3*(1), 86–99.

Azman, N., Sirat, M., & Jantan, M. (2011). Malaysia: Perspectives of university governance and management within the academic profession. In W. Locke, K. Cummings, & D. Fisher (Eds.), *Changing governance and management in higher education: The perspectives of the academy* (pp. 83–106). Dordrecht: Springer.

References

Balbachevsky, E., & Schwartzman, S. (2010). The graduate foundations of Brazilian research. *Higher Education Forum (Hiroshima University), 7*, 85–100.

Balbachevsky, E., & Schwartzman, S. (2011). Brazil: Diverse experience in institutional governance in the public and private sectors. In W. Locke, W. Cummings, & D. Fisher (Eds.), *Changing governance and management in higher education: The perspectives of academy* (pp. 35–56). Dordrecht: Springer.

Chiroleu, A., & Marquina, M. (2010). Argentina. In B. Vlaardingerbroek & N. Taylor (Eds.), *Getting into varsity – Comparability, convergence and congruence*. New York: Cambria Press Inc.

Coates, H., Dobson, I., Edwards, D., Friedman, T., Goedegebuure, L., & Meek, L. (2009). *The attractiveness of the Australian academic profession: A comparative analysis*. Melbourne: LH Martin Institute, EPI & ACER, Melbourne.

Cummings, W. K. (2008). The context for the changing academic profession: A survey of international indicators. In RIHE (Ed.), *The changing academic profession in international comparative and quantitative perspectives* (RIHE International Seminar Reports, Vol. 12, pp. 33–55). Hiroshima: Hiroshima University.

De Weert, E. (2006). The Netherlands. In J. Forest & P. G. Altbach (Eds.), *International handbook of higher education, Part 2: Regions and countries* (pp. 899–918). Dordrecht: Springer.

De Weert, E., Kaiser, F., & Enders, J. (2006). The changing academic profession: The case of the Netherlands. In RIHE (Ed.), *Reports of changing academic profession project workshop on quality, relevance and governance in the changing academia: International perspectives* (pp. 167–183). Hiroshima: Hiroshima University.

DIISRTE. (Various years). *Students: Selected higher education statistics*. Canberra: DIISRTE.

Fernández Lamarra, N., Marquina, M., & Rebello, G. (2011). Argentina: Changes in teachers' involvement in the governance and management of public universities. In W. Locke, W. Cummings, & D. Fisher (Eds.), *Changing governance and management in higher education: The perspectives of academy* (pp. 19–33). Dordrecht: Springer.

Finkelstein, M. J. (2010). Diversification in the academic workforce: The case of the US and implications for Europe. *European Review, 18*(Supplement 1), 141–156.

Finkelstein, M. J., & Frances, C. (2006). The American academic profession: Contact and characteristics. In RIHE (Ed.), *Reports of changing academic profession project workshop on quality, relevance and governance in the changing academia: International perspectives* (COE Publication Series, Vol. 20, pp. 231–254). Hiroshima: Hiroshima University.

Galaz Fontes, J. F., Sevilla García, J. J., Padilla González, L. E., Arcos Vega, J. L., Gil Antón, M., & Martínez Stack, J. (2011). Mexico: A portrait of a managed profession. In W. K. Cummings, & D. Fisher (Eds.), *Changing governance and management in higher education: The perspectives of the academy* (pp. 57–81). New York: Springer.

Galaz-Fontes, J. F., Gil-Antón, M., Padilla-González, L. E., Sevilla-García, J. J., Arcos-Vega, J. L., & Martínez-Stack, J. G. (2009). The academic profession in Mexico: Changes, continuities and challenges derived from a comparison of two national surveys 15 years apart. In RIHE (Ed.), *The changing academic profession over 1992–2007: International, comparative and quantitative perspectives* (RIHE International Seminar Reports, Vol. 13, pp. 193–212). Hiroshima: Hiroshima University.

Gil-Antón, M., Mendoza-Rojas, J., Rodríguez-Gómez, R., & Pérez-García, M. J. (2009). *Cobertura de la educación superior en México: Tendencias, retos y perspectivas* [Student enrollment in higher education in Mexico: Trends, challenges and perspectives]. México: Asociación Nacional de Universidades e Instituciones de Educación Superior.

Huang, F. (2006). The academic profession in Japan: Major characteristics and new changes. In RIHE (Ed.), *Reports of changing academic profession project workshop on quality, relevance and governance in the changing academia: International perspectives* (COE Publication Series, Vol. 20, pp. 195–208). Hiroshima: Hiroshima University.

Huang, F. (2007). Challenges of internationalization of higher education and changes in the academic profession: A perspective from Japan. In M. Kogan & U. Teichler (Eds.), *Key challenges to the academic profession* (Werkstattberichte, Vol. 65, pp. 81–98). Kassel: International Centre for Higher Education Research Kassel.

Kehm, B. M. (2006). Germany. In J. F. Forest & P. G. Altbach (Eds.), *International handbook of higher education. Part 2: Regions and countries* (pp. 729–745). Dordrecht: Springer.

Kehm, B., Michelsen, S., & Vabø, A. (2010). Towards the two-cycle degree structure: Bologna reform and path dependency in German and Norwegian universities. *Higher Education Policy, 23*(2).

Kerr, C. (1990). The internationalization of learning and the nationalization of the purposes of higher education. *European Journal of Education, 25*(1), 5–22.

Lee, S. (1989). The emergency of the modern university in Korea. *Higher Education, 18*, 87–116.

Lee, J. (2002). *Korean higher education: A Confucian perspective*. Seoul: Jimoondang Publishing Company.

Locke, W., Cummings, W., & Fisher, D. (Eds.). (2011). *Changing governance and management in higher education: The perspectives of the academy*. Dordrecht: Springer.

Lomax-Smith, J., Watson, L., & Webster, B. (2011). *Higher education base funding review, final report*. Canberra: Department of Education, Employment and Workplace Relations.

Marquina, M. (2011). Higher education reform in Argentina in the 1990s: Paradoxes of government intervention in a minimalist state model. *Higher Education Forum (Research Institute for Higher Education, Hiroshima University), 8*(3), 93–104.

Marquina, M., & Fernández Lamarra, N. (2008). The academic profession in Argentina: Characteristics and trends in the context of a mass higher education system. In RIHE (Ed.), *The changing academic profession in international comparative and quantitative perspectives* (RIHE International Seminar Reports, Vol. 12, pp. 363–387). Hiroshima: Hiroshima University.

Martinez Cortés, A. M., & Teichler, U. (2010). Higher education in federal systems. In P. Petersen, E. Baker, & B. McGaw (Eds.), *International encyclopedia of education* (Vol. 4, pp. 603–608). Oxford: Elsevier.

May, R. (2011). Casualisation here to stay? The modern university and its divided workforce. In R. Markey (Ed.), *Dialogue downunder, refereed proceedings of the 25th Conference of AIRAANZ*. Auckland: AIRAANZ.

Metcalfe, A. S. (2008). The changing academic profession in Canada: Exploring themes of relevance, internationalization, and management. In RIHE (Ed.), *The changing academic profession in international comparative and quantitative perspectives* (RIHE International Seminar Reports, Vol. 12, pp. 57–73). Hiroshima: Hiroshima University.

Metcalfe, A. S., Fisher, D., Gingras, Y., Jones, G. A., Rubenson, K., & Snee, I. (2011). Canada: Perspectives on governance and management. In W. Locke, W. K. Cummings, & D. Fisher (Eds.), *Governance and management in higher education: The perspectives of the academy* (pp. 151–174). Dordrecht: Springer.

Ministry of Higher Education. (2007). *The national higher education strategic plan 2007–2020*. Putrajaya: Kementerian Pengajian Tinggi Malaysia.

Naidoo, R., & Brennan, J. (2006). The higher education system in the United Kingdom. In RIHE (Ed.), *Reports of changing academic profession project workshop on quality, relevance and governance in the changing academia: International perspectives* (COE Publication Series, Vol. 20, pp. 45–62). Hiroshima: Hiroshima University.

Norton, A. (2012a). *Graduate winners: Assessing the public and private benefits of higher education*. Melbourne: Grattan Institute.

Norton, A. (2012b). *Mapping Australian higher education*. Melbourne: Grattan Institute.

OECD. (2011). *Education at a glance 2011. OECD Indicators*. Paris: OECD.

Postiglione, G. A. (2010). East Asian knowledge systems: Driving ahead amid borderless higher education. In D. W. Chapman, W. K. Cummings, & G. A. Postiglione (Eds.), *Crossing borders in East Asian higher education*. Dordrecht: Springer.

Postiglione, G. A. (2011). The rise of research universities: The case of the Hong Kong University of Science and Technology. In P. Altbach & J. Salmi (Eds.), *The road to academic excellence: Emerging research universities in developing and transition countries*. Washington, DC: The World Bank.

Postiglione, G. A., & Jung, J. (2012). Government frameworks for creating world-class universities: The Hong Kong case. In J. C. Shin & B. M. Kehm (Eds.), *Institutionalization of a world-class university in global competition*. Dordrecht: Springer.

References

RIHE. (2006). *Reports of changing academic profession project workshop on quality, relevance and governance in the changing academia: International perspectives* (COE Publication Series, Vol. 20). Hiroshima: Hiroshima University.

Rostan, M. (2008). The changing academic profession in Italy: Accounts from the past, first insights from the present. In RIHE (Ed.), *The changing academic profession in international comparative and quantitative perspectives* (RIHE International Seminar Reports, Vol. 12, pp. 153–178). Hiroshima: Hiroshima University.

Rostan, M. (2010). Teaching and research in a changing environment: The academic work in Italy. In RIHE (Ed.), *The changing academic profession in international comparative and quantitative perspectives: A focus on teaching & research activities* (RIHE International Seminar Reports, Vol. 15, pp. 61–85). Hiroshima: Hiroshima University.

Rostan, M. (Ed.). (2011). *La professione accademica in Italia: Aspetti, problemi e confronti nel contesto europeo*. Milano: LED Edizioni.

Rubio Oca, J. (Coord.) (2006). *La política educativa y la educación superior en México, 1995–2006: Un balance* [Educational policy and higher education in Mexico, 1995–2006: An appraisal]. México: Secretaría de Educación Pública y Fondo de Cultura Económica.

Schwartzman, S., & Balbachevsky, E. (2009). The academic profession in a diverse institutional environment: Converging or diverging values and beliefs. In RIHE (Ed.), *The changing academic profession over 1992–2007: International, comparative and quantitative perspectives* (RIHE International Seminar Reports, Vol. 13, pp. 145–164). Hiroshima: Hiroshima University.

Shin, J. C. (2012). Higher education development in Korea: Western university ideas, Confucian tradition, and economic development. *Higher Education, 64*(1), 59–72.

Shin, J. C., & Cummings, W. K. (2010). Multilevel analysis of academic publishing across disciplines. Research preference, collaboration, and time on research. *Scientometrics, 85*(2), 581–594

Shin, J. C., & Jang, Y. (2013). World-class university in Korea: Proactive government, responsive university, and procrastinating academics. In J. C. Shin & B. M. Kehm (Eds.), *Institutionalization of world-class university in global competition*. Dordrecht: Springer (forthcoming).

Teichler, U. (1996). Comparative higher education: Potentials and Limits. *Higher Education, 32*(4), 431–465.

Teichler, U., & Bracht, O. (2006). The academic profession in Germany. In RIHE (Ed.), *Reports of changing academic profession project workshop on quality, relevance and governance in the changing academia: International perspectives* (COE Publication Series, Vol. 20, pp. 129–150). Hiroshima: Hiroshima University.

Vabø, A., & Aamodt, P. O. (2008). "Nordic higher education in transition", in structuring mass higher education. In T. Palfreyman & D. Tapper (Eds.), *The role of elite institutions*. New York: Routledge.

Villatoro, P. (2005, Agosto). Programas de transferencias monetarias condicionadas: Experiencias en América Latina [Conditional monetary transfestransfer funds programs: Experiences in Latin America]. *Revista de la CEPAL, 86*, 87–101.

Wheelahan, L., Arkoudis, S., Moodie, G., Fredman, N., & Bexley, E. (2011). *Shaken not stirred? The development of one tertiary education sector in Australia*. Adelaide: National Centre for Vocational Education Research.

Chapter 4
The Academic Career

4.1 Introduction

The academic profession is often portrayed as composed of persons strongly driven by intrinsic motives who concentrate primarily on the substance of teaching and research. They are said to be willing to devote much time to their work and often to forego the conveniences of life outside academia in favour of their interesting and demanding academic work. They are described as isolated from the real world and even absent-minded. Given this portrayal, it can be argued that the employment conditions for academics are less important than for the work of most other occupations.

However, we also note contrasting arguments claiming that the details of biography, employment and work are of outmost importance for the proper functioning of academic work. Some journalists have questioned the propriety of professors spending long periods gliding across oceans on their yachts. Some experts claim that the academic productivity of young researchers is undermined by job insecurity, while others consider their instable employment situation as an incentive mechanism for stimulating high academic achievement. Moreover, the academics themselves seem to be more prone than the majority of professions to pay attention to the rites and symbols associated with their work, for example, titles or memberships in selective academies, and to embark on heated debates on minute distinctions related to academic employment and working conditions (cf. various articles in Enders 2001; Enders and De Weert 2004).

In general, the academic profession is viewed as a highly attractive profession in terms of challenging tasks and leeway to shape one's own work. And in many countries, it is a fairly prestigious profession. However, salaries for academics often are viewed as not matching the demanding job requirements and the high occupational prestige. Moreover, there are obvious hardships in the early career stages before academics attain stable appointments: (a) long periods of concurrent learning and productive work, (b) often accompanied only by part-time employment, short-term contract and relatively limited income, as well as (c) a high degree of selectivity which forces many scholars to move to other occupational areas usually at an age when moves between sectors tend to be rare (Teichler and Schomburg 2008).

Most descriptions of the academic profession focus on the situation in economically advanced countries. There are relatively few reports focusing on low-income and middle-income countries or on countries in an emerging state as far as the maturity of the higher education and research system is concerned. The available studies indicate an enormous diversity in the employment and work situations of the academic profession across countries. The work situation might be more favourable in the economically advanced countries; for example, in economically less favoured countries, research at universities often is an 'endangered species' (see Vessuri and Teichler 2008). On the other hand, academics in some of these countries face less job risks in their early careers than this is the case in most of the economically and academically advanced countries.

Altogether, substantial information is available on the regulatory system affecting the academic profession all over the world, but there is much less information about the actual situation of the academics. Therefore, it is worth describing various issues of the biography, the career, the employment and work of members of the academic profession, that is, issues less well documented in the past. This might help to illustrate the individual situation of the 'productive workers' of the academic system, that is, those in charge of teaching, research and possibly related services (see the analyses in Kogan and Teichler 2007; Locke and Teichler 2007; Research Institute for Higher Education 2008, 2009).

In the presentation of data that follows, differences by *country* will be documented consistently. Thereby, for conceptual and practical reasons, countries will be subdivided into (a) *advanced countries*, that is, those where junior academics as a rule are trained in the home country (autochthonous doctoral education): Canada (CA), the United States of America (US), Finland (FI), Germany (DE), Italy (IT), the Netherlands (NL), Norway (NO), Portugal (PT), the United Kingdom (UK), Australia (AU), Japan (JP), the Republic of Korea (KR) and the Special Administrative Region of Hong Kong (HK) as well as (b) *other countries*, that is, those where a substantial proportion of the brightest academics spend their key years of training, notably their doctoral education, abroad: Argentina (AR), Brazil (BR), Mexico (MX), South Africa (ZA), China (CH) and Malaysia (MY).

The academics of each country will be subdivided by *type of higher education institution* and by staff category. As regards type of higher education institution, a distinction will be made between those employed at *universities* in terms of institutions both in charge of teaching and research and responsible for awarding doctoral degrees (in Europe only these institutions are called 'university'; in the USA, we note references to 'research university', 'doctoral-granting institutions', etc.) and *other institutions of higher education*, that is, those primarily in charge of teaching and usually not in charge of doctoral awards (see the discussion of varying models of diversity in higher education in Teichler 2007).

As regards *staff category*, we present the responses by senior academics or professors, that is, those in the position of professors and associate professors in US terms, on the one hand, and *junior academic staff*, that is, those regularly employed in lower positions (even though some of them might be named professor, that is,

4.1 Introduction

'assistant professor' or 'Junior-Professor'). In some cases, no reference will be made to junior academics in other higher education institutions because the size, the functions and the employment situation of this group is fairly heterogeneous across countries. This reflects the fact that academic careers are characterised in many countries by a long period of concurrent learning and productive work. Often, but not in all countries, this is combined with a clear status distinctions between junior staff and fully established senior staff, with high selectivity of those allowed to pursue the academic career and with a long period of job insecurity. In many countries, the academics are only accepted and stable members of the academic professor when they have reached a senior position. Moreover, the work situation and the assignments for junior staff differ systematically from those for senior staff notably in (a) reflecting the double function of learning and productive work of the former during their 'formative years' (Teichler 2006), (b) having lesser access to resources, (c) having more limited power in their institutions and (d) less often having the opportunity of spending their time in a balanced way both in teaching and research activities. Finally, a split of the respondents according to senior and junior academics staff provides a more realistic comparison of the responses by countries, because the junior to senior ratio varies strikingly by country.

Some of the themes addressed here were also surveyed in the Carnegie Study undertaken in the early 1990s (see Boyer et al. 1994; Altbach 1996). Where this applies, a comparison will be undertaken between the results of that survey with those of the CAP survey. In those cases, findings can be presented consistently for five advanced countries participating in both studies, that is, Australia, Germany, Japan, the United Kingdom and the United States of America, as well as in some cases also for Korea, Hong Kong and Brazil. For convenience's sake, we call it a comparison between the years 1992 and 2007, that is, those years when the majority of national studies were undertaken in the Carnegie Study and in the CAP study, respectively (cf. also Enders and Teichler 1995; Teichler 1996).

Finally, in this chapter, differences by *disciplinary area* as well as by *gender* will only be addressed selectively. Four countries were chosen for this purpose: the USA, Germany, Brazil and Korea. The USA was chosen as an example of an advanced country with a relatively high proportion of female academics as well as a relatively high proportion of academics in the *humanities and social sciences*, while Germany is the case of an advanced country with a relatively low proportion of female academics as well as a relatively high proportion of academics in *science and engineering*. Similarly, Brazil was chosen as an example of another country with a relatively high proportion of female academics as well as a relatively high proportion of academics in the humanities and social sciences, while Korea is the case of a country, which was not viewed as an advanced country when the Carnegie Study was undertaken but is viewed so now, with a relatively low proportion of female academics as well as a relatively high proportion of academics in science and engineering.

A comparison by country, however, reveals enormous variety even among advanced countries. Though academic knowledge transcends borders and academics are among the most international professionals often with 'cosmopolitan' values, the institutional fabrique of the higher education systems, the rules for study programmes, the governance of higher education institutions, the funding of higher education and, last but not least, the institutional frameworks for academic careers and for the employment and work characteristics are strongly shaped nationally (see Research Institute for Higher Education 2006); this even holds true, if many of the supervisory and funding responsibilities rest on smaller geographical entities (e.g. the 'states' in the USA or the 'Länder' in Germany).

4.2 Biography and Career

4.2.1 Gender Distribution

The share of women among academics in the 19 countries (more precisely 18 countries and the Special Administrative Region of Hong Kong) surveyed differs strikingly. In 2007, the share of women among professors at universities in advanced countries is highest in Australia with almost four out of ten (39%), as Fig. 4.1 shows. It is about one-third in the United Kingdom (33%) and the USA (32%). In most of these countries, about one-quarter or slightly more of the university professors are women, while their share is one-fifth or even less in Hong Kong (20%), the Netherlands (19%), Germany (18%), Japan and Korea (13% each). In the other countries, the share of women among university professors is mostly higher: 46% in South Africa, 45% in Brazil and slightly less than 40% in the remaining countries.

In almost all countries, the share of women among junior staff is substantially higher than among professors. Women comprise more than half of the junior academic staff at universities of advanced countries in Australia (63%) as well as in the United Kingdom (52%) and in Norway (50%) and more than two-fifth in all other advanced countries addressed except for Germany (38%), the Netherlands (35%), Korea (20%) and Japan (14%). As concerns the other countries, more than half of the junior academics are women in Argentina (54%) and China (52%), while the other countries reported proportions slightly less than half.

At other institutions of higher education, the share of women among senior staff is lower in several countries than at universities. This is due to the fact that the proportion of fields with high shares of men, for example, engineering, often is larger in other higher education institutions than in the sector of research-oriented universities. In 2007, the share of women among professors at other higher education institutions in advanced countries is almost half in Australia and Portugal (47% each) and one-third or slightly more in the majority of cases, while only one-fifth or less in Germany (20%), Korea (19%) and Japan (17%) are women. As regards other countries, the share of women among the professors at other higher education institutions ranges from 48% in Brazil to 21% in Malaysia. Among junior staff at other higher education institutions, we note again higher percentage of women than among senior academics of this institutional type in most countries and again small shares of those in Germany, Japan and Korea.

4.2 Biography and Career

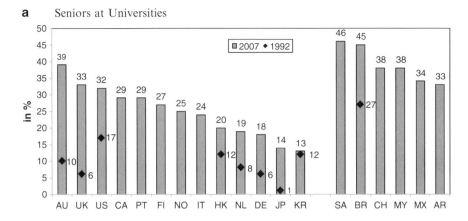

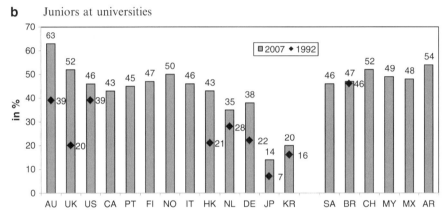

Fig. 4.1 Women academics in 1992 and 2007 (percentage). (**a**) Seniors at universities. (**b**) Juniors at universities (See the country codes on p. 76)

In all the countries selectively included in the analysis by field and gender, we note higher shares of women in the humanities and social sciences than in science and engineering, for example:

- In the USA 41% versus 17% among senior and 48% versus 36% among junior academics
- In Germany 30% versus 3% and 59% versus 22%, respectively
- In Brazil 58% versus 24% and 62% versus 20%
- In Korea 17% versus 7% and 10% versus 11%
- In Japan 22% versus 2% among seniors and 40% versus 0% among junior academics, and in Argentina 27% versus 46% and 62% versus 42% among juniors

In general, we know from available analyses in this area that a lower proportion of women in senior positions than in junior positions often is in part a historical phenomenon: If the share of women is on the increase historically, the relatively higher share of women among junior staff at a certain point in time will lead to an increased representation among senior staff one or two or three decades later. We also know that there is often career selectivity according to gender in many countries: A lower share of women than men move up to higher stages of the career ladder. This survey does not allow us to disentangle these two factors clearly, but a comparison of the findings of 1992 and 2007 provides some relevant information.

Actually, we observe a most striking *change within 15 years* in terms of an increase of women among senior academics at universities, for example, from 10% in 1992 to 39% in 2007 in Australia, from 6 to 33% in the UK, from 6 to 18% in Germany, from 8 to 19% in the Netherlands, and even from 1 to 13% in Japan. In the USA, where already 17% of the senior academics at universities were women in 1992, the increase to 32% is by no means marginal as well; the same holds true for Hong Kong (from 12 to 20%). In contrast, hardly any change occurred in Korea in this respect (12 and 13%). As regards other countries, we also see a substantial increase from 27 to 45% in Brazil.

In comparing the shares of women *among junior staff at universities in 1992* with those of *senior staff in 2007*, we note that the figures are very similar in most of the countries for which data are available. This suggests that almost all of the change observed from 1992 to 2007 is of a historical nature: More or less the same share of men and women being in a junior position in 1992 progressed to a senior position during the period observed. For example, women have comprised only 10% of senior academics in Australia, but 39% of junior academics in 1992; 15 years later, the share of women among senior academics is exactly 39%. In Japan, the share of women among senior academics in 2007 is even more than twice as high as that of junior academics 15 years earlier. In these countries, the findings support the interpretation of a historical catching-up process, but not any 'glass ceiling' or similar interpretation. In the Netherlands, however, we note that the share of senior academics at universities recently (19%) is substantially lower than the share of junior academics in the early 1990s (28%); the same holds true for the USA (32 and 42%, respectively).

4.2.2 Qualifications

For a long time, a **doctoral degree** has been the normal entry qualification for a career at a university in several of the advanced countries analysed. In Germany (95%) and the USA (94%), almost all professors at universities have been doctoral degree holders in 1992, and we note only small changes until 2007 (95% in Germany and 91% in the USA). Actually, in Germany, academics are expected to have passed the habilitation, that is, a kind of second-level doctoral degree, as a requirement for being eligible for an appointment as a professor.

During the period analysed, the doctoral degree has become increasingly a 'must' in Korea (from 79 to 99%), Hong Kong (from 80 to 94%) and Australia (from 85 to 92%). In the United Kingdom, we note only a moderate growth (from 74 to 78%).

In Japan, the respective quota remained constant at 85%. In contrast, the percentage of doctoral degree holders among professors at universities even decreased during that period in the Netherlands (from 90 to 83%). Thus, there is no clear trend towards a doctoral degree as a mandatory entry qualification across all economically advanced countries.

In most of all other advanced countries, almost all university professors are holders of a doctoral degree in 2007 (97% in Portugal, 94% in Canada and 92% in Finland). In Norway, the respective proportion is 85%. Only in Italy (33%), the doctoral award is not the typical entry qualification to a professor position. In the other countries, the share of university professors with a doctoral degree in 2007 is 93% in Brazil, 72% in Malaysia and less than half in Mexico (52%), China (47%), South Africa (44%) and Argentina (31%).

At other institutions of higher education, the doctoral degree increasingly has become a regular entry qualification. In 1992, only about three quarters of professors of these institutions in the USA, about two-thirds in Germany, about half in Japan, less than half in Australia and in the United Kingdom, and close to none in the Netherlands and Korea have had a doctoral degree. In 2007, more than 80% of professors at other institutions of higher education are holders of a doctoral degree in Korea (97%), Australia (92%), the USA (89%), Germany and Norway (86%) and Portugal (82%), while the respective proportion has remained below three quarters in Japan, below half in the United Kingdom and Finland, and even on marginal levels in the Netherlands (17%).

Actually, the **average age at the time of the doctoral award** (arithmetic mean) differs substantially by country. The professors at universities surveyed in 2007 have been on average 30 years in Germany, 31 years in the United Kingdom, 32 years in Italy and 33–35 years in most advanced countries, when they have been awarded a doctoral degree, while the average age at that stage of the academic career had been relatively high in Finland (36 years) and Norway (37 years). The respective average age had been higher in the other countries: 35 years in China, 36 years in Malaysia, 37 years in South Africa, 38 years in Brazil as well as 40 years both in Argentina and Mexico.

The average age at the award of a doctoral degree as a rule is higher among those who later in their career have become professors at other institutions of higher education than among those who later have become university professors. The average age of junior staff is not presented here, because a substantial proportion of those surveyed have not been awarded a doctoral degree at the time the survey has been conducted; therefore, an average of those awarded a degree at the time the survey is conducted would provide a distorted picture.

4.2.3 Professional and Institutional Mobility

Academics do not easily shift back and forth from academic work to other sectors of employment. However, the notion would be misleading as well that more or less all of them spend their whole career within the higher education and

Table 4.1 Senior academics having been employed full-time outside higher education since their first degree (percentage)

	CA	USA	DE	IT	NL	NO	PT	UK	AU	JP	KR	HK	AR	BR	MX	ZA	CH	MY
Universities	32	45	35	25	29	39	33	42	36	13	20	39	90	33	30	44	12	28
Other HEIs	.	40	77	.	63	28	46	a	48	18	14	.	.	36	39	a	8	39

Question A4_a: Since your first degree, how long have you been employed in the following? (only full-time), (other) government or public sector institutions, (other) industry or private sector institutions, self-employed

[a]Too small number of respondents
·No other higher education institutions or no other HEIs not surveyed

research system. A substantial proportion of them have worked for some period of their career in a *research institute*. Moreover, the responses to the CAP questionnaire suggest that senior academics have on average almost 2 years of their career been full-time employed outside higher education and research institutes. However, cross-sector professional mobility of academics varies substantially by country.

Table 4.1 indicates the proportion of senior academics who had been *employed full-time outside higher education* at least for a short period since the award of their first degree. On average across countries, 19% of university professors and 17% of senior academics now employed at other institutions of higher education had been employed for some time at research institutes.

Outside the higher education and research sectors, the respective rates have been 20 and 19%, respectively, in the public sector, 16 and 25% in the private sector as well as 5 and 12% being self-employed. Some period of employment outside higher education and research is more or less customary in the careers of senior academics at other higher education institutions in Germany, the Netherlands and Brazil. In contrast, such type of career mobility is rare among academics both at universities and other higher education institutions in East Asia.

Being employed *the whole academic career within a single institution of higher education* is often viewed with pride if the whole career has been spent at a very prestigious university such as Oxford University or Tokyo University but also is frequently called negatively as 'inbreeding'—possibly an indication of narrow experience and possibly caused by non-meritocratic selection. Definitions of inbreeding vary: whether one has been employed all the time at a single institution of higher education, whether all academic employment has been in a single institution, whether one is employed at the university one has graduated from, etc.

In the framework of this study, information is available about the proportion of academics who have been employed in higher education *only by a single institution* of higher education. This can be viewed as one possible definition of 'inbreeding'; one has to bear in mind, though, that these persons might have been employed full-time somewhere at an institution outside higher education; on the other hand, we do not know whether the respondents have been awarded their degrees at the institution where they are employed at the time the survey has been conducted.

Nine per cent of university professors in Germany report no mobility within higher education during the academic career; a change of career is viewed as obligatory at the moment of first appointment to a professorial rank. The respective rate is also quite small, as Fig. 4.2 shows, among university professors in the USA (13%)

4.2 Biography and Career

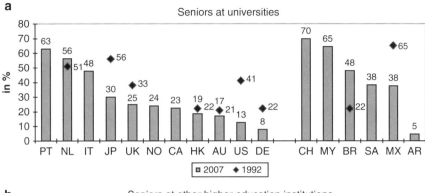

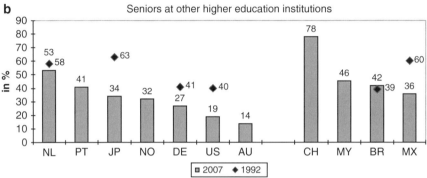

Fig. 4.2 Employed only at a single higher education institution during one's career—1992 and 2007 (percentage). (**a**) Seniors at universities. (**b**) Seniors (for 1992: Senior and junior academics of other higher education institutions combined) at other higher education institutions. Question A5 (2007): By how many higher education institutions or research institutes have you been employed since your first degree?

and quite moderate in various other advanced countries. Inbreeding according this definition is only frequent at universities in Portugal (64%), Italy (48%) and various emerging countries (notably 70% in China). Also, high rates of senior academics at other institutions of higher education not having been professionally mobile within the higher education systems can be found primarily in emerging countries (again notably 78% in China).

Figure 4.2 indicates as well that inbreeding by this definition has declined in most countries since the early 1990s for which respective information is available: For example, in the case of professors at universities in Japan from 56% in 1992 to 30% in 2007 and in the USA from 41 to 13% during the same period. The same holds true for professors at other institutions of higher education. To take the same cases: we note the decline in Japan from 63 to 34% and in the USA from 40 to 19%.

Substantially fewer professors among the 2007 respondents than in the 1992 sample have remained at the same university over their whole career in Germany (from 22 to 9%), Japan (from 56 to 30%) and in Mexico (from 65 to 38%). Today, Germany and the USA are the countries with the highest interuniversity mobility of professors at universities.

Comparing the professor mobility of universities with that of other higher education institutions, we come up with a similar picture—at least where the data is available. The only country notably that is different is Germany, where seniors have stayed more often at other institutions than at universities. Thus, overall institutional mobility has much increased during the last 15 years at universities as well as at other higher education institutions. Germany, the USA and Argentina show the greatest institutional mobility.

4.2.4 International Mobility

To find out how internationally mobile senior and junior staff are or have been during their lifetime, the data describes when the citizenship is or has not been the same as the country of residence at three points in time: at birth (migration background), at the moment of the first degree (student mobility) and currently (foreign staff).

Foreign citizenship, as one can expect, is relatively frequent among advanced countries that are known to accept large numbers of immigrants: 10% of university professors and 22% of junior staff at universities in Canada are foreign citizens at the time of the survey; the respective figures are 8 and 14%, respectively (5% for professors at other higher education institutions), in Australia as well as 9, 8 and 4%, respectively, in the USA. But three other European countries report large proportion of foreign academics, as Table 4.2 shows: the Netherlands, Norway and the United Kingdom. The data show that the respective proportion is even higher in Hong Kong. On the other hand, the number of foreign academics is negligible in Italy, Japan and Korea. The proportion of those born abroad are substantially higher in the immigrant countries: 45% of the university professors in Australia, 36% in Canada and 20% in the USA, while Norway is a country where a higher proportion of university professors were foreigners at the time of the award of the degree than at the time of birth.

In comparing university professors with junior academic staff at universities, we note in almost all European countries a higher proportion of foreigners among the latter (no matter whether we refer to citizenship at birth, at the time of first degree or at the time the survey is conducted). We cannot establish on the basis of these data whether this finding indicates a biographic phenomenon (i.e. substantial numbers of scholars being internationally mobile at the early stages of their career and returning home later) or a historical phenomenon (increase of academic mobility over time). It is interesting to note that the reverse is true for most economically advanced countries outside Europe: a higher proportion of foreign professors than foreign junior staff. Thus, there is no global trend towards the increase of foreign academic staff over time.

In the majority of the economically advanced countries, the proportion of foreign academics at other institutions of higher education is lower than those at universities. As Table 4.2 shows, however, this phenomenon does not consistently apply to all countries. There is about the same ratio of foreigners among professors from

4.2 Biography and Career

Table 4.2 Foreign citizenship[a] at birth, at the award of first degree and currently (percentage)

		CA	USA	FI	DE	IT	NL	NO	PT	UK	AU	KR	HK	AR	BR	MX	ZA	MY
At birth																		
Universities	Seniors	36	20	5	10	1	11	19	1	17	46	0	36	4	3	8	10	6
	Juniors	30	15	12	10	1	22	21	5	22	37	0	25	1	0	6	14	2
Other HEIs	Seniors	.	12	4	8	.	4	23	8	b	38	0	.	.	0	2	b	25
	Juniors	.	18	2	12	.	4	6	5	b	31	0	.	.	2	3	b	9
At the award of first degree																		
Universities	Seniors	33	18	6	10	1	11	22	3	16	35	0	.	3	3	7	7	4
	Juniors	29	14	11	8	1	20	46	6	21	29	3	.	1	0	5	12	2
Other HEIs	Seniors	.	11	4	8	.	3	19	3	b	30	1	.	.	0	3	b	11
	Juniors	.	14	2	12	.	3	47	5	b	26	0	.	.	2	2	b	5
Currently																		
Universities	Seniors	10	9	5	6	0	10	19	0	15	8	1	51	2	2	3	6	5
	Juniors	22	8	10	6	1	19	22	3	20	14	0	35	1	0	5	8	2
Other HEIs	Seniors	.	4	3	2	.	2	19	3	b	5	0	.	.	0	2	b	23
	Juniors	.	11	2	6	.	2	15	2	b	9	1	.	.	1	2	b	8

Question F9: What was/is your nationality/citizenship and your country of residence?
[a]Percentage of respondents whose citizenship is different from country of current employment
[b]Too small number of respondents
. No other HEIs or no other HEIs surveyed

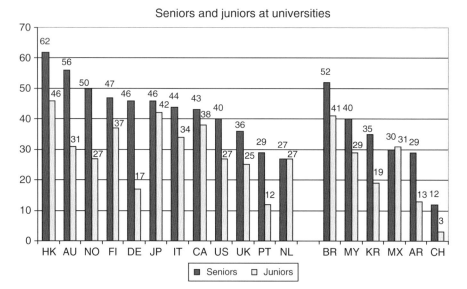

Fig. 4.3 Years spent in other countries—2007 (percentage). Question F13: Since the award of your first degree, how many years have you spent…in other countries (outside the country of your first degree and current employment)?

both types of higher education institutions in Norway, and the proportion of foreigners among staff at other institutions is higher than those at universities in the United Kingdom.

In the emerging countries surveyed in this study, the proportion of foreign staff at other institutions of higher education tends to be low. Only among junior staff at universities in South Africa and among junior staff at other institutions of higher education in Malaysia, do we note sizeable numbers of foreigners.

Figure 4.3 depicts the staff *having spent time outside their country* after their first degree and then coming back to their home country. The Australian university staff and all the Mexican staff have spent the longest time in foreign countries. Also staff from Argentina, Canada, the UK, Portugal and Norway are internationally mobile for relatively longer periods.

One further pointer to internationalisation of academic work is the *language used in teaching and research*. Figure 4.4 depicts the use of a language that is not the first language, by staff members with the citizenship of the country where they are born as well as where they currently live. We can clearly see that a foreign language is much more often used in research than in teaching in all countries. A frequent use of foreign language in teaching indicates widespread provisions of international study programmes; in contrast, we note that foreign languages are employed frequently in countries where the native language is spoken by a relatively small academic community (as in Finland, Italy, Norway, Portugal, Malaysia). Malaysia is the country where a foreign language is used in over three-fourths of the time or more, while in China

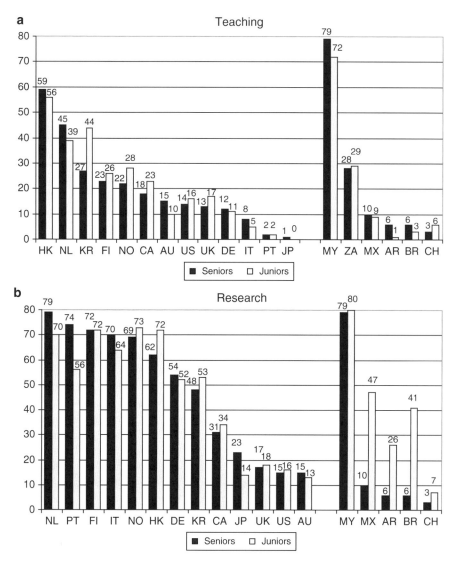

Fig. 4.4 Use of foreign language(s) (language not being the respondents' mother tongue/first language) in teaching and research (percentage of academics at universities whose citizenship is the same of the country of residence). (**a**) Teaching. (**b**) Research. Question F11: Which language do you primarily employ in teaching/research?

and Australia a foreign language is used the least for both teaching and research. Concerning which language is the 'other language', English is most frequently named by the respondents employing a foreign language: 88% in teaching and 95% in research activities.

4.3 Employment Conditions

4.3.1 Part-Time and Short-Term Employment

In many advanced countries, a substantial proportion of academics are employed part-time for some period of their junior career, and employment on a short-term basis is more frequent than for persons of their age in other professional areas. These employment conditions seem to be a function of the long phase of concurrent learning and productive work as well as by the high degree of selectivity which continues up to the promotion to senior positions. Some observers assert that these features of 'precarious' and 'uncertain' employment for junior academic staff are on the increase as the academy becomes more market-driven under the influence of the 'managerial university' (see the overviews on these debates in Enders 2001; Enders and De Weert 2004; Teichler 2006; Finkelstein 2010). In contrast, the full-time employment of professors is customary in advanced countries.

The 'Changing Academic Profession' survey suggests—as documented in Table 4.3—that the prevalence of part-time and short-term employment already varied substantially by country in the early 1990s. It also shows that between the early 1990s and 2007, there were increases in some countries and decreases in others. Obviously, an enormous variety can be observed in this respect in advanced countries, and it would be difficult to conclude that there has been a convergent trend across countries.

Part-time employment of junior academic staff at universities is very low in a substantial number of countries surveyed: None in Korea, 2% each in Canada and Italy and 6% in Finland on the part of the advanced countries. In the other countries, the incidence is 1% in Malaysia, 2% in China, 3% in South Africa and 6% in Mexico. In Japan, for example, the respective rate was 2% in 1992 but has increased to 7% in recent years. In Hong Kong, a substantial decline can be observed (from 26% in 1992 to 10% in 2007). In Australia (5%) and the United Kingdom (6%), part-time employment of juniors was infrequent in 1992, but the rates have doubled and tripled within 15 years (19 and 13%, respectively).

Part-time employment among junior staff at universities was the highest in 1992 in the Netherlands (34%), Germany (25%) and the USA (23%) among the advanced countries that participated in both surveys. According to the recent CAP data, the rate of those employed part-time is 31% in Germany and 30% in the Netherlands. In Germany, the relatively high rate is often explained as being caused by two reasons. First, German universities employ substantial numbers of young academics already during the period of work on doctoral thesis; in that case, part-time employment prevails. Second, employment of young researchers funded by contract funds has increased in the recent two decades; among them, a substantial proportion of the positions created are part-time positions. In the Netherlands, we also have a substantial number of part-time positions for young scholars working on their doctoral thesis. In addition, substantial efforts have been made in the Netherlands to facilitate part-time employment for academics, if they prefer such a solution for a better work-life balance.

4.3 Employment Conditions

Table 4.3 Part-time and short-term employment of academics in 1992 and 2007 (percentage)

		CA	USA	FI	DE	IT	NL	NO	PT	UK	AU	JP	KR	HK	AR	BR	MX	SA	CH	MY
(a) Seniors at universities																					
Part-time	2007	1	2	4	0	3	23	6	3	5	9	0	0	1	75	10	3	11	2	0
	1992	.	3	.	2	.	14	.	.	6	2	0	2	16	.	9	.	.	.	.
Short-term	2007	5	5	34	3	.	17	4	13	2	23	13	23	27	62	2	11	17	21	8
	1992	.	5	.	2	.	3	.	.	9	6	1	31	43	.	7	.	.	.	.
(b) Juniors at universities																					
Part-time	2007	2	15	6	31	2	30	11	12	14	19	7	0	10	88	26	6	3	2	1
	1992	.	23	.	25	.	34	.	.	6	5	2	1	26	.	41	.	.	.	.
Short-term	2007	82	56	50	79	.	41	74	69	28	52	39	86	82	68	15	35	8	23	6
	1992	.	63	.	79	.	44	.	.	28	36	4	33	67	.	33	.	.	.	.
(c) Seniors at other higher education institutions																					
Part-time	2007	.	2	10	6	.	41	10	2	[b]	6	0	0	.	.	65	10	[b]	2	0
	1992[a]	.	12	.	7	.	51	.	.	6	5	.	.	.	.	47	.	.	.	.
Short-term	2007	.	9	8	2	.	11	13	15	[b]	14	9	19	.	.	4	4	[b]	24	29
	1992[a]	.	30	.	6	.	15	.	.	10	26	.	.	.	.	4	.	.	.	.
(d) Juniors at other higher education institutions																					
Part-time	2007	.	14	11	12	.	59	13	6	[b]	11	1	0	.	.	84	16	[b]	2	0
Short-term	2007	.	63	12	41	.	17	61	75	[b]	34	23	80	.	.	5	20	[b]	29	12

Question A7 (2007): How is your employment situation in the current academic year at your higher education institution/research institute? (categories 'part-time employed' and 'part-time employed with payment according to work tasks')
Question A11 (2007): What is the duration of your current employment contract at your higher education institution or research institute? (categories 'fixed-term employed with permanent/continuous employment prospects (tenure-track)' and 'fixed-term employed without permanent/continuous employment prospects')
[a]Senior and junior academics of other higher education institutions combined
[b]Too small number of respondents
. No other HEIs or no other HEIs surveyed

In the USA, part-time employment of junior academic staff has declined over time (to 14%). However, the survey does not show whether part-time employment has been substituted by honorarium-based payments, because persons paid through an honorarium for part-time teaching have not been surveyed.

Short-term employment of junior academic staff at universities prevails in the majority of advanced countries. The highest rates are reported for Korea (86%), Canada and Hong Kong (82% each), Germany (79%), Norway (74%) and Portugal (69%) as well as Argentina on the part of emerging countries (68%). In contrast, less than 10% are short-term employed in Malaysia and South Africa.

For those countries for which information is available both for the early 1990s and for recent years, we do not note any consistent trends. In some cases, short-term employment has increased substantially: For example, in Japan from 4 to 39% and in Hong Kong from 33 to 82%. In some countries, this rate remained more or less constant, for example, in Germany (both 79%), in the Netherlands (44 and 41%) and in the United Kingdom (28%). There are countries as well where a decrease is noted: A modest drop in the USA (from 63 to 56%) and a more substantial drop in Brazil (from 33 to 15%).

There is no consistent pattern across countries for the short-term employment of academic junior staff at universities according to disciplinary group or gender. Altogether, men are slightly more often employed short-term than women. In Germany (98%) and the USA (78%), men in science and engineering and in Korea (82%) and Brazil (15%), men in the humanities and social science report the highest quota of short-term employed among junior staff at universities.

The part-time employment of professors at universities was rare both in 1992 and 2007. It remained on a level of 0–6% in most of the countries analysed. Only in the Netherlands do we note an increase from 14 to 23%. In Australia the increase has been from 2 to 9%. Also in the other advanced countries, the respective ratio has been between 3 and 6%. Among the other countries, the respective ratios is small in most cases, while the Latin American countries stand out with higher ratios of part-time employment among professors: 75% in Argentina, 11% in South Africa, and 10% in Brazil (part-time professors were not surveyed in Mexico).

Short-term employment of senior academics at universities was slightly more frequent in 1992 than part-time employment; the rates ranged from 1% in Japan to 9% in the United Kingdom. Up to 2007, the rates of short-term employment among professors increased substantially in three of the countries: in Australia from 6 to 23%, in the Netherlands from 3 to 17% and in Japan from 1 to 13%. In contrast, it has declined in the United Kingdom from 9 to 2%. In Korea, the rate of short-term employed professors has decreased substantially during that period from 43 to 23%.

In the economically advanced countries with information available only for 2007, Norway (3%) and Canada (5%) report very low rates and Portugal a somewhat higher rate (13%) of short-term employment among senior academics at universities; in contrast, a shift towards short-term contracts for university professors has been realised in Finland (34%). In other countries, ratios between 20 and 30% are often reported, while Argentina (62%) has the highest rate of short-term employed university professors of all the countries analysed.

Part-time employment of professors at other institutions of higher education is quite low (at most 10%) in almost all the countries analysed; a much higher ratio is reported only in the Netherlands (41%) and an extremely high ratio only in Brazil (65%). In many countries, the rate of short-term employment of professors at other institutions of higher education is higher than that at universities. Among advanced countries, we note higher rates than 10% only in Portugal (19%), Australia (16%) and Norway (13%). In other countries, higher rates than 10% dominate (mostly between one-fifth and one-third) with the highest rates in Malaysia (29%).

We have to bear in mind, though, that an international comparison of part-time and short-term employment is difficult because of different employment practices. In some countries, many doctoral candidates are university employees and thus contribute in the statistics to seemingly higher 'unstable employment' while they are financially and socially better off than doctoral students with or without fellowships. In Germany, for example, most of the junior academics are paid only for small tasks over short periods (in contrast to a regular contract) and, thus, contribute to the overall image of high proportions of part-time and short-term employment. In some other cases, persons with similar tasks would be paid through an honorarium and, thus, would not show up in the statistics. In some countries, many affiliated teaching and research assistants are not viewed as regular employees and are not included in the lists of academic staff, while in other countries those tasks are taken over by regular employees. In some countries, part-time professors are regular employees, while in others, part-timers only work on an honorarium basis and therefore are excluded from the CAP survey.

4.3.2 Income

In general, the academic profession is considered as not being as highly paid as various other professions. High intrinsic motivation, interesting work and the leeway to shape one's own work are generally viewed as crucial for the attractiveness of the academic profession. It is often claimed, however, that the opportunity of earning side-income might be an attractive element of the academic profession.

In the CAP questionnaire, the academics were asked to state their *gross annual income*. For comparative purposes, this has been recalculated in US$. The following data have to be viewed with caution. We note substantial differences as regards items included or not included in gross income (e.g. contribution to a pension system). Moreover, the purchasing power of the respective countries is not taken into consideration.

On that basis, we note the following gross annual remuneration of university professors in advanced countries (total sum by their university) is about

- 159,000 US$ in Hong Kong
- 114,000 US$ in the USA
- 98,000 US$ in Japan

- 93,000 US$ in Germany
- Between 76,000 US$ and 83,000 US$ in various other advanced countries
- 60,000 US$ in Korea

In the other countries, the nominal income is lower. It ranged from about 32,000 US$ in Brazil down to about 8,000 US$ in China.

The average income for senior academics at other institutions of higher education is between 60,000 and 80,000 US$ in most advanced countries. As a rule, it is lower than that of university professors except for Japan, where the highest remuneration is reported from professors at teaching-oriented institutions (102,000 US$), and for Finland where the average income of both groups of professors is around 74,000 US$. Among other countries, the professors at other institutions of higher education are exceptions as they earn more than their colleagues at universities (about 29,000 US$ as compared to about 26,000 US$).

Junior academics at universities report on average by country an income ranging from about half to about three quarters of that of senior academics. There is not sufficient information available in the CAP survey about the career stages of the respondents to draw clear conclusions about the typical income differences according to career stages. In absolute figures, junior academic staff at universities are most highly paid in Japan (82,000 US$) and Hong Kong (76,000 US$), while in other advanced countries, the figures range from 41,000 to 64,000 US$.

Junior academics at other higher education institutions have a higher remuneration on average than their peers at universities—a finding certainly linked to the fact that there are more nonprofessorial employment provisions for senior academic staff at these institutions than at universities in many countries. The highest figures are reported for Japan (83,000 US$) and Portugal (71,000 US$).

More than one-third of the academics surveyed in the CAP study have some *income beyond the remuneration from their own university*. Detailed data are not provided here, because they are not suitable for providing a valid picture of the situation across countries. First, the individual countries had different approaches as far as the exclusion and inclusion into the survey of various categories of part-time and honorarium-based academics are concerned. Second, the questions regarding additional employment and income were not equally phrased across countries and obviously not equally understood by the respondents. In one respect, the data show a striking peculiarity in some countries: As already pointed out, the proportion of those having another income is especially high in Latin American countries where part-time teaching in the area of one's major professional expertise and major professional assignment is a widespread phenomenon.

Though many academics do additional work, in the more advanced countries the additional remuneration hardly constitutes a considerable percentage of their overall income. Senior academics at universities report that their additional income is very moderate on average; in most countries, it doesn't exceed much more than 10% of the overall income. The USA is the only exception, where the additional income is in the range of about 20% in 2007, whereby an increase is visible since the early 1990s (see Fig. 4.5). The relatively high side-income reported by US

4.3 Employment Conditions

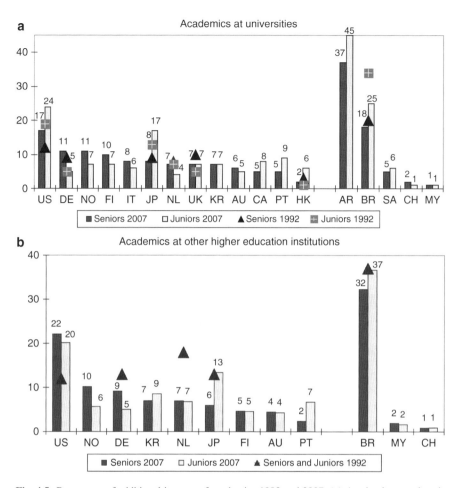

Fig. 4.5 Percentage of additional income of academics 1992 and 2007. (**a**) Academics at universities. (**b**) Academics at other higher education institutions. Question A12 (2007): What is your annual gross income by the following sources? Here: (A12_2 + A12_3)/(A12_1 + A12_2 + A12_3)

senior and junior staff reflects the fact that many academics in the USA do not receive a salary all the year around, but only for 9 of the usual 11 months paid for employees. In addition, junior academic staff in Japan reports a relatively high level of additional income.

As regards emerging countries, the income from other sources is exceptionally high in the Latin American countries. As already stated, a considerable proportion of part-time professors were surveyed in these countries. In Brazil, over 70% report side-income and 10% report an income that constitutes more than two-fifth of their overall gross income. In Argentina, over 40% earn half of their income from additional sources.

4.4 Work Situation

4.4.1 Quality of Facilities and Resources

It is generally assumed that the quality of academic work does not just rely on the talent of the academics. Rather, the *quality of facilities and resources for teaching and research* can be a key for the actual academic performance. Therefore, the academics surveyed have been asked to assess the quality of their resources and facilities.

In Fig. 4.6, the *average ratings* are presented for all the eight major areas of facilities and resources addressed in the survey which allow us to compare across countries, types of higher education institutions and ranks of academics: classroom, technology for teaching, laboratories, research equipment/instruments, computer facilities, library holdings, office space and secretarial support. We note that the university professors from Hong Kong (2.2 on a five-point scale) and from Finland (2.3) give the highest rating to their facilities and resources for teaching and research in 2007. The professors of universities from most of the other advanced countries seem to be quite content as well with their resources (average ratings between 2.5 and 2.7). In contrast, university professors from Italy and the United Kingdom (both 2.9) as well as all those from most of the other countries (ranging in most cases from 2.7 to 3.1) are not impressed by the quality of their working conditions; in Argentina, the professors are the least content in this respect (3.1).

Junior academic staff at universities rates their working conditions about as favourably as the senior academics (both reach an overall average of 2.7). There are a few countries where the juniors' ratings are slightly more positive and other countries where the reverse is true; only in Argentina do junior academic staff consider the facilities and resources clearly worse. The similarity of ratings by junior and senior staff comes as a surprise, because it is widely believed that senior staff have power which they use to obtain a 'bigger piece of the cake'. What does this finding mean: Do junior staff have lower expectations or more or less equal access to these facilities and resources?

Also, the average ratings on the part of academics at other institutions of higher education do not differ substantially from the ratings of their peers at universities. They rate their conditions only slightly lower in the overall average (senior staff 2.8 and junior staff 2.9). There is one exception: Academics at other institutions of higher education in Brazil view their working conditions somewhat more positively than their colleagues at universities.

In examining the university professors' rating of the individual areas of facilities and resources, we might opt for varying perspectives: the appreciations of the different types of facilities across countries, the specific areas emphasised or criticised by professors from countries with an average very positive or a negative view of the resources and facilities in general, and finally the most positive or negative assessments of the individual areas of facilities and resources.

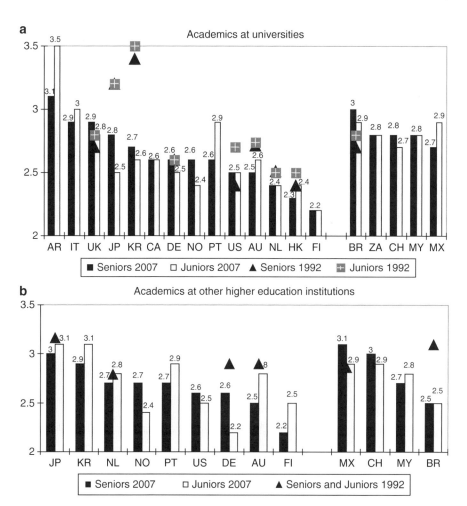

Fig. 4.6 Academics' assessment of facilities and resources 2007 (arithmetic mean, 2007: on a scale for 1 = excellent to 5 = poor, 1992: On a scale for 1 = excellent to 4 = poor). (**a**) Academics at universities. (**b**) Academics at other higher education institutions. Question B3 (2007): At this institution, how would you evaluate each of the following facilities, resources or personnel you need to support your work? Means of eight categories. 1992 Senior and junior academics of other higher education institutions combined

Looking at the *various facilities and resources* addressed across countries, we note that the ratings of the telecommunication (2.2) and library facilities and services computer facilities (2.4 each) are most positive, followed by those of office space, classrooms and technology for teaching (2.6 each). Not so highly appreciated on average are research equipment and instruments (2.8) as well as secretarial support (3.2).

Looking at differences by county, we note:

- Among those university professors from those countries who rate the facilities and resources altogether very positively, the university professors in Hong Kong appreciate the quality of classrooms, technology for teaching, computer facilities and the library facilities as highly appreciated as compared to other countries. The Finnish professors also positively rate the quality of classrooms, the technology for teaching and their office space clearly more often than the average of respondents.
- Among those respondents whose average ratings are close to the average of advanced countries, university professors in the Netherlands often observe good research equipment and instruments as well as good secretarial supports. Respondents from Norway underscore the quality of computer facilities, those from Australia are satisfied with their office space and those from Korea appreciate the telecommunications. In contrast, many university professors in Germany rate the library facilities and services not very positively.
- As the average across the eight areas suggest, university professors from the United Kingdom and Italy formulate critique with respect to various areas addressed. In addition, university professors from Japan relatively often point to deficiencies with regards to classrooms, technology for teaching and computer facilities.
- The university professors from emerging countries on average rate laboratories, research equipment and instruments as well as secretarial support consistently worse than their colleagues from advanced countries. In contrast, university professors from China appreciate the classrooms and the technology for teaching, and those from South Africa, the library facilities and services as well as their office space.

Finally, in looking at the *individual areas of facilities and resources*, we observe some additional noteworthy differences across countries:

- Classrooms are often assessed positively by university professors not only from Finland (75%) and Hong Kong (70%) but also from China (75%) and the Netherlands (74%). Least frequent positive assessments are reported for Japan (30%) and Argentina (31%).
- Technology for teaching seems to excel clearly in Finland and Hong Kong (75%), while positive ratings are less common in Brazil (33%), Italy, Japan (37% each) and Argentina (38%).
- Laboratories are favourably assessed by about half of the professors from universities in Finland, the Netherlands, Hong Kong, Germany and Australia, but by less than one-third in Argentina, Brazil, Italy and Japan.
- More than half of the university professors in Australia, Hong Kong and the Netherlands rate the research equipment and instruments positively in contrast to one-fifth in Argentina and about one-third in Brazil, Italy, China and the United Kingdom.
- Computer facilities are notably praised by university professors from Hong Kong (80%), Norway and Finland and least often appreciated by their colleagues in Brazil (37%), Argentina (43%), Italy (47%), China and the United Kingdom (48% each).

- The working conditions as far as telecommunication is concerned are rated most often positively by university professors in Norway and Hong Kong (84% each), Finland (81%) and the Republic of Korea (80%). Less than half positive ratings can be noted only in Argentina (38%) and China (41%).
- Library facilities are viewed as exceptionally positive in Hong Kong (88%) and Australia (80%). Less than half of the ratings are positive in all emerging countries except for South Africa and among the advanced countries only in Germany (44%).
- Personal office space was most often positively viewed by professors in Finland (78%) and Norway (74%) and least often in Argentina (29%) and China (35%).
- Finally, secretarial support was assessed positively by about half of the university professors in advanced countries: the Netherlands, Hong Kong, Finland and Germany. Positive ratings are seldom—a quarter or less—in all other Asian countries and Norway.

An analysis of change over time cannot be undertaken accurately here. Although the same question was posed in both surveys, a *four-point scale was employed in 1992* as compared to a five-point scale in 2007. Altogether, the data suggest that there has been an improvement of the working conditions for teaching and research in all countries for which information is available at both points in time. Only the ratings of secretarial support are less favourable in 2007 in various countries. The greatest turn towards more positive ratings can be observed for two countries where the ratings had been fairly negative in average in 1992: Japan and even more so Korea.

All the ratings are on average not overwhelmingly positive, but they suggest that it is only a minority of academics in the country surveyed who really complain about their working resources. Moreover, a comparison of the surveys suggests that contemporary academics have a more favourable views of their working resources that they their predecessors in the early 1990s. This holds true both for the majority of academics in economically advanced countries and in the emerging countries surveyed.

4.4.2 Perceived Change of Working Conditions

It should be added, though, that an additional question has been raised in the CAP questionnaire: whether the overall working conditions in higher education have improved or deteriorated since the respondents started their careers. Actually,

- 27% on average of university professors in advanced countries report an improvement and 47% a deterioration; the responses by professors at other institutions of higher education are almost identical on average (30 and 46%). In contrast, 46% of the university professors in emerging countries note an improvement and 25% a deterioration of working conditions; the responses by professors at other institutions of higher education in emerging countries are even more positive (46 vs. 19%).

- Although junior academic staff can only look back at a shorter career span on average, their perceptions of the change of working conditions only differ moderately from those of the professors'. Of the junior staff at universities, 23% on average across advanced countries observe an improvement and 36% a deterioration; the junior staff at other higher education institutions in advanced countries hold a more negative view (19% vs. 42%). Again the respondents from emerging countries observe more often an improvement than a deterioration of the working conditions (40% vs. 27% and 45% vs. 22%, respectively).
- The views of academics from advanced countries vary substantially in the respects. On the one hand, academics from Korea and Portugal predominantly note an improvement. On the other hand, academics from the United Kingdom, Germany and Australia hold the most negative views.

The two findings are incompatible. When a historical analysis of the perceived working conditions with respect to detailed areas of resources for their own work is undertaken through a comparison of surveys conducted at a different point in time, the working conditions for academics seem to have improved moderately on average over time both in economically advanced countries and emerging countries. When academics are asked retrospectively about changes of working conditions in higher education in general during the course of their career, perceptions of improvement only prevail in emerging countries and in a few economically advanced countries which have 'caught up' recently, while the perception of deterioration prevails in the majority of advanced countries. It is justified to assume that retrospective questions as regards higher education in general are more likely to elicit nostalgia to the 'good old days' in the majority of advanced countries rather than a realistic observation.

4.5 Time Budget

4.5.1 Time Committed to Work and Time Distribution Across Work Tasks

Working time has been a frequent theme in discussions about the situation of the academic profession. Two issues are frequently named.

First, the overall working time is frequently addressed. In economically advanced countries, it is widely assumed that most academics are strongly devoted to their work task and spend more time for academic work than officially required. In some developing countries, however, concern is widespread that low wages in higher education necessitate considerable 'moonlighting' at the expense of work time for the academic profession.

Second, there are frequent debates about how to achieve a balance with respect of the time spent for various functions. For example, concerns are voiced in some countries that large numbers of students might enlarge the involvement in teaching and teaching-related activities to such an extent that insufficient time remains for research. Moreover, the critique is widespread among academics themselves that too much time might be spent on administrative matters at the expense of the core functions of teaching and research.

There are complaints that junior staff might not have enough time for research which would be needed to qualify for a professorial position. The critique is frequently heard that the activities required for quality assurance might have gotten out of hand in comparison to the productive working time in the areas of teaching and research. Other issues might be added here. All these discussions suggest that information about the actual working time is relevant.

However, self-ratings of working time are by no means easy and reliable modes of inquiry. The critique has frequently been voiced that self-rating of working time might be too unreliable, notably if undertaken by professionals with very flexible schedules and a high degree of intrinsic motivation. Both of these factors might contribute to exaggerated reports. Moreover, it is not easy to allocate time estimates to the various functions of the academic profession: For example, to what extent does attendances at conferences, reading of books and talking with a colleague contribute to teaching, research or possibly other functions? There might be different views across countries as well: Advice of doctoral candidates is understood as part of the teaching functions in some countries and part of the research functions in other countries. Teaching in the framework of continuing education is viewed as part of teaching in some countries and part of a general service function in other countries.

This study cannot overcome all the problems which call for a cautious interpretation of the findings. The CAP study, however, in the same way as the precursor Carnegie Study, successfully counterbalances one widely spread weakness of surveys of the time budget of academics. Both surveys asked the respondents to estimate the average time spent—altogether and for various functions—separately for the period of the year when classes are in session on the one hand and on the other hand for period when classes are not in session. Comparisons between different surveys suggest that academics if only asked to report their working time without such a distinction tend to think about their working time when classes are in session. As a consequence, they might overestimate in such surveys both the average weekly working time as well as the time spent on teaching. This study, however, provides information about the estimated work time both when classes are in session and when classes are not in session; an aggregate score of the average working time is calculated based on the assumption that classes are in session in about 60% of the working weeks per year and classes are not in session in about 40%.

4.5.2 Weekly Working Hours

In 2007, university professors of the advanced countries on average have worked, according to their own observations, about 48 h per week. This is about 120% of the usual full-time working time in those countries, but it is by no means unusual for a

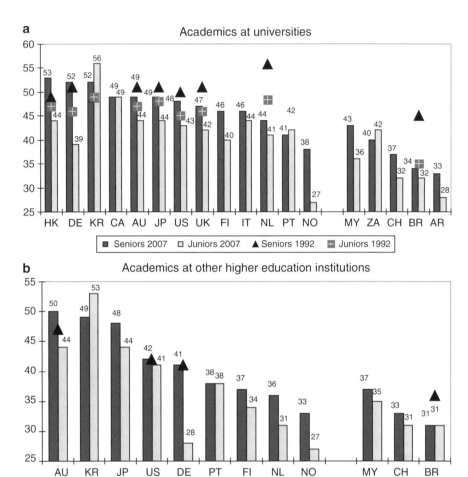

Fig. 4.7 Average weekly working hours (calculated as 60% when classes are in session and 40% when classes are not in session) in 1992 and 2007. (**a**) Academics at universities. (**b**) Academics at other higher education institutions. Question B1 (2007): Considering all your professional work, how many hours do you spend in a typical week on each of the following activities? (hours per week)

profession with high motivation, flexible schedules, room for disposition and a high sense of responsibility. The average working hours differ substantially by country, as Fig. 4.7 shows. Highest working hours are reported by university professors Hong Kong (53 h), Germany and Korea (52 h each). In contrast, university professors in the Netherlands, Norway (44 h) and Portugal (41 h) do not seem to work much more than the usual work time of employees.

The respective figure for university professors in emerging countries is 40 h. The average number of work hours ranges between 41 and 44 in the majority of countries, while lower figures in Brazil (34 h) and Argentina (33 h) reflect the fact that a significant proportion of the respondents are professionals active in higher education on a part-time basis.

Professors at other institutions tend to spend less time on academic work than their colleagues at universities: The average figures are 43 h for advanced countries and 38 h for emerging countries, that is, 5 h less and 2 h less, respectively. Relatively high weekly working hours are only reported by respondents in Australia (50 h), Korea (49 h) and Japan (48 h), while less than 40 h are reported for five countries. As prior studies have shown, academics that are devoted to research on average spend more time on academic activities altogether than those devoted to teaching.

The weekly working hours of junior academic staff at universities seem to be fewer on average than that of seniors: 5 h less (44 h as compared to 48 h) on average of the advanced countries and 3 h less (37 h compared to 40 h) on average of the other countries. Less than half of the difference on average time is due to the fact that larger proportions of junior staff than those of professors are employed part-time. It should be noted, though, that the average weekly working hours of junior staff at universities vary strikingly by country: Very high figures are reported to Korea (56 h) and Canada (49 h), while very low figures hold true for Brazil (34 h), Norway (33 h) and Argentina (29 h).

The average working hours of junior staff at other institutions of higher education are 39 h in advanced countries and 37 h in emerging countries, that is, 5 h less and 1 h less, respectively, than those of the senior staff. Junior staff at teaching-oriented institutions in Korea report the highest average weekly working hours (53 h), that is, more than senior academic staff at these institutions in Korea.

Across countries and functions of the respondents, the academics surveyed in 2007 spend on average 2 weekly hours more when classes are in session than during the periods of the year when classes are not in session. Thereby, schedules vary substantially: While in some cases fewer hours are customary when classes are not in session, the opposite is true in other cases. In the early 1990s, the academics worked on average 4 h more when classes are in sessions than during the periods of the year when classes are not in session.

Altogether, these figures do not confirm the traditionally widespread view that many academics—often highly intrinsically motivated and highly devoted to academic work—are willing to spend substantially more time for work than persons in other occupations. In assuming—somewhat simplistically—that 40 h per week would be the normal working time in well-established blue-collar occupations at most of the countries considered here, we note in 2007 that only university professors in advanced countries report that they invest on average about two-tenths more time for their academic work than one would expect from employees in other sectors. About one-tenth more investment is reported on average by professors from other higher education institutions in advanced countries, junior staff from universities in advanced countries and by university professors in emerging countries. The others—junior staff at other higher education institutions in economically advanced countries as well as all except for university professors in emerging countries—do not work more hours than the typical employee.

In this context, it is interesting to examine changes over time. In the countries which were included both in the comparative survey in the early 1990s and in 2007, only the university professors in Germany and Korea among the advanced countries report an increase of the actual work time (3 h on average in both countries); the same holds true for university professors in Mexico. In the majority of countries, though, we note a reduction of the actual work time—the most dramatic example is the Netherlands (from 56 to 44 h). Also among professors at other higher education institutions as well as junior staff at both types of higher education institutions, we note not a consistent trend across all countries, but more cases of a reduction of work time than cases of an increase.

The dominant trend of a reduction of the academics' actual work time does not come as surprise: The academic profession seems to lose its exceptionality in the course of higher education expansion; moreover, an increasing number of academics seem to care more for a 'work-life balance' rather than for a strong devotion to academic work. On the other hand, we note in many countries the increasing managerial power, a growth of evaluation activities and increasing efforts in recent years to raise the quality and efficiency of higher education through incentives and sanctions. One could have assumed that these changes might have pushed the academics to invest more working time—the resource the academics can control most easily themselves—into their academic work. A comparison of the results of the Carnegie study and the CAP study, however, suggests that fewer academics are mobilised to invest more time in academic work relative to the numbers decreasing their work budget down in the direction of average employees.

4.5.3 Work Time Spent on Teaching and Research

Teaching and research are the core functions of academics. At research-oriented universities, a balance of time spent by professors on both functions is widely assumed as desirable. The functions of junior staff at research-oriented universities might be divergent: Some might be primarily in charge of research, some might be expected to strike a similar balance as professors, and others might be predominantly in charge of teaching. Finally, teaching is viewed generally as the clearly dominant task of professors at other institutions of higher education.

Teaching is the dominant function for university professors in most countries at those periods of the year when classes are in session: During those periods, they spend on teaching among advanced countries on average 38% and on average of emerging countries 46% of their actual working hours. This includes both teaching in classes and teaching-related activities such as preparation for classes, guidance and examinations. However, this proportion varies from 54% in South Africa as one extreme to 31% in Korea and 30% in Australia as the opposite extreme; in the latter two countries and Japan, university professors spend less time on teaching than on research even during the periods when classes are in session.

Research is also a frequent activity of university professors *when classes are in session*. The proportion of time spent on research during those periods is 32% on

4.5 Time Budget

average in advanced countries and 29% in emerging countries. Naturally, it is the prevailing activity when classes are not in session.

In calculating the *overall working time for the whole year*, we note that university professors in all advanced countries on average spend more time on research than on teaching. However, the ratios vary substantially, as Fig. 4.8 shows. The proportion of the overall working time spent on research ranges among advanced countries from 34% in the United Kingdom to 45% each in Korea and Italy, while the time spent on teaching ranges from 23% in Australia to 35% in Portugal. Australian and Korean university professors report that they spend about 1.7 times as much of their working time on research as on teaching; in contrast, university professors in Finland, Portugal and the United Kingdom spend about 1.1 times as much of their working time on research as on teaching. The situation is even more diverse in emerging countries. While university professors in Argentina and China spend somewhat more time on research, teaching dominates the schedules notably in South Africa but also somewhat in Brazil and Malaysia.

We note various pressures to change the balance between teaching and research. Quality assessment activities grew in most countries both in the area of research and teaching. Rising student-teacher ratios in some countries call for more working time of academics in teaching. The growing popularity of ranking of world-class universities mostly underscores the research functions. Political campaigns vary across countries in favour of the research or the teaching function. Altogether, we note the relative time spent on teaching did not change substantially for professors at universities at the countries for which information is available for both points in time. However, changes occurred in different directions in the individual countries. In Germany, where university professors have devoted the highest proportion of their time on teaching in 1992 (33%), and in Australia (25%) the relative time spent on teaching declined up to 2007 (to 29 and 23%, respectively). Thus, the schedules differ less on average by country in 2007 than they have differed in 1992.

We cannot expect the average schedules of *junior staff at universities* to be similar to those of university professors. First, junior staff both in charge of research and teaching are expected to teach fewer hours than senior staff in some countries, more or less the same in other countries, and even more in some countries. Second, some of the junior staff at universities in some countries are employed exclusively for research purposes.

Figure 4.11 actually shows that junior staff at universities in Hong Kong, Australia, Portugal and the USA spends a clearly higher proportion of their actual working hours on teaching than the university professors in those countries. In contrast, junior staff spends a clearly smaller proportion of their work hours on teaching in Japan, Norway, Germany and Finland. Altogether, junior staff in many countries reports that quite some time is spent on research; obviously, a lower proportion of their working hours are absorbed by other activities (administration, services, etc.) than that of the university professors. In almost all emerging countries included in the CAP, junior staff at universities spend, clearly more time on teaching than on research.

From 1992 to 2007, the involvement of junior academic staff at universities in teaching has increased on average. Such an increase is most noteworthy in Hong Kong and in the USA.

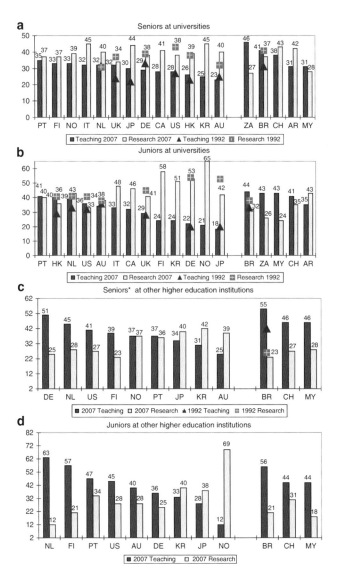

Fig. 4.8 Average (calculated as 60% of the weeks when classes are in session and 40% of the weeks when classes are not in session) percentage of work time spent on teaching and research in Fig. 4.8 (continued) 1992 and 2007. (**a**) Seniors at universities. (**b**) Juniors at universities. (**c**) Seniors (Calculated as 60% of the weeks when classes are in session and 40% of the weeks when classes are not in session) at other higher education institutions. *For 1992: Senior and junior academics of other higher education institutions combined. (**d**) Juniors at other higher education institutions. Question B1 (2007): Considering all your professional work, how many hours do you spend in a typical week on each of the following activities: teaching, research, service, administration, other academic activities?

Teaching is officially the major function of *other types of higher education institutions* in most countries, but in some advanced countries, these institutions have moved towards a substantial research role over time. In 1992, teaching clearly dominated in all countries for which information was available. In 2007, the picture is mixed. In emerging countries for which information is available, teaching is clearly the dominant function for professors at these institutions (55% in Brazil and 46% each in China and Malaysia), but in advanced countries, this is only the case in Germany (51%), the USA (41%) and Finland (39%). In other countries, the weekly hours devoted to teaching equals that to research or is even less; in Australia and Portugal, professors at other institutions even spend lower proportions of their working time for teaching than do university professors.

The role of junior staff at other institutions of higher education is quite diverse. In Finland and Portugal, they spend a clearly higher proportion of their working time than senior academics of these institutions on teaching. In Norway, in reverse, junior academics at other institutions of higher education spend most of their time on research. In Germany, junior staff at these institutions are to a lesser extent involved in teaching than professors at these institutions, but spend more time on service functions.

4.5.4 Work Time Spent on Other Assignments

Teaching and research are the core functions of academics. This does not mean, however, that all of their time is spent on teaching and research. In the CAP survey, for example, university professors in the advanced countries report that they spend 30% of their time on other assignment. The respective rate for the emerging countries is 25%. In the CAP survey, respondents have reported how many of the weekly working hours they actually spend—in addition to teaching and research—on

- **Service**: this has been explained in the questionnaire by services to clients and/ or patients, unpaid consulting, public or voluntary services
- **Administration**: committees, department meetings, paper work
- **Other academic activities**: professional activities not clearly attributable to any of the categories above

Altogether, we note that the time devoted for these additional activities varies even more strongly by country than the time devoted to teaching and research. As regards services, we note the quite varied figures: university professors in Germany report that they spend 7 h per week on average for this function, followed by those in Korea and the USA (6 h); in contrast, the respective figures are only 2 h per week in half a dozen—advanced and emerging—countries. Administrative tasks comprise around 10 h per week in Australia and Hong Kong (11 h each), the United Kingdom and Malaysia (10 h each) and Canada (9 h), while they absorb much less time (5 h or less) in Italy and some emerging countries (Argentina, Brazil and China). Finally, other activities vary on average by country between 2 and 5 h per week.

Junior staff at universities spends on average less time on activities other than teaching and research. The weekly hours spent for these additional functions, however, varies strikingly across countries especially for those who are not university professors. Substantial numbers of hours for services are reported by junior staff from Japan (9 h), Germany and Korea (6 h each). As regards administration, junior academic staff at universities in the United Kingdom (8 h), Australia and Malaysia (7 h each) state a substantial time load. Other activities vary only between 2 and 4 h on average.

Professors at other institutions of higher education spend altogether almost the same proportion of their weekly working hours on activities other than teaching and research as university professors do. However, they spend on average less on service, whereas professors from Korea report the highest number of weekly hours, that is, 5 h on average. Administration is a major function of professors at other institutions of higher education in Australia (12 h) and Finland (11 h). Again, other activities vary moderately between 2 and 4 h on average. Among junior staff at other higher education institutions, service functions are most widely spread in Japan (11 h on average) and administrative functions in the United Kingdom (10 h) as well as in Australia and Mexico (9 h each).

Altogether, the academics' estimates of their working hours suggest that activities beside teaching and learning absorb a substantial proportion of the working time. More detailed descriptions of the actual activities would be needed in future studies in order to explain the enormous differences of the actual types of activities in the various countries.

4.6 Assessment of the Professional Situation

4.6.1 *Reflection of the Professional Situation*

In the 'The Changing Academic Profession' survey, the respondents have been presented with three specific statements to help them examine how they view the professional situation of academics in general:

- 'My job is a source of considerable personal strain'.
- 'This is a poor time for any young person to begin an academic career in my field'.
- 'If I had it to do over again, I would not become an academic'.

Moreover, the academics have been asked to state the extent to which they are satisfied with their overall professional situation. Finally, they have been asked about their views as regards teaching and research as well as their commitments to their discipline, their department and their institution of higher education; the responses to these latter questions will be addressed in the subsequent sections.

Personal Strain: Actually, 45% of university professors on average across the advanced countries consider their job as a source of considerable personal strain. This proportion is even higher among junior academic staff of these countries: 49%. The responses vary substantially by country, as Fig. 4.9 shows. A considerable strain is stated very often by both senior and junior scholars from universities in Korea (64 and 74%) and Japan (61 and 70%) as well as from senior scholars in the United Kingdom (61%). In contrast, less than half the respondents from Italy characterise their job as a source of considerable strain (27 and 35%). Also in Norway (34 and 35%) and the USA (36 and 37%), both senior and junior academics from universities do not often respond affirmatively to this statement. In emerging countries, strain is least often reported—ranging from more than half in China (59 and 51%) to clearly less than a third both of senior and junior academics in Malaysia (23 and 19%), Mexico (25 and 31%) and Argentina (27% each).

The respective proportions were similar or lower among both senior and junior academic staff at other institutions of higher education. Among advanced countries, many respondents from Korea note such a strain (65 and 73%), but relatively few of both senior and junior academics in the USA (30 and 26%) and Germany (34 and 29%), senior academics in Portugal (31%) and Australia (34%) and finally junior academics in Norway (31%). Again, the proportions are lower in some emerging countries, notably Mexico (21% each) as well as Malaysia (18 and 25%).

In the early 1990s, the academics also have been asked to state whether they consider their job as a source of personal strain. As Fig. 4.9 shows, personal strain seems to have increased most among Korean scholars. But in the majority of the other countries, some increase is reported as well. The only clear exceptions are decreases on the part of university professors in Japan (from 65 to 61%) and junior academic staff at US universities (from 42 to 37%).

We have to bear in mind, though, that the term 'strain' has different meanings in the various countries. For example, the term used, for example, in the Japanese language is closer to 'effort' than to 'stress'. Therefore, we cannot simply assume that considering the job as a source of strain has the same negative connotations regarding the academics' own employment and work conditions.

Poor Time: On average across advanced countries, 36% of the university professors and 36% of junior academics at universities state 'This is a poor time for any young person to begin an academic career in my field'. The respective rate is

- Clearly highest in Italy (73 and 77%).
- More than half in Finland (53 and 44%) and the United Kingdom (51% each).
- Between one-third and half in six countries.
- Clearly lower in the USA (21 and 23%) and Korea (22 and 20%).
- By far the lowest in Japan (8 and 7%, respectively).

In emerging countries, this view is shared by substantially fewer academics on average across countries: 21% of university professors and 24% of university junior staff. The respective ratios are 8 and 14% in Malaysia, around 20% in the majority of these countries (except for 10% among junior academic staff in Mexico as well as 34 and 48% in China).

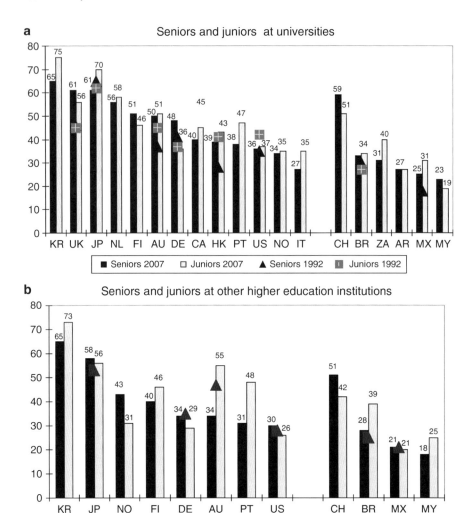

Fig. 4.9 Percentage (responses 1 and 2 on a scale from 1=agree to 5=disagree) of academics stating 'My job is a source of considerable personal strain' in 1992 and 2007. (**a**) Seniors and juniors at universities. (**b**) Seniors and juniors at other higher education institutions (for 1992: Senior and junior academics of other higher education institutions combined). Question B5 (2007): My job is a source of considerable personal strain

The academics at other higher education institutions in advanced countries consider the current period to be a poor time for young academics: Only 24% both of senior academics and junior academics state this on average across countries. The respective figures in emerging countries are even as low as 18 and 21%, respectively. Relatively high proportions hold true only for senior academics of other institutions of higher education in Australia (40%) and the United Kingdom (38%) as well as junior academics in Australia (52%), China (45%) and Portugal (42%).

Would Not Become an Academic Again: Even fewer academics state that they would not choose again to become academics: Only one out of seven on average across countries, institutional types and staff ranks. The respective rates are relatively high—above one fifth on average across institutional types and ranks—in Australia, China, Portugal, South Africa and the United Kingdom. The highest can be observed among junior academic staff at universities in the United Kingdom (30%). In reverse, this is least often stated (between 4 and 7%, respectively) by university professors and university junior academic staff in Argentina, university professors and staff at other institutions in Korea, university junior staff in Japan as well as senior academics at other institutions of higher education in Finland and Germany.

4.7 Commitment to the Discipline, Department and Institution

The 1992 survey indicated that academics in all of the countries felt a strong commitment to their academic discipline. As regards their department and their university, their sense of commitment was lower, though positive on average in most countries. Germany has been the exception in 1992 where the question on commitment to the department and to the university was not positively responded. Altogether, scholars from advanced countries less often stated a strong commitment to their university than scholars from emerging countries.

It is difficult to compare the responses of the 1992 and the 2007 questionnaires by scholars from those countries where information is available on both points in time because a *four-point rating scale was employed in 1992 in contrast to a five-point rating scale in 2007*. We argue though that the commitment to the department and university has increased in the case of German academics, whereas it remained more or less the same in the other countries or somewhat declined, the latter certainly in the United Kingdom. As a consequence, the differences by country are smaller in 2007 than they were in 1992, as Fig. 4.10 shows. In 2007, though, the commitment to the department as well as to the university continues to be somewhat lower in Germany and is now somewhat lower in the United Kingdom and Norway than in the countries addressed here.

Actually, in 2007, about 90% or even more of the professors and the junior academic staff at research-oriented universities express a strong affiliation (1 or 2 on a five-point scale) to their *discipline/field*. The respective share is only lower in four countries: Portugal (76 and 80%), Italy (78% each), China (80% each) and the United Kingdom (83 and 80%). The same holds true for senior academic staff at other institutions of higher education, as far as information is available (79% in China, 80% in Portugal and 81% in the United Kingdom).

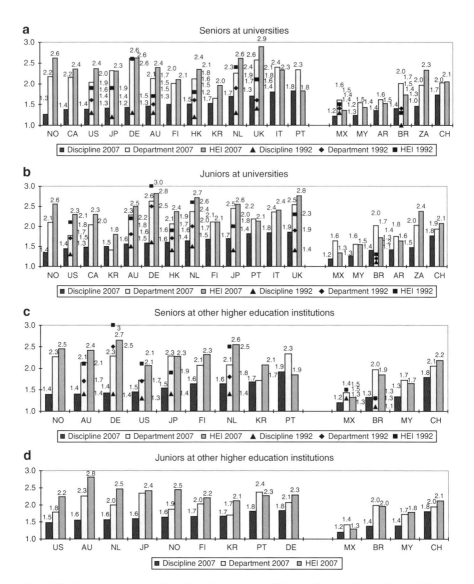

Fig. 4.10 Commitment to the discipline, department and higher education institution in 1992 and 2007. (**a**) Seniors at universities. (**b**) Juniors at universities. (**c**) Seniors at other higher education institutions (for 1992: Senior and junior academics of other higher education institutions combined). (**d**) Juniors at other higher education institutions. Question B4 (2007): Please indicate the degree to which each of the following affiliations is important to you. 2007: Scale from 1 = 'Very important' to 5 = 'Not at all important'; 1992: Scale from 1 = 'Very important' to 4 = 'Not at all important'

A sense of *affiliation to one's department* is most frequently felt (more than 80%) by professors at research-oriented universities in Malaysia, Brazil, Argentina and Mexico. The majority of countries report affirmatively between 60 and 80%. The department is lowest on the agenda for university professors in Germany (49%), the United Kingdom (53%) and Italy (57%). As regards junior staff at research-oriented universities, we observe more or less the same pattern; only the US junior academics have a strong affiliation to their department as well (84%). Among professors of other institutions of higher education, those from Mexico and the United States feel the strongest affiliation to their department, while the lowest affirmative responses were reported by respondents from Germany (54%) and Portugal (56%).

Again, the *affiliation to the university* is most often seen as important by university professors and junior academic staff from other countries, that is, Malaysia (94 and 89%, respectively), Mexico (92 and 95%), Argentina (88 and 87%) and Brazil (83 and 75%). In most countries, it ranges between 50 and 80%, while the lowest scores are reported from the United Kingdom (36 and 39%), Germany (46 and 41%) and Norway (46 and 48%). Many professors from other higher education institutions in Mexico and Malaysia consider their affiliation to their institution of higher education as important, while a very low sense of affiliation is not reported from any other institution of higher education.

Altogether, affiliation to the discipline is rated as more important than affiliation to the department, and the latter is seen as more important than the affiliation to the institution of higher education. Most surprisingly, senior academic staff and junior academic staff at research-oriented universities as well as senior academic staff from other higher education institutions of each individual country harbour very similar views. The differences by status and type of higher education institution do not seem to be highly important for the academics within each country. Clearly, the local affiliation to one's department and institution is most important in newly emerging countries. In contrast, affiliation with one's department or institution is accorded low importance by academics in Germany and the United Kingdom.

4.8 Job Satisfaction

In 2007, senior academics from research-oriented universities rate their overall professional satisfaction on average 2.2 on a scale from 1 = 'very satisfied' to 5 = 'very dissatisfied'. In most countries, between 60 and 80% state that they are satisfied (1 or 2 on the scale), and the proportion of those expressing dissatisfaction (4 or 5 on the scale) ranges in most cases from 1 to 14%. The clear majority is satisfied, but the ratings are by no means enthusiastic. On average, we do not note any differences between the advanced countries and the other countries in this respect. On the one hand, the university professors from Mexico stand out positively with a mean score of 1.8 and 87% positive ratings. On the other hand, satisfaction is on average lowest in the United Kingdom (2.6, 49%), South Africa (2.6, 54%) and China (2.5, 58%).

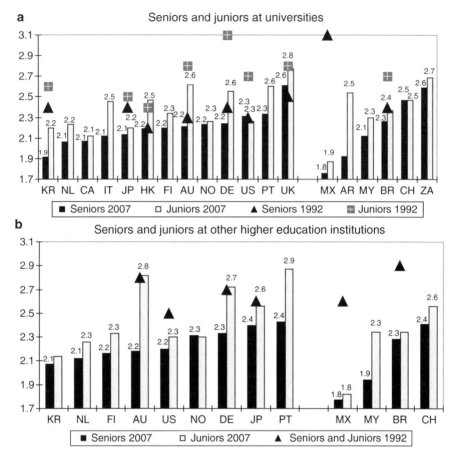

Fig. 4.11 Overall job satisfaction in 1992 and 2007 (arithmetic mean, on a scale from 1 = very satisfied to 5 = very dissatisfied). (**a**) Seniors and juniors at universities. (**b**) Seniors and juniors at other higher education institutions. Question B6 (2007): How would you rate your overall satisfaction with your current job?

In 1992, senior academics from research-oriented universities of those advanced countries, for which information is available at both points in time, have rated their overall professional satisfaction on average 2.4. In 2007, the average score is 2.3, that is, so marginally higher that no clear significant improvement can be observed. Among senior academics, the differences by country are small both in 1992 and 2007, as Fig. 4.11 shows, except for the more negative ratings by professors in the United Kingdom and South Africa in 2007. As regards other countries, we note a substantial increase of satisfaction over time in the Republic of Korea (from 2.4 to 1.9) and a moderate increase in Brazil (from 2.4 to 2.3).

Junior academic staff at research-oriented universities are somewhat less satisfied on average with their professional situation in 2007 than senior academic staff of the same institutional type. Thereby, the ratings by junior academics from advanced countries are less positive on average than those from other countries. The ratings are most positive, again, among junior staff in Mexico (1.9), and the most negative ratings, again, come from the United Kingdom (2.8) and South Africa (2.7) with ratings not better than 2.5 in eight countries.

In 1992, junior academic staff had stated a clearly lower satisfaction with their professional situation than senior academic staff at research-oriented universities. Among the countries for which information is available at both points in time, German junior academics have been clearly less satisfied on average, that is, even slightly lower on average than the scale mean (3.1 as compared to 2.5 of the senior academic staff in Germany). However, German junior academic staff made the biggest leap towards more positive views in 2007 (by 0.6–2.5), even though they remain slightly below the average of junior academic staff and clearly below the average of university professors in their country. We note also moves towards more positive ratings among junior academic staff in some other countries: a substantial change in the USA (from 2.7 to 2.3) and somewhat of a move in Australia (from 2.8 to 2.6), as Fig. 4.11 shows. As regards other countries, a substantial rise of job satisfaction is also visible in the Republic of Korea (from 2.6 to 2.1) and a considerable rise is also seen in Brazil (from 2.7 to 2.4).

On average, job satisfaction is equally high on average among senior academic staff of other higher education institutions as that of their colleagues at research-oriented universities. Positive ratings stand out not only in Mexico (1.8) but also in Malaysia (1.9). In 1992, professors of German *Fachhochschulen* have been clearly less satisfied on average with their professional situation than university professors of Germany, but the formers' satisfaction has increased substantially in comparison to the moderate increase on the part of the latter.

4.9 Summary of Major Findings

In many studies on the academic profession, a substantial gap is depicted between junior academic staff and senior academic staff. High selectivity and a mix between learning and productive work seems to be characteristic of the junior stages of the academic career; as a consequence, short-term contract and part-time employment is widespread. In contrast, most senior academics seem to enjoy a stable employment situation and freedom to shape their own professional activities. Senior academics might not be highly remunerated in comparison to other highly selective and demanding occupations, but they enjoy a relatively high professional reputation, interesting work and leeway to shape their own work.

We have to be cautious in merely reinforcing this 'conventional wisdom'. On average, first, we have more information available on academics in advanced countries, and we tend to address these countries predominantly because they are often viewed as role models for other countries; there is less information available on other countries. Second, the variety existing among advanced countries tends to be underestimated; it is worth analysing the range of practices across countries. Third, most statements on the academic profession have academics in 'research-oriented universities' in mind, that is, universities in which senior academics are expected to serve teaching and research more or less equally. Fourth, there have been indications that the situation of the academic profession has changed in many respects in recent years. In many countries, the power of the university management has been strengthened, and senior academics are put under pressure recently to contribute to an increase of quality, relevance and efficiency of higher education through extended measures of evaluation and a stronger emphasis on incentives and sanctions which also might imply a less stable employment situation. The trend towards a 'knowledge society' might affect academics in various respects; we also hear of measures aimed at making academic careers more attractive.

Two comparative surveys on the academic profession undertaken in 1992 (the 'Carnegie Survey') and in 2007 ('The Changing Academic Profession'—CAP) comprising 14 and 19 countries, respectively, provide a substantial range of information on these issues. However, clearly comparable information at both points in time is only available on eight advanced countries (Australia, Germany, Hong Kong, Japan, Korea, the Netherlands, the United Kingdom and the USA) and to a more limited extent on two emerging countries. Also, information on change over time is limited with respect to other institutions of higher education.

The single most obvious trend as far as the situation of the academic profession is concerned is the rising share of women. Yet remaining differences by country are not at all trivial. To a certain extent, we also note a general trend of the doctoral degree becoming increasingly a 'must' for academic careers, even though there are still enormous differences as far as the rate of doctoral degree holders and as trends towards increasing rates are concerned.

As regards employment stability of junior academic staff at research-oriented universities, the available data suggest the need to be quite cautious with respect to generalisations. The share of part-timers varied in 2007 in advanced countries between 2% in Canada and Italy on the one hand and 31% in Germany on the other hand; thereby, an increase since 1992 could be observed in three countries, no change in one country and a decrease in one country. In other countries, the rates of part-time employment even varied more strikingly from 1% in Malaysia to 88% in Argentina. Also, the rate of short-term contracts ranged from 6% or less in Malaysia and Japan to about 80% or more in Canada and Germany as well as the Republic of Korea and Hong Kong. Where information is available on both points in time, we note an increase of short-term employment in the majority of countries. The data, however, are by no means perfect in mirroring the degree of stability or instability of junior academic careers within the various countries, because they might include many doctoral candidates being employed in some cases and few in others, because short assignments might be done through regular short-term employment contracts included in this study or through auxiliary staff contracts or honorarium contracts not included here.

Professors at research-oriented universities continue to be mostly employed full-time with the exception of Latin American countries, especially Argentina,

4.9 Summary of Major Findings

where part-timers comprise a substantial proportion of the regular professors. Short-term contracts for professors at research-oriented universities increased in many countries. Among advanced countries, short-term contracts only reached high rates in Argentina (62%), Finland (34%) and Hong Kong (27%), while in the majority of the other countries, rates beyond 25% can be observed. More professors at other institutions of higher education seem to be on short-term contracts than professors at research-oriented universities.

Spending more hours on work than the usual contract hours for employees is most pronounced among professors at research-oriented universities in advanced countries: in various countries averages of 50 h weekly or more are reached. We note less additional hours among junior staff in advanced countries as well as a range from some additional hours to less than a normal work schedule among professors at other institutions of higher education in advanced countries as well as among both senior and junior academic staff in other countries.

In the majority of countries, both senior and junior academics at research-oriented universities spend more time in 2007 on research all over the year than on teaching. Where information is available at both points in time, we note increasing activities of research in some cases and increasing teaching activities in other cases with no dominant overall trend. At other institutions of higher education, we observe a considerably higher proportion, and also an increase over time, of research activities in a select number of countries.

Job satisfaction of academics is quite high on average, and in most countries, where respective information is available, on a rise; notably, junior academic staff in various countries are more highly satisfied with their professional situation in 2007 than in 1992. This suggests that the work characteristics and the conditions for academic work—the academics do not report increasing problems as far as the resources for their work are concerned—are more important for the overall assessment of their situation than the employment conditions.

It would be misleading, though, to claim that the academics are generally quite satisfied with their professional situation. About one-sixth or one-seventh of the academics is dissatisfied with their job, and also a similar percentage state that they would not become an academic, if they could choose again. So, there is still room for improvement. Actually, we note relatively consistent findings across the subgroups of academics addressed and the various issues addressed in the questionnaire that academics from certain countries are highly satisfied on average, notably from Mexico and Malaysia, and that academics from certain other countries report below-average levels of satisfaction, notably the United Kingdom, South Africa and to some extent China. In the case of the United Kingdom, available information shows clearly a decline over time; obviously, changes such as increasing expectations to demonstrate more visible research results and to ensure the practical relevance of teaching and research are often viewed as a burden; we also note that the sense of affiliation to one's university and to one's department has declined in this country.

By and large, reports on the work situation from academics in the 'other countries', that is, those not traditionally awarding doctoral degrees to their academics themselves, are at least as positive on average or even slightly more positive as those from advanced countries. Certainly, it would be interesting to know what the basis of these ratings is and what comes into play beyond the working conditions as such: the role of academics in the society, a comparison with other occupations in their country, expectations of future developments, etc. This might be clarified in future analyses.

References

Altbach, P. G. (Ed.). (1996). *The international academic profession: Portraits of fourteen countries*. Princeton: Carnegie Foundation.
Boyer, E. L., Altbach, P. G., & Whitelaw, M. J. (1994). *The academic profession: An international perspective*. Princeton: Carnegie Foundation.
Enders, J. (Ed.). (2001). *Academic staff in Europe: Changing contexts and conditions*. London: Greenwood.
Enders, J., & De Weert, E. (Eds.). (2004). *The international attractiveness of the academic workplace in Europe*. Frankfurt/Main: Gewerkschaft Erziehung und Wissenschaft.
Enders, J. & Teichler, U. (1995). *Der Hochschullehrerberuf im internationalen Vergleich* [The academic profession in international comparison]. Bonn: Bundesministerium für Bildung, Wissenschaft, Forschung und Technologie.
Finkelstein, M. J. (2010). Diversification in the academic work force: The case of the US and implications for Europe. *European Review, 18* (supplement 1), 141–156.
Kogan, M., & Teichler, U. (Eds.). (2007). *Key challenges to the academic profession*. Paris/Kassel: UNESCO Forum on Higher Education, Research and Knowledge and International Centre for Higher Education Research Kassel, University of Kassel.
Locke, W., & Teichler, U. (Eds.). (2007). *The changing conditions for academic work and careers in selected countries*. Kassel: International Centre for Higher Education Research Kassel, University of Kassel.
Research Institute for Higher Education, Hiroshima University (Ed.). (2006). *Reports of changing academic profession project workshop on quality, relevance, and governance in the Changing Academia: International Perspectives*. Hiroshima: Research Institute for Higher Education, Hiroshima University.
Research Institute for Higher Education, Hiroshima University. (Ed.). (2008). *The changing academic profession in international comparative and quantitative perspectives* (RIHE International Seminar Reports No. 12). Hiroshima: Research Institute for Higher Education, Hiroshima University.
Teichler, U. (1996). The conditions of the academic profession: An international comparative analysis of the academic profession in Western Europe, Japan and the USA. In P. A. M. Maassen & F. van Vught (Eds.), *Inside academia: New challenges for the academic profession* (pp. 15–65). Utrecht: Uitgeverij De Tijdstrom.
Teichler, U. (Ed.). (2006). *The formative years of scholars*. London: Portland Press.
Teichler, U. (2007). *Higher education systems: Conceptual frameworks, comparative perspectives, empirical findings*. Rotterdam/Taipei: Sense Publishers.
Teichler, U., & Schomburg, H. (2008). Research careers: Some reflections from Europe. *International Higher Education, 52*, 7–9.
Vessuri, H., & Teichler, U. (Eds.). (2008). *Universities as centres of research and knowledge creation: An endangered species?* Rotterdam/Taipei: Sense Publishers.

Chapter 5
Research and Teaching: The Changing Views and Activities of the Academic Profession

5.1 Conceptual Framework

A close link between teaching and research is widely viewed as desirable by academics throughout the world. Indeed, it is considered to be an essential feature of the modern university over the last about two centuries. However, we note differences across countries and institutions both in the relative emphasis placed on research and teaching as well as in the understanding of the relationship between teaching and research. In the Carnegie International Survey of the Academic Profession undertaken in the early 1990s, Arimoto and Ehara (1996) proposed a tripartite classification of research and teaching orientations: (a) a German type with a prevailing strong research orientation, (b) an Anglo-Saxon type with a more or less balanced emphasis on research and teaching and (c) a Latin American type with a strong teaching orientation.

In the recent public debates on the changing function of higher education, much emphasis has been placed on the research function as the principle characteristic of 'world-class universities', so much so that one might assume that academia in recent years has come to stress the research orientation over teaching. But in contrast is the continuing growth of enrolment rates in higher education which has led to enhanced attention being paid to the teaching function of higher education—in part, because the tertiary level sectors that have experienced the most rapid growth in many countries are those where teaching and learning are paramount—for example, in community colleges, technical institutes and distance educations providers. Particularly in these sectors much attention is being devoted to professionalising the teaching competencies of the professoriate.

As many of the questions posed in the comparative survey of the academic profession conducted in the early 1990s have been asked again in the 2007 'Changing Academic Profession' (CAP) study, it is possible to examine how the roles of research and teaching have changed as well as what the members of the academic professions think about these changes. It is possible, for example, to explore whether the Humboldtian ideal emerging in the early nineteenth century, according to which

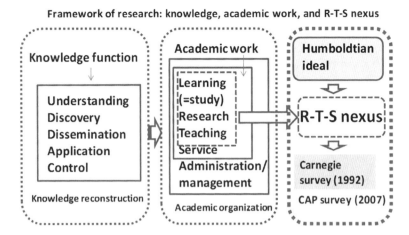

Fig. 5.1 Framework of research, knowledge, academic work and nexus between research, teaching and service. Source: Based on Arimoto 2010

research is the driving force in shaping the relationship between research and teaching, has spread over a larger number of countries and whether research also has become more important in countries which have remained basically within the tradition of the Anglo-Saxon and Latin American types. And it is possible as well to examine whether more elaborate concepts as regards the quality of teaching and learning have taken root recently in countries where teaching traditionally was viewed as subordinate to research (cf. the conceptual framework in Fig. 5.1).

Therefore, the analysis in this chapter will not only address the views and activities as regards teaching and research. Rather, it also will examine how the links between teaching and research are viewed and shaped and what this means for the degree of compatibility between research and teaching in the various countries included in the CAP survey.

The interpretation of the survey findings is based on the conviction that a close link between research and teaching is essential for academic work, as expressed in Fig. 5.1. First, we follow Clark (1983) in assuming that knowledge is the basic component—the raw material for academic work. Knowledge has several dimensions: understanding, discovery, dissemination, application and control. These different dimensions of knowledge have to be translated into learning, research, teaching and service, and they affect management and administration as well. Second, 'academic work' is the most suitable term to translate this function into operation; this work is best described as the discovery of knowledge ('research') and its dissemination ('teaching'). However, the history of the modern university has shown that a close link between research and teaching is not guaranteed. The issue of 'balance', 'compatibility' and 'harmony' between teaching and research is a continuing challenge. According to the Humboldtian ideal underlying the establishment of the University of Berlin at the beginning of the nineteenth century, the 'unity of teaching and research' was realised through the inclusion of students in the process of knowledge generation. The training process of scholars was understood to focus on research, and the seminars and laboratory work were viewed as integrated processes of research, teaching and study (see Von Humboldt 1970; Clark 1997, 2008). Students were an integral part of the research process (Ushiogi 2008, p. 24).

The notion of research being the most pervasive element of universities has spread internationally in the nineteenth and twentieth centuries, but not to the same extent as the Humboldtian concept of the linkage between teaching and research. For example, Geiger (2000, p. 1) argues that the nineteenth century colleges in the USA were 'institutions that conveyed only textbook knowledge to mostly adolescent boys'. Also, other countries adapting elements of the Humboldtian approach realised it to a varying extent (Rudolph 1962; Oleson and Voss 1979; Arimoto 1996). The English tradition of a strong educational approach during the first years of study did not vanish. And the Napoleonic division of labour between teaching and research is often viewed as a third model which spread across many countries. Finally, it is worth noting that many countries have opted for diversification within higher education where different notions of the link between teaching and research shape the most prestigious sectors on the one hand and other sectors of the higher education system on the other hand. For example, Japan successfully established several research universities (Nakayama 1978, pp. 42–43) and thus put research at the apex of the academic function, even though research plays a subordinate role in the majority of universities.

5.2 Preferences for Research and Teaching

It is widely assumed in research on the academic profession that the academics' views as regards the desirable relationships between teaching and research play a powerful role in shaping the actual activities in those domains. Therefore, academics have been asked in the CAP study about their preference as regards teaching and research: whether their interests lie (a) 'primarily in teaching', (b) 'in both, but leaning towards teaching', (c) 'in both, but leaning towards research' and (d) 'primarily in research'.

Actually, academics in all countries point out that they themselves are **in favour of a nexus between teaching and research**. As Table 5.1 shows, the two categories 'in both …' are named as prime interest by academics in all countries surveyed. On average across countries, three-quarters are interested in such a nexus. Thereby, we note that this nexus is most strongly emphasised (more than 80%) by academics in Korea, Italy and in the majority of majority of emerging countries: In contrast, the nexus is underscored by less than two-thirds of academics in Finland, Germany, the Netherlands, Norway, Australia, the UK and the USA. Actually, the nexus between both functions but leaning towards research is more widespread on average across countries (45%) than leaning towards teaching (30%). Leaning towards research prevails in the most advanced countries, while the leaning towards teaching is as frequent as leaning towards research in most emerging countries.

Table 5.1 Preference for teaching and research (per cent)

	CA	US	FI	DE	IT	NL	NO	PT	UK	AU	JP	KR	HK	Avg[a]	AR	BR	MX	ZA	CH	MY	Avg[b]
Primarily in teaching	6	27	15	12	2	22	2	10	10	7	6	3	11	10	13	9	20	18	12	8	13
Both, leaning towards teaching	26	31	20	23	22	28	15	43	23	23	23	29	28	26	36	44	37	35	44	45	40
Both, leaning towards research	54	33	36	39	64	36	51	40	40	40	57	60	49	46	44	42	36	37	39	43	40
Primarily in research	15	10	29	26	12	14	31	7	27	31	14	8	12	18	7	6	7	9	5	4	6

Question B2: Regarding your own preferences, do your interests lie primarily in teaching or in research?
[a]Average among advanced countries
[b]Average among emerging countries

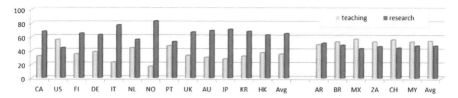

Fig. 5.2 Preference for teaching and research—aggregated categories (per cent, categories 1 and 2 merged to a single category 'teaching', categories 3 and 4 to a single category 'research'). Question B2: Regarding your own preferences, do your interests lie primarily in teaching or in research?

A prime interest in teaching is stated by only 11% of academics on average across countries. This rate is exceptionally high in the United States (27%), the Netherlands (22%) and Mexico (20%)—that is, some of the countries where certain institutional types or certain institutions hardly have any research tasks. The proportion of those with a clear emphasis on research is 14% on average, that is, only moderately higher than that with a clear emphasis on teaching. The clear emphasis on research is most frequent in Australia and Norway (31% each), Finland (29%), the United Kingdom (27%) and Germany (26%)—not only in countries with a strong Humboldtian legacy but also among some Anglo-Saxon countries where rigorous incentive systems in recent years have underscored the research function of higher education.

By combining the responses (c) and (d), we can establish the frequency of a (dominant) research orientation and of a (dominant) teaching orientation. Actually, we note *research orientation* according to this measure among 58% of the respondents on average across the 19 countries. Focusing at the country level (see Fig. 5.2), it can be inferred that a research orientation is:

– *Clearly dominating* (more than 65%) among the academics surveyed by the CAP survey in Norway (83%), Italy (77%), Japan (71%), Australia (69%), Canada and Korea (68% each) and the United Kingdom (67%)
– *Somewhat dominating* (51–65%) in Finland (65%), Germany and Hong Kong (63%), the Netherlands (56%), Portugal (53%) and Argentina (51%)
– *Only true for the minority of academics* (less than 50% of the respondents) in Brazil (48%), Malaysia (47%), South Africa (46%), China and the USA (each 44%) and Mexico (43%)

Obviously, a research orientation is more widely emphasised by academics in advanced countries than in emerging countries. The USA is the clear exception with only a minority of respondents expressing a preference for research.

In the Carnegie International Survey on the Academic Profession, the same question was posed (see Altbach 1996, p. 20). In classifying the countries in the same way as above, we note that among the ten higher education systems participating in both the Carnegie and the CAP survey, a research orientation was clearly (65% and more) evident in 1992 in three countries (the Netherlands, Japan and Germany), and in the recent CAP survey in four countries (Japan, Australia, Korea and the United Kingdom), a research orientation is somewhat prominent (between half and 65%) in 1992 in three countries (Korea, the United Kingdom and Australia) and also in the recent survey in three countries (Germany, Hong Kong and the Netherlands), and research-oriented academics are a minority in the same three countries in both surveys (Mexico, the USA and Brazil).

Among the ten countries participating in both surveys, only Japan is classified at both points of time as strongly research oriented. Germany and the Netherlands have moved from a strong research orientation towards more of a balance between research and teaching, while, in reverse, Korea, Australia and the United Kingdom have moved from a balance towards a strong research orientation. Hong Kong has remained unchanged in the middle position, and Mexico, the USA and Brazil have remained unchanged as countries with a minority emphasis on research. On average of the ten countries, the proportion of research-oriented academics increased from 54% in the early 1990s to 58% in recent years.

In looking at the different types of higher education institutions and the status of the respondents, we note, as was pointed out by Jacob and Teichler (2011), first that professors at 'universities', understood as institutions emphasising both teaching and research, tend to have a strong interest in research. This holds true for more than two-thirds (68% on average across countries) of the respondents in the CAP study (see Table 5.2).

This has been true in the Carnegie Survey in all countries except for Mexico (47%) and Chile (38%) in 1992, and it is true for all of the countries in the CAP survey. Among academics at universities, the research orientation did not change from the early 1990s until recently (68% on average across all countries in both cases).

Table 5.2 shows as well that junior staff at universities tend to have similar preferences as university professors in their respective countries. There are striking exceptions, though. In Finland, junior staff are more interested in research than senior staff (81% vs. 69%); in contrast, a clearly stronger emphasis on research by senior academics at universities than by junior academics is reported for four countries: Australia (87% vs. 70%), Hong Kong (75% vs. 54%), the USA (55% vs. 45%) and Malaysia (55% vs. 41%).

As one might expect, scholars at other institutions of higher education, understood as institutions emphasising teaching predominantly, have a stronger interest in teaching than scholars at universities. However, we note a substantial change over time. While only the academics at teaching-oriented institutions in the single country of Japan differed from the rule in the survey of the early 1990s in being predominantly research oriented, a research orientation also is dominant at the other institutions of higher education in the CAP survey in five cases: Australia, Hong Kong, Japan, Korea and the Netherlands (see Table 5.2).

Thus, altogether, the move towards a slightly stronger research orientation among the academics surveyed is primarily a 'research drift' at teaching-oriented institutions. In contrast, the orientation of academics at universities both in charge of teaching and research hardly changed on average across countries.

5.2 Preferences for Research and Teaching

Table 5.2 Preference for teaching and research—aggregated categories[a]—by type of higher education institution and status group (per cent[a])

	CA	US	FI	DE	IT	NL	NO	PT	UK	AU	JP	KR	HK	Avg[c]	AR	BR	MX	ZA	CH	MY	Avg[d]
All respondents																					
Teaching	32	56	35	38	23	44	17	47	33	30	28	32	37	35	49	53	57	53	56	53	54
Research	68	44	65	63	77	56	83	53	67	69	71	68	63	65	51	48	43	46	44	47	47
Seniors at universities																					
Teaching	32	45	21	25	24	22	20	39	31	13	16	25	25	26	56	40	41	52	50	44	47
Research	68	55	79	75	77	78	80	62	70	87	85	75	75	74	44	60	58	48	49	55	52
Juniors at universities																					
Teaching	30	55	20	29	25	22	16	47	33	29	17	17	45	30	48	47	38	57	55	59	51
Research	70	45	81	71	75	79	84	53	67	70	83	83	54	70	51	53	62	43	45	41	49
Seniors at other HEIs																					
Teaching	.	83	64	77	.	49	25	54	[b]	19	32	36	.	49	.	61	66	[b]	77	49	63
Research	.	16	36	23	.	51	75	46	[b]	81	67	65	.	51	.	39	34	[b]	23	50	37
Juniors at other HEIs																					
Teaching	.	76	85	63	.	83	13	57	[b]	45	32	31	.	52	.	64	65	[b]	66	56	63
Research	.	24	15	37	.	17	88	44	[b]	54	68	69	.	49	.	36	35	[b]	34	43	37

Question B2: Regarding your own preferences, do your interests lie primarily in teaching or in research?
[a]Categories 1 and 2 merged to a single category 'teaching', categories 3 and 4 to a single category 'research'
[b]Too small number of respondents
[c]Average among advanced countries
[d]Average among emerging countries
. No other HEIs or no other HEIs surveyed

5.3 Factors Underlying Research and Teaching Orientation

As the research orientation and the teaching orientation can be viewed as crucial for academic work, an overview will be provided here about the factors which might explain the academics' options for a preference of research versus a preference for teaching. Thereby, differences by country will be taken into consideration. Differences according to the academics' status and type of higher education were considered in the previous section.

First, the *discipline* is relevant for the orientation towards teaching and research. Actually, 62% of the academics in science and engineering—on average across countries—state a preference for research as compared to 56% of the academics in the humanities and social sciences:

- In *science and engineering*, around 70% of academics in most advanced countries state a preference for research; this preference is only more pronounced in Norway (86%) and clearly less pronounced in the USA (50%). In emerging countries, the respective figure is more than 10% lower on average, whereby it ranges from 43% in South Africa to 61% in Argentina.
- In the *humanities and social sciences*, preference for research is most widespread in Italy (76%), and it also dominates in most other advanced countries except for the USA (42%). In emerging countries, the preference for research in the humanities and social sciences dominates only in Argentina (52%), while the respective figure is about 40% in China, Malaysia and Mexico.

The *distinction between the two disciplinary groups* is more pronounced in emerging countries (10% difference on average across countries) than in advanced countries (4%). In Italy, hardly any *distinction* exists among the academics in this respect (77% vs. 76%), while research preference is substantially higher among respondents in science and engineering than those in the humanities and social sciences in the Netherlands (66% vs. 50%), China (53% vs. 40%), Malaysia (52% vs. 40%) and Germany (67% vs. 56%).

These findings are consistent with the argument that there are different cultures embedded in the various academic disciplines. Becher called these 'academic tribes' with their own cultures and territories (Becher 1989; Becher and Trowler 2001), and Clark (1987) referred to the 'small world and different world'. Zuckerman and Merton (1971) pointed out that there is less of a consensus in the humanities and social sciences concerning what might be regarded as creativity and originality. And Arimoto (1981) underscores that values associated with 'universalism' and 'achievement' play a major role in the sciences, while the humanities and social sciences stress values reflecting 'particularism' and 'ascription'. Yet, in comparison to these general assumptions, the preference for research differs only moderately by disciplinary group in the responses to the CAP questionnaire.

Second, the *gender* effect seems to be small. Sixty-three per cent of the men (68% in advanced countries and 52% in emerging countries) and 56% (63 and 41%) of the women surveyed indicate a research orientation. As women in many countries

5.3 Factors Underlying Research and Teaching Orientation

are underrepresented in science and engineering, this relatively small difference is primarily a compositional effect rather than a different gender-based orientation.

There are noteworthy differences, though, by country. On the one hand, slightly more women than men are research oriented in Germany (65% vs. 62%), Norway (84% vs. 82%) and Brazil (49% vs. 47%); on the other hand, women in China are by far less research oriented than men (31% vs. 56%).

Third, in order to examine the possible impact of *age*, the respondents have been subdivided into those being 45 years old or elder and those being younger than 45 years. Actually, older academics (62%) somewhat more frequently expressed a research orientation than younger academics (57%). This holds true both for advanced countries (70% vs. 62%) and for emerging countries (51% vs. 45%). Only in three countries is the reverse true: Germany (57% vs. 68%), Korea (66% vs. 71%) and Norway (81% vs. 86%). Altogether, we note that a research orientation prevails both among older and younger academics.

Fourth, the research orientation does not vary on average by the academics' *income*. In splitting the academics surveyed into a high income and a low income group, we find that those with low income are more strongly research oriented in some countries, while in other countries those with a high income are more strongly research oriented. But on average across countries, income does not help in explaining differences in the strength of the research orientation.

Fifth, having an *advanced academic degree* plays a key role in influencing the research orientation versus the teaching orientation of academics. Seventy-two per cent of the doctoral degree holders (73% on average across advanced countries and 70% in emerging countries) countries express a preference for research in contrast to 43% of those not holding a doctoral degree (46% in advanced countries and 35% in emerging countries).

Such a difference is most pronounced in Mexico (80% vs. 28%), the Netherlands (80% vs. 30%) and Hong Kong (72% vs. 29%). Also in the UK and China, more than twice as many doctoral degree holders than those without a doctoral degree are research oriented. In contrast, this difference hardly exists in Germany (63% vs. 62%), where most academics at higher education institutions without a degree are young scholars working on their dissertation, and it is relatively small in Norway (87% vs. 75%) and Italy (84% vs. 70%)

Sixth, *part-time employed academics* (47% on average, 51% in advanced countries and 37% in emerging countries) show less frequently a preference for research than full-time employed academics (61% on average, thereby 67% in advanced countries and 48% in emerging countries). This holds true for the majority of countries and is very pronounced in Latin American countries where part-timers are often employed for teaching purposes only. Moreover, part-timers are more frequent among persons without a doctoral degree. However, there are four countries where a preference for research is more pronounced by part-timers: in China, Japan, Malaysia and Portugal.

Seventh, *professional mobility* seems to be associated with having a research orientation. Sixty-four per cent (70% in advanced countries and 50% in emerging countries) of those having been active at more than two institutions underscore their preference for research as compared to 58% (64 and 45%, respectively) of the academics who have never moved or moved only once. Research orientation differs most strikingly with the extent of mobility in China (68% of the more mobile vs. 44% of the less mobile or nonmobile respondents), the UK (77% vs. 62%), Hong Kong (71% vs. 58%), Australia (76% vs. 66%) and South Africa (53% vs. 43%). In contrast, those who have been mobile only once or not at all are slightly more research oriented than their mobile peers in Argentina (58% vs. 57%), Brazil (48% vs. 47%) and Norway (84% vs. 83%). The link between professional mobility and the research orientation might be due to the practice among universities to prefer recruiting academics externally who are prominent with respect to their research calibre (see Shinbori 1965; Arimoto 2008).

5.4 Allocation of Working Time to Research and Teaching

Actually, the stronger leaning towards research than towards teaching among academics active at universities both in charge of research and teaching is also reflected in the actual allocation of working time. Both in the Carnegie Survey and in the CAP survey, academics have been asked to estimate the number of weekly hours spent on teaching (and teaching-related activities) and research (and research-related activities) as well as other activities. They have been asked to estimate this both for the period of the year when classes are in session and for the period when classes are not in session. On that basis, the time allocation over the whole year could be calculated.

As shown in detail in Chap. 4, university professors surveyed in the CAP study report on average across countries that they spend 38% of their working time on research and 32% on teaching. There are striking differences by country, though: While university professors in Korea and Australia spend more than one and half times as much of their working hours on research than on teaching, more time is spent on teaching than on research by university professors in South Africa, Brazil and Malaysia.

Junior academics at universities spend a higher proportion of their working time on research and a lower proportion on teaching than university professors on average across countries. A closer look reveals, however, that the time allocation of junior academics and senior academics is similar in various countries. In some countries, though, research activities are clearly more pronounced among junior academic staff than among senior staff at universities: in Norway (65% vs. 39%), Finland (58% vs. 37%) and Germany (53% vs. 38%). Actually, in the countries most clearly shaped by the Humboldtian concept, junior academics are expected to spend substantial time on research in order to qualify for a professoriate.

Senior academics, as one might expect, spend a clearly lower proportion of their work time on research than senior academics at universities on average across countries. The extent to which the time allocation is similar or different, however, varies substantially by country. The most striking differences can be found in

Finland, Germany and the Netherlands where senior academics at other institutions of higher education spend only about two-thirds as much of their overall time budget on research as their colleagues at universities do on average. Again, we note that the functional distinction between universities in charge of research and teaching and other institutions of higher education is most pronounced in countries with a strong emphasis on the Humboldtian understanding of universities.

5.5 Perceived Links Between Research and Teaching Orientation

The actual relationships between research and teaching were addressed in the CAP study by asking the academics to state the extent to which they agreed to two statements:

- 'Your research activities reinforce your teaching'.
- 'Teaching and research are hardly compatible with each other'.

About three quarters of the academics surveyed share the view that their **research activities reinforce their teaching**. As Fig. 5.3 shows, this is stated by more than four-fifth of the academics in seven countries: Korea (85%), Argentina (84%), Canada, Italy, Norway, Mexico (83% each) and Brazil (81%). In contrast, academics in South Africa least often agree to this statement (65%).

University professors are the ones who convinced that their research activities reinforce their teaching, as Table 5.3 shows. Eight-four per cent state this on average across countries; the differences by country are relatively small: They range from 91 to 80% with the exception of South Africa, where such a reinforcement is observed less frequently (68%). Among junior staff at universities, the proportion of those believing in such a reinforcement is clearly lower (73% on average across countries), and the responses vary more substantially between countries (ranging from 60 to 82%). Also at other institutions of higher education, the conviction is widespread that research is reinforcing teaching: It is stated by 76% of the senior academics at these institutions on average, whereby the responses by country range from 65 to 87%.

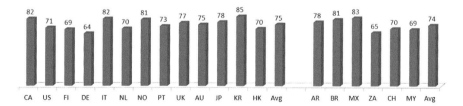

Fig. 5.3 Perceived reinforcement of teaching and research activities (per cent, responses 1 and 2 on a scale from 1 = strongly agree to 5 = strongly disagree). Question C4: Please indicate your views on the following: ... Your research activities reinforce your teaching

Table 5.3 Perception of teaching and research as hardly being compatible with each other by institutional type and status group (per cent[a])

	CA	US	FI	DE	IT	NL	NO	PT	UK	AU	JP	KR	HK	Avg[c]	AR	BR	MX	ZA	CH	MY	Avg[d]
All respondents	20	12	37	34	14	26	14	31	25	28	52	11	27	25	6	7	11	21	42	30	20
Seniors at universities	18	10	37	33	12	18	13	19	25	19	41	8	19	21	10	6	11	21	44	18	18
Juniors at universities	22	13	35	34	17	25	14	28	25	29	61	15	30	27	5	8	14	22	42	37	21
Seniors at other HEIs	.	10	38	47	.	31	20	32	[b]	17	53	12	.	29	.	7	11	.	42	10	14
Juniors at other HEIs	.	11	45	27	.	26	10	36	[b]	36	56	11	.	26	.	8	12	.	39	30	18

Question B5: Please indicate your views on the following: ... Teaching and research are hardly compatible with each other
[a]Responses 1 and 2 on a scale from 1=strongly agree to 5=strongly disagree
[b]Too small number of respondents
[c]Average among advanced countries
[d]Average among emerging countries
. No other HEIs or no other HEIs surveyed

5.5 Perceived Links Between Research and Teaching Orientation

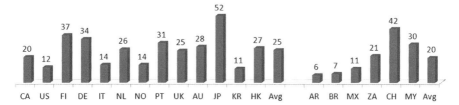

Fig. 5.4 Perception of teaching and research as hardly being compatible with each other (per cent, responses 1 and 2 on a scale from 1 = strongly agree to 5 = strongly disagree). Question B5: Please indicate your views on the following: ... Teaching and research are hardly compatible with each other

The responses of junior academic staff at these institutions are somewhat similar as those senior academics with exceptions. In Finland, Germany and the Netherlands, only a minority states such a reinforcing value. One has to bear in mind that the number of junior academics at other institutions of higher education is relatively low, whereby a substantial proportion of them are not employed for regular teaching and research purposes, but rather for various service functions.

On average across countries, 23% of the academics surveyed have come to the conclusion that **teaching and research are hardly compatible**. There are striking differences by county. The notion that teaching and research are hardly compatible is least frequent, as Fig. 5.4 shows, in Argentina (6%), Brazil (7%), Korea, Mexico (each 11%) and the USA (12%). In contrast, the problem of the incompatibility between teaching and research is somewhat more frequently noted by academics in Japan (51%), China (42%), Finland (38%), Germany (33%) and Malaysia (30%).

Actually, problems of compatibility between teaching and research are named most often in countries characterised by a strong research orientation. In contrast, problems of compatibility are seldom named in countries characterised by a strong teaching orientation of the academics. This pattern, however, does not hold true for all countries. For example, academics in Italy and Korea are strongly research oriented but seldom name problems of compatibility between teaching and research.

Taking into account the institutional type and status of the respondent, we note that only one-fifth of university professors note problems of compatibility between teaching and research as compared to one-fourth of junior staff at universities and as compared to one-fourth of academics at other institutions (see Table 5.3). The finding certainly is due to the fact that senior academics in charge of both research and teaching have more flexibility in shaping the teaching-research nexus according to their intentions than other academics. Among the countries where such problems of compatibility are named frequently, we note that junior academics at universities state these clearly more often than university professors (61% as compared to 41%). In Malaysia, such a difference between junior and seniors holds true for both institutional types. Finally, senior academics at other institutions of higher education in Germany note more often problems of compatibility between teaching and research than senior academics at universities (43% vs. 33%).

These responses to the themes addressed in this section suggest that the relationship between research and teaching is not without tensions, but that the majority of academics note a productive relationship. However, we have to take into consideration that academics have been asked whether research reinforces teaching, but not whether teaching reinforces research.

5.6 Factors Affecting Compatibility Between Research and Teaching

Building on the above review of the factors associated with the academics' preference for research or teaching, a similar review has been undertaken of several factors that were thought to be associated with the academics' belief in the compatibility of research and teaching.

First, the proportion of respondents considering research and teaching as hardly compatible does not differ by *disciplinary group*. Slightly less than a quarter of academics in the humanities and social sciences as well as in science and engineering note a compatibility problem. In Japan—the country where academics most frequently raise doubts about the compatibility of teaching a research—this notion is almost equally spread across all disciplines (52% in the humanities and social sciences as compared to 50% in science and engineering).

Second, *gender* as well does not seem to be associated with the belief in the compatibility of teaching and research. Overall, only 2% of women question such compatibility more often than men.

Third, the influence of *age* seems to be small as well. The proportion of those noting problems of compatibility between research and teaching is only 4% higher among young academics (up to age 45) than among older respondents (45 years and older). The younger ones notably in Malaysia (34% vs. 17%), Australia (31% vs. 18%) and Hong Kong (31% vs. 20%) see more problems of compatibility.

Fourth, those not holding a *doctoral degree* are only slightly more likely to mention a compatibility problem between teaching and research (3% difference, i.e. 25% vs. 22%) than those holding a doctoral degree. Those not holding a doctoral degree mention most often such a problem as compared to doctoral degree holders in Korea (26% vs. 11%), Malaysia (33% vs. 24%), Australia (35% vs. 26%) and Portugal (33% vs. 25%). The reverse is true in Italy: Doctoral degree holders perceive more often a compatibility problem with research and teaching than those not holding a doctoral degree (16% vs. 12%).

Fifth, *employment conditions* also do not matter much as regards the notion of compatibility of research and teaching. South Africa is a notable exception: Full-time employed academics are clearly more sceptical as regards the compatibility of research and teaching than part-timers (22% vs. 11%).

Sixth, academics' *income* is somewhat more linked to compatibility between research and teaching than the previously discussed factors. Those with relatively low income raise doubts as regards compatibility more often (6%) than those with a relatively high income. This is most pronounced in Hong Kong (30% vs. 20%) and China (46% vs. 38%).

Seventh, those persons who have been *professionally mobile* several times view research and teaching as slightly more compatible than those who have little or no mobility. There is not a striking difference in any of the countries surveyed.

Thus, altogether the factors that have been taken into account above fail to adequately account for the likelihood that an academic will express the belief that research and teaching are compatible. One might assume that the perception of compatibility problems depends on specific conditions that cannot be generalised.

5.7 Teaching Approaches

In the CAP survey, the academics have been asked to characterise their *teaching approaches* with respect to five dimensions:

- Practice-oriented approach ('Practically oriented knowledge and skills are emphasised in your teaching')
- International approach ('In your courses you emphasise international perspectives or content')
- Value-oriented approach ('You incorporate discussions of values and ethics into your course content')
- Honesty approach ('You inform students of the implications of cheating and plagiarism in your courses')
- Meritocratic approach ('Grades in your courses strictly reflect levels of student achievement')

Slightly more than two-thirds of all the academics surveyed—on average across countries—consider their teaching as *practice oriented*. As Table 5.4 shows, this is more typically the case for academics from emerging countries (more than three-quarters) than from advanced countries. Rates of four-fifths or even more are stated by academics in Mexico (88%), Brazil (81%), Argentina (80%) as well as Germany (80%), that is, the highest ratio among advanced countries. While, in contrast, only about half of the respondents in Finland, Italy, Norway and Japan describe their teaching as practice oriented.

In some countries, a practice orientation is considered typical for other institutions of higher education, while the academics at universities place their emphasis on theories as contrasted to practice. This is most pronounced in Finland, where only 31% of the university professors describe themselves as practice oriented as compared to 79% of the senior staff at other institutions of higher education, and the Netherlands, where the respective figures are 40 and 84%. A clearly more moderate difference in the same direction can be observed in Germany (75% vs. 93%), Australia (65% vs. 81%) and Japan (38% vs. 55%), while such a distinction between a more theoretically and practically oriented institutional type does not seem to hold true at all for the majority of countries.

Sixty-two per cent of the academics on average across countries view their teaching as *internationally oriented*. There are no substantial differences between

Table 5.4 Teaching approaches by type of higher education institution and status group (per cent[a])

	CA	US	FI	DE	IT	NL	NO	PT	UK	AU	JP	KR	HK	Avg[c]	AR	BR	MX	ZA	CH	MY	Avg[d]
All respondents																					
Practice-oriented approach	60	71	54	79	54	70	50	79	68	74	53	76	69	66	80	81	88	76	76	68	78
International approach	60	49	50	55	61	53	65	79	64	67	53	74	71	62	48	53	77	59	65	62	61
Value-oriented approach	64	68	48	41	38	59	41	67	70	71	48	61	63	57	66	85	79	69	61	71	72
Honesty approach	77	83	44	45	31	61	37	80	90	85	49	66	79	64	54	82	81	86	70	82	76
Meritocratic	84	86	92	63	80	48	74	53	83	80	57	76	79	73	72	56	78	75	31	83	66
Seniors at universities																					
Practice-oriented approach	56	68	31	75	54	40	49	75	69	65	38	71	65	58	89	80	82	76	78	71	79
International approach	60	51	63	79	62	64	69	90	66	75	59	81	77	69	67	62	80	59	70	71	68
Value-oriented approach	64	67	53	57	40	48	45	71	69	68	48	58	63	58	81	80	72	68	59	75	73
Honesty approach	77	81	41	53	32	53	36	78	94	82	42	63	86	63	64	71	76	84	72	85	75
Meritocratic	86	85	95	72	79	54	78	55	87	87	60	81	83	77	79	59	80	75	35	85	69
Juniors at universities																					
Practice-oriented approach	65	74	48	77	54	42	51	77	67	75	53	71	71	63	79	77	86	79	76	63	77
international approach	60	46	46	50	60	60	60	82	60	64	58	75	67	61	46	52	77	59	63	58	59
Value-oriented approach	62	66	41	36	34	44	36	71	70	68	44	34	62	51	64	83	79	73	60	71	72
Honesty approach	77	84	38	41	28	58	36	88	86	82	32	64	76	61	52	81	80	88	69	81	75
Meritocratic	80	87	89	59	81	59	71	53	79	78	33	76	78	71	72	61	81	78	28	84	67
Seniors at other HEIs																					
Practice-oriented approach	.	72	79	93	.	84	57	81	[b]	81	55	75	.	76	.	86	90	.	77	74	65
International approach	.	51	52	60	.	58	61	68	[b]	77	56	71	.	62	.	50	76	.	67	75	74
Value-oriented approach	.	73	53	54	.	71	39	73	[b]	78	50	59	.	64	.	91	83	.	70	66	82
Honesty approach	.	89	60	58	.	67	41	72	[b]	89	53	65	.	69	.	88	83	.	83	86	88
Meritocratic	.	87	98	80	.	42	80	47	[b]	81	59	76	.	73	.	53	77	.	35	88	71

5.7 Teaching Approaches

Juniors at other HEIs

Practice-oriented approach	.	76	80	99	.	90	70	82	b	77	59	81	.	79	.	81	91	.	71	82	65
International approach	.	52	45	40	.	38	64	75	b	65	37	76	.	58	.	45	76	.	54	59	47
Value-oriented approach	.	78	57	21	.	62	48	62	b	78	42	68	.	59	.	86	80	.	64	65	59
Honesty approach	.	82	55	81	.	62	60	75	b	91	47	70	.	72	.	89	83	.	67	81	64
Meritocratic	.	86	95	76	.	44	52	51	b	81	54	73	.	70	.	52	76	.	25	79	.

Question C4: Please indicate your views on the following:

[a] Responses 1 and 2 on a scale of answer from 1 = strongly agree to 5 = strongly disagree

Items: Practically oriented knowledge and skills are emphasised in your teaching

In your courses you emphasise international perspectives or content

You incorporate discussions of values and ethics into your course content

You inform students of the implications of cheating or plagiarism in your courses

Grades in your courses strictly reflect levels of student achievement

[b] Too small number of respondents

[c] Average among advanced countries

[d] Average among emerging countries

. No other HEIs or no other HEIs surveyed

advanced and emerging countries in this respect, but international dimensions are very strongly emphasised in selected countries: Portugal (81%), Mexico (77%), Korea (74%) and Hong Kong (72%). In contrast, only slightly more than half of the respondents in Japan, Finland, the USA, Brazil and the Netherlands report that they place an emphasis on this dimension.

In Portugal (90% vs. 68%) and Germany (79% vs. 60%), senior academics at universities are clearly more strongly internationally oriented than are senior academics at other institutions of higher education. This holds true to a moderate extent as well for Finland and Korea, while we note the reverse in Malaysia.

A strong *value orientation* in teaching—reported by slightly less than two-thirds of all respondents—varies more substantially by country than the practice and international orientations. On average across countries, academics in emerging countries (73%) appreciate values and ethics in teaching more often than do academics in advanced countries (58%). This is most pronounced in Brazil (81%) and Mexico (77%) among the former countries, while among the latter this is emphasised by over half of the academics in Anglo-Saxon countries and Portugal and by less than half of the academics in Italy, Norway, the Netherlands and Japan.

In only a single country, the Netherlands, do we note a striking gap between senior academics at universities and at other institutions of higher education. Seventy-one per cent of the Dutch professors at other institutions consider the teaching of values to be important compared to 48% of the professors at universities.

The strength of the *anti-plagiarism approach* varies even more by country. Almost all academics in the United Kingdom (94%) underscore that they inform students about the consequences of cheating and plagiarism. This rate is also high among academics in advanced countries with an Anglo-Saxon tradition of teaching—Hong Kong (86%), Australia (82%) and the United States (81%)—and in South Africa (88%), Brazil, Malaysia (each 81%) and Mexico (80%) as well. In contrast, we note quite a low rate in Italy (32%), Norway (36%), Finland (41%) and Japan (42%).

In many countries, senior academics at other higher education institutions are slightly more likely to address cheating and plagiarism than senior academics at universities. This is quite pronounced in Germany (60% vs. 41%), the Netherlands (67% vs. 53%) and Japan (53% vs. 42%).

Finally, about 70% of the respondents underscore that their *grading is meritocratically based*. Affirmative responses are rare in China (31%) and only slightly above half in the Netherlands (51%), Portugal (55%) and Brazil (56%). In only two of the latter countries is such a meritocratic approach somewhat less frequent among senior academics at other institutions of higher education than among senior academics at universities: in China (25% vs. 35%) and in the Netherlands (42% vs. 54%).

By and large, junior academics hold similar views as senior academics as regards the desirable approaches for teaching and learning. There is no gap between generations in this respect.

5.8 Teaching Modes

Lecturing in classes is a common mode of teaching all over the world. Many experts argue, though, that more diverse modes of teaching and learning are needed. Among others, more complex modes of teaching are advocated to mobilise and motivate the rising number of students and notably the 'nontraditional students'. New activities are seen as critical for increasing the societal relevance of higher education. Last but not least, new technologies provide new options for communication between the teachers and their students.

In the CAP survey, academics were asked to state whether they have been involved in the current year in several modes of teaching and communication with students—other than merely lecturing in classes. As Table 5.5 shows, the academics surveyed report on average that had been involved in 3.8 of these seven modes. On average the same *frequency of varied teaching modes* is reported for advanced and emerging countries. The country averages range from 4.5 in Mexico, 4.4 in Malaysia as well as 4.4 in Australia and the United Kingdom at the top to 2.8 in Germany at the bottom end. On average, academics at other institutions of higher education report a somewhat greater variety of teaching modes than academics at universities. We also note that junior academics—irrespective of type or higher education—are involved on average in a somewhat smaller range of teaching modes than senior academics.

As Table 5.5 indicates, the variety of teaching modes hardly differs by institutional type. However, junior academics at both types of institutions are involved in a slightly smaller variety of teaching modes than senior academics. This is not surprising because junior academics in various countries are to a lesser extent involved in teaching than senior academics.

Three of the modes of teaching and communication are reported by more than 70% of the respondents: *face-to face interaction with students outside class, electronic communication (e-mail) with students and individualised instruction*. As one might expect, these figures are high across all countries. The few exceptions visible in the Appendix Table 5.11 might be named here: Individual instruction is not common in Portugal (20%) and Argentina (42%), and only about half of the German academics report frequent face-to-face international with students outside class (50%) or the use of electronic communication with students (52%).

About half of the respondents are involved in *practice instruction/laboratory work* (49%) and in *learning in projects/project groups* (47%). The former is named least by academics in the Netherlands (29%) and the latter by respondents in China (26%).

ICP-based learning/computer-assisted learning is only named as a current practice by about one-third and 'distance education' by one-sixth of the respondents. The former is only affirmed by 11% in Korea. Distance education is a rare responsibility for academics in many countries, while South Africa is the exception with almost one-half of the respondents involved.

In addition, almost 70% of the academics surveyed report that they have been involved in the *development of course material*, and almost 60% have been involved in *curriculum/programme development*. Japanese academics are the least likely to engage in these latter practices—only about one-quarter each.

Table 5.5 Variety of teaching modes (mean[a]) by type of higher education institution and status group

	CA	US	FI	DE	IT	NL	NO	PT	UK	AU	JP	KR	HK	Avg[c]	AR	BR	MX	ZA	CH	MY	Avg[d]
All respondents	3.9	4.0	4.1	2.2	3.7	3.4	3.7	3.5	4.2	4.2	3.2	3.2	3.9	3.6	2.7	3.9	4.7	3.8	3.0	4.4	3.7
Seniors at universities	3.9	4.0	4.4	2.6	3.7	3.0	4.0	3.2	4.5	3.8	3.2	3.4	4.1	3.7	3.6	4.1	4.4	3.8	3.1	4.5	3.9
Juniors at universities	3.85	3.9	3.6	2.0	3.7	3.1	3.3	3.6	3.9	4.2	2.5	2.8	3.7	3.4	2.8	3.7	4.5	3.8	2.9	4.6	3.7
Seniors other HEIs	.	4.1	5.1	3.1	.	3.7	3.7	3.4	[b]	4.1	3.3	3.2	.	3.8	.	3.8	4.4	.	3.0	3.9	3.8
Juniors other HEIs	.	4.3	4.8	2.6	.	3.4	3.0	3.6	[b]	4.7	2.9	3.3	.	3.7	.	3.7	4.7	.	2.9	4.2	3.9

Question C2: During the current (or previous) academic year, have you been involved in any of the following teaching activities?
[a]Average of 7 items: Individualized instruction; Learning in projects/project groups; Practice instruction/laboratory work ICT-based learning/computer-assisted learning; Distance education; Development of course material Curriculum/program development; Face-to-face interaction with students outside of class Electronic communication (e-mail) with students
[b]Too small number of respondents
[c]Average among advanced countries
[d]Average among emerging countries
. No other HEI or nor other HEIs surveyed

5.9 Notions and Approaches to Research and Scholarship

The academics' views of the character of their research were addressed in the CAP questionnaire by two questions. First, they have been asked to state whether research and scholarship is to be understood ('is best defined') as original research, the synthesis of academic knowledge, and/or as the application of knowledge in real-life settings. Second, they have been asked more directly linked to their own activities whether the research they undertake is basic/theoretical, practically oriented, international in scope and as mono-disciplinary or multidisciplinary. These questions are posed because academics have a choice between different approaches, but expectations have grown in recent years for more attention to the societal relevance of research. In other words, some observers argue for an increased emphasis to be placed on the dissemination of knowledge, the 'transfer' of knowledge, to move from 'mode 1' to 'mode 2' research (Gibbons et al. 1994) or to engage in more 'applied' and 'commercial' research.

Figure 5.5 suggests that many academics do not see research to be geared in a single major direction. Rather, while three quarters of the respondents support the applied nature of academic research, two-thirds support the 'basic' and 'theoretical' character of research, and two-thirds also support the need for the synthesis of major findings.

It is surprising to note that the function of **basic research** is about as often stressed by academics from emerging countries as by academics from advanced countries. One could have expected that academics from advanced countries would emphasise this more strongly, because they certainly have better means as a rule to be active in basic research as well as in any kind of research with a theoretical emphasis. In contrast, the application of knowledge as well as commercially and transfer-oriented research are somewhat more frequently named as customary by academics from emerging countries, and this is even more pronounced as far as socially relevant research is concerned.

There are, however, noteworthy differences between individual countries. For example, as Appendix Table 5.12 shows, among the advanced countries basic

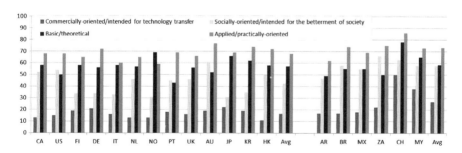

Fig. 5.5 Prime character of research (per cent, responses 1 and 2 on a scale of answer from 1 = very much to 5 = not at all). Question D2: How would you characterise the emphasis of your primary research this (or the previous) academic year?

research is least supported by academics from Finland (57% as compared to 69–90% in other advanced countries); in contrast, more of Malaysia's academics put a strong emphasis on the importance of basic research than their colleagues in the other emerging countries (78% as compared to 37–64%). The theoretical and basic nature of research is in some countries more often stressed by academics at universities than by those at other institutions of higher education. This difference is most pronounced among senior academics in Germany (83% vs. 56%), followed by the USA (74% vs. 57%), Finland (68% vs. 54%), the Netherlands (80% vs. 67%) and Norway (92% vs. 80%).

Application of knowledge is viewed as typical for scholarship by the majority of academics in all countries except for the Netherlands (46%). Otherwise, the rates range from 60% in Italy to over 80% in the three advanced and four emerging countries (with the highest rate of 86% in Mexico). A stronger emphasis on the application of knowledge can be observed among academics at other institutions of higher education compared to those at universities. Among senior academics, this difference is most pronounced in Norway (88% vs. 59%), the Netherlands (87% vs. 62%) and Germany (87% vs. 62%).

Synthesis of research findings is considered to be an important task of scholarship, as already pointed out, by about two-thirds of the academics surveyed. This mode is most frequently highlighted by the academics from Korea (91%), while it is exceptionally low in the Netherlands (45%) and Italy (46%). In this case, the responses differ by type of higher education institution to a lesser extent than the responses to the two research emphases already discussed.

In examining the responses by type of higher education institution and by status groups we note that the responses hardly differ on average between senior and junior academics at universities; the same holds true for senior and junior academics at other institutions. Therefore, we concentrate on responses of senior academics of the two institutional types. On average across countries the differences are smaller than one might have expected. University professors put somewhat more emphasis on basic research (61% vs. 47%) and somewhat less on applied research (69% vs. 78%), **commercial and transfer-oriented research** (20% vs. 24%) and socially relevant research (46% vs. 49%). As already shown above, there is only a small number of the countries addressed in the CAP survey where the functional profile between universities and other institutions of higher education is clearly polarised; this holds true notably for Finland, Germany and the Netherlands:

- Sixty-one per cent of the university professors as compared to 24% of the professors at other institutions of higher education in Finland underscore basic and theoretical research. The respective figures for Germany are 64 and 27% and for the Netherlands 62 and 34%.
- In contrast, an applied research emphasis is clearly more widespread at other institutions of higher education than at universities in these three countries, even though the affirmative responses by university professors are remarkably high: 89% versus 66% in Finland, 94% versus 67% in Germany and 93% versus 62% in the Netherlands.

5.9 Notions and Approaches to Research and Scholarship

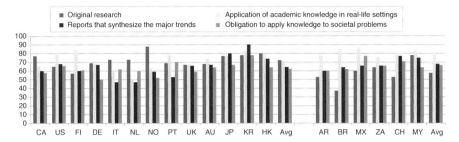

Fig. 5.6 Academics' notion of scholarship as generation, synthesis and application of knowledge (per cent, responses 1 and 2 on a scale of answer 1=strongly agree to 5=strongly disagree). Question B5: Please indicate your views on the following. Items: Scholarship is best defined as the preparation and presentation of findings on original research; Scholarship includes the application of academic knowledge in real-life settings; Scholarship includes the preparation of reports that synthesise the major trends and findings of my field; Faculty in my discipline have a professional obligation to apply their knowledge to problems in society

- The same holds true for commercially oriented and transfer-oriented research in the former two countries: 32% versus 16% in Finland and 43% versus 15% in Germany. In the Netherlands, the respective figure is 15% each for both senior academics at universities and other institutions of higher education.
- The emphasis on **socially relevant research** is not clearly divided by institutional type. In the case of these three countries, socially relevant research is more often emphasised by professors at universities as by those at other institutions of higher education in Germany (48% vs. 37%), about as often in Finland (33% vs. 32%) and less frequently in the Netherlands (39% vs. 69%).

Academics were asked in the CAP questionnaire as well to indicate their **general views on scholarship**. In contrast to the previous question, this question does not address the character of their current activities, but rather their view on research and scholarship. The responses to four categories posed in the questionnaire are shown in Fig. 5.6:

- 'Scholarship is best defined as the preparation and presentation of original research'.
- 'Scholarship includes the application of academic knowledge in real-life settings'.
- 'Scholarship includes the preparation of reports and synthesis of the trends and findings of my field'.
- 'Faculty in my discipline have a professional obligation to apply their knowledge to problems in society'.

The function of *original research* is emphasised by 68% of the academics on average across countries. As one might expect, this is more often the case in economically advanced countries (73% on average across countries) than in emerging countries (58%). By far the highest rate is stated, as Fig. 5.6 shows, by academics from Norway (90%) and by far the lowest by their colleagues from Brazil (37%).

The *applied research* function is highlighted by three quarters of all academics. As one might expect from the previous responses, applied research is named more often by academics from emerging countries (81% on average across countries) than from advanced countries (71%). It is most often selected by Chinese academics (86%) but also is selected by more than 70% of the academics in four advanced countries and four additional emerging countries. Altogether, the responses vary to a lesser extent by country than those regarding original research. The lowest rate as regards applied research is almost 60% (59% in Norway).

The *synthesising research function* finally is selected on average across countries by 65% of the academics, and the differences between advanced countries and emerging countries are small (64% vs. 67%). Differences by country range from 91% in Korea and 81% in Japan on the one hand to less than half in Italy and the Netherlands on the other hand.

In response to the query on multidisciplinary scholarship, 65% on average across countries describe their current primary research activities as *multi-/interdisciplinary* and 39% as *based on a single discipline.* Thus, only about 5% select both descriptors. In most of the countries, a majority describes the research as multidisciplinary. But in Norway (68%) and Japan (60%), the reverse is true, and also in the Netherlands (51%) and Mexico (55%), slightly more than half of the respondents characterise their research as mono-disciplinary.

In examining the differences by type of higher education institution and status group (see Appendix Table 5.13), we note a similar pattern as in the responses to the previous question. The responses between junior academics and senior academics are similar at universities as at other institutions of higher education. The differences according to type of higher education institution, therefore, will be illustrated only with respect to senior academics. As one might expect, university professors define scholarship more often as linked to original research than do professors at other institutions (72% vs. 65%) and less often to application (72 and 80%) and to the synthesis of findings (66% vs. 69%). But these differences with regard to their general views are even smaller than those in response to the previous question addressing their activities.

In this case, we note the most striking differences as regards original research and application again occur in Germany and the Netherlands. Clearly, more university professors than senior academics at other institutions consider scholarship is linked to original research in Germany (83% vs. 56%), whereas the respective difference is smaller in the Netherlands (80% vs. 67%). In contrast, more senior academics at other institutions of higher education than at universities underscore the importance of application in Germany (87% vs. 62%) and in the Netherlands (63% vs. 41%). In other countries, differences tend to be smaller.

5.10 Research Activities

Reports about the research function of higher education mostly address the output of research, notably publications, while the research activities as such often remain a 'black box'. In the CAP survey, the process of research is probed with the help of several questions. While these do not cover all aspects of the research activities, they do touch on several interesting aspects.

Table 5.6 shows that about half of the respondents have been involved recently in *preparing proposals for research projects*. One-third say they have been involved in

5.10 Research Activities   141

Table 5.6 Research activities by type of higher education institution and status group (per cent[a])

	CA	US	FI	DE	IT	NL	NO	PT	UK	AU	JP	KR	HK	Avg[c]	AR	BR	MX	ZA	CH	MY	Avg[d]
All respondents																					
Preparing experiments	61	42	58	59	55	37	52	37	31	38	62	61	39	49	56	40	38	17	36	45	39
Conducting experiments	63	0	51	54	53	34	43	35	28	36	70	71	43	45	54	40	39	19	47	47	41
Supervising assistants	61	41	40	49	61	30	39	25	27	39	46	54	53	43	43	28	28	31	26	43	33
Publishing results	81	67	66	75	80	45	79	54	51	66	81	88	79	70	82	64	54	59	61	64	64
Technology transfer	17	13	26	17	15	8	12	12	11	14	13	13	12	14	27	9	11	13	19	17	16
Calls for proposals	67	50	52	55	70	32	74	23	39	50	69	90	63	56	66	42	31	33	61	53	48
Managing research	58	30	31	44	43	13	37	19	25	37	45	65	52	38	29	22	18	18	16	36	23
Purchasing supplies	52	32	39	43	58	10	34	29	23	30	68	46	42	39	47	29	33	16	27	44	33
Seniors at universities																					
Preparing experiments	58	52	70	59	54	54	51	37	45	47	65	68	43	54	50	53	52	18	36	53	44
Conducting experiments	61	0	54	48	50	46	44	36	41	44	69	74	51	48	49	53	53	19	52	59	48
Supervising assistants	62	57	79	75	69	57	51	41	45	72	56	70	72	62	50	51	46	31	39	73	48
Publishing results	80	77	83	84	80	69	83	62	73	86	91	94	93	81	78	88	79	56	70	82	76
Technology transfer	21	18	29	22	15	16	15	18	17	23	15	21	15	19	27	13	12	13	25	27	20
Calls for proposals	63	60	73	76	72	51	79	38	58	78	85	96	77	70	56	70	49	31	73	78	60
Managing research	58	43	61	69	51	25	50	35	44	69	59	81	69	55	31	41	33	17	22	60	34
Purchasing supplies	51	42	49	57	59	15	37	35	37	46	81	56	53	48	45	53	51	17	36	64	44
Juniors at universities																					
Preparing experiments	65	36	57	64	59	57	50	36	38	47	69	69	34	52	46	47	53	16	34	46	40
Conducting experiments	66	0	52	64	59	54	40	35	37	46	77	84	36	50	46	46	52	15	38	48	41
Supervising assistants	58	33	38	36	52	46	16	17	28	40	67	75	37	42	23	28	35	35	11	40	29
Publishing results	83	54	74	77	78	69	71	50	61	74	91	97	67	73	71	70	74	68	47	65	66
Technology transfer	13	14	28	11	13	10	7	11	8	15	16	8	8	12	21	11	5	15	10	13	13
Calls for proposals	75	42	56	48	68	50	64	18	41	56	89	98	50	58	53	47	45	35	43	52	46
Managing research	59	24	26	33	32	18	15	12	19	39	56	85	37	35	17	21	21	20	8	33	20
Purchasing supplies	57	31	45	38	59	16	27	25	29	34	76	58	32	41	31	32	46	17	17	43	31
Preparing experiments	65	36	57	64	59	57	50	36	38	47	69	69	34	52	46	47	53	16	34	46	40

(continued)

142   5 Research and Teaching: The Changing Views and Activities…

Table 5.6 (continued)

	CA	US	FI	DE	IT	NL	NO	PT	UK	AU	JP	KR	HK	Avg[c]	AR	BR	MX	ZA	CH	MY	Avg[d]
Seniors at other HEIs																					
Preparing experiments	.	29	63	42	.	37	59	38	b	39	57	59	.	46	.	33	34	.	39	36	28
Conducting experiments	.	0	59	38	.	33	40	30	b	36	66	72	.	40	.	33	34	.	53	35	31
Supervising assistants	.	15	29	30	.	15	46	27	b	55	42	51	.	33	.	15	21	.	14	50	40
Publishing results	.	53	59	54	.	40	84	51	b	85	77	85	.	62	.	51	46	.	64	80	68
Technology transfer	.	7	36	25	.	4	6	22	b	11	11	16	.	18	.	5	12	.	14	22	17
Calls for proposals	.	30	38	38	.	27	81	24	b	60	59	88	.	47	.	29	24	.	62	60	55
Managing research	.	13	38	28	.	9	44	23	b	52	40	60	.	33	.	13	12	.	8	47	36
Purchasing supplies	.	18	40	35	.	9	38	27	b	33	61	45	.	34	.	16	26	.	19	48	28
Preparing experiments	.	29	63	42	.	37	59	38	b	39	57	59	.	46	.	33	34	.	39	36	28
Juniors at other HEIs																					
Preparing experiments	.	30	43	40	.	7	70	27	b	31	65	61	.	42	.	25	29	.	42	31	25
Conducting experiments	.	0	41	35	.	7	51	25	b	30	73	68	.	37	.	25	31	.	37	33	25
Supervising assistants	.	20	6	22	.	2	27	10	b	26	30	47	.	22	.	13	19	.	5	31	14
Publishing results	.	50	23	37	.	6	60	41	b	64	70	87	.	49	.	42	39	.	44	49	41
Technology transfer	.	7	20	19	.	3	9	7	b	13	4	10	.	12	.	4	10	.	9	15	8
Calls for proposals	.	28	14	26	.	2	51	9	b	40	59	94	.	36	.	17	21	.	33	39	29
Managing research	.	19	10	38	.	1	25	6	b	28	27	63	.	25	.	8	11	.	6	22	16
Purchasing supplies	.	21	17	45	.	1	44	20	b	20	55	48	.	31	.	12	22	.	9	29	14
Preparing experiments	.	21	17	45	.	1	44	20	b	20	55	48	.	31	.	12	22	.	9	29	14

Question D3: Have you been involved in any of the following research activities during this (or the previous) academic year?
[a]Items: Preparing experiments, inquiries etc.; conducting experiments, inquiries etc; supervising a research team or graduate research assistants; writing academic papers that contain research results or findings; involved in the process of technology transfer, answering calls for proposals or writing research grants; managing research contracts and budgets, purchasing or selecting equipment and research supplies
[b]Too small number of respondents
. Too small number of respondents
[c]Average among advanced countries
[d]Average among emerging countries
. No other HEIs or no other HEIs surveyed

various aspects of *starting and carrying out research*: preparing experiments and inquiries, purchasing relevant materials, managing projects, supervising other researchers and actually conducting inquiries. Finally, about two-thirds are involved in *writing up the results* of research. As one might expect, the responses to these three questions are intertwined. We note that academics active in preparing research proposals are also more likely to indicate that they are involved in the research process and in reporting results.

Turning to differences across countries, on the one hand, there is a group of research active countries (Korea, Norway, Italy, Japan and Canada) where research proposals are written by more than two-thirds of the academics and on the other hand are a group of countries (Portugal, Mexico, the Netherlands and South Africa) where relatively few academics spend time preparing proposals. Activities of preparing and conducting research are distributed similarly. The differences by country in writing up research results are smaller, because many scholars publish books and articles that do not depend on the acquisition of research grants and the availability of substantial resources for research.

We might also expect substantial differences in the research activities between senior and junior academics at *universities*, that is, institutions both more or less equally in charge of teaching and research:

– Actually, 54% of junior academics at universities are involved in the *writing of research proposals* in comparison to 66% of the professors. In 11 countries, a smaller proportion of junior staff than of senior academics are involved in these activities, with the most pronounced differences in Portugal (18% vs. 38%) and China (43% vs. 73%). In the eight other countries, there were no substantial differences.
– As one might expect, senior academics at universities are more likely than their junior colleagues to have a **supervisory role in research activities**. In fact, there is on average across all countries a gap of 58–38%.
– Overall, half of the senior academics and junior academics report that they are *actually involved in the process of inquiry*. There are only two countries where a clearly lower proportion of senior academics at universities are involved in the research process itself than of junior academics: in Germany (48% vs. 64%) and Korea (74% vs. 84%).
– Finally, across countries 79% of the senior academics and 71% of the junior academics report that they have recently been involved in *writing the research results* for publications.

In many countries, academics at *other institutions of higher education* are involved in research to a lesser extent than are the academics at universities. Among those countries for which information is available on the two types of higher education institutions, 48% of professors at other institutions of higher education are involved in writing research proposals as compared to 69% of the university professors; the respective rates for research supervision are 38% versus 59%, for actual research activities 40% versus 48%, and for writing the research results for publication 66% versus 81%.

Three quarters of the academics report that they *collaborate with other persons in their research activities*. This is not confined to their own institution of higher education, as Table 5.7 shows: six out of ten of those collaborating have research

Table 5.7 Collaboration in research by type of higher education institution and status group (per cent of all undertaking research)

	CA	US	FI	DE	IT	NL	NO	PT	UK	AU	JP	KR	HK	Avg[b]	AR	BR	MX	ZA	CH	MY	Avg[c]
All respondents																					
Working individually	65	71	16	65	45	73	31	40	53	78	52	37	51	52	42	39	39	64	66	29	47
Project collaboration	85	79	89	67	82	86	80	57	84	89	61	74	83	78	77	77	77	63	72	86	75
National collaboration	68	61	68	58	77	59	56	65	67	67	49	64	53	62	63	60	55	53	33	56	53
International collaboration	63	33	69	44	59	52	60	45	60	59	22	29	57	50	43	28	35	41	10	32	32
Seniors at universities																					
Working individually	64	71	9	65	42	75	27	28	59	86	44	29	52	50	34	32	36	62	74	24	44
Project collaboration	84	85	93	74	83	93	84	71	84	96	76	83	87	84	83	89	82	62	75	91	80
National collaboration	70	70	83	82	79	73	65	80	72	80	61	71	60	73	70	72	62	51	43	69	61
International collaboration	67	49	87	75	62	77	72	70	68	85	38	44	71	67	52	41	46	37	16	51	41
Juniors at universities																					
Working individually	67	66	16	66	51	78	36	38	47	75	32	42	50	51	43	42	40	61	57	28	45
Project collaboration	85	78	90	68	80	90	75	56	84	89	77	81	80	79	76	75	82	63	73	88	76
National collaboration	65	59	66	54	73	67	48	61	64	66	51	68	48	61	62	54	63	56	25	49	52
International collaboration	57	24	68	40	54	74	50	46	58	55	25	44	49	50	41	28	40	45	6	23	31
Seniors at other HEIs																					
Working individually	.	75	19	66	.	69	21	27	[a]	82	54	40	.	50	.	41	39	.	73	33	47
Project collaboration	.	68	83	46	.	82	93	71	[a]	92	57	72	.	74	.	75	74	.	67	76	73
National collaboration	.	45	67	57	.	50	79	77	[a]	79	49	60	.	63	.	51	49	.	34	48	46
International collaboration	.	16	56	26	.	26	65	59	[a]	68	20	27	.	40	.	19	27	.	6	42	24

5.10 Research Activities

Juniors at other HEIs																	
Working individually	.	75	23	56	.	73	34	45	a	76	56	34	.	52	.	46	40	.	65	46	49
Project collaboration	.	67	77	71	.	65	82	53	a	81	57	72	.	69	.	58	70	.	58	71	64
National collaboration	.	50	60	50	.	32	48	64	a	56	39	68	.	52	.	48	42	.	25	53	42
International collaboration	.	17	51	27	.	11	61	39	a	43	13	25	.	32	.	12	22	.	6	25	16

Question D1: How would you characterise your research efforts undertaken during this (or the previous) academic year?
Scale from 1 = yes to 2 = no
Items: Are you working individually/without collaboration on any of your research projects? Do you have collaborators in any of your research projects? Do you collaborate with persons at other institutions in your country? Do you collaborate with international colleagues?
[a]Too small number of respondents
[b]Average among advanced countries
[c]Average among emerging countries
. No other HEIs or no other HEIs surveyed

partners abroad, and eight out of ten who are collaborating have research partners in their country but outside their own institution. Half of the respondents state that they undertake research work individually; this suggests that many scholars are concurrently involved in collaborative research and in undertaking research on their own.

5.11 Research Output

In the CAP questionnaire, the academics are asked to state the numbers of publications, papers and other research output they have produced during the last 3 years. The question addresses simply the quantity of the various products without any effort to elicit information that might be used for an in-depth assessment of academic productivity, for example, co-authorship and publication in select journals, because it seemed impossible to acquire additional information which could be used to weigh the research productivity according to criteria valid across all countries, disciplines and types of institutions.

Altogether, the responses of all academics—average across countries—show (see Tables 5.8 and 5.9) that:

- Sixty-five per cent have published articles in academic books and journals—on average 5.1 articles over the past 3 years.
- Sixty-three per cent have presented papers at scholarly conferences—on average 4.6.
- Thirty-five per cent have written research reports/monographs—on average 1.1 reports.
- Twenty-five per cent have authored or co-authored a scholarly books—on average 0.5 books.
- Sixteen per cent have edited or coedited scholarly books—on average 0.3 books.
- Twenty-five per cent have written professional articles for newspapers and magazines—on average 1.1 articles.
- Five per cent or less each have produced other research results, such as patents (4%—on average 0.1), computer programmes for public use (4%—on average 0.1), artistic work (5%—on average 0.3), films (4%—on average 0.1) and others (5%—on average 0.3).
- Twenty per cent have not produced any visible research results within the recent 3 years.

An aggregate *publication index* was created by counting the authorship and editorship of books as 3, the authorship of articles in scholarly books and journals as well as research reports as 2, and finally conference papers and articles for newspapers and magazines as 1. According to this index, the average score for all academics—21—does not explain very much, because it varies substantially not

5.11 Research Output

Table 5.8 Research activities (means of all respondents)

	CA	US	FI	DE	IT	NL	NO	PT	UK	AU	JP	KR	HK	Avg[a]	AR	BR	MX	ZA	CH	MY	Avg[b]
Books (co-)authored	0.3	0.2	0.4	0.3	1	0.4	0.4	0.5	0.3	0.3	1.8	1	0.5	0.6	0.5	0.6	0.5	0.4	0.7	0.8	0.6
Books (co-)edited	0.2	0.2	0.3	0.3	0.5	0.3	0.2	0.5	0.2	0.2	0.5	0.7	0.4	0.3	0.3	0.2	0.2	0.2	0.7	0.4	0.3
Articles published	6.4	4.2	4.6	6.2	9.1	5.9	4.8	4.2	5.4	6.9	8.9	11.3	8.7	6.7	3.8	4.4	3	3	7.3	5	4.4
Report for funded project	1.4	1.6	1.3	1.7	1.6	1.1	0.6	1.3	1.2	1.5	1.1	2.6	1.5	1.4	1.8	1.4	0.7	0.8	1.2	1.6	1.3
Conference paper	8.2	5.2	4.3	5.4	7.7	4.2	4.3	6.4	4.9	5.7	4.8	7.9	7	5.8	5.8	5.5	3.8	3.4	2.2	5.9	4.4
Professional article	1.3	1.5	1.1	1.3	1.9	1.8	1.4	1.1	0.7	1.3	1.0	1.0	2.1	1.3	1.3	1.6	1.4	0.6	0.9	1.2	1.2
Patent secured	0.1	0.1	0.1	0.2	0.1	0.1	0.1	0.1	0.1	0.1	0.3	0.8	0.2	0.2	0	0	0	0	0.3	0.2	0.1
Computer programme written	0.1	0.1	0.1	0.1	0.1	0.2	0.2	0.1	0.2	0.1	0.1	0.1	0.1	0.1	0.1	0.1	0.2	0.1	0.3	0.1	0.2
Artistic work exhibited	0.3	1.7	0.3	0.5	0.1	0.2	0.5	0.5	0.2	0.4	1.2	0.5	0.2	0.5	0.2	0.3	0.5	0.2	0.1	0.2	0.3
Film produced	0.1	0.2	0.1	0.3	0.1	0	0.2	0.1	0.1	0.1	0.1	0.1	0.1	0.1	0.1	0.2	0.2	0.1	0.1	0.2	0.2
Others	0.6	0.9	0.3	0.3	0.2	0.1	0.6	0.4	0.4	0.2	0	0.5	0.6	0.4	0	1.0	0.6	0.3	0.1	0.4	0.4

Question D4: How many of the following scholarly contributions have you completed in the past 3 years?
Items: Scholarly books you authored or co-authored, Scholarly books you edited or coedited, Articles published in an academic book or journal, Research report/monograph written for a funded project, Paper presented at a scholarly conference, Professional article written for a newspaper or magazine, Patent secured on a process or invention, Computer programme written for public use, Artistic work performed or exhibited, Video or film produced, Others
[a]Average among advanced countries
[b]Average among emerging countries

Table 5.9 Number of research output (means for respondents with any respective research output)

	CA	US	FI	DE	IT	NL	NO	PT	UK	AU	JP	KR	HK	Avg[a]	AR	BR	MX	ZA	CH	MY	Avg[b]
Books (co-)authored	1.4	1.3	1.5	1.4	2.0	1.4	1.7	2.1	1.4	1.4	3.1	2.1	1.6	1.7	1.5	1.8	1.8	1.7	2.4	2.4	1.9
Books (co-)edited	1.4	1.6	1.7	2.2	1.8	1.8	1.5	2.4	1.4	1.5	2.3	2.3	1.6	1.8	1.5	1.8	1.7	1.5	2.1	1.9	1.8
Articles published	7.1	5.9	6.2	7.6	9.6	7.5	5.7	5.8	6.1	7.9	10.3	11.5	9.6	7.8	5.1	5.7	5.1	4.1	9.0	7.1	6.0
Report for funded project	3.2	5.2	3.3	3.0	3.3	3.0	2.9	2.8	3.1	3.7	2.6	3.5	3.2	3.3	2.9	3.2	2.4	2.9	3.8	3.3	3.1
Conference paper	8.8	6.6	5.6	7.0	9.1	6.0	5.5	8.2	5.7	6.4	8.2	9.4	7.8	7.3	6.7	7.6	5.7	4.3	4.3	7.4	6.0
Professional article	3.4	5.3	3.4	4.6	6.6	3.7	3.9	3.3	2.7	4.4	3.5	4.4	6.7	4.3	3.1	4.6	4.3	2.6	5.1	5.7	4.2
Patent secured	1.7	1.7	1.7	2.1	1.9	2.0	1.6	2.0	1.8	1.7	2.5	3.7	2.6	2.1	1.2	1.6	1.4	2.2	2.7	3.7	2.1
Computer programme written	2.0	2.0	1.9	1.6	2.1	2.6	3.5	1.9	3.2	1.6	2.6	1.8	1.7	2.2	1.7	1.7	2.2	2.6	3.3	2.1	2.3
Artistic work exhibited	6.2	14.0	7.4	11.5	5.8	5.7	9.3	9.5	5.3	6.8	7.8	9.4	4.7	8.0	2.7	6.8	7.9	4.8	5.5	3.6	5.2
Film produced	1.9	4.0	1.6	3.9	4.5	1.3	3.3	2.5	2.3	1.8	1.7	2.4	2.1	2.6	1.3	3.4	3.5	2.4	4.7	2.9	3.0
Others	6.6	10.1	4.1	7.2	5.1	1.5	5.8	3.3	4.4	6.4	0	10.4	12.5	6.5	0	7.6	7.1	6.0	3.4	7.7	6.4

Question D4: How many of the following scholarly contributions have you completed in the past 3 years?
Items: Scholarly books you authored or co-authored, Scholarly books you edited or co-edited, Articles published in an academic book or journal, Research report/monograph written for a funded project, Paper presented at a scholarly conference, Professional article written for a newspaper or magazine, Patent secured on a process or invention, Computer programme written for public use, Artistic work performed or exhibited, Video or film produced, Others
[a] Average among advanced countries
[b] Average among emerging countries

5.11 Research Output

only by country but also by the academics' status and type of higher education institution. Actually, the average score is:

- 37 for university professors
- 21 for junior staff at universities
- 19 for senior academics at other institutions of higher education
- 11 for junior academics at other institutions of higher education

According to this index, university professors publish almost twice as much as junior staff at universities and as senior academics at other institutions of higher education. Junior academics at other institutions publish substantially less.

Among *university professors*, as Table 5.13 shows, academic productivity, according to the index chosen, is:

- Very high in Korea (61), Germany (56) and Japan (50)
- High in Australia (49), Portugal (47), Hong Kong (46) and the Netherlands (41)
- Close to the average in Italy (39), Finland (38), Malaysia (36), China (34) and Canada (31)
- Low in the Argentina, Brazil and the UK (29), Norway (28), the USA (27) and Mexico (22)
- Very low in South Africa (14)

On average, the score is one and a half times as high in advanced countries as in emerging countries. The score is higher in 8 of the 13 advanced countries than in the emerging country with the highest score (Table 5.10).

Among *junior staff at universities*, who publish slightly more than half as much as senior academics, the score is exceptionally high in Japan (45) and Korea (37); both of these countries have an exceptionally small proportion of academics with junior level appointments. The score is high as well in Italy (29) and in the Netherlands (27), while it is very low in South Africa (12) and Norway (11). In half of the countries, the academic productivity of junior staff at universities is less than half of that of university professors.

Among *senior academics at other institutions of higher education*, the scores vary even more widely by country. The highest scores are reported for Malaysia (59), Portugal (42) and Korea (40). In contrast, the scores are exceptionally low in the Netherlands (7), the USA (9) and Finland (10).

Among *junior academics at other institutions of higher education*, who publish clearly least, the highest scores are reported in Korea (36) and Japan (20), where again the exceptionally small number of these junior staff positions in the two countries comes into play. In contrast, the score is exceptionally low in the Netherland (5) and Finland (7)—that is, countries with a strong polarisation of the research function between universities that are expected to stress research in contrast to a more limited role for academics at other institutions of higher education.

The academics included in the CAP survey have been asked to provide some additional information about the modes of publications. Four issues are worth reporting.

Table 5.10 Index[a] of academic productivity by type of higher education institution and status group (arithmetic mean)

	CA	US	FI	DE	IT	NL	NO	PT	UK	AU	JP	KR	HK	Avg[c]	AR	BR	MX	ZA	CH	MY	Avg[d]
All respondents	26.7	19.4	19.2	24.4	35.4	22.2	18.5	21.4	20.4	25.2	32.9	41.9	32.0	26.1	20.5	21.2	14.8	13.5	24.6	23.7	19.7
Seniors at universities	30.9	26.8	37.7	55.8	39.4	41.3	27.8	47.0	28.6	49.3	50.2	60.7	46.2	41.7	29.3	29.1	21.8	14.0	34.0	36.2	27.4
Juniors at universities	19.5	17.9	16.2	19.5	28.8	27.4	11.4	22.6	15.0	20.4	44.8	36.7	20.9	23.2	19.3	18.4	16.6	11.6	15.9	17.5	16.6
Seniors other HEIs	.	8.9	9.9	19.2	.	7.1	21.3	41.6	b	32.5	30.7	40.4	.	24.1	.	16.7	11.9	.	25.2	58.8	25.2
Juniors other HEIs	.	8.7	6.8	8.8	.	5.3	8.5	15.6	b	15.8	20.4	35.9	.	14.0	.	12.9	8.6	.	11.9	13.5	11.6

Question D4: How many of the following scholarly contributions have you completed in the past 3 years?

[a]Scores built by giving different weights to different sorts of publications (3 for scholarly books (co-)authored, scholarly books (co-)edited, 2 for articles published in an academic book or journal, a research report/monograph written for a funded project, and 1 for papers presented at scholarly conference, professional articles written for a newspaper or magazine)

[b]Too small number of respondents

[c]Average among advanced countries

[d]Average among emerging countries

. No other HEIs or no other HEIs surveyed

About three quarters of the respondents report that their publications have been *peer reviewed*. This holds true—according to the academics' responses—on average across countries for 82% of the publications published by authors in advanced countries and 65% in emerging countries. 'Peer reviewed' is high in Canada (95%), the UK, Australia (94%) and Argentina (91%), while it is low in China (35%), Brazil and Malaysia (54% each).

About three quarters of the publications are reported to be *co-authored by colleagues of the country of employment*, while about one-third are *co-authored by colleagues of other countries*. The latter is most often stated by academics in the Netherlands (57%), Norway (50%) and Hong Kong (49%), and least often in China (3%), Brazil (19%) and South Africa (21%).

Slightly more than half of the publications are 'published in a *language* different from the language of instruction at your current institution'. This is most often the case among academics in Norway (94%), the Netherlands (90%) and Italy (86%), while it is seldom the case in Australia (6%), the USA (10%) and the UK (12%).

5.12 Concluding Observations

The framework of the study, which underlined the relationship between knowledge and academic work, first, pointed out that academic work was located at the core of discovery and dissemination. Accordingly, in the processes of academic work, research and teaching are the most important vehicles. In fact, in modern universities, where a research orientation was institutionalised together with the teaching orientation that had existed since the medieval universities, these two functions had the potential for generating conflicts so the search for their intentional and systematic nexus became inevitable. The Humboldtian ideal, attempting to clarify their integration, is an aim to be realised in modern universities.

Second, fostering harmony between the research and teaching functions is often a challenge, as both are established activities of the contemporary university and as in most major universities both have their distinctive administrative settings. The former has been the role of higher education institutions since the middle ages; the latter has entered the university in conjunction with the institutionalisation of modern sciences and the scientific community. Integration of the values of both research and teaching has presented a great deal of difficulty as shown by the fact that cross-nationally there are several types in terms of academics' consciousness. In the 1992 Carnegie survey, three types were identified, with the German type stressing research. By the time of the 2007 survey, arguably most systems had converged into one type, the research orientation type, or the German type. Arguably because, just at the same time that systems such as the UK system were heightening their stress on research, others such as the US and Japanese systems were striving to fortify their teaching orientation.

Third, recognising these ambiguities, still it is useful to ask why national systems and their academics might strengthen the research orientation at the expense of the teaching orientation. Modern universities are intrinsically committed to a research orientation. Moreover, the results of the emerging university rankings since the early twenty-first century have affected every system, bringing about a trend of identifying world-class universities, COEs and global universities. Finally, the market mechanism of university ranking, which was started originally in the USA, has emerged internationally in connection with the globalisation and marketisation of the knowledge society and has extended to almost all of the countries in the world.

At a time when the research orientation is itself becoming more pronounced, one has to ask, fourth, whether the integration between research and teaching has been adequately fostered. The Humboldtian ideal is, as it were, an abstract theory so there is no guarantee of its actual implementation. In reality, Germany, where this ideal was initially introduced, has been and is still going further towards a research orientation without realising the ideal. Despite the US system's recent efforts to favour quality teaching, the compatibility of teaching and research has a shaky foundation there. This is perhaps because the USA initially constructed a system realising both differentiation and integration simultaneously. However, even in the USA, the integration between teaching and research is continually confronted with constraints in which the deliberate pursuit of a teaching orientation is not attainable.

In this regard, Japan's trend is noteworthy because it is the country with the lowest compatibility of research and teaching. Recent higher education policies, especially the Faculty Development (FD) policy, seek to transform higher education in Japan from a research orientation to a teaching orientation. But these policies have encountered difficulties due to insufficient consideration of the scholarship on the factors that foster the compatibility of teaching and research. It would appear that the Japanese approach to faculty development has experienced a setback (Arimoto 2010).

This article, fifth, has testified to the compatibility of research and teaching in nineteen countries on the basis of the CAP survey. The factors highly associated with a research orientation are as follows: male gender, older age group, doctoral degree, sciences discipline, higher income, full-time employment and greater mobility. In contrast, factors associated with a teaching orientation are as follows: female gender, younger age group, lower level degree than doctorate, humanities and social sciences discipline, lower income, part-time employment and lower mobility. Based on these results, five countries are revealing high compatibility and five other countries are revealing low compatibility. The other countries are situated in between. It is realistic to say that there is the likelihood in the future of witnessing a decline in the compatibility of teaching and research.

Appendix

Table 5.11 Types of teaching modes by type of higher education institution and status group (per cent)

	CA	US	FI	DE	IT	NL	NO	PT	UK	AU	JP	KR	HK	Avg[b]	AR	BR	MX	ZA	CH	MY	Avg[c]
All respondents																					
Individualised instruction	78	79	79	37	95	66	86	21	82	80	77	56	78	96	34	89	78	75	69	72	96
Project groups	45	54	45	38	33	66	49	44	57	50	25	45	59	70	32	45	58	41	24	78	70
Practice instruction	39	40	66	45	53	29	42	79	44	41	59	51	38	47	44	60	63	34	52	66	46
ICT-based learning	24	23	39	13	16	25	20	28	42	41	31	7	29	48	31	17	67	26	31	49	53
Distance education	11	24	32	2	9	11	7	15	20	35	5	12	9	26	12	18	15	48	5	15	37
Development of course material	88	86	75	33	85	78	46	85	82	87	28	63	77	15	62	50	76	86	25	70	19
Curriculum development	62	73	65	29	33	68	61	74	69	74	25	49	62	70	37	45	66	70	38	68	62
Face-to-face outside of class	94	92	65	42	83	72	78	77	83	85	67	85	88	57	61	80	86	83	67	86	54
E-mail with students	96	92	86	45	85	69	86	91	93	92	55	66	89	78	72	81	79	77	52	78	77
Seniors at universities																					
Individualised instruction	80	83	92	43	96	71	97	17	88	82	79	58	84	97	44	96	76	73	74	73	97
Project groups	44	51	54	39	33	44	58	43	66	45	32	54	64	75	41	54	53	42	30	76	73
Practice instruction	39	40	62	29	49	22	38	70	48	33	54	50	37	48	44	69	59	32	54	70	49
ICT-based learning	25	25	40	20	15	23	25	18	44	29	23	7	29	44	52	14	65	28	31	46	55
Distance education	11	23	29	2	10	9	9	9	21	21	3	15	9	25	22	15	13	45	5	18	39
Development of course material	87	83	84	37	84	70	51	85	89	84	26	59	81	13	79	55	76	84	30	71	20
Curriculum development	61	72	80	60	38	61	73	74	78	79	24	48	76	71	68	47	64	67	49	76	66
Face-to-face outside of class	95	91	75	61	86	68	85	79	89	82	67	83	93	63	79	83	90	83	68	85	62
E-mail with students	96	92	92	64	86	63	93	88	97	90	61	73	95	81	81	81	83	75	50	78	81

(continued)

Table 5.11 (continued)

	CA	US	FI	DE	IT	NL	NO	PT	UK	AU	JP	KR	HK	Avg[b]	AR	BR	MX	ZA	CH	MY	Avg[c]
Juniors at universities																					
Individualised instruction	76	72	74	35	92	71	73	21	76	81	61	52	74	94	33	89	76	76	64	73	96
Project groups	46	55	32	34	32	46	40	47	51	52	23	47	56	66	31	46	54	41	21	80	69
Practice instruction	39	39	64	47	60	35	45	82	41	44	58	41	37	43	44	65	60	42	50	69	46
ICT-based learning	23	21	26	12	18	27	16	33	40	39	14	0	30	49	28	11	65	25	30	52	55
Distance education	12	23	21	1	8	5	5	13	18	28	8	6	9	23	11	13	19	38	5	15	35
Development of course material	91	85	65	32	86	71	39	85	73	87	10	55	74	12	60	40	81	87	19	67	17
Curriculum development	63	68	49	18	24	45	46	69	60	70	7	37	54	66	33	49	64	77	28	65	59
Face-to-face outside of class	93	91	60	35	78	67	71	81	78	85	42	80	84	47	59	83	88	83	64	88	53
E-mail with students	96	89	80	39	85	64	79	88	91	91	43	58	85	73	71	79	87	75	54	80	78
Seniors at other HEIs																					
Individualised instruction	.	83	80	30	.	73	90	18	a	79	80	53	.	95	.	87	77	76	72	64	98
Project groups	.	62	73	69	.	75	43	58	a	43	24	41	.	65	.	41	59	41	18	62	75
Practice instruction	.	37	78	49	.	29	52	65	a	19	58	52	.	54	.	56	65	42	57	51	45
ICT-based learning	.	17	56	19	.	24	20	29	a	47	34	7	.	49	.	21	69	25	31	44	57
Distance education	.	23	56	12	.	16	7	14	a	47	6	14	.	28	.	23	13	38	3	7	41
Development of course material	.	90	89	43	.	79	59	81	a	82	31	62	.	22	.	50	77	87	30	69	12
Curriculum development	.	81	85	73	.	81	69	69	a	73	28	48	.	68	.	44	66	77	46	73	57
Face-to-face outside of class	.	96	73	70	.	75	73	72	a	86	71	85	.	67	.	75	85	83	72	81	57
E-mail with students	.	97	97	66	.	76	90	86	a	90	56	65	.	78	.	78	76	75	46	82	78

Appendix

Juniors at other HEIs

Individualised instruction	.	81	76	19	.	55	75	22	a	79	69	60	.	91	.	83	85	.	70	67	96
Project groups	.	54	61	64	.	81	36	41	a	52	23	50	.	62	.	36	66	.	15	76	76
Practice instruction	.	45	73	66	.	30	48	80	a	46	67	51	.	52	.	52	64	.	50	55	48
ICT-based learning	.	27	65	0	.	24	13	28	a	53	33	7	.	55	.	21	72	.	34	45	55
Distance education	.	29	54	7	.	9	7	16	a	54	3	9	.	28	.	20	21	.	5	13	43
Development of course material	.	94	87	31	.	83	34	85	a	91	18	68	.	21	.	47	80	.	22	81	15
Curriculum development	.	80	84	38	.	71	47	76	a	78	22	53	.	67	.	41	69	.	27	70	58
Face-to-face outside of class	.	96	62	55	.	75	65	76	a	88	54	88	.	61	.	79	86	.	65	85	52
E-mail with students	.	99	93	50	.	68	58	93	a	96	45	66	.	74	.	84	80	.	56	75	79

Question C2: During the current (or previous) academic year, have you been involved in any of the following teaching activities?

Items: Individualised instruction, Learning in projects/project groups, Practice instruction/laboratory work, ICT-based learning/computer-assisted learning, Distance education, Development of course material, Curriculum/programme development, Face-to-face interaction with students outside of class, Electronic communication (e-mail) with students

[a]Too small number of respondents
[b]Average among advanced countries
[c]Average among emerging countries
. No other HEIs or no other HEIs surveyed

Table 5.12 Prime character of research by type of higher education institution and status group (per cent[a])

	CA	US	FI	DE	IT	NL	NO	PT	UK	AU	JP	KR	HK	Avg[c]	AR	BR	MX	ZA	CH	MY	Avg[d]
All respondents																					
Commercially oriented	13	15	19	21	16	13	13	18	16	19	22	19	11	17	17	17	18	22	50	38	27
Socially oriented	52	54	34	34	33	46	31	45	46	61	31	35	50	42	47	58	55	66	63	58	58
Basic/theoretical	58	50	58	56	58	57	69	43	56	52	66	62	58	57	49	55	55	50	78	65	59
Applied/practically oriented	68	68	65	72	60	65	59	69	66	77	69	74	72	68	62	74	69	75	86	73	73
Seniors at universities																					
Commercially oriented	58	53	61	64	60	62	72	41	58	57	76	68	59	61	46	57	58	53	81	68	61
Socially oriented	68	68	66	67	60	56	57	76	68	72	62	76	74	67	59	71	65	72	87	76	72
Basic/theoretical	16	17	16	15	14	15	12	22	18	25	19	21	11	17	20	15	16	22	51	39	27
Applied/practically oriented	45	51	33	48	33	39	32	50	37	58	32	23	54	41	53	50	55	65	65	62	58
Juniors at universities																					
Commercially oriented	58	57	62	60	52	67	65	42	55	54	57	62	60	58	53	50	52	42	73	68	56
Socially oriented	71	68	63	67	62	57	60	69	64	76	72	69	68	67	52	63	68	81	86	71	70
Basic/theoretical	11	22	21	18	17	12	15	17	15	19	14	27	10	17	14	17	8	25	52	36	25
Applied/practically oriented	54	49	29	26	34	41	29	52	42	62	25	16	46	39	46	55	41	68	60	62	55
Seniors at other HEIs																					
Commercially oriented	.	36	24	27	.	34	60	50	[b]	52	62	58	.	45	.	64	51	.	81	58	64
Socially oriented	.	69	89	94	.	93	61	62	[b]	82	69	73	.	77	.	82	73	.	83	88	82
Basic/theoretical	.	11	32	43	.	15	8	21	[b]	6	20	22	.	20	.	22	20	.	42	33	29
Applied/practically oriented	.	48	34	37	.	69	18	47	[b]	70	35	30	.	43	.	74	59	.	67	54	64

Appendix 157

Juniors at other HEIs

Commercially oriented	.	50	20	35	.	24	70	41	b	40	61	64	.	43	.	48	53	.	68	61	58
Socially oriented	.	67	80	96	.	88	61	60	b	83	67	77	.	77	.	82	69	.	79	74	76
Basic/theoretical	.	21	25	65	.	19	17	18	b	16	11	18	.	26	.	16	21	.	46	36	30
Applied/practically oriented	.	46	33	25	.	42	18	47	b	63	27	40	.	39	.	59	56	.	62	47	56

Question D2: How would you characterise the emphasis of your primary research this (or the previous) academic year?

[a]Responses 1 and 2 on a scale of answer from 1 = very much to 5 = not at all
[b]Too small number of respondents
[c]Average among advanced countries
[d]Average among emerging countries
. No other HEIs or no other HEIs surveyed

Table 5.13 Academics' notion of scholarship as generation, synthesis and application of knowledge by type of higher education institution and status group (per cent[a])

	CA	US	FI	DE	IT	NL	NO	PT	UK	AU	JP	KR	HK	Avg[c]	AR	BR	MX	ZA	CH	MY	Avg[d]
All respondents																					
Original research	77	65	57	69	73	73	88	69	67	68	77	78	80	72	53	37	60	64	53	78	58
Application of academic knowledge	66	79	84	68	59	50	63	78	67	74	77	83	79	71	78	85	86	76	81	83	82
Reports synthesise the major trends	60	68	60	67	47	47	59	53	66	67	80	90	74	64	60	64	66	66	77	75	68
Obligation to apply their knowledge	58	66	61	50	62	60	52	70	59	64	67	78	64	62	60	62	77	66	71	64	67
Seniors at universities																					
Original research	77	74	68	83	73	80	92	81	68	76	83	76	84	78	54	35	64	63	56	82	59
Application of academic knowledge	65	81	74	62	57	41	59	77	69	67	72	81	78	68	82	77	79	75	81	85	80
Reports synthesise the major trends	61	72	69	61	45	44	56	59	68	71	85	90	72	66	59	61	66	65	75	78	67
Obligation to apply their knowledge	55	63	65	61	62	45	50	73	58	67	62	79	62	62	63	56	69	62	70	67	65
Juniors at universities																					
Original research	76	61	61	69	74	82	86	74	66	69	73	79	78	73	53	39	70	66	52	79	60
Application of academic knowledge	66	76	84	67	64	42	65	76	65	75	74	85	79	71	77	83	83	79	82	86	82
Reports synthesise the major trends	58	64	59	67	49	41	61	62	63	65	86	88	74	64	60	60	58	67	79	78	67
Obligation to apply their knowledge	64	68	58	44	61	46	51	73	59	60	67	72	64	61	59	59	72	70	72	66	66
Seniors at other HEIs																					
Original research	.	57	54	56	.	67	88	80	[b]	68	77	78	.	69	42	55	.	50	75	.	56
Application of academic knowledge	.	83	92	87	.	63	56	88	[b]	67	78	82	.	77	94	88	.	81	79	.	86
Reports synthesise the major trends	.	71	75	72	.	53	68	57	[b]	67	80	89	.	70	69	68	.	78	63	.	70
Obligation to apply their knowledge	.	67	78	63	.	74	56	66	[b]	71	65	79	.	69	67	82	.	71	51	.	68

Appendix 159

Juniors at other HEIs

Original research	.	62	35	49	.	67	81	64	b	59	72	79	.	61	31	59	.	43	69	.	51
Application of academic knowledge	.	80	91	84	.	46	70	80	b	78	78	86	.	75	86	93	.	78	74	.	83
Reports synthesise the major trends	.	67	54	83	.	48	63	47	b	68	75	91	.	66	65	67	.	73	63	.	67
Obligation to apply their knowledge	.	66	64	75	.	63	74	68	b	69	77	76	.	71	67	80	.	73	54	.	69

Question B5: Please indicate your views on the following:

[a] Responses 1 and 2 on a scale of answer 1 = strongly agree to 5 = strongly disagree

Items: Scholarship is best defined as the preparation and presentation of findings on original research. Scholarship includes the application of academic knowledge in real-life settings. Scholarship includes the preparation of reports that synthesise the major trends and findings of my field. Faculty in my discipline have a professional obligation to apply their knowledge to problems in society

[b] Too small number of respondents

[c] Average among advanced countries

[d] Average among emerging countries

. No other HEIs or no other HEIs surveyed

Table 5.14 Proportion of respondents producing different research outputs in the past 3 years (per cent of all respondents, multiple responses)

	CA	US	FI	DE	IT	NL	NO	PT	UK	AU	JP	KR	HK	Avgᵇ	AR	BR	MX	ZA	CH	MY	Avgᶜ
Seniors at universities																					
Books (co-)authored	24	19	32	34	51	25	40	36	27	32	69	46	35	36	38	37	35	14	23	40	31
Books (co-)edited	18	17	36	39	32	27	21	27	21	22	35	42	38	29	23	17	22	7	26	30	21
Articles published	77	78	87	87	94	68	85	60	72	84	89	97	93	82	70	82	76	40	49	75	65
Report for funded project	41	35	38	67	50	28	24	45	34	41	56	81	50	45	61	53	36	14	24	60	41
Conference paper	77	80	85	81	84	63	77	58	70	80	64	86	89	76	76	74	75	46	35	80	64
Professional article	38	28	47	40	30	41	38	28	23	32	38	25	38	34	48	37	36	14	10	27	29
Patent secured	6	5	6	17	6	5	5	7	3	10	15	25	10	9	2	5	4	1	8	9	5
Computer programme written	6	5	4	5	3	5	3	5	5	6	3	1	5	4	5	5	9	2	6	6	6
Artistic work exhibited	4	8	1	8	1	2	5	2	2	3	18	4	4	5	5	5	4	2	1	4	4
Film produced	3	5	3	9	3	3	4	4	3	4	6	4	5	4	4	5	6	4	1	7	5
Others	7	9	8	3	5	1	8	4	9	3	0	3	5	5	0	12	8	3	1	6	5
No research activity stated	15	6	4	4	2	28	8	34	21	15	4	1	4	11	14	9	7	43	42	9	21
Juniors at universities																					
Books (co-)authored	13	12	20	15	41	23	10	17	9	13	64	29	17	22	26	19	24	17	9	21	19
Books (co-)edited	9	7	11	8	17	13	6	11	5	7	19	13	10	10	14	9	9	6	10	12	10
Articles published	77	55	66	68	91	71	68	49	58	71	95	100	63	72	65	68	73	52	32	50	57
Report for funded project	30	23	33	47	43	30	15	32	23	31	41	88	31	36	53	36	30	18	9	34	30
Conference paper	83	59	69	67	84	65	66	54	56	73	49	80	64	67	76	65	78	57	18	60	59
Professional article	27	23	25	21	23	33	25	23	15	20	41	16	19	24	36	27	34	18	7	13	23
Patent secured	3	6	4	7	5	4	1	3	2	3	11	25	4	6	2	0	6	1	2	3	2
Computer programme written	3	4	7	6	4	7	4	4	4	4	7	1	3	4	6	2	5	1	4	2	3
Artistic work exhibited	5	10	3	3	2	2	4	4	2	4	16	1	4	5	8	3	6	4	1	5	5
Film produced	2	4	3	5	3	1	4	4	1	4	4	0	4	3	4	3	6	3	1	4	4
Others	11	5	5	4	4	2	9	10	4	2	0	2	3	5	0	9	10	3	1	3	4
No research activity stated	13	24	14	16	3	27	13	37	35	20	0	0	27	18	15	19	9	32	59	25	27

Appendix

	1	2	3	4	5	6	7	8	9	10	11	12	13	14	15
Seniors at other HEIs															
Books (co-)authored	13	15	23	9	43	22 [a]	33	55	55	28	16	17	21	29	21
Books (co-)edited	9	11	16	4	7	20 [a]	21	20	31	16	6	10	23	11	13
Articles published	50	38	51	28	86	56 [a]	85	80	97	61	41	41	40	64	47
Report for funded project	20	32	35	18	18	33 [a]	39	38	76	33	22	19	18	36	24
Conference paper	67	33	41	26	74	55 [a]	84	55	83	56	41	50	20	59	43
Professional article	25	34	29	23	43	30 [a]	30	25	25	29	21	26	12	27	22
Patent secured	0	3	5	0	2	10 [a]	0	10	20	5	1	2	2	11	4
Computer programme written	3	3	6	2	7	5 [a]	6	2	4	4	3	6	1	4	4
Artistic work exhibited	10	3	3	2	14	0 [a]	7	13	4	7	3	5	2	4	4
Film produced	6	1	5	2	7	5 [a]	4	5	3	5	2	4	0	6	3
Others	12	3	3	3	5	2 [a]	4	0	6	4	6	7	0	4	4
No research activity stated	13	29	31	51	2	39 [a]	11	8	0	22	45	31	51	16	36
Juniors at other HEIs															
Books (co-)authored	7	7	7	1	12	12 [a]	9	47	40	15	14	12	4	13	11
Books (co-)edited	6	2	0	1	0	11 [a]	5	10	28	6	3	7	5	6	5
Articles published	44	12	32	5	66	40 [a]	58	73	99	48	36	38	21	38	33
Report for funded project	18	14	21	2	25	23 [a]	28	33	67	25	19	17	5	19	15
Conference paper	61	12	32	4	44	44 [a]	62	49	83	44	32	45	7	47	33
Professional article	23	9	20	4	27	16 [a]	22	26	21	20	18	24	5	9	14
Patent secured	3	0	11	0	7	1 [a]	2	5	20	5	1	2	1	1	1
Computer programme written	5	0	5	1	0	5 [a]	2	1	5	3	2	5	2	3	3
Artistic work exhibited	19	5	2	0	10	3 [a]	6	14	7	7	1	6	0	4	3
Film produced	8	2	2	0	5	3 [a]	2	3	2	3	3	4	0	2	2
Others	6	4	16	1	17	8 [a]	2	0	6	6	11	8	0	6	6
No research activity stated	21	67	44	89	18	41 [a]	26	9	0	36	47	33	75	41	49

Question D4: How many of the following scholarly contributions have you completed in the past 3 years?

[a] Too small number of respondents
[b] Average among advanced countries
[c] Average among emerging countries
. No other HEIs or no other HEIs surveyed

References

Altbach, P. G. (Ed.). (1996). *The international academic profession: Portraits of fourteen countries*. Princeton: Carnegie Foundation.

Arimoto, A. (1981). *Daigakujin no shakaigaku* [Sociology of academics]. Tokyo: Gakubunsha Publishing Co.

Arimoto, A. (Ed.) (1996). *Gakumon chûshinshi no kenkyû: Sekai to Nihon niokeru gakumonteki seisansei to sono jôken* [A Study of centers of learning: Academic productivity and its conditions in the world and Japan]. Tokyo: Toshindo Publishing Co.

Arimoto, A. (Ed.) (2008). *Henbôsuru Nihon no daigaku kyôjushoku* [The changing academic profession in Japan]. Tokyo: Tamagawa University Press.

Arimoto, A. (2010). Differentiation and integration of research, teaching and learning in the knowledge society: From the perspective of Japan. In Research Institute for Higher Education (Ed.), *The changing academic profession in international and quantitative perspectives: A focus on teaching & research activities* (pp. 1–28). Hiroshima: RIHE.

Arimoto, A., & Ehara, T. (Eds.) (1996). *Daigaku kyôshoku no kokusai hikaku* [International comparison of academic profession]. Tokyo: Tamagawa University Press.

Becher, T. (1989). *Academic tribes and territories: Intellectual enquiry and the culture of disciplines*. Milton Keynes/Bristol: Society for Research Higher Education and Open University Press.

Becher, T., & Trowler, P. (2001). *Academic tribes and territories: Intellectual enquiry and the culture of disciplines* (2nd ed.). Buckingham: Society for Research into Higher Education and Open University Press.

Clark, B. R. (1983). *The higher education system: Academic organization in cross-national perspective*. Berkeley: University of California Press.

Clark, B. R. (1987). *The academic life: Small worlds, different worlds*. Princeton: Carnegie Foundation.

Clark, B. R. (1997). The modern integration of research activities with teaching and learning. *Journal of Higher Education, 68*(3), 241–255.

Clark, B. R. (2008). *On higher education: Selected writings 1956–2006*. Baltimore: John Hopkins University Press.

Geiger, R. (Ed.). (2000). *The American college in the nineteenth century*. Nashville: Vanderbilt University Press.

Gibbons, M., Limoges, C., Nowotny, H., Schwartzman, S., Scott, P., & Trow, M. (1994). *The new production of knowledge: The dynamics of science and research in contemporary societies*. London: Sage.

Jacob, A. K., & Teichler, U. (Eds.). (2011). *Der Wandel des Hochschullehrerberufs im internationalen Vergleich: Ergebnisse einer Befragung in den Jahren 2007/08* [Change of the academic profession in international comparison: Results of the survey of the years 2007–08]. Bonn/Berlin: Bundesministerium fur Bildung und Forschung. http://www.uni-kassel.de/wz1/pdf/BMBF_Hochschullehrerstudie2011_Druck.pdf

Nakayama, S. (1978). *Teikoku daigaku no tanjô* [Birth of imperial university]. Tokyo: Chuoukoron Publishing Co.

Oleson, A., & Voss, J. (Eds.). (1979). *The organization of knowledge in modern America, 1860–1920*. Baltimore: Johns Hopkins University Press.

Rudolph, F. (1962). *The American college and university*. New York: Knopf.

Shinbori, M. (1965). *Nihon no daigaku kyôju shijô* [Academic marketplace in Japan]. Tokyo: Toyokan Publishing Co.

Ushiogi, M. (2008). *Humboldt rinen no shûen: Gandai daigaku no shinjigen* [The end of Humboldtian ideal: New dimension of modern university]. Tokyo: Toshindo Publishing Co.

Von Humboldt, W. (1970). On the spirit and the organizational framework of intellectual institutions in Berlin (E. Shils, Trans.). *Minerva 8*, 242–250.

Zuckerman, H., & Merton, R. K. (1971). Patterns of evaluation in science: Institutionalization, structure and functions of the referee system. *Minerva, 9*(1), 66–100.

Chapter 6
Faculty Perceptions of the Efficacy of Higher Educational Governance and Management

6.1 Introduction

In the medieval university, academics were prominent in the governance and management of institutions of higher education, especially in Northern Europe. In contrast, students in Southern Europe had an important role in many decisions. Over time the shift to faculty control extended across the continent. In more recent times as national and local governments have increased their role in the support of higher education, these public entities have sought to have more influence—through boards of trustees, the selection of CEOs and other means. As national systems of higher education have sought to become more relevant and to expand, strains have emerged concerning the respective roles of academics, managers and other stakeholders. In the original planning for the CAP study (the unpublished CAP concept paper formulated in 2004, p. 3), this tension was described as follows:

> New systemic and institutional processes such as quality assurance have been introduced which also change traditional distributions of power and values within academe and may be a force for change in academic practice. The project will examine both the rhetorics and the realities of academics' responses to such managerial practices in higher education.
>
> A number of views can be discerned about recent attempts at the management of change in higher education and the responses of academics to such changes. One view would see a victory of managerial values over professional ones with academics losing control over both the overall goals of their work practices and their technical tasks. Another view would see the survival of traditional academic values against the managerial approach. This does not imply that academic roles fail to change, but that change does not automatically mean that interests and values are weakened. A third view would see a 'marriage' between professionalism and managerialism with academics losing some control over the goals and social purposes of their work but retaining considerable autonomy over their practical and technical tasks. The desirability or otherwise of these three different positions is also subject to a range of different views.

6.2 The CAP Approach

The CAP team sought through a survey instrument both to determine what academics perceived to be the governance and management practices at their institutions and how academics evaluated these practices. *Concerning actual practice,* academics were asked who, from a list of six potential decision-makers, actually had 'the primary influence' on each of 11 areas of decisions. Academics were also asked if they personally were influential in shaping key academic policies and if there was good communication between managers and academics. And they were asked several questions about special themes in decision-making such as the emphasis on institutional mission, the stress on performance, the support for teaching activities and the support for research activities. Similarly concerning their *evaluation of these practices,* academics were asked several questions focusing on the competence of managers, the efficiency of management practices and the administration's record on protecting academic freedom. Finally, drawing on the above statement from the CAP concept paper, the bottom line in the evaluation of governance and management practice is the level of commitment of academics to their workplaces. Is this strong or weak, and to what extent is the level influenced by recent trends in governance and management?

This chapter initially will present the findings on each of the above items at the country level, relying on an analytic framework to be described in the next section. And as with previous chapters, it will pay special attention to differences by type of institution and by academic rank. Finally, two different comparative perspectives will be introduced to suggest additional ways of thinking about the findings: a comparison of mature versus emerging systems and a comparison of the impact of coordination systems (professorial-state-market).

6.3 A Framework for Analysis

During the 1970s particularly in the USA, the norm of 'shared governance' was proposed wherein academic decisions were to be made primarily by academics and most of the other decisions primarily by managers (AAUP 2006; Baldridge et al. 1978; Birnbaum 1988). While the original proposal was normative, the underlying question of who decides what is descriptive (Gumport 1997). Drawing on the logic of the shared governance perspective, we outline a simple model of governance/management in Fig. 6.1: *Faculty participation* is the cornerstone accompanied by communicative management leading to operationally oriented support of academics, protection of academic freedom and ultimately to the loyalty of academics both to their fields and their institutions and hence to their engagement in the governance and managerial activities of their institutions.

Fig. 6.1 The faculty participation in governance model

6.4 Decision-Making and the Academic's Perception of Their Participation

Higher educational governance encompasses a wide range of issues, from choosing the top officers to modifying current academic programmes. The CAP instrument identifies 11 important issues (9 will be discussed in this section and two more in the next section) and asks the participating academics to specify who at their institution 'has the primary influence on each of these decisions'. The questionnaire provides a list of six possible *decision-makers*:

– Government and external stakeholders
– Institutional managers
– Academic unit managers
– Faculty committee/boards
– Individual faculty
– Students

One has to bear in mind, though, that the questions posed in the CAP questionnaire are not specific enough to provide information on the levels and sequences of decision-making. For example, the government might decide in one country about the funds allocated for staff remuneration, while faculty committees might decide about the distribution of funds for the material costs of teaching and research; in such a case, some might consider the government most influential, while others might conclude the faculty committee has more power.

Actually, the responses provided by the academics show that the prime influence of actors varies substantially according to the area of *decision-making*:

1. *Budget decisions* are in most countries the domain of institutional managers, but not consistently within the various countries: The responses range from 40% in Italy to 78% in Korea. There are two exceptions: Government is most frequently named in Mexico and academic unit managers most often in the Netherlands.
2. The selection of *key administrators* is in most countries determined primarily by institutional managers. Only in Mexico, governmental influence prevails, and only

in Argentina, faculty committees are most frequently named. Faculty committees also play a role in various instances in Canada and Japan. One should bear in mind, though, that academics of the individual countries do not provide uniform reports. Among the countries where institutional managers seem to be most influential in the area, the percentage of academics stating this ranges from only 39% in Japan to 75% in Italy.

3. The prime influence of *setting admission standards* is among the least consistent across and within countries. Influence of institutional managers is most frequent in almost half of the countries surveyed, but this influence dominates (more than 50% of the responses) in only three countries: the USA, Korea and China. The faculty committees are most influential in this respect in European countries but only seem to dominate clearly in two countries: Japan and Italy. Institutional managers are named most frequently in almost all emerging countries as well as in Germany. Academic unit managers seem to be most influential in Malaysia as are faculty committees in the case of the Netherlands.

4. Similarly, the *approval of new academic programmes* is primarily influenced either by institutional managers or by faculty committees. In most countries, the dominant view is held by less than half of the respondents, and academic unit managers are not a negligible force in some countries. Finally, governmental influence prevails in China.

5. The *primary influence on setting research priorities* seems to be more varied across countries than in most other areas of decision-making addressed here. Institutional managers, academic unit managers and individual faculty are named as most influential in about the same number of countries, while prime influence of faculty committees is exceptional. There are only three countries where the majority of respondents identify a most influential type of actor: individual faculty in Italy and Germany as well as institutional management in China.

6. *Establishing international linkages* is in the USA, Japan, Korea and most emerging countries the domain of institutional managers. In most European countries, individual faculty are viewed as the major force for establishing those ties. In Portugal, the responses are spread over various actors, academic unit managers are viewed as most influential in the Netherlands, and government seems to be highly influential in this respect in Mexico.

7. The *teaching load of faculty* is determined in most of the surveyed countries primarily by academic unit managers. But also in countries where this prevails, modes of decision-making are quite diverse. Moreover, faculty committees are most influential in Portugal, Italy and Japan, and institutional managers in Korea and Norway. In Finland, individual faculty are named as most influential. Finally, this question was not posed in Germany, because the norms set by government are assumed to be upheld so much that respondents would not be sure whether to refer to the general norm setting or to the few individual exceptions.

8. The *choice of new faculty* is most frequently influenced by faculty committees. However, there are variations within all countries: Among the countries where faculty committees seem to be most influential in this respects, the affirmative responses are less than half on average and range from 32% in Norway to 78% in

6.4 Decision-Making and the Academic's Perception of Their Participation

Canada. Moreover, there are four countries where the strongest influence rests with academic unit managers: notably China, Malaysia, Brazil and the Netherlands. In South Africa, institutional managers are most influential as regards the appointment of new faculty. In Finland, in reverse, individual faculty are named most frequently as the key decision-makers in this respect.

9. The *promotion and tenure decisions* as well as the decisions of the choice of new faculty are conducted in different ways across the participating countries. In about half of the countries, faculty committees are viewed as most influential. In various other countries, academic unit managers have the strongest say, and in three countries (Korea, Norway and South Africa), institutional managers have the major influence in this area.

As regards *executive power*, we note that the *government and external stakeholders* are viewed as playing a dominant role in Mexico regarding the selection of key administrators, determining the budget and establishing international linkages.

The *institutional managers* are named as most influential in seven of the nine areas addressed above in Brazil, Korea and South Africa. They also play a role in six areas in China and in five areas in Norway and the USA. In contrast, the institutional managers are seldom named as dominant by academics from the Netherlands, Italy and the United Kingdom.

Finally, *academic unit managers* most often play a dominant role in the Netherlands (in seven areas). They are also frequently named by academics from Malaysia (in five areas).

Drawing on the *shared governance concept*, the areas of decision-making can be divided between:

– Those that are primarily managerial or external
– Those that are strongly influenced by academics (individual faculty and faculty committees)

Table 6.1 shows, first, that academics in most of the countries are more likely to perceive that they have authority, either individually or through academic committees and boards, over such matters as choosing new faculty, making faculty promotion and tenure decisions and approving new academic programmes. Influence seems to be divided between academics and managers, as already pointed out above, in matters of teaching load, admissions, research priorities and international linkages. In contrast, managers clearly dominate in decisions regarding budget priorities and the selection of key administrators.

Table 6.1 shows *the variation between the countries* surveyed. Across the nine areas of decision-making addressed, academics in Italy and Japan are most powerful. To a somewhat lesser extent, also academics in Finland, Canada and the United Kingdom are influential. In contrast, they have hardly any say at all in China, and they believe that they have little power as well in Malaysia and Brazil.

The *differences by institutional type and academic rank* are not consistently the same across all countries. For example, concerning the selection of key administrators, the academics at other higher education institutions indicate they are left out, whereas

Table 6.1 Faculty participation[a] in their institution's decisions (percentage of all respondents)

	CA	US	FI	DE	IT	NL	NO	PT	UK	AU	JP	KR	AR	BR	MX	SA	CH	MY
Selection of managers	35	8	22	25	10	2	18	25	29	19	44	8	33	27	10	18	3	4
New faculty	86	62	67	47	60	43	52	61	54	43	83	45	37	22	38	33	9	12
Promotion	66	51	57	38	57	24	38	50	53	51	76	40	32	24	37	31	22	9
Budget	7	2	38	13	27	9	22	6	30	23	36	8	17	6	7	18	4	8
Teaching load	21	11	63	.	53	33	28	54	39	38	68	25	22	18	29	38	15	23
Admissions	39	22	50	32	58	40	46	46	51	32	67	22	30	23	28	37	9	22
New programmes	41	36	37	28	75	40	0	62	61	46	65	32	25	27	42	34	4	15
Research priorities	52	43	59	64	78	36	39	59	53	45	42	36	43	35	52	49	5	27
International linkages	51	41	69	62	77	37	76	41	56	51	36	18	25	17	16	38	5	6
Mean**	45	31	51	39	55	29	35	45	48	39	57	26	29	22	29	34	8	14

Question E1: At your institution, which actor has the primary influence on each of the following decisions?

Hong Kong is not included because this question was phrased differently

[a]Faculty committees, individual faculty or the university senate are prime decision-makers

**Mean of responses to the nine areas of decision-making (not included: decision-making as regards evaluation of teaching and research)

.Not Surveyed

a modest fraction of those at universities believe that academics do have influence. Concerning the selection of new faculty, in the majority of systems, senior faculty both at universities and other higher education institutions are more likely to say that they have influence than do their junior rank colleagues. On average, however, the academics at research universities are more likely to perceive academics as having the primary influence than are academics at other institutions; this difference is, for example, only 3% on average of the areas of decision-making addressed in Germany but 7% in the USA. Also senior academics tend to believe more often than junior academics that academics have a say; this difference is 6% on average in Germany but only 2% in the USA.

Based on these findings, can we say that faculty participation in governance is prevalent in academia? Clearly in some areas such as the selection of top officers, academics in nearly all of the countries included in the survey report they are powerless. Concerning the three areas we have identified as core academic areas (choosing new faculty, making faculty promotion and tenure decisions and approving new academic programmes), academics in a majority of the systems believe that they and their colleagues have influence. This inclination is slightly more pronounced in the case of academics at universities relative to other higher education institutions and even to a smaller extent more pronounced on the part of senior ranks than on junior ranks, but these differences are small as compared to country differences. So as a starting point for the analysis to follow, we can say that the faculty role in governance is mixed.

6.5 The Evaluation of Teaching and Research

In the list of the 11 areas of decision-making addressed in the CAP survey, the *evaluation of teaching* and the *evaluation of research* are also named. One could argue, though, that these two categories do not fit in this list. It is not clear, whether the respondents have decision-making regarding the undertaking of evaluation, the processes of evaluation or the impact of the evaluation in mind. Actually, we note that respondents in the individual countries vary substantially in their responses. In almost all cases, a minority names institutional managers, academic unit managers, faculty committees or individual faculty as most influential and in the case of teaching evaluations the students. But there are only a few cases where the majority of respondents name certain actors as most influential: as regards the evaluation of teaching, the institutional managers in Malaysia and the students in Korea, and as regards research evaluation, the institutional managers in China and the academics themselves in Italy.

To obtain a more complete indication of who is involved in the evaluation of teaching and research, a further question allowed respondents to list all of the actors involved in these evaluations. That is, respondents were allowed to go beyond identifying a single category of actors to list as many actors as seemed appropriate: Given this opportunity, most respondents identified between two and three relevant actors for each area as illustrated in Table 6.2.

Table 6.2 Evaluators of teaching and research (percent of all respondents; multiple responses)

	CA	US	FI	DE	IT	NL	NO	PT	UK	AU	JP	KR	HK	AR	BR	MX	SA	CH	MY
Evaluators of teaching																			
Your peers in your department or unit	35	51	35	21	20	51	25	41	64	33	20	21	39	46	46	45	46	54	30
The head of your department or unit	70	81	54	17	33	57	26	42	50	67	30	24	71	45	63	62	57	62	66
Members of other departments or units at this institution	11	16	5	4	4	8	5	27	11	11	5	7	10	15	18	26	20	21	14
Senior admin. staff at this institution	29	33	11	11	3	15	17	32	9	17	32	31	30	30	27	25	15	37	17
Your students	91	91	82	77	86	91	88	60	92	85	50	80	93	62	80	82	75	67	83
External reviewers	8	8	11	4	9	23	11	44	32	6	9	4	25	20	11	25	28	21	20
Yourself (formal self-assessment)	39	57	0	38	24	39	29	31	53	53	40	21	46	41	47	52	55	37	49
No one at or outside my institution	3	1	3	9	6	2	6	12	3	4	8	3	0	8	5	1	8	6	3
Evaluators of research																			
Your peers in your department or unit	41	41	51	47	38	40	52	20	47	36	17	29	36	24	33	34	39	25	30
The head of your department or unit	61	65	67	17	31	56	30	12	64	70	31	20	79	21	27	42	51	52	62
Members of other departments or units at this institution	16	17	23	9	8	15	8	9	21	16	4	16	20	28	23	33	25	17	28
Senior admin. staff at this institution	31	31	16	19	3	16	9	13	21	22	38	42	38	28	21	21	20	38	25
Your students	3	3	3	3	2	5	5	55	5	4	2	3	2	3	9	4	7	11	6
External reviewers	60	38	52	37	43	50	37	24	62	55	15	36	57	73	33	47	58	25	35
Yourself (formal self-assessment)	36	51	0	41	24	34	26	26	54	43	43	29	48	26	29	40	49	37	46
No one at or outside my institution	5	11	7	13	18	7	13	20	6	3	11	9	1	4	29	4	9	8	5

Question E3: By whom is your teaching, research and service regularly evaluated?

Concerning *teaching*, overall 'your students' was most frequently identified followed by yourself, the head of your department or unit and peers in your department in that order. In the cases of Germany, Italy, Norway, Japan and Korea, the latter two groups tended to have a minor role. Members of other departments, senior administrative staff and external reviewers were rarely mentioned as prominent evaluators of teaching.

Concerning *research,* there was a somewhat similar pattern except that external reviewers moved to the top of the list for the majority of countries while 'your students' was rarely mentioned. Also senior administrative staff were often identified as important actors, especially in the East Asian settings of Korea, Hong Kong, Japan and China.

Appendix Tables 6.11.1, 6.11.2, 6.11.3, and Table 6.11.4 display the response patterns to these questions by type and rank. Overall there are few striking differences by type or rank. Relative to the academics at universities, those at other institutions are more likely to perceive teaching evaluations being seriously reviewed by their peers. In contrast, those at universities are more likely to perceive research as being evaluated by peers both in their departments and in other departments. Junior rank faculty, both at universities and other institutions, are more likely than senior rank faculty to see department heads taking a prominent role in teaching evaluations.

6.6 Influence

An alternate measure of the strength of faculty participation in governance is the extent to which *faculty regard themselves as having personal influence* in shaping key academic policies. As one might expect, a relatively high percentage in all countries see themselves as influential *at the department level*—actually 49% on average across countries. This is particularly the case, as Table 6.3 shows, in the Netherlands (80%) and also clearly above average in Brazil (67%), the USA and Mexico (65% each), Canada and Korea (62% each) and Germany and South Africa (60% each). In contrast, only one quarter in Argentina and little more than one-third in China and Norway consider themselves influential on this level.

In comparing these findings to those in the previous sections, we can draw the conclusion that academics in most of the countries surveyed indicate that they personally have greater influence on decisions at the department level than does the professoriate on average. Obviously, they consider themselves individually to be more influential than the average academics and also more influential than academics as a formal constituency.

Yet when we extend the examination of personal influence beyond the department to policy decisions made at the level of the faculty or school and to the institution as a whole, we find that the number of countries where faculty regard themselves as having a high level of personal influence is small. As regards *influence on the faculty level*, the average figure across countries is 32%, and even the highest figure is below

Table 6.3 Self-*perceived* influence of academics in helping to shape key academic policies (percentage[a])

		CA	US	FI	DE	IT	NL	NO	PT	UK	AU	JP	KR	HK	AR	BR	MX	SA	CH	MY
At departmental level																				
	Total	62	66	43	60	43	80	36	47	40	44	50	62	39	25	67	66	60	34	48
Universities	Seniors	67	77	75	89	55	85	52	73	58	75	57	55	63	57	78	71	61	44	63
	Juniors	53	46	30	51	23	71	21	40	28	32	14	45	25	21	67	66	66	26	38
Other HEIs	Seniors	.	89	68	85	.	86	60	79	[b]	77	57	70	.	.	69	63	[b]	51	60
	Juniors	.	66	48	67	.	74	32	42	[b]	38	22	50	.	.	50	67	[b]	27	52
At the faculty level																				
	Total	28	42	20	24	22	40	12	22	20	19	30	31	18	13	43	48	37	34	32
Universities	Seniors	36	50	40	64	32	51	21	40	30	42	32	32	34	31	56	52	37	40	43
	Juniors	14	27	10	11	5	18	4	17	15	8	10	15	8	10	36	47	42	30	25
Other HEIs	Seniors	.	69	38	67	.	53	22	53	[b]	52	35	38	.	.	45	47	[b]	39	55
	Juniors	.	33	20	39	.	33	16	17	[b]	14	12	18	.	.	28	48	[b]	27	35
At the institutional level																				
	Total	12	19	12	11	7	10	11	14	10	8	15	23	8	6	25	26	13	30	14
Universities	Seniors	17	25	21	27	10	12	16	23	12	16	12	21	11	19	26	26	15	30	21
	Juniors	3	10	6	4	2	4	6	7	9	3	0	12	6	5	17	15	13	30	9
Other HEIs	Seniors	.	30	35	30	.	19	25	47	[b]	31	18	27	.	.	32	26	[b]	38	30
	Juniors	.	18	10	24	.	4	7	14	[b]	5	8	15	.	.	19	28	[b]	28	17

Question E2: How influential are you, personally, in helping to shape key academic policies?
Faculty committees, individual faculty or the university senate are prime decision-makers
[a]Responses 1 and 2 on a scale from 1 = very influential to 4 = not at all influential
[b]Too small number of respondents
. No other HEIs or no other HEIs surveyed

half. Personal influence at this level is most often perceived by respondents from Mexico (48%), Brazil (43%), the USA (42%) and the Netherlands (40%). In contrast, influence at this level is least often perceived by academics in Norway (12%) and Argentina (13%).

Finally, as one might expect, the personal influence is the lowest on average as regards **the institutional level**—4% on average across countries. Influence on this level is most often reported by academics from China (30%)—this is surprising, because hardly any influence has been reported in response to the preceding questions regarding the individual areas of decision-making. Influence on the institutional level is also reported relatively often in Mexico (26%) and Brazil (25%). In contrast, influence at the institutional level is seldom perceived in Argentina (6%), Italy (7%) and Australia and Hong Kong (8% each).

Across all three levels, academics in Mexico, Brazil and the Netherlands consider their personal influence to be quite high. In contrast, those from Norway, Hong Kong, the United Kingdom and Australia consider their personal influence to be modest—only about half the level of the academics in the former countries.

Table 6.3 shows the perceptions of *personal influence according to institutional type and academic rank*. Not surprisingly, in nearly all of the comparisons, senior professors are more likely than junior professors to believe they have personal influence; this difference by rank between university professors and junior academics at universities is most noticeable in Germany but also is considerable in Finland, Australia and Japan. In contrast, junior academics at universities in South Africa consider themselves to be even slightly more influential than university professors, and those in China and Brazil do not consider themselves considerably less influential than university professors. By and large, the gap of influence is higher in mature systems than in emerging countries; this finding may reflect an exceptional level of tension in some countries between the all powerful senior professors and the junior faculty who feel their voice is not heard sufficiently.

On average across the countries for which information is available, professors at other institutions of higher education rate their influence higher than professors at universities. This is not true for influence at the departmental level, but is true to some extent for influence at the faculty level (4% higher on average of the countries surveyed) and clearly so for influence at the institutional level: On average across countries, 30% of the professors at other institutions as compared to 20% of the professors at universities consider themselves influential on that level. This might be due to the fact that other institutions of higher education are often smaller than universities, and thus, it is easier for senior academics to be known at the institutional level.

6.7 Perceptions of Teaching and Research Strategies

Distinct from who makes decisions is the content of decisions. CAP respondents were given examples of four decisions relating to funding, four relating to personnel and two relating to external relations. They were asked which of these were characteristic of their institutions. In general the decisions tended to be those characteristic of a pragmatic institution that was seeking to balance its expenses with tuition revenue and that carefully scrutinised the teaching, research and service contributions of its faculty members. Table 6.4 presents the percentage of faculty who indicated the items were characteristic of the decision-making process in their country.

First, it can be observed that no 'cell' in Table 6.4 is empty, though those focused on external relations are least frequently noted. Also, while funding of departments based on their student numbers is common, especially for the academic systems of the more advanced countries, it appears that the funding of departments based on the number of graduates is relatively uncommon—Netherlands and Norway are exceptions. In contrast, possibly the most common decisions are those that focus on the quality of research and the quality of teaching (but not the practical relevance of an individual's work).

By country, the ten decisions of Table 6.4 seem to fit the culture of some countries relatively well—notably China, the Netherlands and Germany. In these countries for the majority of the decisions, the country level was above the average level for all 19 countries. But they appear to be a poor fit for Argentina, South Africa and Korea; for example, in the case of Argentina, the country level for all of the decisions was below the average level.

Appendix Tables 6.12.1, 6.12.2, 6.12.3, and 6.12.4 report the distributions by type and rank. Given the differences in the goals of research universities and other types of higher educational institutions, it is understandable that there are several differences by type—for example, a greater emphasis in the other types of higher educational institutions on student enrolments in determining the allocation of funds and on allocations based on evaluations. Also there is a greater emphasis on quality teaching and on recruiting faculty with outside work experience in the other types. In contrast, there are no obvious reasons for expecting differences by academic rank.

6.8 Communication-Oriented Management

Governance and management reflect the decision-making rules and processes that link the actors at the various organisational levels. The academics have been asked to assess the prevailing management style at their institution of higher education in various respects.

The first group of issues addressed might be summarised as the **communication styles of management**. The following items have been presented in the questionnaire in this domain:

- 'Good communication between management and academics'.
- 'A top-down management style'.
- 'Collegiality in the decision-making process'.
- 'I am kept informed about what is going on at this institution'.

Some of this decision-making may involve extensive consultation between actors and have a collegial character, while other decisions tend to be top-down. Fewer than two out of every five respondents in the CAP survey say there is 'collegiality in decision-making'. Over half describe the management style at their institution as

6.8 Communication-Oriented Management

Table 6.4 Strong perceptions of teaching and research-related institutional strategies (percent[a] of all respondents)

	CA	US	FI	DE	IT	NL	NO	PT	UK	AU	JP	KR	HK	AR	BR	MX	SA	CH	MY	MEAN
Funding decisions																				
Performance-based allocation	34	38	55	49	30	37	53	16	47	49	31	35	57	16	29	37	33	51	35	39
Evaluation-based allocation	21	0	35	26	23	26	23	15	33	36	30	33	50	16	29	37	28	45	37	29
Funding based on numbers of students	70	49	46	45	54	75	51	40	70	70	59	62	67	35	36	35	49	52	41	53
Funding based on numbers of graduates	34	27	70	25	23	66	55	20	30	38	6	23	34	10	15	22	45	36	34	32
Personnel decisions																				
Considering the research quality	50	48	39	50	23	38	34	22	62	51	57	33	68	22	28	36	40	57	40	42
Considering the teaching quality	33	52	28	26	12	39	26	17	31	28	38	23	44	28	38	34	31	50	45	33
Considering the practical relevance/applicability of the work of colleagues	19	31	31	22	11	31	20	15	29	25	26	15	27	26	28	28	25	54	38	26
Recruiting faculty who have work experience outside of academia	15	30	25	34	7	39	13	33	23	26	21	18	22	21	30	25	25	48	38	26
External relations decisions																				
Encouraging academics to adopt service activities	17	38	20	50	15	27	14	32	30	36	28	28	23	12	20	28	25	32	35	27
Encouraging individuals, businesses, foundations, etc. to contribute more to higher education	42	65	19	45	22	37	20	29	36	51	18	28	46	17	34	34	37	54	41	36

Question E6: To what extent does your institution emphasise the following practices? (Scale of answer 1 = very much to 5 = not at all)
Mean: The national percentages summed up and divided by the number of countries (overall mean cannot be calculated since we do not have national weights in the data set)

[a]Responses 1 and 2 on a scale from 1 = very much to 5 = not at all

top-down. Overall the academics in the CAP countries believe current decision-making is far more top-down than is appropriate and far less collegial than is desirable.

Altogether, as Table 6.5 shows, less than one-third of the academics on average of the countries surveyed state that there is good communication between management and academics (30%), that collegiality prevails in decision-making (30%) and that the respondents feel they are kept informed about what is going on at their institution. In contrast, a top-down management style is perceived by 55% of the respondents on average across countries.

In considering the first three dimensions of communication styles as typical for 'communication-oriented management' and calculating the mean responses to these three dimensions, we can argue that '*communication-oriented management*' is accordingly

- Most widespread in Malaysia (45%)
- Fairly widespread as well in Argentina (40%), Brazil (39%), Canada, China and Mexico (38% each)
- Above average in the Netherlands (36%), Norway and the USA (35% each) as well as Japan (33%)
- Around average (28–32%) in Finland, Germany, Portugal, Hong Kong, Australia and Italy
- Below average in the United Kingdom (27%), South Africa (25%) and Korea (23%)

The respective responses of junior and senior academics are similar in most countries. Substantial differences are visible in only three cases. A communicative management style is clearly less frequently observed on the one hand by junior academics at universities in Japan (25% as compared to 33% among university professors) and the Netherlands (27% as compared to 36%). On the other hand, junior academics in Korea more often note a communicative management style than do senior academics of their country (35% as compared to 23%).

Professors at other institutions of higher education perceive more frequently a communicative management style than do university professors on average across countries. This is clearly visible in Norway, the United States, Portugal and China. In reverse, university professors perceive this more often in Japan and Korea than do professors at other institutions of higher education.

A *top-down management style* is

- Most frequently perceived by academics in Australia (74%) and Hong Kong (72%)
- Also clearly above average perception in South Africa and the United Kingdom (68% each) as well as in the United States (65%)
- Around average in nine countries
- Below average in Germany (43%), Argentina (44%), China (45%) and Portugal (48%)
- By far most seldom in Norway (29%)

A top-down management style is as often perceived by junior academic staff at universities as by university professors on average across the 19 countries. There are substantial differences (at least 10%), however, in some countries: A top-down

6.8 Communication-Oriented Management

Table 6.5 Academics' perceptions of communication styles prevailing at their institution of higher education (percentage[a])

		CA	US	FI	DE	IT	NL	NO	PT	UK	AU	JP	KR	HK	AR	BR	MX	SA	CH	MY
Good communication																				
	Total	30	30	30	21	26	27	34	29	23	23	24	20	26	33	41	39	21	35	50
Universities	Seniors	30	26	33	28	27	28	35	32	21	28	28	29	24	55	36	37	21	31	49
	Juniors	32	27	32	17	24	18	33	31	21	23	23	23	28	30	36	33	19	39	51
Other HEIs	Seniors	.	42	31	35	.	29	40	39	[b]	23	23	17	.	.	48	38	[b]	40	52
	Juniors	.	42	25	39	.	28	44	27	[b]	20	23	20	.	.	45	45	[b]	32	38
Top-down management style																				
	Total	55	65	56	43	52	54	29	48	68	74	57	54	72	44	55	54	68	45	60
Universities	Seniors	57	66	52	43	49	51	24	46	76	75	50	55	80	34	41	49	69	48	57
	Juniors	53	65	52	44	57	58	33	50	64	71	40	40	69	45	45	62	70	42	61
Other HEIs	Seniors	.	64	65	35	.	51	10	52	[b]	86	61	53	.	.	66	56	[b]	48	76
	Juniors	.	62	70	36	.	56	29	47	[b]	76	53	57	.	.	66	54	[b]	47	57
Collegiality in decision-making																				
	Total	38	33	23	28	16	36	25	34	20	19	45	17	25	36	29	41	20	36	42
Universities	Seniors	36	29	28	28	18	33	27	39	19	24	54	17	20	45	36	48	20	34	41
	Juniors	42	33	24	27	12	28	21	36	20	19	21	28	27	35	32	42	19	38	43
Other HEIs	Seniors	.	37	23	41	.	38	37	47	[b]	25	45	19	.	.	25	35	[b]	40	40
	Juniors	.	38	16	33	.	41	32	31	[b]	14	40	12	.	.	24	43	[b]	32	33
Kept informed																				
	Total	45	43	43	47	41	44	40	32	38	42	30	41	37	52	46	35	35	45	43
Universities	Seniors	44	40	52	56	43	55	35	46	40	43	37	47	35	69	45	35	35	42	44
	Juniors	47	40	42	45	39	36	41	37	30	45	30	56	38	50	51	38	34	47	42
Other HEIs	Seniors	.	47	53	54	.	48	53	56	[b]	46	30	36	.	.	46	32	[b]	50	39
	Juniors	.	57	38	50	.	39	68	25	[b]	34	22	44	.	.	45	40	[b]	46	42

Question E4: At my institution there is…
Question E5: Please indicate your views on the following issues
[a]Responses 1 and 2 on a scale from 1 = strongly agree to 5 = strongly disagree
[b]Too small number of respondents
. No other HEIs or no other HEIs surveyed

management style is more often perceived by junior academics at universities in Mexico and Argentina than by university professors, while it is less often perceived by junior academics in Korea, the United Kingdom, Hong Kong and Japan.

Professors at other institutions of higher education report a top-down style of management across countries 5% more than university professors. The respective ratings are clearly higher among the former in Brazil, Finland, Malaysia, Australia and Japan, while they are lower in Norway as in the case of university professors.

If we aggregate and average the above three items and add the reverse of top-down management, we can create an **index of communication-oriented management**. We note the following ratings of communication-oriented management:

- High in Argentina, Norway (44% each), Malaysia (43%) and China (41%)
- Above average in Brazil (39%), Canada and Mexico (38% each) as well as Germany and the Netherlands (36% each)
- Around average in Portugal (34%) as well as in Finland, Japan and the USA (32% each)
- Below average in Italy (29%),
- Low in South Africa (21%) as well as in Australia, Hong Kong, Korea and the United Kingdom

We note, however, that the responses to the three dimensions of communication named above are not necessarily in contrast to the responses as regards top-down management. For example:

- Malaysia stands out in the three communicative dimensions, but top-down management is reported close to average.
- The USA is above average both in the communicative dimensions and in top-down management.
- Australia and Hong Kong are close to average in the communicative dimensions and very high in top-down management.
- Korea, in contrast, is close to average in top-down management but very low in the three communicative dimensions.

Thus, we do not find the expected contrast between the responses as regards the communicative dimensions and top-down management in five of the 19 cases. We can argue, for example, that a communicative management style sometimes seems to coexist with a top-down management style, even though these are often thought to be incompatible.

6.9 Operationally Oriented Management Style

Distinct from the communicative dimensions of management, the second group of issues addressed might be summarised as targeted operationally oriented arrangements of management. Is the management strategic, competent, efficient and

6.9 Operationally Oriented Management Style

supportive? The following items have been presented in the questionnaire in this domain:

- 'A strong performance orientation'
- 'A strong emphasis on the institution's mission'
- 'A cumbersome administrative process' (in reverse used as indicating 'smooth' administrative processes)
- 'A supportive attitude of administrative staff towards teaching activities'
- 'A supportive attitude of administrative staff towards research activities'
- 'Top-level administrators are providing competent leadership'

A *strong performance orientation* of their institution is noted, as Table 6.6 indicates, by slightly more than half of the academics on average across countries (51%). Highest ratings (more than 10% above average) hold true for Australia (70%), the United Kingdom (68%), Hong Kong (64%) and Korea (62%). In contrast, a performance orientation is seldom reported for Italy (22%), Portugal (29%) and Argentina (34%). The notions of university professors and junior staff at universities are similar on average. However, the junior staff at Canadian universities perceive a stronger performance orientation than do university professors, while the opposite holds true for Korea. On average, other institutions of higher education are viewed as less performance oriented: On the one hand, the ratings are clearly lower in this respect in Japan, the Netherlands and the United States; in contrast, the respective ratings are higher in Brazil.

A *strong emphasis on the institution's mission* is perceived by slightly more than half the academics across the 19 countries (55%). This is reported most often for Malaysia (75%) and the United States (69%) and, in contrast, seems to play only a small role in Italy (20%), Germany (36%) and Norway (43%).

Smooth administrative processes are slightly more frequently noted: 58% on average across countries (or more precisely, cumbersome processes have been reported by 42% of the academics). This quality of administration seems to apply most often to Australia (76%), the United Kingdom (73%) as well as Germany and Japan (69% each), while it is least often the case in Malaysia (41%) as well as Brazil and Mexico (44% each). Junior academics at universities rate the administrative processes equally on average across the 19 countries, whereby the ratings by senior academics in Hong Kong are clearly more positive than those by junior academics, and the reverse holds true for Argentina and Mexico. Ratings by academics at other higher education institutions are slightly more negative than by those at universities. Professors at other higher education institutions consider the administrative processes to be less smooth than do their colleagues at universities; this is especially notable in Brazil and the United States, while the opposite is true for the Netherlands.

A *supportive attitude of administration towards teaching activities* is less frequently perceived: Across the 19 countries, only 39% of the academics observe this support. The ratings are most positive in this respect in Japan (59%) and the United States (52%) and most critical in Italy (19%), Finland (25%) and Germany (28%). The average ratings of university professors and junior academics staff at universities are similar across countries with relatively negative notions by junior academics in Australia and Argentina and relatively positive notions of junior academics in

Table 6.6 Academics' perceptions of targeted and operationally orientated management styles prevailing at their institution of higher education (percentage[a])

		CA	US	FI	DE	IT	NL	NO	PT	UK	AU	JP	KR	HK	AR	BR	MX	SA	CH	MY
Performance orientation																				
Universities	Total	51	49	60	b	22	52	50	29	68	70	51	62	64	34	46	46	51	60	57
	Seniors	45	52	67	b	23	68	50	40	69	81	70	80	70	34	39	47	50	62	54
	Juniors	62	50	58	b	21	67	51	36	67	75	72	69	61	34	40	49	50	61	58
Other HEIs	Seniors	.	37	60	b	.	51	45	22	c	71	44	56	.	.	53	43	c	57	64
	Juniors	.	43	58	b	.	33	53	23	c	52	54	65	.	.	49	52	c	49	54
Smooth administration																				
Universities	Total	65	56	59	69	53	62	55	58	73	76	69	50	60	54	44	44	61	53	41
	Seniors	64	59	59	62	53	56	57	64	79	76	73	53	68	41	51	43	59	56	46
	Juniors	66	58	57	72	53	54	55	56	71	74	65	49	56	56	53	57	67	51	40
Other HEIs	Seniors	.	48	65	62	.	73	50	58	c	79	69	48	.	.	37	43	c	51	47
	Juniors	.	53	62	54	.	60	47	60	c	79	66	53	.	.	35	43	c	51	41
Supportive for teaching																				
Universities	Total	49	52	25	28	19	43	44	29	41	39	57	29	44	34	43	41	30	49	45
	Seniors	51	51	20	30	20	46	43	30	44	47	63	38	38	51	35	39	29	44	44
	Juniors	46	49	27	26	17	45	44	30	38	36	55	39	47	31	36	44	30	55	46
Other HEIs	Seniors	.	58	30	29	.	42	40	21	c	34	57	27	.	.	54	39	c	39	48
	Juniors	.	57	19	39	.	39	40	28	c	41	52	28	.	.	45	48	c	46	39
Supportive for research																				
Universities	Total	48	49	25	23	17	27	36	12	32	37	36	26	39	23	29	35	27	49	37
	Seniors	49	51	17	34	19	32	33	26	34	48	47	38	41	32	32	36	26	45	35
	Juniors	46	56	27	22	14	34	38	13	30	37	51	28	39	22	30	40	29	55	38
Other HEIs	Seniors	.	38	21	17	.	23	27	16	c	32	33	25	.	.	29	31	c	39	42
	Juniors	.	35	25	27	.	21	41	9	c	28	33	21	.	.	24	39	c	43	33

6.9 Operationally Oriented Management Style

Competent leadership

		Total																		
Universities	Seniors	39	45	38	31	33	40	38	41	25	32	55	27	35	32	52	42	28	63	49
	Juniors	40	40	42	36	36	41	33	49	25	41	63	42	34	44	44	40	29	62	47
Other HEIs	Seniors	39	48	40	30	28	36	39	42	22	33	61	51	35	30	52	48	29	65	50
	Juniors	.	50	36	37	.	43	50	42	c	37	52	23	.	.	56	37	c	64	39
		.	50	33	31	.	38	47	37	c	23	53	24	.	.	57	52	c	55	46

Question E4: At my institution there is…

Question E5: Please indicate your views on the following issues

[a] Responses 1 and 2 on a scale from 1 = strongly agree to 5 = strongly disagree

[b] This question was not asked in Germany

[c] Too small number of respondents

. No other HEIs or no other HEIs surveyed

China. Professors at other institutions of higher education also do not differ on average across countries in this rating: However, professors at other institutions of higher education are relatively less satisfied in this respect in Australia and Korea, whereas in Brazil they indicate more favourable ratings.

A supportive attitude of administration towards research activities is even less frequently noted: only by 31% of the academics on average across countries. Administrative support for research is most often reported in Canada and China (49% each) as well as in the United States (48%), while little support in this respect is perceived in Portugal (12%) and Italy (17%). University professors report administrative support for research slightly more often than junior academic staff across countries; this difference is greatest in Portugal and Australia. As one might expect, university professors clearly note more administrative support for research than do professors at other institutions of higher education: This difference is most obvious in the United States, Germany and Australia.

Competent leadership is not prevalent at institutions of higher education in the view of the academics: 39% on average of countries rate this affirmatively. The most positive ratings can be found in China (63%), Japan (55%) and Brazil (52%), but are rare in the United Kingdom (25%), Korea (27%) and South Africa (28%). University professors have a more negative view than junior staff; only in Argentina do university professors consider their institution's leaders in a more positive light than do junior academics. The respective ratings also do not differ substantially on average between university professors and professors at other institutions of higher education; university professors hold relatively positive views in Korea and Japan and relatively negative views in Norway and Brazil.

Altogether, we note that about half of the academics surveyed on average across the countries included in the CAP study consider their institution's management to be smooth, mission oriented and performance oriented. In contrast, only about four out of ten rate their leadership as competent and consider the administration as being supportive of teaching. And only three out of ten view their administration as being supportive for research. When we create an overall score by calculating the average of the responses to these six dimensions, we find that 46% of the academics observe a **targeted and operationally oriented management style at** their institution of higher education.

Actually,

- In eight cases, half or more of the academics note such a management style—notably in the Anglo-Saxon and Asian countries: China (56%), the United States (55%), Japan (54%), Australia (53%), Malaysia (51%) as well as Canada, the United Kingdom and Hong Kong (50% each).
- Ratings close to the average are made primarily by some European and some emerging countries outside Asia: Brazil (46%), the Netherlands and Mexico (45% each), Finland, Norway and South Africa (44%) and finally Korea (41%).
- Finally, management is least often rated as targeted and operationally oriented by academics in Italy (27%) and also clearly less than average in Portugal (36%), Germany (37%) and Argentina (38%).

This does not mean that high ratings of targeted and operationally oriented management styles are consistently positive ratings and that low ratings in this area are consistently negative ratings. For example, academics might be convinced that the emphasis on the institution's mission might endanger the diversity of academic activities and that a performance orientation might encourage short-term perspectives and undermine efforts to strive for fundamental breakthroughs. But in terms of the currently fashionable management philosophies, higher education management in China might be the darling and that in Italy old-fashioned.

6.10 Protection of Academic Freedom

The guarantee of academic freedom is a cherished value for academics. Academics were asked in the survey to report the extent to which they agree to the statement: 'The administration supports academic freedom'.

The phrasing of the question is unfortunate in the framework of an international survey. In some countries, 'administration' might comprise all the executives of an institution of higher education, while in many other countries—notably European countries—it refers only to the administrative apparatus, often even derogatively named the bureaucracy.

On average across countries, as Table 6.7 shows, 46% of the academics note academic freedom to be supported by their administration. This is most strongly underscored in Mexico (76%), the United States (61%), Canada (60%) and Argentina (58%). In contrast, it is seldom noted in Finland (23%), South Africa (26%), Norway (31%) and Germany (34%), but this finding might be artificial as a consequence of the different meanings of 'administration'.

Junior academics at universities observe a slightly lower level of support for academic freedom. This difference is most striking in Argentina, Australia and Korea, while junior academics in Japan and Malaysia note more of this support than do university professors in their respective countries.

Professors at other institutions of higher education note an even lower level of support for academic freedom. This is most pronounced in the Netherlands, Brazil, Japan, Mexico and Australia.

6.11 Institutional Affiliation and Engagement

Both in the Carnegie survey undertaken in 1992 (see Altbach 1996) and in the recent CAP study, academics were asked to respond to the following question: 'Please indicate the degree to which each of the following affiliations is important for you: My academic discipline/field, My department (at this institution), My institution'.

Most academics in all of the 19 countries considered themselves to be affiliated with an academic discipline or to an academic field defined otherwise (e.g. by the object

Table 6.7 Academics' perceptions of support of academic freedom by the administration of their institution of higher education (percentage[a])

		CA	US	FI	DE	IT	NL	NO	PT	UK	AU	JP	KR	HK	AR	BR	MX	SA	CH	MY
	Total	60	61	23	34	47	37	31	36	39	39	55	50	53	58	47	76	26	54	41
Universities	Seniors	61	61	19	40	49	51	32	49	42	51	68	61	58	81	57	76	25	53	39
	Juniors	60	59	26	33	44	47	30	40	39	39	82	50	51	55	52	88	26	55	41
Other HEIs	Seniors	.	64	18	43	.	30	24	58	[b]	41	53	52	.	.	39	74	[b]	49	37
	Juniors	.	61	17	36	.	24	33	30	[b]	28	47	43	.	.	40	76	[b]	51	38

Question E5: Please indicate your views on the following issues
[a]Responses 1 and 2 on a scale from 1 = strongly agree to 5 = strongly disagree
[b]Too small number of respondents
. No other HEIs or no other HEIs surveyed

of their study (organisational research)). But there were enormous differences by country in the extent to which affiliation with an institution is viewed as important.

The importance of academics' affiliation to their institution of higher education can be linked to the management of higher education institutions in both directions. On the one hand, the management style—for example, a 'communication-oriented management style'—might increase the academics' affiliation to their institution. On the other hand, academics with a strong affiliation to their institutions might perceive the management differently and interact with the management in a more positive way than those with a not so strong affiliation.

As Table 6.8 shows,

- 90% of academics on average across countries have affirmed the high importance of their discipline/field.
- 72% affirm their department.
- 64% affirm their institution of higher education.

The high *importance of the discipline* is stated in most countries. There are only three European countries differing from this pattern—78% in Italy and 81% each in Portugal and the United Kingdom—as well as one Asian country: 80% in China. Within the individual countries, the responses do differ substantially by type of higher education institution and by status group.

Almost three quarters on average across countries consider *their department* as highly important, when asked about their affiliation. Thereby, differences by country are noteworthy: On the one hand, the respective proportion is very high in Korea (89%) as well as in various emerging countries: Mexico (90%), Malaysia (89%) and Argentina (82%). On the other hand, the affiliation to one's department is not so often named as important by academics in four European countries: Germany (51%), the United Kingdom (54%), Italy (57%) and Portugal (60%).

Within the individual countries, the responses do differ substantially by type of higher education institution and by status group, but there are some noteworthy differences within individual countries: In the United States, the affiliation to one's department is clearly lower among university professors than among junior staff at universities and academics at other higher education institutions. Somewhat similar, academics at universities (both senior and junior) in Germany (almost to the same extent in the Netherlands) consider their department less important than do academics at other institutions of higher education. In contrast, the department plays a relatively important role for academics at universities in Norway and Malaysia.

Less than two-thirds on average across countries underscore their *institutional affiliation*. The differences by countries are even more striking in this case. On the one hand, the academics in two-thirds of the emerging countries surveyed consider their institution of higher education as important in this respect: Mexico (93%), Malaysia (88%), Argentina (86%) and Brazil (79%). On the other hand, almost the same countries where the affiliation to the department was stated as relatively low, the affiliation to one's institution of higher education was stated again as relatively low—of course in this case even lower as far as the actual figures are concerned: United Kingdom (39%), Germany (43%), Norway (48%) and the Netherlands (50%).

Table 6.8 Academics stating high importance of affiliation to their discipline, department and institution (percentage[a])

		CA	US	FI	DE	IT	NL	NO	PT	UK	AU	JP	KR	HK	AR	BR	MX	SA	CH	MY
Discipline/field	Total	92	91	89	92	78	88	95	81	81	89	94	89	90	93	94	97	93	80	96
Universities	Seniors	92	92	93	93	78	86	97	76	84	91	95	92	92	92	94	97	93	80	97
	Juniors	91	91	88	91	78	86	96	80	80	88	86	89	89	94	92	98	92	81	97
Other HEIs	Seniors	.	92	88	94	.	87	87	80	[b]	94	93	89	.	.	96	97	[b]	79	93
	Juniors	.	87	89	81	.	93	79	82	[b]	89	94	89	.	.	94	96	[b]	78	95
Department	Total	69	79	72	51	57	73	70	60	54	67	64	89	73	82	73	90	76	74	89
Universities	Seniors	67	71	76	47	57	68	67	59	53	69	61	89	72	86	72	86	75	72	90
	Juniors	74	84	71	49	58	63	72	67	56	67	54	95	72	82	71	87	76	76	90
Other HEIs	Seniors	.	85	75	64	.	76	55	56	[b]	68	65	89	.	.	75	91	[b]	71	77
	Juniors	.	85	73	75	.	80	77	57	[b]	65	64	88	.	.	73	93	[b]	76	86
Institution	Total	59	60	67	43	58	50	48	64	39	51	64	73	60	86	79	93	60	68	88
Universities	Seniors	59	56	72	46	60	48	46	76	36	56	63	75	60	86	84	93	60	69	94
	Juniors	61	59	67	40	55	42	49	65	39	53	43	92	59	86	80	95	58	68	90
Other HEIs	Seniors	.	71	63	52	.	48	44	80	[b]	56	66	72	.	.	79	93	[b]	63	82
	Juniors	.	66	64	50	.	58	54	62	[b]	42	61	73	.	.	72	94	[b]	63	78

Question B4: Please indicate the degree to which each of the following affiliations is important to you
[a]Responses 1 and 2 on a scale from 1 = very important to 5 = not at all important
[b]Too small number of respondents

6.11 Institutional Affiliation and Engagement

Table 6.9 Change in level of academics' affiliation to their discipline, department and institution in selected countries[a] from 1992 to 2007 (percentage[b] of all respondents)

	DE	UK	US	JP	KO	HK	BR	MX	AU
In 2007									
My academic discipline/field	92	81	91	94	89	90	94	97	89
My department (at this institution)	50	54	79	64	89	73	73	90	67
My institution	43	39	60	64	73	60	79	93	51
In 1992									
My academic discipline/field	91	93	96	96	99	93	99	98	94
My department (at this institution)	52	66	89	85	88	87	95	95	87
My institution	34	84	90	80	97	78	96	94	74

Question B4 (2007): Please indicate the degree to which each of the following affiliations is important to you
[a]The countries that participated in the two surveys
[b]Percent who responded very important or important on a five-item scale

Within the individual countries, respondents from universities in the United States express a clearly lower institutional affiliation than respondents from other institutions of higher education in that country. Junior academics in Portugal at both institutional types and junior academics in Japan at universities place a relatively low importance on their institutions, while the reverse is true for junior academics at universities in Korea.

One of the most striking findings of the comparison between the Carnegie study and the CAP study is the decline of the level of affiliation of academics, particularly with their institution. This can be demonstrated for nine countries (including Hong Kong), where data are available both for 1992 and for 2007 (see Table 6.9).

First, the level of *affiliation to one's discipline or field* has declined from 95 to 91% on average across countries. Of course, most academics continue to consider their discipline as important, but the share of those not considering it important has almost doubled. The most dramatic change has occurred in the United Kingdom, where the respective figure has declined from 93 to 81%.

Second, the level of *affiliation to one's department* is clearly lower as well. It has declined from 83% in 1992 to 72% about 15 years later on average across countries. Substantially lower figures hold true in two-thirds of the cases: Most substantially lower in Brazil and Australia but also noteworthy in Japan, Hong Kong, the United States and the United Kingdom.

Third, the level of *affiliation to one's institution of higher education* has dropped enormously within 15 years: on average across countries for which information is available at both points in time, from 80 to 63%. There is a clear decline in seven cases—thereby most exceptionally in the United Kingdom from 84% to less than half, that is, 38%. There are two exceptions: First, only in Mexico did almost all academics state a strong affiliation both in 1992 and 2007. Second, the level of institutional affiliation increased in Germany: It was by far the lowest in 1992 (34%) and increased at least to a higher level than in the United Kingdom, namely, to 51%.

In looking specifically at the affiliation to one's department and one's institution, we note a substantial decline in six cases out of nine as regards the former and in seven cases as regards the latter. Correlates of low institutional commitment or loyalty include a perception that the prevailing management style is top-down, a perception that facilities are inadequate and a perception that support services are too bureaucratic (Cummings and Finkelstein 2011). The emerging countries of Brazil and Mexico are the exceptions with high levels of institutional loyalty expressed in both 1992 and 2007. The decline in institutional loyalty is particularly steep in the four systems that are market coordinated—specifically the UK, Australia, the USA and Hong Kong.

The decline in institutional loyalty appears to have consequences. Academics who express low institutional loyalty are more likely to favour research over teaching, are more likely to devote a greater percentage of their time to research and a lesser percentage of their time to teaching and are less likely to engage in university service and administrative tasks.

The presumption in Fig. 6.1 is that participatory consultative efficient governance/management influences institutional loyalty and engagement in institution specific activities. In most of the mature systems, less than two out of three academics expressed a positive level of commitment when asked to rate the importance of their affiliation to their institution. In the UK, less than four out of ten expressed this sentiment. This contrasts with several of the emerging countries like Argentina, Brazil, Malaysia and Mexico where between 80 and 90% expressed a positive sense of institutional commitment.

6.12 Conclusion: Variations in the Model's Applicability

This chapter began with the introduction of a hypothetical model of the governance and management of higher educational systems and institutions. The overall pattern of results suggests the applicability of this model, at least for the higher education systems in the more advanced societies. For these higher education systems, it may be that a significant minority of academics, demoralised by current decision-making processes and by what they perceive to be an inadequate working environment, are reducing the effort they devote to the required tasks of teaching and routine administration. Thus, these systems may be losing valuable academic energy.

Of course, depending on national circumstances and traditions, there may be interesting variations in the model. One variation is between university systems in more advanced societies as contrasted with those in transitional or emerging societies (Locke et al. 2011). In the former settings, many of the institutions have been around for some time and are staffed both by eminent professors and experienced managers, enabling an atmosphere of mutual respect and a reasonable sharing of power. In contrast, in the university systems of emerging societies, many of the

6.12 Conclusion: Variations in the Model's Applicability

institutions may be newer and more fragile, reflecting the greater uncertainty of enrolments and the part-time status of many professors; hence, the owners and managers may seek to assert greater authority in decision-making.

Several qualifications of the relations suggested in Fig. 6.1 can be attributed to the advanced versus emerging system distinction. For example, faculty in the emerging countries have relatively little power yet they believe they are consulted, they give managers high marks on efficiency and the protection of academic freedom, and they express a high level of loyalty not only to their disciplines and departments but also to their institutions. So an important reason for the muted relation between faculty power and the other variables noted earlier stems from this divergent emerging country pattern.

A second dimension of variation, proposed by Burton Clark (1987), concerns the principle basis for the coordination of national systems. Clark has proposed three distinctive patterns: coordination resting primarily in the hands of senior professors as in Germany, Italy and Portugal; coordination provided by the state as in the cases of Japan, Korea and Brazil; and coordination signalled by the market as in the USA, Australia and lately in the UK. There are no striking differences in terms of faculty participation in governance by coordinating principle, but concerning the perceived level of personal influence, academics in the professorial systems feel they have the least influence. This finding may reflect an exceptional level of tension in institutions coordinated by the professorial system between the all powerful senior professors and the junior faculty who feel their voice is not heard. Suggestive of this interpretation is the finding that across all three coordination systems but especially in professorial coordinated systems, junior faculty believe they have a much lower level of personal influence than do senior faculty—indeed this difference is one of the most striking findings of the CAP study.

Decisions are described as more top-down in market-coordinated systems. The perception of a strong performance orientation varies widely, but it is most evident in market-coordinated systems being exceptionally high in the USA (see Finkelstein and Cummings 2011). And it is perceived as least prevalent in the professorial coordinated systems such as Italy and Portugal. Particularly notable is the perception in the market systems that teaching is supported. But at the same time, the market systems are notable for the perception that the bureaucracy is cumbersome. Managers in the market systems are the least likely to be considered competent. Also notable is the low level of institutional affiliation expressed by academics in the systems of the market coordination group.

Appendix

Table 6.10.1 Selecting key administrators (percentage)

	CA	US	FI	DE	IT	NL	NO	PT	UK	AU	JP	KR	HK	AR	BR	MX	SA	CH	MY
Seniors at universities																			
Government or external stakeholders	4	6	2	8	4	27	2	2	2	2	2	2	22	5	21	62	6	26	37
Institutional managers	47	73	69	53	78	64	57	36	66	64	22	66	53	24	23	21	65	63	51
Academic unit managers	13	15	5	12	8	8	24	39	11	17	15	22	11	28	5	4	13	10	10
Faculty committees/boards	31	7	21	23	7	1	15	19	14	14	51	7	4	34	10	10	11	1	1
Individual faculty	4	0	3	4	3	0	3	5	7	3	12	3	1	7	36	2	5	0	1
Students	0	0	0	1	0	0	0	0	0	0	0	0	0	2	4	1	0	0	0
Juniors at universities																			
Government or external stakeholders	6	6	3	8	9	24	1	5	1	2	0	0	19	9	21	54	10	22	28
Institutional managers	46	65	59	49	70	62	64	43	49	58	16	50	41	30	30	25	62	64	51
Academic unit managers	15	21	9	18	11	12	17	27	13	18	20	22	16	27	6	8	8	10	16
Faculty committees/boards	29	8	23	20	8	2	18	17	26	16	62	25	7	29	16	10	15	4	4
Individual faculty	5	0	7	4	3	1	2	8	10	7	2	3	2	3	22	4	6	0	1
Students	0	0	0	0	0	0	0	0	0	0	0	0	1	3	5	1	0	0	0
Seniors at other HEIs																			
Government or external stakeholders	.	8	3	8	.	18	3	0	a	2	1	0	.	.	6	60	a	37	11
Institutional managers	.	78	91	52	.	69	72	49	a	83	45	90	.	.	70	23	a	58	77
Academic unit managers	.	6	2	7	.	9	21	21	a	11	16	4	.	.	11	7	a	5	9
Faculty committees/boards	.	8	2	29	.	1	3	27	a	5	30	4	.	.	7	7	a	1	2
Individual faculty	.	1	3	5	.	2	0	3	a	0	8	1	.	.	7	2	a	0	0
Students	.	0	0	0	.	2	0	0	a	0	0	0	.	.	1	2	a	0	0
Juniors at other HEIs																			
Government or external stakeholders	.	6	4	24	.	19		2	a	3	1	1	.	.	4	54	a	19	16
Institutional managers	.	71	88	49	.	67	65	38	a	77	38	81	.	.	83	29	a	64	47
Academic unit managers	.	10	3	9	.	13	16	32	a	6	17	8	.	.	5	6	a	12	32
Faculty committees/boards	.	14	3	18	.	1	13	15	a	11	40	7	.	.	5	8	a	4	4
Individual faculty	.	0	3	0	.	0	7	11	a	3	4	2	.	.	2	2	a	0	2
Students	.	0	0	0	.	1	0	0	a	0	0	0	.	.	1	1	a	0	0

Question E1: At your institution, which actor has the primary influence on each of the following decisions?
Additional category, asked only in HK: University senate: 9% by seniors at universities, 16% by juniors at universities
[a] Too small number of respondents
. No other HEIs or no other HEIs surveyed

Appendix

Table 6.10.2 Choosing new faculty (percentage)

	CA	US	FI	DE	IT	NL	NO	PT	UK	AU	JP	KR	HK	AR	BR	MX	SA	CH	MY
Seniors at universities																			
Government or external stakeholders	0	0	1	2	2	0	1	0	0	0	0	0	0	1	17	9	1	1	6
Institutional managers	4	4	7	16	4	1	21	8	13	16	2	13	10	18	23	17	37	22	33
Academic unit managers	11	31	16	18	31	45	19	22	33	38	3	22	54	43	24	21	27	68	46
Faculty committees/boards	77	59	37	57	39	50	35	66	34	40	89	60	31	25	33	50	25	8	13
Individual faculty	9	6	41	7	24	4	25	5	20	7	7	5	2	12	4	3	10	1	3
Students	0	0	0	0	0	0	0	0	0	0	0	0	0	1	0	0	0	0	0
Juniors at universities																			
Government or external stakeholders	1	0	0	4	4	0	2	0	1	0	0	0	5	1	10	11	3	1	1
Institutional managers	3	3	8	29	6	3	26	8	16	25	0	3	15	8	28	15	35	23	34
Academic unit managers	11	37	12	25	36	31	23	40	27	27	14	27	45	53	31	30	27	66	54
Faculty committees/boards	79	55	31	35	27	57	31	48	33	39	77	65	23	21	29	41	29	8	10
Individual faculty	6	5	49	6	27	9	17	5	23	8	9	5	3	16	2	3	6	1	2
Students	0	0	0	0	0	0	0	0	0	0	0	0	0	1	0	0	0	1	0
Seniors at other HEIs																			
Government or external stakeholders	.	0	0	4	.	0	0	0	a	0	0	0	.	.	1	14	a	2	0
Institutional managers	.	9	46	9	.	7	21	0	a	24	11	31	.	.	15	22	a	44	34
Academic unit managers	.	32	20	20	.	61	31	21	a	44	8	28	.	.	73	35	a	47	59
Faculty committees/boards	.	55	11	63	.	28	24	79	a	25	74	38	.	.	10	27	a	6	5
Individual faculty	.	4	23	5	.	2	24	0	a	6	7	4	.	.	0	2	a	1	2
Students	.	0	0	0	.	2	0	0	a	0	0	0	.	.	0	1	a	0	0
Juniors at other HEIs																			
Government or external stakeholders	.	0	1	19	.	0	0	0	a	1	0	0	.	.	0	9	a	2	2
Institutional managers	.	14	46	34	.	7	26	4	a	40	10	28	.	.	15	23	a	33	31
Academic unit managers	.	29	20	9	.	57	55	31	a	26	12	33	.	.	76	37	a	56	56
Faculty committees/boards	.	55	5	38	.	30	19	56	a	25	72	33	.	.	8	27	a	5	8
Individual faculty	.	3	29	0	.	5	0	9	a	9	6	5	.	.	0	4	a	2	4
Students	.	0	0	0	.	1	0	0	a	0	0	0	.	.	0	0	a	2	0

Question E1: At your institution, which actor has the primary influence on each of the following decisions?
Additional category, asked only in HK: University senate: 3% by seniors at universities, 9% by juniors at universities
[a] Too small number of respondents
. No other HEIs or no other HEIs surveyed

Table 6.10.3 Making faculty promotion and tenure decisions (percentage)

	CA	US	FI	DE	IT	NL	NO	PT	UK	AU	JP	KR	HK	AR	BR	MX	SA	CH	MY
Seniors at universities																			
Government or external stakeholders	0	0	0	2	4	0	2	0	0	0	0	0	0	3	16	13	1	4	8
Institutional managers	11	15	22	27	4	1	38	11	34	27	6	29	27	22	28	18	44	46	64
Academic unit managers	22	29	13	24	33	55	21	23	16	15	5	25	44	43	12	9	22	27	20
Faculty committees/boards	64	52	48	13	37	38	33	64	44	55	85	45	23	26	41	58	27	23	9
Individual faculty	3	4	17	35	21	5	6	2	7	4	4	1	1	5	3	2	6	1	0
Students	0	0	0	0	0	0	0	0	0	0	0	0	0	1	0	0	0	0	0
Juniors at universities																			
Government or external stakeholders	0	0	0	2	4	0	3	1	0	0	0	0	2	3	10	15	1	5	4
Institutional managers	15	17	17	18	5	4	40	24	27	27	5	14	20	23	35	23	48	45	47
Academic unit managers	21	36	10	39	39	56	20	26	17	16	11	38	41	41	18	20	24	29	40
Faculty committees/boards	62	45	48	13	27	30	33	47	43	52	77	43	27	25	36	41	26	22	9
Individual faculty	2	2	25	27	25	10	5	3	12	5	7	5	2	8	2	1	2	0	0
Students	0	0	0	0	0	0	0	0	0	0	0	0	0	0	0	0	0	0	0
Seniors at other HEIs																			
Government or external stakeholders	.	0	0	4	.	0	3	0	a	0	0	0	.	.	1	19	a	15	5
Institutional managers	.	24	80	40	.	11	45	3	a	60	19	50	.	.	60	31	a	51	71
Academic unit managers	.	22	11	30	.	78	17	33	a	8	7	9	.	.	31	24	a	13	21
Faculty committees/boards	.	54	5	19	.	7	21	64	a	30	71	35	.	.	8	24	a	19	5
Individual faculty	.	0	5	8	.	2	14	0	a	2	2	6	.	.		2	a	1	0
Students	.	0	0	0	.	2	0	0	a	0	0	0	.	.	0	0	a	0	0
Juniors at other HEIs																			
Government or external stakeholders	.	0	1	12	.	0	9	4	a	1	0	0	.	.	0	16	a	10	2
Institutional managers	.	28	71	41	.	7	44	24	a	43	19	54	.	.	53	35	a	52	43
Academic unit managers	.	29	11	32	.	74	28	24	a	19	12	12	.	.	40	24	a	22	47
Faculty committees/boards	.	43	6	9	.	13	19	44	a	34	67	33	.	.	6	24	a	13	5
Individual faculty	.	1	12	6	.	6	0	4	a	3	2	1	.	.	0	2	a	1	2
Students	.	0	0	0	.	0	0	0	a	0	0	0	.	.	0	0	a	2	0

Question E1: At your institution, which actor has the primary influence on each of the following decisions?
Additional category, asked only in HK: University senate: 5% by seniors at universities, 8% by juniors at universities
[a]Too small number of respondents
. No other HEIs or no other HEIs surveyed

Appendix 195

Table 6.10.4 Determining budget priorities (percentage)

	CA	US	FI	DE	IT	NL	NO	PT	UK	AU	JP	KR	HK	AR	BR	MX	SA	CH	MY
Seniors at universities																			
Government or external stakeholders	3	1	6	2	2	0	2	5	3	2	0	3	1	9	11	34	2	5	9
Institutional managers	61	53	42	67	42	25	50	34	61	49	36	67	41	36	64	39	60	66	50
Academic unit managers	31	44	7	17	29	60	25	45	14	28	18	25	44	38	14	17	22	25	34
Faculty committees/boards	5	2	25	12	21	13	21	11	15	17	43	3	9	17	10	9	12	3	7
Individual faculty	0	0	20	1	6	2	3	5	7	5	3	2	2	1	1	1	5	1	1
Students	0	0	0	0	0	0	0	0	0	0	0	0	0	0	0	0	0	0	0
Juniors at universities																			
Government or external stakeholders	5	3	4	7	2	2	2	8	3	2	0	3	8	14	9	40	7	6	6
Institutional managers	53	46	40	59	37	28	54	48	46	49	18	47	28	43	63	34	53	59	43
Academic unit managers	33	49	12	21	33	53	22	35	16	22	27	42	41	27	17	19	22	30	43
Faculty committees/boards	9	2	25	11	19	14	19	8	29	19	55	8	12	16	11	7	12	5	8
Individual faculty	0	0	20	3	9	4	3	1	7	8	0	0	0	1	0	0	6	0	1
Students	0	0	0	0	0	0	0	0	0	0	0	0	0	0	0	1	0	0	0
Seniors at other HEIs																			
Government or external stakeholders	.	1	5	3	.	1	7	3	[a]	2	0	0	.	.	3	40	[a]	7	7
Institutional managers	.	77	66	75	.	44	52	61	[a]	75	50	83	.	.	87	39	[a]	77	49
Academic unit managers	.	22	9	10	.	48	23	33	[a]	14	16	8	.	.	7	14	[a]	12	38
Faculty committees/boards	.	0	9	10	.	4	19	3	[a]	5	32	8	.	.	3	6	[a]	4	2
Individual faculty	.	0	11	3	.	0	0	0	[a]	5	2	1	.	.	0	1	[a]	0	4
Students	.	0	0	0	.	3	0	0	[a]	0	0	0	.	.	1	0	[a]	0	0
Juniors at other HEIs																			
Government or external stakeholders	.	3	3	3	.	3	6	8	[a]	1	0	2	.	.	2	42	[a]	6	6
Institutional managers	.	53	72	84	.	37	41	53	[a]	69	47	78	.	.	89	37	[a]	72	54
Academic unit managers	.	39	10	6	.	55	31	35	[a]	12	26	12	.	.	7	16	[a]	17	34
Faculty committees/boards	.	5	5	6	.	4	6	4	[a]	13	26	8	.	.	2	4	[a]	5	5
Individual faculty	.	0	10	0	.	2	13	0	[a]	5	1	0	.	.	0	1	[a]	0	1
Students	.	0	0	0	.	0	3	0	[a]	0	0	0	.	.	0	0	[a]	0	0

Question E1: At your institution, which actor has the primary influence on each of the following decisions?
Additional category, asked only in HK: University senate: 3% by seniors at universities, 9% by juniors at universities
[a]Too small number of respondents
. No other HEIs or no other HEIs surveyed

Table 6.10.5 Determining the overall teaching load of faculty (percentage)

	CA	US	FI	DE	IT	NL	NO	PT	UK	AU	JP	KR	HK	AR	BR	MX	SA	CH	MY
Seniors at universities																			
Government or external stakeholders	0	1	3	a	2	0	3	0	0	0	0	1	2	6	3	11	1	1	3
Institutional managers	20	24	12	a	14	4	33	6	24	12	8	47	11	22	19	14	17	30	12
Academic unit managers	59	65	9	a	29	45	34	34	44	53	10	32	64	45	46	33	40	55	65
Faculty committees/boards	17	9	19	a	48	42	21	56	17	26	56	13	18	25	29	29	20	10	14
Individual faculty	4	1	57	a	6	9	9	3	15	9	26	7	4	2	3	13	21	3	6
Students	0	0	0	a	0	0	0	0	0	0	0	0	0	0	0	0	0	1	0
Juniors at universities																			
Government or external stakeholders	0	1	4	a	2	0	4	1	2	1	0	3	0	3	4	5	2	1	1
Institutional managers	24	23	13	a	12	10	41	8	23	17	12	44	11	42	27	15	24	28	10
Academic unit managers	55	66	11	a	36	42	28	43	30	37	7	33	61	34	41	38	43	54	63
Faculty committees/boards	20	9	27	a	42	40	22	46	24	28	58	19	18	18	24	29	14	14	21
Individual faculty	2	1	45	a	8	8	5	2	20	17	23	0	3	3	4	13	17	3	6
Students	0	0	0	a	0	0	0	0	1	0	0	0	0	0	0	0	0	1	0
Seniors at other HEIs																			
Government or external stakeholders	.	4	3	a	.	0	3	3	b	3	0	1	.	.	0	11	b	1	0
Institutional managers	.	53	38	a	.	12	40	.	b	35	14	55	.	.	20	19	b	30	7
Academic unit managers	.	33	20	a	.	65	33	26	b	38	21	18	.	.	75	49	b	57	77
Faculty committees/boards	.	10	14	a	.	20	20	68	b	18	42	16	.	.	5	17	b	11	9
Individual faculty	.	0	26	a	.	2	3	3	b	6	23	10	.	.	1	5	b	1	7
Students	.	0	0	a	.	2	0	0	b	0	0	0	.	.	0	0	b	0	0
Juniors at other HEIs																			
Government or external stakeholders	.	1	3	a	.	1	6	1	b	1	1	1	.	.	0	8	b	2	2
Institutional managers	.	44	45	a	.	13	44	11	b	33	16	50	.	.	20	20	b	27	9
Academic unit managers	.	39	18	a	.	62	38	31	b	37	23	26	.	.	73	51	b	58	74
Faculty committees/boards	.	17	9	a	.	17	13	52	b	16	35	17	.	.	6	17	b	9	9
Individual faculty	.	0	25	a	.	7	0	5	b	13	25	7	.	.	0	4	b	4	6
Students	.	0	0	a	.	0	0	0	b	0	0	0	.	.	0	0	b	1	0

Question E1: At your institution, which actor has the primary influence on each of the following decisions?
Additional category, asked only in HK: University senate: 1% seniors at universities, 7% juniors at universities
aNot included in the survey because this is determined by the government
bToo small number of respondents
. No other HEIs or no other HEIs surveyed

Appendix   197

Table 6.10.6 Setting admission standards for undergraduate students (percentage)

	CA	US	FI	DE	IT	NL	NO	PT	UK	AU	JP	KR	HK	AR	BR	MX	SA	CH	MY
Seniors at universities																			
Government or external stakeholders	2	3	7	11	7	7	10	14	2	3	1	6	3	2	4	30	6	21	17
Institutional managers	40	60	24	31	22	17	36	14	29	44	14	57	23	27	46	22	39	60	22
Academic unit managers	22	13	5	17	13	39	9	28	24	20	10	15	27	29	18	12	19	12	34
Faculty committees/boards	36	23	49	39	56	35	41	44	31	31	71	22	35	39	30	34	26	6	25
Individual faculty	2	1	15	2	2	2	4	0	14	3	4	0	3	2	1	2	11	0	2
Students	0	0	0	0	0	0	0	0	1	0	0	0	1	1	0	0	0	1	0
Juniors at universities																			
Government or external stakeholders	1	2	10	10	5	3	15	13	5	7		6	2	4	4	24	3	16	8
Institutional managers	41	61	24	39	16	20	30	17	31	42	14	51	18	36	48	19	39	61	32
Academic unit managers	17	13	8	24	21	35	9	27	12	14	23	26	28	30	16	17	22	14	38
Faculty committees/boards	38	23	41	26	52	38	41	39	36	26	61	17	34	24	29	40	23	9	21
Individual faculty	2	1	17	1	6	3	6	3	18	11	2	0	4	4	2	0	14	1	1
Students	0	0	0	0	0	1	0	0	0	0	0	0	1	2	1	0	0	0	0
Seniors at other HEIs																			
Government or external stakeholders	.	4	32	4	.	7	3	3	a	2	0	2	.	.	2	29	a	29	16
Institutional managers	.	71	42	31	.	15	62	12	a	64	19	62	.	.	54	33	a	51	28
Academic unit managers	.	5	11	19	.	39	3	12	a	20	14	15	.	.	30	15	a	13	35
Faculty committees/boards	.	19	8	45	.	31	24	73	a	6	63	20	.	.	14	21	a	4	9
Individual faculty	.	0	8	1	.	5	7	0	a	8	4	1	.	.	.	1	a	1	12
Students	.	0	0	0	.	3	0	0	a	0	0	0	.	.	1	0	a	2	0
Juniors at other HEIs																			
Government or external stakeholders	.	4	32	0	.	9	6	10	a	4		1	.	.	2	30	a	17	7
Institutional managers	.	73	35	19	.	15	50	22	a	55	21	48	.	.	54	34	a	57	35
Academic unit managers	.	13	10	32	.	30	6	21	a	16	20	24	.	.	30	18	a	18	43
Faculty committees/boards	.	11	8	48	.	40	38	47	a	20	53	24	.	.	15	17	a	8	13
Individual faculty	.	0	15	0	.	5	0	0	a	5	7	3	.	.	0	1	a	1	2
Students	.	0	0	0	.	2	0	0	a	0	0	0	.	.	0	0	a	0	0

Question E1: At your institution, which actor has the primary influence on each of the following decisions?
Additional category, asked only in HK: University senate: 9% seniors at universities, 12% juniors at universities
[a]Too small number of respondents
. No other HEIs or no other HEIs surveyed

Table 6.10.7 Approving new academic programmes (percentage)

	CA	US	FI	DE	IT	NL	NO	PT	UK	AU	JP	KR	HK	AR	BR	MX	SA	CH	MY
Seniors at universities																			
Government or external stakeholders	.	8	14	4	2	4	a	5	1	1	2	2	3	5	3	29	12	50	25
Institutional managers	37	39	28	42	8	12	a	14	30	38	13	45	19	42	35	11	31	38	49
Academic unit managers	16	14	5	14	13	59	a	31	10	10	11	23	17	20	24	7	20	9	12
Faculty committees/boards	39	37	47	36	72	24	a	49	56	49	68	27	26	33	37	51	31	3	15
Individual faculty	1	1	6	4	5	1	a	2	5	3	6	2	2	0	1	1	5	0	0
Students	0	0	0	0	1	1	a	0	0	0	0	0	0	0	0	0	0	0	0
Juniors at universities																			
Government or external stakeholders	7	5	14	9	3	6	a	7	3	1	0	6	6	12	3	22	15	42	20
Institutional managers	35	44	34	47	8	9	a	14	25	35	12	33	16	47	35	21	31	42	45
Academic unit managers	17	20	7	20	16	47	a	20	8	14	24	25	23	18	26	12	19	10	20
Faculty committees/boards	41	30	38	22	64	33	a	54	54	44	62	33	28	24	36	46	28	5	14
Individual faculty	0	1	6	3	8	5	a	4	9	6	2	3	1	0	1	0	7	0	1
Students	0	0	0	0	1	0	a	0	0	0	0	0	1	1	0	0	0	0	0
Seniors at other HEIs																			
Government or external stakeholders	.	7	55	7	.	1	a	.	b	2	1	2	.	.	2	33	b	59	11
Institutional managers	.	33	36	35	.	12	a	6	b	48	19	45	.	.	53	18	b	25	48
Academic unit managers	.	14	6	21	.	38	a	27	b	13	17	20	.	.	28	14	b	11	14
Faculty committees/boards	.	45	2	33	.	42	a	64	b	36	57	33	.	.	17	34	b	5	23
Individual faculty	.	1	2	5	.	5	a	3	b	2	6	1	.	.	0	1	b	1	5
Students	.	0	0	0	.	3	a	0	b	0	0	0	.	.	0	0	b	0	0
Juniors at other HEIs																			
Government or external stakeholders	.	8	48	19	.	1	a	9	b	3	1	1	.	.	2	29	b	42	20
Institutional managers	.	46	38	36	.	8	a	13	b	48	17	44	.	.	56	24	b	41	44
Academic unit managers	.	15	4	19	.	44	a	12	b	12	20	25	.	.	28	10	b	12	27
Faculty committees/boards	.	31	5	19	.	41	a	60	b	34	54	29	.	.	15	35	b	3	8
Individual faculty	.	1	5	7	.	5	a	7	b	2	8	2	.	.	0	3	b	2	1
Students	.	0	0	0	.	1	a	0	b	0	0	0	.	.	0	0	b	1	0

Question E1: At your institution, which actor has the primary influence on each of the following decisions?
Additional category, asked only in **HK**: University senate: 34% seniors at universities, 26% juniors at universities
[a]Not asked in Norway
[b]Too small number of respondents
. No other HEIs or no other HEIs surveyed

Appendix

Table 6.10.8 Evaluating teaching (percentage)

	CA	US	FI	DE	IT	NL	NO	PT	UK	AU	JP	KR	HK	AR	BR	MX	SA	CH	MY
Seniors at universities																			
Government or external stakeholders	0	0	4	4	1	3	3	2	2	1	4	0	1	3	4	7	4	42	3
Institutional managers	11	9	19	26	9	9	17	19	14	26	17	30	13	21	23	10	17	40	10
Academic unit managers	25	39	11	24	14	48	19	21	24	20	20	11	34	35	27	15	30	12	56
Faculty committees/boards	18	23	23	22	37	34	20	29	27	19	39	6	19	31	35	35	19	4	22
Individual faculty	5	3	28	2	4	1	15	5	21	14	14	3	2	5	8	2	19	1	9
Students	42	26	15	22	35	6	28	24	12	19	7	49	29	5	3	31	12	1	0
Juniors at universities																			
Government or external stakeholders	0	0	6	4	1	4	1	4	5	1	5	0	0	5	7	8	3	38	2
Institutional managers	7	4	16	18	8	5	20	20	13	23	15	22	7	20	19	10	22	43	10
Academic unit managers	25	48	9	22	17	34	19	26	14	18	15	11	38	38	24	18	28	10	59
Faculty committees/boards	21	23	23	24	31	35	20	23	31	20	50	3	15	22	36	33	21	7	24
Individual faculty	4	6	30	7	5	5	16	5	26	17	10	3	2	11	7	0	13	1	6
Students	44	20	16	26	38	16	24	23	10	22	5	62	35	5	7	31	14	1	0
Seniors at other HEIs																			
Government or external stakeholders	.	0	10	4	.	0	3	7	a	0	2	0	.	.	4	14	a	45	3
Institutional managers	.	12	22	28	.	2	20	.	a	46	25	27	.	.	26	17	a	34	3
Academic unit managers	.	46	18	26	.	37	23	13	a	22	33	6	.	.	37	22	a	9	77
Faculty committees/boards	.	28	13	22	.	40	13	55	a	16	26	9	.	.	18	21	a	8	12
Individual faculty	.	2	24	10	.	13	10	.	a	5	9	2	.	.	9	2	a		6
Students	.	13	14	10	.	8	30	26	a	11	5	56	.	.	6	23	a	3	0
Juniors at other HEIs																			
Government or external stakeholders	.	0	10	13	.	1	6	6	a	1	0	0	.	.	3	13	a	35	2
Institutional managers	.	9	28	20	.	3	13	15	a	31	27	29	.	.	33	19	a	41	5
Academic unit managers	.	44	12	30	.	35	16	32	a	23	27	6	.	.	32	22	a	13	67
Faculty committees/boards	.	17	6	17	.	45	16	30	a	16	35	7	.	.	17	17	a	7	18
Individual faculty	.	7	30	7	.	12	28	6	a	14	5	1	.	.	9	5	a	0	8
Students	.	22	14	13	.	4	22	11	a	14	7	56	.	.	6	23	a	3	0

Question E1: At your institution, which actor has the primary influence on each of the following decisions?
Additional category, asked only in HK: University senate: 3% seniors at universities, 3% juniors at universities
aToo small number of respondents
. No other HEIs or no other HEIs surveyed

Table 6.10.9 Actors having the primary influence on setting internal research priorities (percent)

	CA	US	FI	DE	IT	NL	NO	PT	UK	AU	JP	KR	HK	AR	BR	MX	SA	CH	MY
Seniors at universities																			
Government or external stakeholders	2	1	1	3	3	0	1	2	2	1	0	1	a	1	1	11	1	3	2
Institutional managers	27	21	28	14	6	11	31	13	22	34	34	47	a	26	20	13	22	82	22
Academic unit managers	19	35	12	19	13	51	28	26	22	19	23	16	a	32	22	12	28	10	46
Faculty committees/boards	18	19	13	11	13	26	15	30	20	21	24	31	a	16	32	34	24	4	22
Individual faculty	34	24	46	53	65	12	24	29	33	24	18	5	a	25	24	31	25	0	8
Students	0	0	0	0	0	0	0	0	0	0	0	0	a	0	0	0	0	0	0
Juniors at universities																			
Government or external stakeholders	3	1	1	3	3	1	2	1	1	1	0	4	a	3	1	7	2	5	3
Institutional managers	28	16	17	11	4	5	33	11	22	26	24	20	a	20	22	13	31	79	26
Academic unit managers	20	43	12	22	15	34	27	29	22	21	20	45	a	38	30	18	22	11	45
Faculty committees/boards	20	22	16	13	11	34	16	32	21	22	38	28	a	12	26	33	22	5	19
Individual faculty	28	18	54	51	67	26	23	27	35	30	18	3	a	28	20	28	22	0	7
Students	0	0	0	0	0	0	0	0	0	0	0	0	a	0	0	1	0	0	0
Seniors at other HEIs																			
Government or external stakeholders	.	0	0	1	.	0	3	10	b	0	0	0	a	.	1	17	b	3	2
Institutional managers	.	29	50	23	.	17	26	4	b	56	38	49	a	.	52	19	b	81	26
Academic unit managers	.	32	16	6	.	51	29	17	b	20	25	12	a	.	29	16	b	8	35
Faculty committees/boards	.	16	13	8	.	23	22	32	b	13	21	33	a	.	14	33	b	9	23
Individual faculty	.	23	22	61	.	8	20	37	b	11	16	6	a	.	4	15	b	0	13
Students	.	0	0	0	.	1	0	0	b	0	0	0	a	.	0	0	b	0	0
Juniors at other HEIs																			
Government or external stakeholders	.	0	2	0	.	1	0	3	b	1	0	1	a	.	0	17	b	2	2
Institutional managers	.	17	56	14	.	9	30	15	b	47	27	57	a	.	51	21	b	78	28
Academic unit managers	.	30	16	27	.	64	28	26	b	16	28	12	a	.	31	20	b	12	46
Faculty committees/boards	.	25	8	2	.	22	14	29	b	23	25	26	a	.	15	28	b	7	14
Individual faculty	.	27	18	57	.	4	28	26	b	12	19	4	a	.	4	14	b	1	10
Students	.	0	0	0	.	0	0	0	b	0	0	0	a	.	0	0	b	0	0

Question E1: At your institution, which actor has the primary influence on each of the following decisions?
[a] Not asked in Hong Kong
[b] Too small number of respondents
. No other HEIs or no other HEIs surveyed

Appendix

Table 6.10.10 Actors having the primary influence on evaluating research (percent)

	CA	US	FI	DE	IT	NL	NO	PT	UK	AU	JP	KR	HK	AR	BR	MX	SA	CH	MY
Seniors at universities																			
Government or external stakeholders	9	3	10	15	16	13	21	53	16	7	11	4	a	16	9	13	4	18	3
Institutional managers	13	9	39	30	13	9	18	9	21	33	19	11	a	35	22	17	19	63	25
Academic unit managers	23	35	14	23	16	47	10	10	21	16	18	15	a	23	19	11	31	13	34
Faculty committees/boards	33	39	20	21	34	27	17	21	23	24	31	8	a	20	41	53	30	5	35
Individual faculty	21	14	17	11	22	4	34	7	18	20	20	62	a	7	9	5	15	0	3
Students	0	0	0	0	0	0	0	1	0	0	0	0	a	0	0	0	0	0	0
Juniors at universities																			
Government or external stakeholders	8	3	15	9	13	17	19	24	17	11	13	4	a	14	6	13	6	20	2
Institutional managers	12	6	25	20	10	10	22	15	19	26	3	9	a	28	23	15	24	57	29
Academic unit managers	19	40	15	26	21	30	15	19	20	19	12	17	a	28	23	15	27	15	36
Faculty committees/boards	42	42	20	20	31	34	18	30	26	22	54	13	a	19	41	50	31	8	28
Individual faculty	18	8	25	24	26	8	27	11	17	22	18	56	a	11	8	7	12	1	5
Students	0	1	0	0	0	0	0	0	0	0	0	0	a	0	0	0	0	0	0
Seniors at other HEIs																			
Government or external stakeholders	.	5	6	7	.	1	28	25	b	12	1	1	.	.	1	21	b	15	2
Institutional managers	.	9	39	44	.	12	21	14	b	50	29	29	.	.	40	22	b	64	24
Academic unit managers	.	29	13	6	.	40	20	16	b	17	33	8	.	.	32	17	b	10	39
Faculty committees/boards	.	42	19	12	.	39	18	30	b	11	23	10	.	.	25	35	b	12	28
Individual faculty	.	15	24	31	.	7	14	15	b	11	13	51	.	.	2	5	b	0	7
Students	.	0	0	0	.	1	0	0	b	0	0	0	.	.	0	0	b	0	0
Juniors at other HEIs																			
Government or external stakeholders	.	4	6	6	.	1	12	12	b	9	0	1	.	.	1	19	b	12	3
Institutional managers	.	14	46	33	.	9	20	13	b	36	30	31	.	.	41	28	b	61	24
Academic unit managers	.	23	22	27	.	51	25	24	b	18	26	11	.	.	35	16	b	16	41
Faculty committees/boards	.	40	6	3	.	33	26	34	b	24	29	10	.	.	20	29	b	9	26
Individual faculty	.	19	19	31	.	6	17	17	b	13	15	47	.	.	3	8	b	2	5
Students	.	0	0	0	.	1	0	0	b	0	0	0	.	.	0	0	b	0	0

Question E1: At your institution, which actor has the primary influence on each of the following decisions?
[a]Not asked in Hong Kong
[b]Too small number of respondents
. No other HEIs or no other HEIs surveyed

201

Table 6.10.11 Actors having the primary influence on establishing international linkages (percent)

	CA	US	FI	DE	IT	NL	NO	PT	UK	AU	JP	KR	HK	AR	BR	MX	SA	CH	MY
Seniors at universities																			
Government or external stakeholders	1	1	0	0	1	1	0	1	0	2	1	0	a	2	5	32	1	14	7
Institutional managers	36	40	18	22	12	19	11	29	27	31	46	71	a	58	47	32	42	68	59
Academic unit managers	11	17	13	15	10	43	12	29	17	15	17	10	a	22	14	11	19	13	21
Faculty committees/boards	5	11	8	6	6	17	4	12	10	9	22	5	a	3	16	6	12	2	6
Individual faculty	46	30	61	56	71	20	72	29	46	42	14	13	a	14	19	19	26	4	7
Students	0	1	0	0	0	1	0	1	0	0	0	0	a	0	0	0	0	0	0
Juniors at universities																			
Government or external stakeholders	3	0	0	0	1	2	0	1	0	3	4	0	a	6	5	25	4	18	7
Institutional managers	38	38	10	20	11	10	10	25	27	24	17	47	a	40	63	39	44	66	59
Academic unit managers	9	20	11	17	12	27	17	27	16	17	26	34	a	31	10	13	17	12	21
Faculty committees/boards	6	12	9	6	5	21	4	15	10	11	35	3	a	5	11	6	7	3	7
Individual faculty	44	29	69	57	70	39	69	32	47	46	18	16	a	18	11	17	28	2	6
Students	0	0	1	0	1	1	0	0	0	0	0	0	a	0	0	1	1	0	0
Seniors at other HEIs																			
Government or external stakeholders	.	1	1	1	.	0	0	0	b	0	0	1	.	.	3	46	b	20	2
Institutional managers	.	54	31	30	.	23	17	36	b	38	51	75	.	.	84	32	b	74	54
Academic unit managers	.	16	19	14	.	52	7	22	b	24	15	8	.	.	10	9	b	5	27
Faculty committees/boards	.	8	12	8	.	15	4	10	b	1	20	4	.	.	2	5	b	1	5
Individual faculty	.	20	37	46	.	9	71	33	b	35	13	12	.	.	1	6	b	1	11
Students	.	1	0	0	.	1	0	0	b	1	0	0	.	.	0	0	b	0	0
Juniors at other HEIs																			
Government or external stakeholders	.	0	0	0	.	2	0	1	b	0	0	0	.	.	2	42	b	21	3
Institutional managers	.	49	39	28	.	20	15	32	b	46	46	73	.	.	81	34	b	65	58
Academic unit managers	.	5	19	24	.	50	12	33	b	15	19	8	.	.	10	12	b	10	27
Faculty committees/boards	.	18	8	8	.	16	10	11	b	10	20	7	.	.	6	5	b	3	8
Individual faculty	.	27	34	40	.	11	64	22	b	29	16	11	.	.	2	6	b	1	4
Students	.	1	0	0	.	1	0	1	b	0	0	0	.	.	0	0	b	0	0

Question E1: At your institution, which actor has the primary influence on each of the following decisions?

[a] Not asked in Hong Kong
[b] Too small number of respondents
. No other HEIs or no other HEIs surveyed

Appendix

Table 6.11.1 Evaluators of teaching at universities (percent; multiple responses)

	CA	US	FI	DE	IT	NL	NO	PT	UK	AU	JP	KR	HK	AR	BR	MX	SA	CH	MY
Seniors at universities																			
Your peers in your department or unit	32	51	28	11	18	42	19	43	66	26	22	18	37	45	59	42	47	53	21
The head of your department or unit	65	77	59	26	30	42	30	48	51	67	21	34	72	47	47	51	58	58	61
Members of other departments or units at this institution	9	14	5	4	4	7	5	31	10	9	2	5	10	15	19	21	23	20	7
Senior administrative staff at this institution	28	34	19	10	3	18	18	26	7	15	16	23	37	32	17	17	17	39	13
Your students	91	87	92	88	87	93	92	48	94	80	52	81	91	65	73	79	76	69	82
External reviewers	7	6	18	7	9	30	11	29	30	6	21	9	24	28	10	18	26	21	18
Yourself (formal self-assessment)	34	54	0	32	23	24	29	27	50	44	48	16	46	51	39	43	52	35	37
No one at or outside my institution	3	1	1	5	5	0	5	14	1	5	10	3	0	8	9	2	7	6	4
Juniors at universities																			
Your peers in your department or unit	38	48	37	24	24	41	31	44	66	36	14	34	40	48	51	54	34	50	32
The head of your department or unit	79	86	49	15	37	38	21	48	47	70	21	41	71	47	52	51	50	65	66
Members of other departments or units at this institution	13	15	5	4	4	9	6	30	9	11	0	3	11	14	22	24	16	21	15
Senior administrative staff at this institution	30	25	8	10	3	17	14	36	9	17	20	32	26	23	20	21	14	34	16
Your students	93	93	77	73	85	92	84	62	90	86	36	86	94	60	73	89	76	62	84
External reviewers	9	10	6	3	8	16	10	52	30	6	11	2	25	11	12	21	32	22	19
Yourself (formal self-assessment)	46	55	0	41	26	27	28	25	53	51	29	22	47	38	42	60	53	40	51
No one at or outside my institution	3	0	5	10	7	1	8	10	5	5	18	2	0	12	6	0	12	6	2

Question E3: By whom is your teaching, research and service regularly evaluated?

Table 6.11.2 Evaluators of research at universities (percent; multiple responses)

	CA	US	FI	DE	IT	NL	NO	PT	UK	AU	JP	KR	HK	AR	BR	MX	SA	CH	MY
Seniors at universities																			
Your peers in your department or unit	37	51	41	15	32	40	31	15	36	27	22	44	36	22	51	40	38	24	25
The head of your department or unit	58	76	65	22	27	61	26	5	61	67	24	35	77	14	27	44	52	51	64
Members of other departments or units at this institution	14	19	21	8	7	11	6	6	22	11	3	15	22	28	32	37	27	18	26
Senior administrative staff at this institution	30	38	26	16	2	11	11	9	23	30	22	33	48	28	18	17	22	41	27
Your students	2	3	3	1	2	0	6	72	4	4	3	5	3	2	8	4	7	10	6
External reviewers	61	48	71	55	48	68	47	22	63	59	34	43	70	74	54	50	54	24	37
Yourself (formal self-assessment)	31	52	0	35	23	22	22	15	51	37	49	26	44	28	31	37	48	38	38
No one at or outside my institution	5	4	5	18	19	1	20	19	4	3	10	9	1	4	15	3	9	7	4
Juniors at universities																			
Your peers in your department or unit	48	35	60	57	47	52	70	19	51	41	7	62	37	31	46	39	36	25	33
The head of your department or unit	66	58	72	17	38	57	31	13	64	76	14	45	80	34	31	50	45	57	62
Members of other departments or units at this institution	18	16	25	10	10	12	10	7	19	18	5	21	19	26	31	38	21	15	32
Senior administrative staff at this institution	33	21	11	19	4	17	7	9	18	16	23	31	31	25	23	30	15	30	24
Your students	3	3	2	4	3	2	4	59	7	4	0	6	2	4	6	2	5	10	8
External reviewers	57	32	51	36	36	52	29	25	59	54	22	40	49	57	38	51	62	26	35
Yourself (formal self-assessment)	43	49	0	43	25	23	29	26	54	45	47	29	50	30	31	56	45	37	49
No one at or outside my institution	5	18	5	9	16	5	8	17	7	4	14	5	2	5	17	2	12	9	5

Question E3: By whom is your teaching, research and service regularly evaluated?

Appendix

Table 6.11.3 Evaluators of teaching at other institutions of higher education (percent; multiple responses)

	US	FI	DE	NL	NO	PT	AU	JP	KR	BR	MX	CH	MY
Seniors at other HEIs													
Your peers in your department or unit	46	31	9	53	15	65	24	19	19	42	43	67	23
The head of your department or unit	76	60	22	65	30	25	57	31	19	77	69	69	65
Members of other departments or units at this institution	22	5	2	8	0	37	6	5	6	15	28	22	20
Senior admin. staff at this institution	51	8	13	16	29	26	19	36	31	34	28	37	15
Your students	88	92	91	89	90	43	90	49	79	89	84	74	71
External reviewers	10	27	11	25	15	52	6	7	4	11	28	17	16
Yourself (formal self-assessment)	62	0	40	49	30	16	55	39	20	55	55	39	43
No one at or outside my institution	1	1	2	2	0	0	1	8	4	3	1	8	4
Juniors at other HEIs													
Your peers in your department or unit	63	32	30	62	51	39	29	36	23	27	31	59	36
Your peers in your department or unit	84	63	19	70	23	41	28	63	35	25	78	67	72
Members of other departments or units at this institution	23	6	0	6	6	24	27	13	8	10	17	26	16
Senior admin. staff at this institution	37	14	16	10	30	31	0	16	36	35	35	31	20
Your students	98	92	77	90	75	61	82	86	54	81	86	67	83
External reviewers	7	16	0	21	7	42	26	6	5	2	12	22	24
Yourself (formal self-assessment)	64	0	34	48	44	34	52	63	39	24	54	42	54
No one at or outside my institution	1	2	13	3	7	15	2	3	6	2	3	8	4

Question E3: By whom is your teaching, research and service regularly evaluated?

Table 6.11.4 Evaluators of research at other institutions of higher education (percent; multiple responses)

	US	FI	DE	NL	NO	PT	UK	AU	JP	KR	BR	MX	CH	MY
Seniors at other HEIs														
Your peers in your department or unit	30	20	6	37	30	28	18	18	15	22	20	30	26	20
The head of your department or unit	57	52	9	56	44	5	63	62	32	15	28	40	47	56
Members of other departments or units at this institution	18	21	5	22	3	0	8	14	3	14	16	29	22	16
Senior admin. staff at this institution	39	35	14	21	32	9	6	38	42	42	20	20	45	25
Your students	1	6	3	11	6	56	13	9	2	2	10	5	12	5
External reviewers	29	39	19	42	57	28	33	61	11	35	21	47	19	45
Yourself (formal self-assessment)	51	0	37	50	25	22	49	46	42	30	27	41	39	49
No one at or outside my institution	10	14	37	5	5	13	28	6	12	9	40	4	11	2
Juniors at other HEIs														
Your peers in your department or unit	36	25	49	22	55	20	72	35	23	31	15	29	22	26
The head of your department or unit	54	48	28	41	47	12	81	62	37	18	24	41	51	56
Members of other departments or units at this institution	15	22	0	14	11	10	33	17	5	20	15	30	17	27
Senior admin. staff at this institution	25	19	18	10	7	16	50	25	43	51	24	24	40	20
Your students	2	7	0	5	10	51	0	4	3	3	11	4	13	4
External reviewers	38	33	41	31	26	21	76	51	8	32	16	41	20	35
Yourself (formal self-assessment)	51	0	38	38	27	28	60	43	39	28	27	39	35	48
No one at or outside my institution	14	18	14	27	11	25	2	3	10	9	43	7	8	6

Question E3: By whom is your teaching, research and service regularly evaluated?

Appendix

Table 6.12.1 Strong perceptions of teaching and research-related institutional strategies (percent[a]): seniors at universities

	CA	US	FI	DE	IT	NL	NO	PT	UK	AU	JP	KR	HK	AR	BR	MX	SA	CH	MY	Mean
Funding decisions																				
Performance-based allocation	32	43	70	61	30	65	54	19	56	60	44	33	62	24	30	42	29	50	30	44
Evaluation-based allocation	17	0	44	41	24	42	24	14	37	39	47	24	55	20	28	40	25	43	32	31
Funding based on numbers of students	71	51	33	50	55	67	53	57	76	76	65	43	70	37	30	32	47	53	50	53
Funding based on numbers of graduates	33	25	74	33	23	58	57	23	30	41	9	27	31	11	13	23	44	36	37	33
Personnel decisions																				
Considering the research quality	46	54	55	57	24	69	34	28	69	56	76	43	74	27	28	44	39	57	44	49
Considering the teaching quality	33	46	32	28	13	37	24	17	35	33	39	27	43	37	27	33	34	49	40	33
Considering the practical relevance/ applicability of the work of colleagues	18	27	26	18	11	20	14	14	24	19	21	16	18	39	17	26	24	52	37	23
Recruiting faculty who have work experience outside of academia	14	26	18	27	7	19	11	23	18	22	20	13	15	35	15	16	25	45	34	21
External relations decisions																				
Encouraging academics to adopt service activities	18	33	19	55	16	20	17	38	31	37	26	18	21	28	14	23	25	30	29	26
Encouraging individuals, businesses, foundations, etc. to contribute more to higher education	43	64	25	52	25	23	22	39	41	60	28	37	47	33	26	27	35	54	38	38

Question E6: To what extent does your institution emphasise the following practices?
Mean: The national percentages summed up and divided by the number of countries
[a] Responses 1 and 2 on a scale from 1 = very much to 5 = not at all

Table 6.12.2 Strong perceptions of teaching and research-related institutional strategies (percent[a]): juniors at universities

	CA	US	FI	DE	IT	NL	NO	PT	UK	AU	JP	KR	HK	AR	BR	MX	SA	CH	MY	Mean
Funding decisions																				
Performance-based allocation	38	39	58	49	29	51	52	17	39	47	22	46	55	15	31	44	36	54	36	40
Evaluation-based allocation	28	0	38	26	22	35	23	17	30	36	27	49	48	15	26	42	34	47	38	31
Funding based on numbers of students	69	48	39	42	52	64	49	47	68	62	28	48	65	35	25	33	54	52	38	48
Funding based on numbers of graduates	35	29	71	21	23	60	55	27	32	41	8	30	36	10	8	26	49	37	37	33
Personnel decisions																				
Considering the research quality	56	56	44	53	20	59	35	21	59	55	68	48	65	21	34	46	35	62	42	46
Considering the teaching quality	33	46	21	21	10	28	26	15	28	28	37	18	44	26	32	37	28	53	46	30
Considering the practical relevance/applicability of the work of colleagues	22	38	28	20	10	17	24	10	32	27	20	21	31	24	23	31	25	58	39	26
Recruiting faculty who have work experience outside of academia	18	38	15	26	9	19	14	27	27	27	23	6	26	19	22	31	24	52	37	24
External relations decisions																				
Encouraging academics to adopt service activities	16	42	16	49	12	15	12	26	30	35	23	26	23	10	16	20	29	34	38	25
Encouraging individuals, businesses, foundations, etc. to contribute more to higher education	41	68	19	44	19	22	19	33	32	52	15	30	45	15	28	25	42	54	41	34

Question E6: To what extent does your institution emphasise the following practices?
Mean: The national percentages summed up and divided by the number of countries
[a] Responses 1 and 2 on a scale from 1 = very much to 5 = not at all

Appendix

Table 6.12.3 Strong perceptions of teaching and research-related institutional strategies (percent[a]): seniors at other HEIs

	US	FI	DE	NL	NO	PT	AU	JP	KR	BR	MX	CH	MY	Mean
Funding decisions														
Performance-based allocation	25	41	42	24	74	18	51	28	32	29	33	39	32	36
Evaluation-based allocation	0	21	14	23	25	18	41	25	31	32	34	41	41	27
Funding based on numbers of students	51	77	65	81	45	37	84	65	67	42	35	53	50	58
Funding based on numbers of graduates	26	71	41	75	45	11	36	6	23	20	19	25	28	33
Personnel decisions														
Considering the research quality	24	9	25	27	39	31	48	54	28	27	29	42	37	32
Considering the teaching quality	71	54	51	53	39	15	41	39	22	50	31	43	56	43
Considering the practical relevance/applicability of the work of colleagues	29	45	36	46	31	18	35	28	12	39	26	47	37	33
Recruiting faculty who have work experience outside of academia	21	62	88	50	7	26	36	22	17	43	26	42	51	38
External relations decisions														
Encouraging academics to adopt service activities	41	40	61	39	13	33	48	27	27	26	28	22	17	32
Encouraging individuals, businesses, foundations, etc. to contribute more to higher education	59	15	45	52	15	44	57	15	27	43	36	48	49	39

Question E6: To what extent does your institution emphasise the following practices?
Mean: The national percentages summed up and divided by the number of countries
[a]Responses 1 and 2 on a scale from 1 = very much to 5 = not at all

Table 6.12.4 Strong perceptions of teaching and research-related institutional strategies (percent[a]): juniors at other HEIs

	US	FI	DE	NL	NO	PT	AU	JP	KR	BR	MX	CH	MY	Mean
Funding decisions														
Performance-based allocation	27	35	51	18	37	14	45	34	41	28	32	44	42	35
Evaluation-based allocation	0	17	17	10	16	13	31	31	40	28	37	41	41	23
Funding based on numbers of students	44	69	66	83	55	34	77	39	63	47	40	54	41	53
Funding based on numbers of graduates	27	61	39	65	47	17	31	4	20	18	21	39	24	30
Personnel decisions														
Considering the research quality	33	15	55	9	31	21	36	45	37	25	33	47	28	33
Considering the teaching quality	73	34	57	34	28	19	20	31	26	43	41	45	48	38
Considering the practical relevance/applicability of the work of colleagues	25	42	47	33	37	17	21	25	19	34	34	47	38	33
Recruiting faculty who have work experience outside of academia	33	49	71	54	22	39	25	20	24	39	36	50	47	38
External relations decisions														
Encouraging academics to adopt service activities	37	29	46	26	18	36	34	32	35	24	36	32	38	32
Encouraging individuals, businesses, foundations, etc. to contribute more to higher education	68	14	49	40	7	24	42	18	27	41	41	51	43	36

Question E6: To what extent does your institution emphasise the following practices?
Mean: The national percentages summed up and divided by the number of countries
[a]Responses 1 and 2 on a scale from 1 = very much to 5 = not at all

References

AAUP (2006). *1958 Statement on college and university governance*. Washington, DC: AAUP.

Altbach, P. G. (Ed.). (1996). *The international academic profession: Portraits of fourteen countries*. Princeton: Carnegie Foundation.

Baldridge, J. V., Curtis, D. V., Ecker, G., & Reilly, G. L. (1978). *Policy making and effective leadership: A national study of academic management*. San Francisco: Jossey-Bass Publishers.

Birmbaum, R. (1988). *How colleges work*. San Francisco: Jossey-Bass Publishers.

Clark, B. (1987). *The higher education system*. Berkeley: University of California Press.

Cummings, W. K., & Finkelstein, M. (2011). *Scholars in the changing American academy: New contexts, new rules, and new roles*. Dordrecht: Springer.

Finkelstein, M., & Cummings, W. K. (2011). The U.S. of America: Perspectives on faculty governance 1992–2007. In W. Locke, W. K. Cummings, & D. Fisher (Eds.), *Changing governance and management in higher education: The perspectives of the academy* (pp. 199–222). Dordrecht: Springer.

Gumport, P. (1997). Academic restructuring: Organizational change and institutional imperatives. *Higher Education, 39*(1), 67–91.

Locke, W., Cummings, W. K., & Fisher, D. (Eds.). (2011). *Changing governance and management in higher education: The perspectives of the academy*. Dordrecht: Springer.

Appendix

The Changing Academic Profession: Questionnaire

Final Version 21 November 2006

A. Career and professional situation

A1 For each of your degrees, please indicate the year of completion and the country in which you obtained it

Degree	Year	Earned in country of current employment	If no, please specify country
First degree [NATCAT]	☐☐☐☐	Yes ☐ No ☐	....
Second degree (if applicable) [NATCAT]	☐☐☐☐	Yes ☐ No ☐	....
Doctoral degree (if applicable) [NATCAT]	☐☐☐☐	Yes ☐ No ☐	....
Postdoctoral degree (if applicable) [NATCAT]	☐☐☐☐	Yes ☐ No ☐	....

A2   Please identify the academic discipline or field of your…

Check one in each column

Highest degree	Current acad unit	Current teaching	
1☐	1☐	1☐	Teacher training and education science
2☐	2☐	2☐	Humanities and arts
3☐	3☐	3☐	Social and behavioural sciences
4☐	4☐	4☐	Business and administration, economics
5☐	5☐	5☐	Law
6☐	6☐	6☐	Life sciences
7☐	7☐	7☐	Physical sciences, mathematics, computer sciences
8☐	8☐	8☐	Engineering, manufacturing and construction, architecture
9☐	9☐	9☐	Agriculture
10☐	10☐	10☐	Medical sciences, health-related sciences, social services
11☐	11☐	11☐	Personal services, transport services, security services
12☐	12☐	12☐	Other (please specify): ………………………………… (Please specify)
13☐	13☐	13☐	Not applicable

A3   How would you characterise the training you received in your doctoral degree? (If you do not hold a doctoral degree, please go to question A4)

Check all that apply

1☐ You were required to take a prescribed set of courses
2☐ You were required to write a thesis or dissertation
3☐ You received intensive faculty guidance for your research
4☐ You chose your own research topic
5☐ You received a scholarship or fellowship
6☐ You received an employment contract during your studies (for teaching or research)
7☐ You received training in instructional skills or learned about teaching methods
8☐ You were involved in research projects with faculty or senior researchers
9☐ You served on an institutional or departmental (unit) committee

Appendix

A4 Since your first degree, how long have you been employed in the following? [If '0', so indicate]

Full time	Part time	
☐☐	☐☐	Higher education institutions
☐☐	☐☐	Research institutes
☐☐	☐☐	(Other) government or public sector institutions
☐☐	☐☐	(Other) industry or private sector institutions
☐☐	☐☐	Self-employed

☐☐☐☐ If you reported some nonacademic employment, since how many years do you work in academe without interim phases of employment in other occupational areas?

A5 By how many institutions have you been employed since your

First degree	Highest degree	
☐☐	☐☐	Higher education institutions or research institutes
☐☐	☐☐	Other institutions (including self-employment)

A6 Please indicate the following

☐☐☐☐ Year of your first full-time appointment (beyond research and teaching assistant) in the higher education/research sector

☐☐☐☐ Year of your first appointment to your current institution (beyond research and teaching assistant)

☐☐☐☐ Year of your appointment/promotion to your current rank at your current institution

☐☐ For how many years have you interrupted your service at your current institution for family reasons, personal leave or full-time study? [If '0', so indicate]

A7 How is your employment situation in the current academic year at your higher education institution/research institute? [Check one only]

1☐ Full-time employed
2☐ Part-time employed   ☐☐ % of full time
3☐ Part time with payment according to work tasks
4☐ Other (please specify): ....

A8		Do you work for an additional employer or do additional remunerated work in the current academic year?
	1☐	No
	2☐	In addition to your current employer, you also work at another research institute or higher education institution
	3☐	In addition to your current employer, you also work at a business organisation outside of academe
	4☐	In addition to your current employer, you also work at a non-profit organisation or government entity outside of academe
	5☐	In addition to your current employer, you are also self-employed
	6☐	Other: ....
		(Please specify)
A9		How would you describe your current institution?
		Check one only
	☐	NATCATs to identify (a) higher education institution or research institute and (b) type of higher education institution and (c) type of research institution
A10		What is your academic rank (if you work in a research institution with ranks differing from those at higher education institutions, please choose the rank most closely corresponding to yours)?
	1☐	NATCAT
	2☐	NATCAT
	3☐	NATCAT
	4☐	NATCAT
	5☐	NATCAT
	6☐	NATCAT
	7☐	NATCAT
	8☐	Other: ....
		(Please specify)
A11		What is the duration of your current employment contract at your higher education institution or research institute? [Check only one]
		Check only one
	1☐	Permanently employed (tenured)
	2☐	Continuously employed (no preset term, but no guarantee of permanence)
	3☐	Fixed-term employment *with* permanent/continuous employment prospects (tenure track)
	4☐	Fixed-term employment *without* permanent/continuous employment prospects
	5☐	Other: ....
		(Please specify)

A12	What is your overall annual gross income (including supplements) from the following sources?
☐☐☐☐	Your current higher education institution/research institute [NATCAT: currency and number of boxes]
☐☐☐☐	All other concurrent employers [NATCAT: currency and number of boxes]
☐☐☐☐	Other income (e.g. self-employment) [NATCAT: currency and number of boxes]

A13 During the current academic year, have you done any of the following?

Check all that apply

1. ☐ Served as a member of national/international scientific committees/boards/bodies
2. ☐ Served a peer reviewer (e.g. for journals, research sponsors, institutional evaluations)
3. ☐ Served as an editor of journals/book series
4. ☐ Served as an elected officer or leader in professional/academic associations/organisations
5. ☐ Served as an elected officer or leader of unions
6. ☐ Been substantially involved in loc.l, national or international politics
7. ☐ Been a member of a community organisations or participated in community-based projects
8. ☐ Worked with local, national or international social service agencies
9. ☐ Other: ....

(Please specify)

A14 Within the last 5 years, have you considered a major change in your job? And did you take concrete actions to make such a change? [If yes, check all that apply in both columns A and B. If no, so indicate in column A and skip to B1]

Considered	Concrete action taken	
1 ☐	1 ☐	To a management position in your higher education/research institution
2 ☐	2 ☐	To an academic position in another higher education/research institute within the country
3 ☐	3 ☐	To an academic position in another country
4 ☐	4 ☐	To work outside higher education/research institutes
5 ☐		No, I have not considered making any major changes in my job

B. General work situation and activities

B1 Considering all your professional work, how many hours do you spend in a typical week on each of the following activities? [If you are not teaching during the current academic year, please reply to the second column only]

Hours per week when classes are in session	Hours per week when classes are <u>not</u> in session	
☐☐	☐☐	Teaching (preparation of instructional materials and lesson plans, classroom instruction, advising students, reading and evaluating student work)
☐☐	☐☐	Research (reading literature, writing, conducting experiments, fieldwork)
☐☐	☐☐	Service (services to clients and/or patients, unpaid consulting, public or voluntary services)
☐☐	☐☐	Administration (committees, department meetings, paperwork)
☐☐	☐☐	Other academic activities (professional activities not clearly attributable to any of the categories above)

B2 Regarding your own preferences, do your interests lie *primarily* in teaching or in research?

Check only one

¹☐ Primarily in teaching
²☐ In both, but leaning towards teaching
³☐ In both, but leaning towards research
⁴☐ Primarily in research

B3 At this institution, how would you evaluate each of the following facilities, resources or personnel you need to support your work?

Excellent				Poor	
1	2	3	4	5	
☐	☐	☐	☐	☐	Classrooms
☐	☐	☐	☐	☐	Technology for teaching
☐	☐	☐	☐	☐	Laboratories
☐	☐	☐	☐	☐	Research equipment and instruments
☐	☐	☐	☐	☐	Computer facilities
☐	☐	☐	☐	☐	Library facilities and services

continued

Appendix

B3 continued

1	2	3	4	5	
☐	☐	☐	☐	☐	Your office space
☐	☐	☐	☐	☐	Secretarial support
☐	☐	☐	☐	☐	Telecommunications (Internet, networks and telephones)
☐	☐	☐	☐	☐	Teaching support staff
☐	☐	☐	☐	☐	Research support staff
☐	☐	☐	☐	☐	Research funding

B4 Please indicate the degree to which each of the following affiliations is important to you

Very important			Not at all important		
1	2	3	4	5	
☐	☐	☐	☐	☐	My academic discipline/field
☐	☐	☐	☐	☐	My department (at this institution)
☐	☐	☐	☐	☐	My institution

B5 Please indicate your views on the following

Strongly agree			Strongly disagree		
1	2	3	4	5	
☐	☐	☐	☐	☐	Scholarship is best defined as the preparation and presentation of findings on original research
☐	☐	☐	☐	☐	Scholarship includes the application of academic knowledge in real-life settings
☐	☐	☐	☐	☐	Scholarship includes the preparation of reports that synthesise the major trends and findings of my field
☐	☐	☐	☐	☐	This is a poor time for any young person to begin an academic career in my field
☐	☐	☐	☐	☐	If I had it to do over again, I would not become an academic
☐	☐	☐	☐	☐	My job is a source of considerable personal strain
☐	☐	☐	☐	☐	Teaching and research are hardly compatible with each other
☐	☐	☐	☐	☐	Faculty in my discipline have a professional obligation to apply their knowledge to problems in society

B6 How would you rate your overall satisfaction with your current job?

Very high			Very low	
1	2	3	4	5
☐	☐	☐	☐	☐

B7 Since you started your career, have the overall working conditions in higher education and research institutes improved or declined?

Very much improved			Very much deteriorated		
1	2	3	4	5	
☐	☐	☐	☐	☐	Working conditions in higher education
☐	☐	☐	☐	☐	Working conditions in research institutes

C. Teaching (Refer to the current academic year or the previous academic year (if you do not teach in this academic year). If you do not/did not teach in this or the previous academic year, go to section D)

C1 Please indicate the proportion of your teaching responsibilities during the current academic year that are devoted to instruction at each level below and the approximate number of students you instruct at each of these levels

Percent of instruction time	Approximate average number of students per course	
☐☐	☐☐☐	(NATCAT) undergraduate programmes
☐☐	☐☐☐	(NATCAT) master programmes
☐☐	☐☐☐	(NATCAT) doctoral programmes
☐☐	☐☐☐	(NATCAT) continuing professional education programmes
☐☐	☐☐☐	Others

C2 During the current (or previous) academic year, have you been involved in any of the following teaching activities?

Check all that apply

1☐ Classroom instruction/lecturing
2☐ Individualised instruction
3☐ Learning in projects/project groups
4☐ Practice instruction/laboratory work
5☐ ICT-based learning/computer-assisted learning
6☐ Distance education
7☐ Development of course material
8☐ Curriculum/programme development
9☐ Face-to-face interaction with students outside of class
10☐ Electronic communications (e-mail) with students

Appendix

C3 Does your institution set quantitative load targets or regulatory expectations for individual faculty for the following?

Check all that apply

1. ☐ Number of hours in the classroom
2. ☐ Number of students in your classes
3. ☐ Number of graduate students for supervision
4. ☐ Percentage of students passing exams
5. ☐ Time for student consultation

C4 Please indicate your views on the following

Strongly agree				Strongly disagree	
1	2	3	4	5	
☐	☐	☐	☐	☐	You spend more time than you would like teaching basic skills due to student deficiencies
☐	☐	☐	☐	☐	You are encouraged to improve your instructional skills in response to teaching evaluations
☐	☐	☐	☐	☐	At your institution there are adequate training courses for enhancing teaching quality
☐	☐	☐	☐	☐	Practically oriented knowledge and skills are emphasised in your teaching
☐	☐	☐	☐	☐	In your courses you emphasise international perspectives or content
☐	☐	☐	☐	☐	You incorporate discussions of values and ethics into your course content
☐	☐	☐	☐	☐	You inform students of the implications of cheating or plagiarism in your courses
☐	☐	☐	☐	☐	Grades in your courses strictly reflect levels of student achievement
☐	☐	☐	☐	☐	Since you started teaching, the number of international students has increased
☐	☐	☐	☐	☐	Currently, most of your graduate students are international
☐	☐	☐	☐	☐	Your research activities reinforce your teaching
☐	☐	☐	☐	☐	Your service activities reinforce your teaching

C5 During the current (or previous) academic year, are you teaching any courses

Check all that apply

1. ☐ Abroad
2. ☐ In a language different from the language of instruction at your current institution

D. Research (Refer to the current academic year or the previous academic year (if you are not active in research in this academic year). If you are not/ were not active in research in this or the previous academic year, go to section E)

D1 How would you characterise your research efforts undertaken during this (or the previous) academic year?

Yes	No	
1☐	1☐	Are you working individually/without collaboration on any of your research projects?
2☐	2☐	Do you have collaborators in any of your research projects?
3☐	3☐	Do you collaborate with persons at other institutions in your country?
4☐	4☐	Do you collaborate with international colleagues?

D2 How would you characterise the emphasis of your primary research this (or the previous) academic year?

Very much   Not at all

1	2	3	4	5	
☐	☐	☐	☐	☐	Basic/theoretical
☐	☐	☐	☐	☐	Applied/practically oriented
☐	☐	☐	☐	☐	Commercially oriented/intended for technology transfer
☐	☐	☐	☐	☐	Socially oriented/intended for the betterment of society
☐	☐	☐	☐	☐	International in scope or orientation
☐	☐	☐	☐	☐	Based in one discipline
☐	☐	☐	☐	☐	Multi-/interdisciplinary

D3 Have you been involved in any of the following research activities during this (or the previous) academic year?

Check all that apply

1☐ Preparing experiments, inquiries, etc.
2☐ Conducting experiments, inquiries, etc.
3☐ Supervising a research team or graduate research assistants
4☐ Writing academic papers that contain research results or findings
5☐ Involved in the process of technology transfer
6☐ Answering calls for proposals or writing research grants
7☐ Managing research contracts and budgets
8☐ Purchasing or selecting equipment and research supplies

D4 How many of the following scholarly contributions have you completed in the past 3 years?

(Number completed in the past 3 years)

☐☐	Scholarly books you authored or co-authored
☐☐	Scholarly books you edited or coedited
☐☐	Articles published in an academic book or journal
☐☐	Research report/monograph written for a funded project
☐☐	Paper presented at a scholarly conference
☐☐	Professional article written for a newspaper or magazine
☐☐	Patent secured on a process or invention
☐☐	Computer program written for public use
☐☐	Artistic work performed or exhibited
☐☐	Video or film produced
☐☐	Others (please specify): ....

(Please specify)

D5 Which percentage of your publications in the last 3 years were

☐☐☐	Published in a language different from the language of instruction at your current institution
☐☐☐	Co-authored with colleagues located in the country of your current employment
☐☐☐	Co-authored with colleagues located in other (foreign) countries
☐☐☐	Published in a foreign country
☐☐☐	Online or electronically published
☐☐☐	Peer-reviewed

D6 Please indicate your views on the following

Strongly agree				Strongly disagree	
1	2	3	4	5	
☐	☐	☐	☐	☐	Restrictions on the publication of results from my publicly funded research have increased since my first appointment
☐	☐	☐	☐	☐	Restrictions on the publication of results from my privately funded research have increased since my first appointment
☐	☐	☐	☐	☐	External sponsors or clients have no influence over my research activities

continued

D6 continued

Strongly agree				Strongly disagree	
☐	☐	☐	☐	☐	The pressure to raise external research funds has increased since my first appointment
☐	☐	☐	☐	☐	Interdisciplinary research is emphasised at my institution
☐	☐	☐	☐	☐	Your institution emphasises commercially oriented or applied research
☐	☐	☐	☐	☐	Your research is conducted in full compliance with ethical guidelines
☐	☐	☐	☐	☐	Research funding should be concentrated (targeted) on the most productive researchers
☐	☐	☐	☐	☐	High expectations to increase research productivity are a threat to the quality of research
☐	☐	☐	☐	☐	High expectations of useful results and application are a threat to the quality of research

D7 In the current (or previous) academic year, which percentage of the funding for your research came from

☐☐☐ Your own institution
☐☐☐ Public research funding agencies
☐☐☐ Government entities
☐☐☐ Business firms or industry
☐☐☐ Private not-for-profit foundations/agencies
☐☐☐ Others: ....
(Please specify)

D8 In the current (or previous) academic year, which percentage of the external funding for your research came from

☐☐☐ National organisations/entities
☐☐☐ International organisations/entities
(Please specify)

E. Management

E1 At your institution, which actor has the primary influence on each of the following decisions (please check only one column on each decision)?

Government or external stakeholders	Institutional managers	Academic unit managers	Faculty committees/ boards	Individual faculty	Students	
☐	☐	☐	☐	☐	☐	Selecting key administrators
☐	☐	☐	☐	☐	☐	Choosing new faculty
☐	☐	☐	☐	☐	☐	Making faculty promotion and tenure decisions
☐	☐	☐	☐	☐	☐	Determining budget priorities
☐	☐	☐	☐	☐	☐	Determining the overall teaching load of faculty
☐	☐	☐	☐	☐	☐	Setting admission standards for undergraduate students
☐	☐	☐	☐	☐	☐	Approving new academic programmes
☐	☐	☐	☐	☐	☐	Evaluating teaching
☐	☐	☐	☐	☐	☐	Setting internal research priorities
☐	☐	☐	☐	☐	☐	Evaluating research
☐	☐	☐	☐	☐	☐	Establishing international linkages

E2 How influential are *you*, personally, in helping to shape key academic policies?

Very influential	Somewhat influential	A little influential	Not at all influential	Not applicable	
☐	☐	☐	☐	☐	At the level of the department or similar unit
☐	☐	☐	☐	☐	At the level of the faculty, school or similar unit
☐	☐	☐	☐	☐	At the institutional level

E3 By whom is your teaching, research and service regularly evaluated?

Check all that apply

Your teaching	Your research	Your service	
1☐	1☐	1☐	Your peers in your department or unit
2☐	2☐	2☐	The head of your department or unit
3☐	3☐	3☐	Members of other departments or units at this institution
4☐	4☐	4☐	Senior administrative staff at this institution
5☐	5☐	5☐	Your students
6☐	6☐	6☐	External reviewers
7☐	7☐	7☐	Yourself (formal self-assessment)
8☐	8☐	8☐	No one at or outside my institution

E4 At my institution there is…

Strongly agree				Strongly disagree	
1	2	3	4	5	
☐	☐	☐	☐	☐	A strong emphasis on the institution's mission
☐	☐	☐	☐	☐	Good communication between management and academics
☐	☐	☐	☐	☐	A top-down management style
☐	☐	☐	☐	☐	Collegiality in decision-making processes
☐	☐	☐	☐	☐	A strong performance orientation
☐	☐	☐	☐	☐	A cumbersome administrative process
☐	☐	☐	☐	☐	A supportive attitude of administrative staff towards teaching activities
☐	☐	☐	☐	☐	A supportive attitude of administrative staff towards research activities
☐	☐	☐	☐	☐	Professional development for administrative/management duties for individual faculty

E5 Please indicate your views on the following issues

Strongly agree				Strongly disagree	
1	2	3	4	5	
☐	☐	☐	☐	☐	Top-level administrators are providing competent leadership
☐	☐	☐	☐	☐	I am kept informed about what is going on at this institution
☐	☐	☐	☐	☐	Lack of faculty involvement is a real problem
☐	☐	☐	☐	☐	Students should have a stronger voice in determining policy that affects them
☐	☐	☐	☐	☐	The administration supports academic freedom

Appendix

E6 To what extent does your institution emphasise the following practices?

Very much			Not at all		
1	2	3	4	5	
☐	☐	☐	☐	☐	Performance-based allocation of resources to academic units
☐	☐	☐	☐	☐	Evaluation-based allocation of resources to academic units
☐	☐	☐	☐	☐	Funding of departments substantially based on numbers of students
☐	☐	☐	☐	☐	Funding of departments substantially based on numbers of graduates
☐	☐	☐	☐	☐	Considering the research quality when making personnel decisions
☐	☐	☐	☐	☐	Considering the teaching quality when making personnel decisions
☐	☐	☐	☐	☐	Considering the practical relevance/applicability of the work of colleagues when making personnel decisions
☐	☐	☐	☐	☐	Recruiting faculty who have work experience outside of academia
☐	☐	☐	☐	☐	Encouraging academics to adopt service activities/ entrepreneurial activities outside the institution
☐	☐	☐	☐	☐	Encouraging individuals, businesses, foundations, etc. to contribute more to higher education

F. Personal background and professional preparation

F1 What is your gender?
¹☐ Male
²☐ Female

F2 Year of birth

☐☐☐☐ Year

F3 What is your familial status
¹☐ Married/partner
²☐ Single
³☐ Other: ....
(Please specify)

F4 If married/partner, is she/he employed?
¹☐ Yes, full time
²☐ Yes, part time
³☐ No

F5 Is your spouse/partner also an academic?

¹☐ Yes
²☐ No

F6 Do you have children living with you?

¹☐ Yes, 1 child
²☐ Yes, 2 children
³☐ Yes, 3 or more children
⁴☐ No

F7 Did you ever interrupt your employment in order to provide child or elder care in the home?

¹☐ Yes
²☐ No
☐☐ If yes, for how many years?

F8 What is your parents' highest and, if applicable, partner's highest education level?

Father	Mother	Partner	
¹☐	¹☐	¹☐	Entered and/or completed tertiary education
²☐	²☐	²☐	Entered and/or completed secondary education
³☐	³☐	³☐	Entered and/or completed primary education
⁴☐	⁴☐	⁴☐	No formal education
⁵☐	⁵☐	⁵☐	Not applicable

F9 What was/is your nationality/citizenship and your country of residence

	Citizenship	Country of residence
At birth	....	....
At the time of your first degree	....	....
Currently	....	....
	(Please specify)	(Please specify)

F10 What is your first language/mother tongue?

....
(Please specify)

F11 Which language do you primarily employ in teaching?

¹☐ First language/mother tongue
²☐ Other:..
(Please specify)

Appendix

F12 Which language do you primarily employ in research?

1☐ First language/mother tongue
2☐ Other: ....
(Please specify)

F13 Since the award of your first degree, how many years have you spent

☐☐ In the country of your first degree
☐☐ In the country in which you are currently employed if different from the country of your first degree
☐☐ In other countries (outside the country of your first degree and current employment)

Bibliography

Publications of the Project "The Changing Academic Profession" (CAP)[1]

Compiled by Ester Ava Höhle

Aarrevaara, T. (2009). Akateeminen ura ja laajentuva korkeakoulutus [Academic career and expanding of higher education]. In M.-L. Huotari & A. Lehto (Eds.), *Johtamishasteena muutos – Kirjasto akateemisessa yhteisössä* [Change as a challenge for leadership] (pp. 19–37). Tampere: Tampere University Press.

Aarrevaara, T. (2010). Academic freedom in a changing academic world. *European Review, 18*(Supplement 1), 55–69.

Aarrevaara, T. (2011). A global profession? – A comparative perspective on academic work in China and Finland. In Y. Cai & J. Kivistö (Eds.), *Higher education reforms in China and Finland. Experiences and challenges in post-massification era* (pp. 367–380). Tampere: Tampere University Press.

Aarrevaara, T., & Dobson, I. (2010). Do engineering academics in Finland have job satisfaction? *World Transactions on Engineering and Technology Education, 3,* 250–255.

Aarrevaara, T., & Dobson, I. R. (2013a). Finland: Satisfaction guaranteed! A tale of two systems. In P. Bentley, H. Coates, I. Dobson, L. Goedegebuere, & V. L. Meek (Eds.), *Job satisfaction around the academic world* (The changing academy – The changing academic profession in international comparative perspective, Vol. 7). Dordrecht: Springer.

Aarrevaara, T., & Dobson, I. R. (2012b). Movers and shakers: Academics as stakeholders – Do they control their own work? In U. Teichler & E. A. Höhle (Eds.), *The work situation of the academic profession: Findings of a survey in twelve European countries* (The changing academy – The changing academic profession in international comparative perspective, Vol. 6, pp. 159–181). Dordrecht: Springer [EUROAC].

Aarrevaara, T., Dobson, I. R., & Postareff, L. (2013) (forthcoming). The scholarly question in Finland: To teach or not to teach. In J. C. Shin, A. Arimoto, W. K. Cummings, & U. Teichler (Eds.),

---

[1] The list also comprises publications of the Project "The Academic Profession in Europe – Responses to Societal Challenges" (EUROAC) that was undertaken in close cooperation with the CAP project.

Teaching and research in contemporary higher education: Systems, activities, and rewards. Dordrecht: Springer.

Aarrevaara, T., Dobson, I., & Pekkola, E. (2011). Finland: CAPtive academics – An examination of the binary divide. In W. Locke, W. Cummings, & D. Fisher (Eds.), *Changing governance and management in higher education: The perspectives of the academy* (The changing academy – The changing academic profession in international comparative perspective, Vol. 2, pp. 243–262). Dordrecht: Springer.

Aarrevaara, T., & Hölttä, S. (2007). Finland: Massification, steering-by-results and new divisions of labor. In W. Locke & U. Teichler (Eds.), *The changing conditions for academic work and careers in select countries* (Werkstattberichte/International Centre for Higher Education Research Kassel, Vol. 66, pp. 195–209). Kassel: Jenior.

Aarrevaara, T., & Hölttä, S. (2008). Finnish academic profession reflect reforms in higher education. In RIHE (Ed.), *The changing academic profession in international comparative and quantitative perspectives* (RIHE international seminar reports, Vol. 12, pp. 117–130). Hiroshima: Hiroshima University.

Aarrevaara, T., & Pekkola, E. (2010). *Muuttuva akateeminen professio suomessa – Maaraportti* [Changing academic profession in Finland, national report] (Higher Education Finance and Management Series). Tampere: Tampere University Press.

Aarrevaara, T., & Pekkola, E. (2012). A comparative perspective on the work content of the academic profession. In S. Ahola & D. M. Hoffman (Eds.), *Higher education and research in Finland: Emerging structures and contemporary issues*. Jyväskylä: University of Jyväskylä.

Aiello, M. (2012). ¿El camino del éxito? La internacionalisación en la profesión académica en Argentina [The road to success? Internationalization of the academic profession in Argentina]. In N. Fernández Lamarra & M. Marquina (Eds.), *El futuro de la profesión académica: Desafíos para los países emergentes* [The future of the academic profession: Challenges for emerging countries] (pp. 329–338). Tres de Febrero: EDUNTREF.

Aiello, M., & Marquina, M. (2009). La profesión académica en las universidades públicas [The academic profession in public universities]. *Revista Sudamericana de Educación, Universidad y Sociedad* [South American Journal of Education, University and Society], 1(1).

Aiello, M., & Rebello, G. (2012). Consideraciones metodológicas sobre el proyecto CAP en Argentina [Methodical considerations about the CAP project in Argentina]. In N. Fernández Lamarra & M. Marquina (Eds.), *El futuro de la profesión académica: Desafíos para los países emergentes*. [The future of the academic profession: Challenges for emerging countries] (pp. 452–458). Tres de Febrero: EDUNTREF.

Albero, B., Lameul, G., & Loisy, C. (Eds.). (2013). *Les mutations de l'enseignement supérieur: grandes tendances et pratiques émergentes* [Changes of the work tasks in higher education: Tendencies and upcoming practices]. Pédagogie universitaire et numérique.

Amano, T. (2011). Kyūyo (Salary). In A. Arimoto (Ed.), *Henbō suru sekai no daigaku kyōjushoku* [The changing academic profession in the world] (pp. 201–213). Tamagawa: Tamagawadaigakushuppanbu (Tamagawa University Press).

Arimoto, A. (2006a). Institutionalization of faculty development with a focus on Japan. In RIHE (Ed.), *Reports of changing academic profession project workshop on quality, relevance and governance in the changing academia: International perspectives* (COE publication series, Vol. 20, pp. 3–20). Hiroshima: Hiroshima University.

Arimoto, A. (2006b). The changing academic profession in Japan: Its origins, heritage and current situation. In RIHE (Ed.), *Reports of changing academic profession project workshop on quality, relevance and governance in the changing academia: International perspectives* (COE publication series, Vol. 20, pp. 183–194). Hiroshima: Hiroshima University.

Arimoto, A. (2007a). Japan: Origins, history and transition to a universal higher education system. In W. Locke & U. Teichler (Eds.), *The changing conditions for academic work and careers in select countries* (Werkstattberichte/International Centre for Higher Education Research Kassel, Vol. 66, pp. 113–126). Kassel: Jenior.

Arimoto, A. (2007b). Reflections on the changing relevance of academic profession in Japan. In M. Kogan & U. Teichler (Eds.), *Key challenges to the academic profession* (Werkstattberichte/ International Centre for Higher Education Research Kassel, Vol. 65, pp. 29–47). Kassel: Jenior.

Arimoto, A. (2008). International implications of the changing academic profession in Japan. In RIHE (Ed.), *The changing academic profession in international comparative and quantitative perspectives* (RIHE international seminar reports, Vol. 12, pp. 1–32). Hiroshima: Hiroshima University.

Arimoto, A. (2009). Changing academic profession in the world from 1992 to 2007. In RIHE (Ed.), *The changing academic profession over 1992–2007: International, comparative and quantitative perspectives* (RIHE international seminar reports, Vol. 13, pp. 1–37). Hiroshima: Hiroshima University.

Arimoto, A. (2010a). Differentiation and integration of research, teaching and learning in the knowledge society: From the perspective of Japan. In RIHE (Ed.), *The changing academic profession in international and quantitative perspectives: A focus on teaching & research activities: Report of the international conference on the changing academic profession project 2010* (RIHE international seminar reports, Vol. 15, pp. 1–28). Hiroshima: Hiroshima University.

Arimoto, A. (2010b). The academic profession and the managerial university: An international comparative study from Japan. *European Review, 18*(Supplement 1), 117–139.

Arimoto, A. (Ed.). (2011a). *Henbō suru sekai no daigaku kyōjushoku* [The changing academic profession in the world]. Tamagawa: Tamagawa: Tamagawadaigakushuppanbu (Tamagawa University Press).

Arimoto, A. (2011b). Japan: Effects of changing governance and management on the academic profession. In W. Locke, W. Cummings, & D. Fisher (Eds.), *Changing governance and management in higher education: The perspectives of the academy* (The changing academy – The changing academic profession in international comparative perspective, Vol. 2, pp. 281–320). Dordrecht: Springer.

Arimoto, A. (Ed.). (2011c). *Henbō suru sekai no daigaku kyōjushoku* [The changing academic profession in the world]. Tamagawa: Tamagawadaigakushuppanbu (Tamagawa University Press). http://tamagawa.hondana.jp/book/b91427.html

Arimoto, A. (2011d). International trends in the academic profession from a Japanese perspective. In RIHE (Ed.), *The changing academic profession in Asia: Contexts, realities and trends: Report of the international conference on the changing academic profession project 2011* (RIHE international seminar reports, Vol. 17, pp. 15–56). Hiroshima: Hiroshima University.

Arimoto, A. (2011e). Daigaku kyōjushoku no tenbō [The prospect of academic profession]. In A. Arimoto (Ed.), *Henbō suru sekai no daigaku kyōjushoku* [The changing academic profession in the world] (pp. 291 ff). Tamagawa: Tamagawadaigakushuppanbu (Tamagawa University Press).

Arimoto, A. (2011f). Hennbō suru sekai no daigaku kyōjushoku [The changing academic profession in the world]. In A. Arimoto (Ed.), *Henbō suru sekai no daigaku kyōjushoku* [The changing academic profession in the world] (pp. 11–51). Tamagawa: Tamagawadaigakushuppanbu (Tamagawa University Press).

Arimoto, A., & Daizen, T. (2013). Japan: Factors determining academics' job satisfaction from the perspective of role diversification. In P. Bentley, H. Coates, I. Dobson, L. Goedegebuere, & V. L. Meek (Eds.), *Job satisfaction around the academic world* (The changing academy – The changing academic profession in international comparative perspective, Vol. 7, pp. 145–165). Dordrecht: Springer.

Arimoto, A. (2013) (forthcoming). The teaching and research nexus in the third wave age. In J. C. Shin, A. Arimoto, W. K. Cummings, & U. Teichler (Eds.), *Teaching and research in contemporary higher education: Systems, activities, and rewards*. Dordrecht: Springer.

Arnaut, A., & Giorguli, S. (Eds.). (2010). *Los grandes problemas de México. Vol. II Educación* [The great problems of Mexico. Vol. VII Education]. México City: El Colegio de México. http://2010.colmex.mx/16tomos/VII.pdf

Asonuma, A. (2011). Chikishikishakai no inpakuto [The impact of the knowledge society]. In A. Arimoto (Ed.), *Henbō suru sekai no daigaku kyōjushoku* [The changing academic profession in the world] (pp. 68–85). Tamagawa: Tamagawadaigakushuppanbu (Tamagawa University Press).

Ates, G., & Brechelmacher, A. (2012). Academic career paths. In U. Teichler & E. A. Höhle (Eds.), *The work situation of the academic profession: Findings of a survey in twelve European countries* (The changing academy – The changing academic profession in international comparative perspective, Vol. 6, pp. 13–35). Dordrecht: Springer [EUROAC].

Azman, N., Jantan, M., & Sirat, M. (2010). The transformation of the academic profession in Malaysia: Trends and issues on institutional governance and management. *Journal of the World Universities Forum, 2*(5), 123–138.

Azman, N., Pang, V., Sirat, M., & Yunus, A. S. (2013) (forthcoming). Teaching and research in Malaysian public universities: Synergistic or antagonistic? In J. C. Shin, A. Arimoto, W. K. Cummings, & U. Teichler (Eds.), *Teaching and research in contemporary higher education: Systems, activities, and rewards*. Dordrecht: Springer.

Azman, N., Sirat, M., & Jantan, M. (2011). Malaysia: Perspectives of university governance and management within the academic profession. In W. Locke, W. K. Cummings, & D. Fisher (Eds.), *Changing governance and management in higher education: The perspectives of the academy* (The changing academy – The changing academic profession in international comparative perspective, Vol. 2, pp. 83–106). Dordrecht: Springer.

Azman, N., Sirat, M., & Samsudin, M. A. (2013). Malaysia: An academic career in Malaysia – A wonderful life, or satisfaction not guaranteed? In P. Bentley, H. Coates, I. Dobson, L. Goedegebuere, & V. L. Meek (Eds.), *Job satisfaction around the academic world* (The changing academy – The changing academic profession in international comparative perspective, Vol. 7, pp. 167–186). Dordrecht: Springer.

Balbachevsky, E., & Schwartzman, S. (2007). Brazil: A typology of the academic profession and the impact of recent government and institutional policies. In W. Locke & U. Teichler (Eds.), *The changing conditions for academic work and careers in select countries* (Werkstattberichte/ International Centre for Higher Education Research Kassel, Vol. 66, pp. 93–111). Kassel: Jenior.

Balbachevsky, E., & Schwartzman, S. (2011). Brazil: Diverse experiences in institutional governance in the public and private sectors. In W. Locke, W. K. Cummings, & D. Fisher (Eds.), *Changing governance and management in higher education: The perspectives of the academy* (The changing academy – The changing academic profession in international comparative perspective, Vol. 2, pp. 35–56). Dordrecht: Springer.

Balbachevsky, E., & Schwartzman, S. (2012). Instituições carreiras e perfis acadêmicos na experiência brasileira [Institutions, programs and the academic profile of the Brasilian experience]. In N. Fernández Lamarra & M. Marquina (Eds.), *El futuro de la profesión académica: Desafios para los países emergentes* [The future of the academic profession: Challenges for emerging countries] (pp. 287–299). Tres de Febrero: EDUNTREF.

Balbachevsky, E., & Schwartzman, S. (2013). Brazil: Job satisfaction in a diverse institutional environment. In P. Bentley, H. Coates, I. Dobson, L. Goedegebuere, & V. L. Meek (Eds.), *Job satisfaction around the academic world* (The changing academy – The changing academic profession in international comparative perspective, Vol. 7, pp. 55–81). Dordrecht: Springer.

Balbachevsky, E., Schwartzman, S., Novaes Alves, N., Felgueiras dos Santos, D. F., & Birkholz Duarte, T. S. (2008). Brazilian academic profession: Some recent trends. In RIHE (Ed.), *The changing academic profession in international comparative and quantitative perspectives* (RIHE international seminar reports, Vol. 12, pp. 327–344). Hiroshima: Hiroshima University.

Bennion, A., & Locke, W. (2010). The early career paths and employment conditions of the academic profession in 17 countries. *European Review, 18*(Supplement 1), 7–33.

Bentley, P. J. (2012). Gender differences and factors affecting publication productivity among Australian university academics. *Journal of Sociology, 48*(1), 85–103.

Bentley, P. J., Goedegeburre, L., & Meek, V. L. (2013) (forthcoming). Australian academics, teaching and research: History, vexed issues and potential changes. In J. C. Shin, A. Arimoto, W. K. Cummings, & U. Teichler (Eds.), *Teaching and research in contemporary higher education: Systems, activities, and rewards*. Dordrecht: Springer.

Bentley, P., & Kyvik, S. (2010). Academic staff and public communication: A survey of popular science publishing across 13 countries. *Sage Journals online: Public Understanding of Science*, 1–16.

Bentley, P. J., & Kyvik, S. (2012). Academic work from a comparative perspective: A survey of faculty working time across 13 countries. *Higher Education, 63*(4), 529–547.

Bentley, S., Kyvik, A., Vabø, A., & Waagene, E. (2010). *Forskningsvilkår ved norske universiteter i et internasionalt perspektiv. En undersøkelse av 7 land* [Research conditions at Norwegian universities from a comparative perspective. An investigation of 7 countries]. Oslo: NIFU STEP. http://www.forskerforbundet.no/upload/23506/NIFU_STEP_Rapport_8-2010.pdf

Bentley, P., Coates, H., Dobson, I. R., Goedegebuure, L., & Meek, V. L. (2013a). Conclusion: Academic job satisfaction from an international comparative perspective. Factors associated with satisfaction across 12 countries. In P. Bentley, H. Coates, I. Dobson, L. Goedegebuere, & V. L. Meek (Eds.), *Job satisfaction around the academic world* (The changing academy – The changing academic profession in international comparative perspective, Vol. 7, pp. 239–262). Dordrecht: Springer.

Bentley, P. J., Coates, H., Dobson, I. R. G. L., & Meek, V. L. (2013b). Australia: Factors associated with job satisfaction amongst Australian university academics and future workforce implications. In P. Bentley, H. Coates, I. Dobson, L. Goedegebuere, & V. L. Meek (Eds.), *Job satisfaction around the academic world* (The changing academy – The changing academic profession in international comparative perspective, Vol. 7, pp. 29–53). Dordrecht: Springer.

Bentley, P. J., Coates, H., Dobson, I. R., Goedegebuure, L., & Meek, V. L. (2013c). Introduction: Satisfaction around the world? In P. Bentley, H. Coates, I. Dobson, L. Goedegebuere, & V. L. Meek (Eds.), *Job satisfaction around the academic world* (The changing academy – The changing academic profession in international comparative perspective, Vol. 7, pp. 1–11). Dordrecht: Springer.

Bentley, P., Coates, H., Dobson, I., Goedegebuere, L., & Meek, V. L. (Eds.). (2013d). *Job satisfaction around the academic world* (The changing academy – The changing academic profession in international comparative perspective, Vol. 7). Dordrecht: Springer.

Bernasconi, A. (2012). Gestión del cuerpo académico en un contexto de mercado: el caso de Chile [Management of academic body in Chilean Universities: The institutionalization of the academic profession in a market context]. In N. Fernández Lamarra & M. Marquina (Eds.), *El futuro de la profesión académica: Desafíos para los países emergentes* [The future of the academic profession: Challenges for emerging countries] (pp. 153–167). Tres de Febrero: EDUNTREF.

Bežovan, G., Ledić, J., & Zrinščak, S. (2011). Civilno društvo u sveučilišnoj nastavi [Civil society in university classes]. *Hrvatska i komparativna javna uprava, 11*(1), 173–202 [EUROAC].

Bracht, O., & Teichler, U. (2008). Hochschullehrernachwuchs [Junior academic staff]. In Bundesministerium für Bildung und Forschung (Ed.), *Bundesbericht zur Förderung des wissenschaftlichen Nachwuchses (BuWiN)* [Federal report for the advancement of young researchers] (pp. 87–92). Bonn/Berlin: BMBF. http://www.bmbf.de/pub/buwin_08.pdf

Brennan, J. (2006). The changing academic profession: The driving forces. In RIHE (Ed.), *Reports of changing academic profession project workshop on quality, relevance and governance in the changing academia: International perspectives* (COE publication series, Vol. 20, pp. 37–44). Hiroshima: Hiroshima University.

Brennan, J. (2007). The academic profession and increasing expectations of relevance. In M. Kogan & U. Teichler (Eds.), *Key challenges to the academic profession* (Werkstattberichte/ International Centre for Higher Education Research Kassel, Vol. 65, pp. 19–28). Kassel: Jenior.

Brennan, J., Locke, W., & Naidoo, R. (2007). United Kingdom: An increasingly differentiated profession. In W. Locke & U. Teichler (Eds.), *The changing conditions for academic work and careers in select countries* (Werkstattberichte/International Centre for Higher Education Research Kassel, Vol. 66, pp. 163–176). Kassel: Jenior.

Cai, Y., & Kivistö, J. (Eds.). (2011). *Higher education reforms in China and Finland: Experiences and challenges in post-massification era*. Tampere: Tampere University Press.

Campbell, D. (2013). New university governance: How the academic profession perceives the evaluation of research and teaching. In U. Teichler & E. A. Höhle (Eds.), *The work situation of the academic profession: Findings of a survey in twelve European countries* (The changing academy – The changing academic profession in international comparative perspective, Vol. 6, pp. 205–227). Dordrecht: Springer [EUROAC].

Campbell, D., & Carayannis, E. (2013). *Epistemic governance in higher education: Quality enhancement of universities for development*. Dordrecht: Springer [EUROAC].

Carvalho, T., Santiago, R., & Bruckman, S. (2012). Trabalho académico em Portugal: O que há de novo no campo? [The academic work in Portugal: Is there anything new in the field?]. In T. Glades & D. Leite (Eds.), *Avaliação institucional e ação política na universidade: Perspectivas internacionais* [Institutional evaluation and political action in the University: International perspectives]. Santa Maria/RS/BR: Editora UFSM (Universidade Federal de Santa Maria/BR).

Cavalli, A. (2011). Origine sociale e formazione del ceto accademico [Social and educational background of academics]. In M. Rostan (Ed.), *La professione accademica in Italia: Aspetti, problemi e confronti nel contesto europeo* [The academic profession in Italy: Aspects, problems and comparisons within the European Context] (pp. 51–62). Milano: Edizione Universitarie di Lettere Economia Diritto.

Cavalli, A., & Moscati, R. (2010). Academic systems and professional conditions in five European countries. *European Review, 18*(Supplement 1), 35–53.

Cavalli, A., & Teichler, U. (2010). The academic profession: A common core, a diversified group or an outdated idea? *European Review, 18*(Supplement 1), 1–5.

Cedillo Nakay, R., Cruz Santana, A. L., & de Rodríguez García, R. G. (2010). *Una perspectiva global de los académicos de la Universidad de Colima: Reporte institucional del sobremuestreo* [A global perspective of academics of the University of Colima: Institutional report of the over-sample]. Colima: Universitdad de Colima.

Centeno, C. P. (2012). Profesión académica y docencia en la universidad argentina (Academic profession and teaching in the Argentinean university). In N. Fernández Lamarra & M. Marquina (Eds.), *El futuro de la profesión académica: Desafios para los países emergentes* [The future of the academic profession: Challenges for emerging countries] (pp.387–410). Tres de Febrero: EDUNTREF.

Chiroleu, A. (2012). Comentarios sobre los casos de Brasil, México y Argentina. [Commentary about the cases Brasil, Mexico and Argentina]. In N. Fernández Lamarra & M. Marquina (Eds.), *El futuro de la profesión académica: Desafios para los países emergentes* [The future of the academic profession: Challenges for emerging countries] (pp. 81–87). Tres de Febrero: EDUNTREF.

Clarke, M., Hyde, A., & Drennan, J. (2013). Professional identity in higher education. In B. M. Kehm & U. Teichler (Eds.), *The academic profession in Europe – New tasks and new challenges: The changing academic profession in international comparative perspective* (The changing academy – The changing academic profession in international comparative perspective, Vol. 5, pp. 7–22). Dordrecht: Springer [EUROAC].

Coates, H. B., Goedegebuure, L., van der Lee, J., & Meek, V. L. (2008a). The Astralian academic profession in 2007: A first analysis of the survey results. *Higher Education Research*, 1–8.

Coates, H. B., van der Lee, J., & Meek, V. L. (2008b). The Australian academic profession: A first overview. In RIHE (Ed.), *The changing academic profession in international comparative and quantitative perspectives* (RIHE international seminar reports, Vol. 12, pp. 179–202). Hiroshima: Hiroshima University.

Coates, H. B., Dobson, I., Edwards, D., Friedman, T., Goedegebuure, L., & Meek, V. L. (2009a). *The attractiveness of the Australian academic profession: A comparative analysis*. Melbourne and Canberra: LH Martin Institute for Higher Education Leadership and Management; Educational Policy Institute; Australian Council for Educational Research. http://www.educationalpolicy.org/pdf/CAP_Australian_briefing_paper.pdf.

Coates, H. B., Dobson, I., Goedegebuure, L., & Meek, V. L. (2009b). Australia's casual approach to its academic teaching workforce. *People & Place, 17*(4), 47–54.

Coates, H. B., Dobson, I., Goedegebuure, L., & Meek, V. L. (2010). Across the great divide: What do Australian academics think of university leadership? Advice from the CAP Survey. *Journal of Higher Education Policy and Management, 32*(4), 379–387.

Coates, H. B., Dobson, I., Goedegebuure, L., & Meek, V. L. (2011). Australia: The changing academic profession – An enCAPulsation. In W. Locke, W. K. Cummings, & D. Fisher (Eds.), *Changing governance and management in higher education: The perspectives of the academy* (The changing academy – The changing academic profession in international comparative perspective, Vol. 2, pp. 129–150). Dordrecht: Springer.

Coates, H., Dobson, I.R., Goedegebuure, L., & Meek, V. L. (2013) (forthcoming). The international dimension of teaching and learning. In F. Huang, M. Finkelstein, & M. Rostan (Eds.), *The internationalization of the academy: Changes, realities and prospects*. Dordrecht: Springer.

Ćulum, B., & Ledić, J. (2010a). Civilna misija sveučilišta: element u tragovima? [University civic mission: An element in traces?]. Rijeka: Filozofski fakultet u Rijeci [EUROAC].

Ćulum, B., & Ledić, J. (2010b). Učenje zalaganjem u zajednici – integracija viskoškolske nastave i zajednice u procesu obrazovanja društveno odgovornih i aktivnih građana [Service-learning – The integration of higher education and the community in the process of education of socially responsible and active citizens]. *Revija za socijalnu politiku, 17*(1), 71–88 [EUROAC].

Ćulum, B., & Ledić, J. (2011). Sveučilišni nastavnici i civilna misija sveučilišta. [Academics and university civic mission]. Rijeka: Filozofski fakultet u Rijeci [EUROAC].

Culum, B., Rončević, N., & Ledić, J. (2013a). Facing new expectations – Integrating third mission activities into the university. In B. M. Kehm & U. Teichler (Eds.), *The academic profession in Europe – New tasks and new challenges: The changing academic profession in international comparative perspective* (The changing academy – The changing academic profession in international comparative perspective, Vol. 5, pp. 163–196). Dordrecht: Springer [EUROAC].

Culum, B., Rončević, N., & Ledić, J. (2013b). The academic profession and the role of the service function. In U. Teichler & E. A. Höhle (Eds.), *The work situation of the academic profession: Findings of a survey in twelve European countries* (The changing academy – The changing academic profession in international comparative perspective, Vol. 6, pp. 137–158). Dordrecht: Springer [EUROAC].

Cummings, W. K. (2006). The third revolution of higher education: Becoming more relevant. In RIHE (Ed.), *Reports of changing academic profession project workshop on quality, relevance and governance in the changing academia: International perspectives* (COE publication series, Vol. 20, pp. 209–222). Hiroshima: Hiroshima University.

Cummings, W. (2008). The context for the changing academic profession: A survey of international indicators. In RIHE (Ed.), *The changing academic profession in international comparative and quantitative perspectives* (RIHE international seminar reports, Vol. 12, pp. 33–56). Hiroshima: Hiroshima University.

Cummings, W. K. (2009a). Teaching versus research in the contemporary academy. In RIHE (Ed.), *The changing academic profession over 1992–2007: International, comparative and quantitative perspectives* (RIHE international seminar reports, Vol. 13, pp. 39–56). Hiroshima: Hiroshima University.

Cummings, W. K. (2009b). The internationalization of the U.S. academy. *Asia Pacific Education Review, 1*(1), 14–26.

Cummings, W. K. (2010). Comparing the academic research productivity of selected societies. In RIHE (Ed.), *The changing academic profession in international and quantitative perspectives: A focus on teaching & research activities: Report of the international conference on the changing academic profession project 2010* (RIHE international seminar reports, Vol. 15, pp. 29–40). Hiroshima: Hiroshima University.

Cummings, W. K. (2011). The rise of Asian research universities: Focus on the context. In RIHE (Ed.), *The changing academic profession in Asia: Contexts, realities and trends: Report of the international conference on the changing academic profession project 2011* (RIHE international seminar reports, Vol. 17, pp. 57–78). Hiroshima: Hiroshima University.

Cummings, W. K. (2012). Estrategias de fortalecimiento de capacidades y profesión académica: aproximaciones de Asia del Este [Capacity building strategies and academic profession: East Asian approaches]. In N. Fernández Lamarra & M. Marquina (Eds.), *El futuro de la profesión académica: Desafíos para los países emergentes* [The future of the academic profession: Challenges for emerging countries] (pp. 31–60). Tres de Febrero: EDUNTREF.

Cummings, W. K., Bain, O, Postiglione, G., & Jung, J. (2013) (forthcoming). Trends in the internationalization of the academy: Rhetoric, realities and prospects. In F. Huang, M. Finkelstein, & M. Rostan (Eds.), *The internationalization of the academy: Changes, realities and prospects*. Dordrecht: Springer.

Cummings, W. K., & Bain, O. (2012). El declive de la productividad académica en los Estados Unidos [The increase of acadeic productivity in the United States]. In N. Fernández Lamarra & M. Marquina (Eds.), *El futuro de la profesión académica: Desafíos para los países emergentes* [The future of the academic profession: Challenges for emerging countries] (pp. 215–225). Tres de Febrero: EDUNTREF.

Cummings, W. K. (2013) (forthcoming). The research role in comparative perspective. In J. C. Shin, A. Arimoto, W. K. Cummings, & U. Teichler (Eds.), *Teaching and research in contemporary higher education: Systems, activities, and rewards*. Dordrecht: Springer.

Cummings, W. K., & Finkelstein, M. J. (2012). *Scholars in the changing American academy: New contexts, new rules and new roles* (The changing academy – The changing academic profession in international comparative perspective, Vol. 4). Dordrecht/New York: Springer.

Cummings, W. K., & Kim, M. (2011). Faculty time allocation for teaching and research in Korea and the United States: A comparative perspective. *Korean Social Science Journal, 38*(1), 1–39.

Cummings, W. K., Fisher, D., & Locke, W. (2011). Introduction. In W. Locke, W. K. Cummings, & D. Fisher (Eds.), *Changing governance and management in higher education: The perspectives of the academy* (The changing academy – The changing academic profession in international comparative perspective, Vol. 2, pp. 1–18). Dordrecht: Springer.

Cummings, W. K., & Shin, J. (2013) (forthcoming). Teaching and research in contemporary higher education: An overview. In J. C. Shin, A. Arimoto, W. K. Cummings, & U. Teichler (Eds.), *Teaching and research in contemporary higher education: Systems, activities, and rewards*. Dordrecht: Springer.

Daizen, T. (2011). Kenkyū gyōseki no kokusai hikaku [The international comparison of the research achievement]. In A. Arimoto (Ed.), *Henbō suru sekai no daigaku kyōjushoku* [The changing academic profession in the world] (pp. 222–238). Tamagawa: Tamagawadaigakushuppanbu (Tamagawa University Press).

Daizen, T., & Yamanoi, A. (2008). The changing academic profession in an era of university reform in Japan. In RIHE (Ed.), *The changing academic profession in international comparative and quantitative perspectives* (RIHE international seminar reports, Vol. 12, pp. 293–326). Hiroshima: Hiroshima University.

de Fanelli, A. M. G. (2012). Comentarios sobre los casos e Europa y los Estados Unidos [Comment on the European cases and the United States]. In N. Fernández Lamarra & M. Marquina (Eds.), *El futuro de la profesión académica: Desafíos para los países emergentes* [The future of the academic profession: Challenges for emerging countries] (pp. 209–214). Tres de Febrero: EDUNTREF.

de Fátima Costa Paula, M. (2012). Comentarios sobre carrera académica, trayectorias y condiciones de trabajo [Commentary about academic careers, paths and working conditions]. In N. Fernández Lamarra & M. Marquina (Eds.), *El futuro de la profesión académica: Desafíos para los países emergentes* [The future of the academic profession: Challenges for emerging countries] (pp. 255–261). Tres de Febrero: EDUNTREF.

De Weert, E., Kaiser, F., & Enders, J. (2006). The changing academic profession: The case of the Netherlands. In RIHE (Ed.), *Reports of changing academic profession project workshop on quality, relevance and governance in the changing academia: International perspectives* (COE poublication series, Vol. 20, pp. 167–182). Hiroshima: Hiroshima University.

De Weert, E., & van der Kaap, H. (2013) (forthcoming). The changing balance of teaching and research in the Dutch binary higher education system. In J. C. Shin, A. Arimoto, W. K. Cummings, & U. Teichler (Eds.), *Teaching and research in contemporary higher education: Systems, activities, and rewards*. Dordrecht: Springer.

Dénes, I. Z. (2010). Liberty versus common good. *European Review, 18*(Suppl 1), 89–97.

Dias, D., de Lourdes Machado-Taylor, M., Santiago, R., Carvalho, T., & Sousa, S. (2013). Portugal: dimensions of academic job satisfaction. In P. Bentley, H. Coates, I. Dobson, L. Goedegebuure, & V. L. Meek (Eds.), *Job satisfaction around the academic world* (The changing academy – The changing academic profession in international comparative perspective, Vol. 7). Dordrecht: Springer.

Diversification of higher education and the academic profession (special issue). (2010). *European Review, 18(Suppl. 1)*. http://journals.cambridge.org/action/displayIssue?jid=ERW&volumeId=18&seriesId=0&issueId=S1

Drennan, J., Clarke, M., Hyde, A., & Politis, Y. (2013). The research function of the academic profession in Europe. In U. Teichler & E. A. Höhle (Eds.), *The work situation of the academic profession: Findings of a survey in twelve European countries* (The changing academy – The changing academic profession in international comparative perspective, Vol. 6, pp. 109–136). Dordrecht: Springer [EUROAC].

Du, C., & Shen, H. (2008). yanjiu piaoyi shiyu xia de xueshu zhiye dingxiang [Academic profession in the view of research drift]. Jiangsu gaojiao [Jiangsu Higher Education], *2*, 26–28.

Ehara, T. (2006). Governing Japanese higher education institutions. In RIHE (Ed.), *Reports of changing academic profession project workshop on quality, relevance and governance in the changing academia: International perspectives* (COE Publication Series, Vol. 20, pp. 255–266). Hiroshima: Hiroshima University.

Ehara, T. (2011). Kankyō no henka [The world trend of the university reform]. In A. Arimoto (Ed.), *Henbō suru sekai no daigaku kyōjushoku* [The changing academic profession in the world] (pp. 52–67). Tamagawa: Tamagawadaigakushuppanbu (Tamagawa University Press).

Estévez-Nénninger, E., & Martínez García, J. M. (2011). El peso de la docencia y la investigación desde la visión de los académicos de una universidad pública mexicana. El caso de la Universidad de Sonora. The weight of teaching and research from the perspective of academics at a Mexican public university. The case of the University of Sonora. *Archivos Analíticos de Políticas Educativas, 19*(12).

Estévez-Nenninger, E., & Martínez-Stack, J. (2012). La actividad docente en la educación tertiaria mexicana: La perspectiva de sus académicos [The teaching activities in the Mexican tertiary education from their academic views]. In N. Fernández Lamarra & M. Marquina (Eds.), *El futuro de la profesión académica: Desafios para los países emergentes* [The future of the academic profession: Challenges for emerging countries] (pp. 371–386). Tres de Febrero: EDUNTREF.

Fengqiao, Y., & Yuan, C. (2008). Analyses of the educational backgrounds and career paths of faculty in higher education institutions in Beijing Municipality, China. In RIHE (Ed.), *The changing academic profession in international comparative and quantitative perspectives* (RIHE international seminar reports, Vol. 12, pp. 265–292). Hiroshima: Hiroshima University.

Fernández Lamarra, N., & Marquina, M. (Eds.). (2012). *El futuro de la profesión académica: Desafios para los países emergentes* [The future of the academic profession: Challenges for emerging countries]. Tres de Febrero: EDUNTREF.

Fernández Lamarra, N., Marquina, M., & Rebello, G. (2010). Gobierno, gestión y participación docente en la universidad pública: un desafío pendiente [Governance, Management and teacher participation in public university: a pending challenge]. *Revista del Institutto de Investigaciones en Ciencias de la Educación (IICE)* [Journal of the Research Institute of Educational Sciences], *27*.

Fernández Lamarra, N., Marquina, M., & Rebello, G. (2011). Argentina: Changes in academics' involvement in the governance and management of public universities. In W. Locke, W. K. Cummings, & D. Fisher (Eds.), *Changing governance and management in higher education: The perspectives of the academy* (The changing academy – The changing academic profession in international comparative perspective, Vol. 2, pp. 19–34). Dordrecht: Springer.

Finkelstein, M. J. (2007). The "new" look of academic careers in the United States. In M. Kogan & U. Teichler (Eds.), *Key challenges to the academic profession* (Werkstattberichte/International Centre for Higher Education Research Kassel, Vol. 65, pp. 145–158). Kassel: Jenior.

Finkelstein, M. J. (2010a). Diversification in the academic workforce: The case of the US and implications for Europe. *European Review, 18*(Supplement 1), 141–156.

Finkelstein, M. J. (2010b). The balance between teaching and research in the work life of American academies, 1992–2007: Is it changing? In RIHE (Ed.), *The changing academic profession in international and quantitative perspectives: A focus on teaching & research activities: Report of the international conference on the changing academic profession project 2010* (RIHE international seminar reports, Vol. 15, pp. 213–234). Hiroshima: Hiroshima University.

Finkelstein, M. J. (2011). USA. The U.S. as a prototype for an Asian academic profession: What does that prototype really look like? In RIHE (Ed.), *The changing academic profession in Asia: Contexts, realities and trends: Report of the international conference on the changing academic profession project 2011* (RIHE international seminar reports, Vol. 17, pp. 229–244). Hiroshima: Hiroshima University.

Finkelstein, M. (2013) (forthcoming). The balance between teaching and research in the work life of American academics. In J. C. Shin, A. Arimoto, W. K. Cummings, & U. Teichler (Eds.), *Teaching and research in contemporary higher education: Systems, activities, and rewards*. Dordrecht: Springer.

Finkelstein, M., & Cummings, W. (2008). The changing academic profession in the United States: 2007. In RIHE (Ed.), *The changing academic profession in international comparative and quantitative perspectives* (RIHE international seminar reports, Vol. 12, pp. 75–88). Hiroshima: Hiroshima University.

Finkelstein, M. J., & Frances, C. (2006). The American academic profession: Contact and characteristics. In RIHE (Ed.), *Reports of changing academic profession project workshop on quality, relevance and governance in the changing academia: International perspectives* (COE publication series, Vol. 20, pp. 231–254). Hiroshima: Hiroshima University.

Finkelstein, M. J., Walker, E., & Chen, R. (2009). USA. The internationalization of the American faculty: Where are we, what drives or deters us? In RIHE (Ed.), *The changing academic profession over 1992–2007: International, comparative and quantitative perspectives* (RIHE international seminar reports, Vol. 13, pp. 113–144). Hiroshima: Hiroshima University.

Finkelstein, M. J., Ju, M., & Cummings, W. K. (2011). The United States of America: Perspectives on faculty governance, 1992–2007. In W. Locke, W. K. Cummings, & D. Fisher (Eds.), *Changing governance and management in higher education: The perspectives of the academy* (The changing academy – The changing academic profession in international comparative perspective, Vol. 2, pp. 199–222). Dordrecht: Springer.

Finkelstein, M., Rostan, M., & Huang, F. (2013) (forthcoming). The changing academic profession survey: Concepts and methods. In F. Huang, M. Finkelstein, & M. Rostan (Eds.), *The internationalization of the academy: Changes, realities and prospects*. Dordrecht: Springer.

Finkelstein, M., & Sethi, W. (2013) (forthcoming). Patterns of academic internationalization: A predictive model. In F. Huang, M. Finkelstein, & M. Rostan (Eds.), *The internationalization of the academy: Changes, realities and prospects*. Dordrecht: Springer.

Fisher, D., Locke, W. K., & Cummings, W. K. (2011). Comparative perspectives: Emerging findings and further investigations. In W. Locke, W. K. Cummings, & D. Fisher (Eds.), *Changing governance and management in higher education: The perspectives of the academy* (The changing academy – The changing academic profession in international comparative perspective, Vol. 2, pp. 369–380). Dordrecht: Springer.

Forčić, G., & Ćulum, B. (2010). Civic involvement in the knowledge society – The case of volunteering in Primorsko-Goranska county (Croatia). In J. Langer, N. Alfirević, & Vlasić G. (Eds.), *Knowledge region: Alps-Adriatic challenges* (II: Actors and Cases). Frankfurt am Main: Peter Lang GmbH [EUROAC].

Fujimura, M. (2011). Kanriunei [Management]. In A. Arimoto (Ed.), *Henbō suru sekai no daigaku kyōjushoku* [The changing academic profession in the world] (pp. 144–165). Tamagawa: Tamagawadaigakushuppanbu (Tamagawa University Press).

Fukudome, H. (2011a). Japan. The academic profession in Japan: Work, careers and scholarship. In RIHE (Ed.), *The changing academic profession in Asia: Contexts, realities and trends: Report of the international conference on the changing academic profession project 2011* (RIHE international seminar reports, Vol. 17, pp. 133–148). Hiroshima: Hiroshima University.

Fukudome, H. (2011b). Kenkyū to kyōku no kankei [The relationship of research and education]. In A. Arimoto (Ed.), *Henbō suru sekai no daigaku kyōjushoku* [The changing academic profession in the world] (pp. 254–274). Tamagawa: Tamagawadaigakushuppanbu (Tamagawa University Press).

Fukudome, H., & Daizen, T. (2009). Japan. Education and research activities of the academic profession in Japan. In RIHE (Ed.), *The changing academic profession over 1992–2007: International, comparative and quantitative perspectives* (RIHE international seminar reports, Vol. 13, pp. 165–192). Hiroshima: Hiroshima University.

Fukudome, H., & Kimoto, N. (2010). Teaching and research in the Japanese academic profession: A focus on age and gender. In RIHE (Ed.), *The changing academic profession in international and quantitative perspectives: A focus on teaching & research activities: Report of the international conference on the changing academic profession project 2010* (RIHE international seminar reports, Vol. 15, pp. 135–158). Hiroshima: Hiroshima University.

Galaz-Fontes, J. F., & Gil Antón, M. (2009). La profesión académica en México: Un oficio en proceso de reconfiguración [The academic profession in Mexico: A trade in a restructuring process]. *Revista Electrónica de Investigación Educativa, 11*(2).

Galaz-Fontes, J. F., Padilla-Gonzáles, L., & Gil-Antón, M. (2007). The increasing expectation of relevance for higher education and the academic profession: Some reflections on the case of Mexico. In M. Kogan & U. Teichler (Eds.), *Key challenges to the academic profession* (Werkstattberichte/International Centre for Higher Education Research Kassel, Vol. 65, pp. 49–62). Kassel: Jenior.

Galaz-Fontes, J., Gil-Antón, M., Padilla-González, L., Sevilla-García, J., Arcos-Vega, J., Martínez-Stack, J., et al. (2008a, November 21). *Los académicos mexicanos a principios del siglo XXI: Una primera exploración sobre quiénes son y cómo perciben su trabajo, sus instituciones y algunas políticas públicas*. Documento presentado en la XXXII Sesión Ordinaria del Consejo de Universidades Públicas e Instituciones Afines (CUPIA), de la Asociación Nacional de Universidades e Instituciones de Educación Superior. Villahermosa, Tabasco [Mexican academics at the turn of the XXI Century: A first exploration regarding who they are and how they perceive their work, their institutions and some public policies].

Galaz-Fontes, J. F., Padilla-Gonzáles, L. E., Gil-Antón, M., & Sevilla-García, J. J. (2008b). Los dilemas del profesorado en la educación superior Mexicana [The dilemmas of the professorship in Mexican higher education]. *Calidad en la educación, 28*, 53–69.

Galaz-Fontes, J., Padilla-González, L., Gil-Antón, M., Sevilla-García, J., Arcos-Vega, J., Martínez-Stack, J., Martínez-Romo, S., Sánchez-de-Aparicio-y-Ben´tez, G. A., Jiménez-Loza, L., & Barrera-Bustillos, M. E. (2008c). Mexican academics at the turn of the twenty-first century: Who are they and how do they perceive their work, institutions and public policies (a preliminary analysis). In RIHE (Ed.), *The changing academic profession in international comparative and quantitative perspectives* (RIHE international seminar reports, Vol. 12, pp. 345–362). Hiroshima: Hiroshima University.

Galaz-Fontes, J. F., Gil-Antón, M., Padilla-Gonzáles, L. E., Sevilla-Garcia, J., Martinez-Stack, J., & Arcos-Vega, J. L. (2009a). Mexican higher education at a crossroads: Topics for a new agenda in public policies. *Higher Education Forum [Hiroshima University], 6*, 86–101.

Galaz-Fontes, J. F., Gil-Antón, M., Padilla-Gonzáles, L. E., Sevilla-García, J. J., Arcos-Vega, J. L., & Martínez-Stack, J. G. (2009b). Mexico. The academic profession in Mexico: Changes, continuities and challenges derived from a comparison of two national surveys 15 years apart. In RIHE (Ed.), *The changing academic profession over 1992-2007: International, comparative and quantitative perspectives* (RIHE international seminar reports, Vol. 13, pp. 193–212). Hiroshima: Hiroshima University.

Galaz-Fontes, J. F., Martinez-Stack, J. G., Estévez-Nénninger, E. H., De-la-Cruz-Santana, A. L., Padilla-González, L. E., Gil-Antón, M., Sevilla-García, J. J., & Arcos-Vega, J. L. (2010). The divergent worlds of teaching and research among Mexican faculty: Tendencies and implications. In RIHE (Ed.), *The changing academic profession in international and quantitative perspectives: A focus on teaching & research activities: Report of the international conference on the changing academic profession project 2010* (RIHE international seminar reports, Vol. 15, pp. 191–212). Hiroshima: Hiroshima University.

Galaz-Fontes, J. F., Sevilla-García, J. J., Padilla-Gonzáles, L. E., Acros-Vega, J. L., Gil-Antón, M., & Martinez-Stack, J. (2011). México: A portrait of a managed profession. In W. Locke, W. Cummings, & D. Fisher (Eds.), *Changing governance and management in higher education: The perspectives of the academy* (The changing academy – The changing academic profession in international comparative perspective, Vol. 2, pp. 57–82). Dordrecht: Springer.

Galaz-Fontes, J., Gil-Antón, M., González, L., Sevilla García, J., Vega, J., & Stack, J. (Eds.). (2012a). *La reconfiguración de la profesión académica en México* [The reconfiguration of the academic profession in Mexico]. Culiacán/Sinaloa: Universidad autónoma de Sinaloa/ Universidad autónoma de Baja California.

Galaz-Fontes, J. F., La Cruz Santana, A., Rodríguez García, R., Cedillo Nakay, R., & Villaseñor Amézquita, M. (2012b). El académico mexicano miembro del sistema nacional del investigadores: una primera exploración con base en los resultados de la encuesta "La reconfiguración de la profesíon académica en México" [The academic researcher: A first exploration on the basis of RPAM survey]. In N. Fernández Lamarra & M. Marquina (Eds.), *El futuro de la profesión académica: Desafíos para los países emergentes* [The future of the academic profession: Challenges for emerging countries] (pp. 344–355). Tres de Febrero: EDUNTREF.

Galaz-Fontes, J. F., Martinez-Stack, J. G., Estévez-Nénninger, E. H., Padilla-González, L. E., Gil-Antón, M., Sevilla-García, J. J., & Arcos-Vega, J. L. (2013) (forthcoming). The divergent worlds of teaching and research among Mexican faculty: Tendencies and implications. In J. C. Shin, A. Arimoto, W. K. Cummings, & U. Teichler (Eds.), *Teaching and research in contemporary higher education: Systems, activities, and rewards*. Dordrecht: Springer.

Gil-Antón, M. (2010). El oficio académico: Los límites del dinero [The academic trade: The limits of money]. In A. Arnaut & S. Giorguli (Eds.), *Los grandes problemas de México. Vol. II Educación* [The great problems of Mexico. Vol. VII: Education] (pp. 419–447). México City: El Colegio de México. http://2010.colmex.mx/16tomos/VII.pdf

Gil-Antón, M. (2012). La educación superior en México entre 1990 y 2010: Una conjetura para comprender su transformación [Mexican higher education between 1990 and 2012: A hypothesis to understand its transformation]. *Estudios Sociológicos, 30*(89), 549–566.

Gil-Antón, M., Galaz-Fontes, J. F., & others (2012). La profesión académica en México: continuidad, cambio y renovación [The academic profession in Mexico: Continuity, change and renovation]. In N. Fernández Lamarra & M. Marquina (Eds.), *El futuro de la profesión académica: Desafíos para los países emergentes* [The future of the academic profession: Challenges for emerging countries] (pp. 104–125). Tres de Febrero: EDUNTREF.

Glades, T., & Leite, D. (Eds.). (2012) (forthcoming). *Avaliação institucional e ação política na universidade: Perspectivas internacionais* [Institutional evaluation and political action in the University: International perspectives]. Santa Maria/RS/BR: Editora UFSM (Universidade Federal de Santa Maria/BR).

Goastellec, G., & Pekari, N. (2013a). Gender in academia between differences and inequalities: Findings in Europe. In U. Teichler & E. A. Höhle (Eds.), *The work situation of the academic profession: Findings of a survey in twelve European countries* (The changing academy – The changing academic profession in international comparative perspective, Vol. 6, pp. 55–78). Dordrecht: Springer [EUROAC].

Goastellec, G., & Pekari, N. (2013b). The internationalisation of academic markets, careers and profession. In U. Teichler & E. A. Höhle (Eds.), *The work situation of the academic profession: Findings of a survey in twelve European countries* (The changing academy – The changing academic profession in international comparative perspective, Vol. 6, pp. 229–248). Dordrecht: Springer [EUROAC].

Goastellec, G., & von Crettaz Rotten, F. (2013). (forthcoming). The societal embeddedness of academic markets: From sex to gender in the Swiss context. In M. Soares, U. Teichler, & M. Machado-Taylor (Eds.), *Approaches to the academic career in Europe: Challenges*. Porto: Issues and Developments.

Goastellec, G., Park, E., Ates, G., & Toffel, K. (2013). Academic markets, academic careers. In B. M. Kehm & U. Teichler (Eds.), *The academic profession in Europe – New tasks and new challenges: The changing academic profession in international comparative perspective* (The changing academy – The changing academic profession in international comparative perspective, Vol. 5, pp. 93–120). Dordrecht: Springer [EUROAC].

Goedegebuure, L., Coates, H. B., van der Lee, J., & Meek, L. V. (2009a). Australia. International dimensions of the Australian academic profession. In RIHE (Ed.), *The changing academic profession over 1992–2007: International, comparative and quantitative perspectives* (RIHE international seminar reports, Vol. 13, pp. 79–96). Hiroshima: Hiroshima University.

Goedegebuure, L., Coates, H. B., van der Lee, J., & Meek, V. L. (2009b). Diversity in Australian higher education: An empirical analysis. *Australian Universities Review, 51*(2), 49–61.

Gulbrandsen, M., & Kyvik, S. (2010). Are the concepts basic research, applied research and experimental development still useful? An empirical investigation among Norwegian academics. *Science and Public Policy, 37*, 343–353.

Harman, G., & Meek, V. L. (2007). Australia: Adjustment to the new management and entrepreneurial environment. In W. Locke & U. Teichler (Eds.), *The changing conditions for academic work and careers in select countries* (Werkstattberichte/International Centre for Higher Education Research Kassel, Vol. 66, pp. 127–146). Kassel: Jenior.

Hasegawa, Y. (2011). Seikatsujikan [Lifetime]. In A. Arimoto (Ed.), *Henbō suru sekai no daigaku kyōjushoku* [The changing academic profession in the world] (pp. 180–200). Tamagawa: Tamagawadaigakushuppanbu (Tamagawa University Press).

Hasegawa, Y., & Ogata, N. (2009). Japan. The changing academic profession in Japan. In RIHE (Ed.), *The changing academic profession over 1992–2007: International, comparative and quantitative perspectives* (RIHE international seminar reports, Vol. 13, pp. 271–287). Hiroshima: Hiroshima University.

Hasegawa, Y., & Ogata, N. (2010). Convergence and divergence of teaching and research activities in the Japanese academic profession. In RIHE (Ed.), *The changing academic profession in international and quantitative perspectives: A focus on teaching & research activities: Report of the international conference on the changing academic profession project 2010* (RIHE international seminar reports, Vol. 15, pp. 113–134). Hiroshima: Hiroshima University.

Hawkins, J. N. (2006). Remaining competitive: Faculty recruitment and retention in the University of California. In RIHE (Ed.), *Reports of changing academic profession project workshop on quality, relevance and governance in the changing academia: International perspectives* (COE publication series, Vol. 20, pp. 223–230). Hiroshima: Hiroshima University.

Henkel, M. (2007). Shifting boundaries and the academic profession. In M. Kogan & U. Teichler (Eds.), *Key challenges to the academic profession* (Werkstattberichte/International Centre for Higher Education Research Kassel, Vol. 65, pp. 191–204). Kassel: Jenior.

Herzog, M. (2011). Karriere in der Lehre? Die Lehrorientierung wissenschaftlicher Mitarbeiter und ihre Bedeutung für die Wettbewerbsarena Lehre [Making a career by teaching? The preferences for teaching among junior researchers and its relevance for the competitive arena of teachling]. *Die Hochschule [The higher education institution], 21*(2), 233–244 [EUROAC].

Higgs, P., Higgs, L. G., Ntshoe, I., Wolhuter, C. C., & International Seminar Reports, R. I. H. E. (2010a). Teaching and research in higher education in South Africa: Transformation issues. In RIHE (Ed.), *The changing academic profession in international and quantitative perspectives: A focus on teaching & research activities: Report of the international conference on the changing academic profession project 2010* (Vol. 15, pp. 87–100). Hiroshima: Hiroshima University.

Higgs, L. G., Ntshoe, I. M., Higgs, P., & Wolhuter, C. C. (2010b). Lifelong learning and social inclusion: A South African perspective. In N. Popov, C. C. Wolhuter, B. Leutwyler, M. Mihova, & J. Ogunleye (Eds.). *Comparative education, teacher education, education policy, school leadership and social inclusion* (pp. 423–429). Sofia: Bureau for Educational Services/University of Sofia. http://bces.conference.tripod.com/sitebuildercontent/sitebuilderfiles/8th.bces.conference.2010.book.vol.8.pdf

Higgs, P., Wolhuter, C. C., Higgs, L. G., & Ntshoe, I. M. (2010c). The South African academic profession in comparative perspective. In C. C. Wolhuter & H. D. Herman (Eds.), *Education in hard times*. Potchefstroom: The Platinum Press.

Höhle, E. A., Jacob, A. K., & Teichler, U. (2012). Das Paradies nebenan? (The paradise next door?). *Beiträge zur Hochschulforschung (IHF Bayern) (Contributions to higher education research)* (2), 8–29.

Höhle, E. A., & Teichler, U. (2011). Is there an Asian academic profession? Common and diverse features in comparative perspective. In RIHE (Ed.), *The changing academic profession in Asia: Contexts, realities and trends: Report of the international conference on the changing academic profession project 2011* (RIHE international seminar reports, Vol. 17, pp. 79–96). Hiroshima: Hiroshima University.

Höhle, E. A., & Teichler, U. (2012). Auf dem Weg zu einem europäischen Hochschullehrerberuf? [On the way to a European academic profession?]. In B. M. Kehm, H. Schomburg, & U. Teichler (Eds.), *Funktionswandel der Universitäten: Differenzierung, Relevanzsteigerung, Internationalisierung* [Functional changes of the universities: Differentiation, increase of relevance, internationalisation] (pp. 405–420). Frankfurt: Campus [EUROAC].

Höhle, E. A., & Teichler, U. (2013a). Determinants of academic job satisfaction in Germany. In P. Bentley, H. Coates, I. Dobson, L. Goedegebuere, & V. L. Meek (Eds.), *Job satisfaction around the academic world* (The changing academy – The changing academic profession in international comparative perspective, Vol. 7, pp. 125–143). Dordrecht: Springer.

Höhle, E. A., & Teichler, U. (2013b). The academic profession in the light of comparative surveys. In B. M. Kehm & U. Teichler (Eds.), *The academic profession in Europe – New tasks and new challenges: The changing academic profession in international comparative perspective* (The changing academy – The changing academic profession in international comparative perspective, Vol. 5, pp. 23–38). Dordrecht: Springer [EUROAC].

Höhle, E. A., & Teichler, U. (2013c). The European academic profession or academic professions in Europe? In U. Teichler & E. A. Höhle (Eds.), *The work situation of the academic profession: Findings of a survey in twelve European countries* (The changing academy – The changing academic profession in international comparative perspective, Vol. 6, pp. 249–271). Dordrecht: Springer [EUROAC].

Höhle, E. A., & Teichler, U. (2013d). The teaching function of the academic profession. In U. Teichler & E. A. Höhle (Eds.), *The work situation of the academic profession: Findings of a survey in twelve European countries* (The changing academy – The changing academic profession in international comparative perspective, Vol. 6, pp. 79–108). Dordrecht: Springer [EUROAC].

Huang, F. (2006). The academic profession in Japan: Major characteristics and new changes. In RIHE (Ed.), *Reports of changing academic profession project workshop on quality, relevance and governance in the changing academia: International perspectives* (COE publication series, Vol. 20, pp. 195–208). Hiroshima: Hiroshima University.

Huang, F. (2007). Challenges of internationalization of higher education and changes in the academic profession: A perspective from Japan. In M. Kogan & U. Teichler (Eds.), *Key challenges to the academic profession* (Werkstattberichte/International Centre for Higher Education Research Kassel, Vol. 65, pp. 81–98). Kassel: Jenior.

Huang, F. (2008). Conclusion: Preliminary findings and discussions about the characteristics of the changing academic profession in fifteen countries and regions: An international, comparative and quantitative perspective. In RIHE (Ed.), *The changing academic profession in international comparative and quantitative perspectives* (RIHE international seminar reports, Vol. 12, pp. 401–404). Hiroshima: Hiroshima University.

Huang, F. (2009a). Japan. The internationalisation of Japan's academic profession 1992–2007: Facts and views. In RIHE (Ed.), *The changing academic profession over 1992–2007: International, comparative and quantitative perspectives* (RIHE international seminar reports, Vol. 13, pp. 97–112). Hiroshima: Hiroshima University.

Huang, F. (2009b). The internationalization of the academic profession in Japan. *Journal of Studies in International Education, 13*(2), 143–158.

Huang, F. (2010). Changes and realities in teaching and research activities of the academy. In RIHE (Ed.), *The changing academic profession in international and quantitative perspectives: A focus on teaching & research activities: Report of the international conference on the changing academic profession project 2010* (RIHE international seminar reports, Vol. 15, pp. 235–238). Hiroshima: Hiroshima University.

Huang, F. (2011a). Conclusion: Changes in and issues of academic profession in Asia. In RIHE (Ed.), *The changing academic profession in Asia: Contexts, realities and trends: Report of the international conference on the changing academic profession project 2011* (RIHE international seminar reports, Vol. 17, pp. 245–248). Hiroshima: Hiroshima University.

Huang, F. (2011b). Japan. The academic profession in East Asia: Changes and realities. In RIHE (Ed.), *The changing academic profession in Asia: Contexts, realities and trends: Report of the international conference on the changing academic profession project 2011* (RIHE international seminar reports, Vol. 17, pp. 113–132). Hiroshima: Hiroshima University.

Huang, F. (2011c). Gurōbaruka kokusaika [Globalization and internationalization]. In A. Arimoto (Ed.), *Henbō suru sekai no daigaku kyōjushoku* [The changing academic profession in the world] (pp. 86–98). Tamagawa: Tamagawadaigakushuppanbu (Tamagawa University Press).

Huang, F. (2013) (forthcoming). The internationalization of the academic profession. In F. Huang, M. Finkelstein, & M. Rostan (Eds.), *The internationalization of the academy: Changes, realities and prospects*. Dordrecht: Springer.

Huang, F. (2013) (forthcoming). Teaching and curriculum development across countries. In J. C. Shin, A. Arimoto, W. K. Cummings, & U. Teichler (Eds.), *Teaching and research in contemporary higher education: Systems, activities, and rewards*. Dordrecht: Springer.

Huang, F., & Li, M. (2010). Teaching and research activities of the Chinese academics. In RIHE (Ed.), *The changing academic profession in international and quantitative perspectives: A focus on teaching & research activities: Report of the international conference on the changing academic profession project 2010* (RIHE international seminar reports, Vol. 15, pp. 101–112). Hiroshima: Hiroshima University.

Huang, F., Finkelstein, M. J., & Rostan, M. (Eds.). (2013). *The internationalisation of the academy: Changes, realities and prospects* (The changing academy – The changing academic profession in international comparative perspective, Vol. 9). Dordrecht: Springer.

Huang, F., Teichler, U., & Galaz-Fontes, J. F. (2013) (forthcoming). Regionalization of higher education and the academic profession in Asia, Europe and North America. In F. Huang, M. Finkelstein, & M. Rostan (Eds.), *The internationalization of the academy: Changes, realities and prospects*. Dordrecht: Springer.

Huotari, M.-L., & Lehto, A. (Eds.). (2009). *Johtamishasteena muutos – Kirjasto akateemisessa yhteisössä* (Change as a challenge for leadership). Tampere: Tampere University Press.

Hyde, A., Clarke, M., & Drennan, J. (2013). The changing role of academics and the rise of managerialism. In B. M. Kehm & U. Teichler (Eds.), *The academic profession in Europe – New tasks and new challenges: The changing academic profession in international comparative perspective* (The changing academy – The changing academic profession in international comparative perspective, Vol. 5, pp. 39–52). Dordrecht: Springer [EUROAC].

Izqierdo, M., & Gómez, G. M. (2012). Exclusividad entre los académicos mexicanos (Exclusivity of academics in Mexican IES). In N. Fernández Lamarra & M. Marquina (Eds.), *El futuro de la profesión académica: Desafíos para los países emergentes* ([The future of the academic profession: Challenges for the emerging countries], pp. 273–286). Tres de Febrero: EDUNTREF.

Jacob, A. K. (2011). *Beschäftigungsverhältnisse an Hochschulen: Ein problemorientierter Ländervergleich Deutschland – Norwegen* [Employment conditions at higher education institutions: A problem oriented country comparison Germany-Norway]. Dissertation, University of Flensburg, Flensburg.

Jacob, A. K., & Teichler, U. (2009). Germany: The changing employment and work situation of the academic profession in Germany. In RIHE (Ed.), *The changing academic profession over 1992–2007: International, comparative and quantitative perspectives* (RIHE international seminar reports, Vol. 13, pp. 253–269). Hiroshima: Hiroshima University.

Jacob, A. K., & Teichler U. (Eds.) (2011). *Der Wandel des Hochschullehrerberufs im internationalen Vergleich: Ergebnisse einer Befragung in den Jahren 2007/08* [Change of the academic profession in international comparison: Results of the survey of the years 2007–08]. Bonn/Berlin: Bundesministerium für Bildung und Forschung. http://www.uni-kassel.de/wz1/pdf/BMBF_Hochschullehrerstudie2011_Druck.pdf

Jacob, A.K., & Teichler, U. (2012). Der Hochschullehrerberuf im internationalen Vergleich [The academic profession in international comparison]. In B. M. Kehm, H. Schomburg, & U. Teichler (Eds.), *Funktionswandel der Universitäten: Differenzierung, Relevanzsteigerung, Internationalisierung* [Functional changes of the universities: Differentiation, increase of relevance, internationalisation] (pp. 387–403). Frankfurt: Campus.

Jayaram, N. (2006). The academic profession in India. In RIHE (Ed.), *Reports of changing academic profession project workshop on quality, relevance and governance in the changing academia: International perspectives* (COE publication series, Vol. 20, pp. 151–166). Hiroshima: Hiroshima University.

Jones, G., Gopaul, B., Weinrib, J., Metcalfe, A. S., Fisher, D., Gingras, Y., & Rubenson, K. (2013) (forthcoming). Teaching, research and the Canadian Professoriate. In J. C. Shin, A. Arimoto, W. K. Cummings, & U. Teichler (Eds.), *Teaching and research in contemporary higher education: Systems, activities, and rewards*. Dordrecht: Springer.

Jung, J., Kooij, R., & Teichler, U. (2013) (forthcoming). Internationalization and the new generation of academics. In F. Huang, M. Finkelstein, & M. Rostan (Eds.), *The internationalization of the academy: Changes, realities and prospects*. Dordrecht: Springer.

Kearney, M.-L. (2007). Foreword. In M. Kogan & U. Teichler (Eds.), *Key challenges to the academic profession* (Werkstattberichte/International Centre for Higher Education Research Kassel, Vol. 65, pp. 7–8). Kassel: Jenior.

Kehm, B. M. (2007). The changing role of graduate and doctoral education as a challenge to the academic profession: Europe and North Amercia compared. In M. Kogan & U. Teichler (Eds.), *Key challenges to the academic profession* (Werkstattberichte/International Centre for Higher Education Research Kassel, Vol. 65, pp. 111–124). Kassel: Jenior.

Kehm, B. M., & Teichler, U. (2013a). Introduction. In B. M. Kehm & U. Teichler (Eds.), *The academic profession in Europe – New tasks and new challenges: The changing academic profession in international comparative perspective* (The changing academy – The changing academic profession in international comparative perspective, Vol. 5, pp. 1–6). Dordrecht: Springer [EUROAC].

Kehm, B. M., & Teichler, U. (Eds.). (2013b). *The academic profession in Europe – New tasks and new challenges: The changing academic profession in international comparative perspective* (The changing academy – The changing academic profession in international comparative perspective, Vol. 5). Dordrecht: Springer [EUROAC].

Kimoto, N. (2011). Jendābaiasu – kyōn no raifu sutairu [Gender bias — the life style of the faculty]. In A. Arimoto (Ed.), *Henbō suru sekai no daigaku kyōjushoku* [The changing academic profession in the world] (pp. 123–143). Tamagawa: Tamagawadaigakushuppanbu (Tamagawa University Press).

Kogan, M. (2007). The academic profession and its interface with management. In M. Kogan & U. Teichler (Eds.), *Key challenges to the academic profession* (Werkstattberichte/International Centre for Higher Education Research Kassel, Vol. 65, pp. 159–173). Kassel: Jenior.

Kogan, M., & Teichler, U. (Eds.). (2007a). *Key challenges to the academic profession* (Werkstattberichte/International Centre for Higher Education Research Kassel, Vol. 65). Kassel: Jenior. http://www.gbv.de/dms/hebis-darmstadt/toc/187222819.pdf.

Kogan, M., & Teichler, U. (2007b). Key challenges to the academic profession and its interface with management: Some introductory thoughts. In M. Kogan & U. Teichler (Eds.), *Key challenges to the academic profession* (Werkstattberichte/International Centre for Higher Education Research Kassel, Vol. 65, pp. 9–15). Kassel: Jenior.

Kovač, V., & Turk, M. (2012). Review of new university education policy implementation in Croatia. In E. J. Groccia, A. M. Alsudairi, & W. Buskist (Eds.), *Handbook of college and university teaching: A global perspective*. Washington, DC: [EUROAC].

Kuzuki, K. (2011). Kyōiku katudō [Education programs]. In A. Arimoto (Ed.), *Henbō suru sekai no daigaku kyōjushoku* [The changing academic profession in the world] (pp. 239–253). Tamagawa: Tamagawadaigakushuppanbu (Tamagawa University Press).

Kwiek, M. (2003). Academe in transition: Transformations in the Polish academic profession. *Higher Education, 45*(4), 455–476.

Kwiek, M. (2012). The growing complexity of the academic enterprise in Europe: A panoramic view. *European Journal of Higher Education, 2*(2).

Kwiek, M., & Antonowicz, D. (2013). Academic work, working conditions and job satisfaction. In U. Teichler & E. A. Höhle (Eds.), *The work situation of the academic profession: Findings of a survey in twelve European countries* (The changing academy – The changing academic profession in international comparative perspective, Vol. 6, pp. 37–54). Dordrecht: Springer [EUROAC].

Kyvik, S. (2009). Tid til forskning ved universitetene [Time allocated to research within universities]. In NIFU STEP (Ed.), *Det norske forsknings- og innovasjonssystemet – statistikk og indikatorer 2009* [Norwegian research and innovation system – statistics and indicators 2009] (pp. 122–123). Oslo: NIFU STEP.

Kyvik, S. (2010a). Hvorfor professorene er misfornøyde [On why professors are dissatisfied]. *Forskerforum* [Research Forum], 5/2010, 34.

Kyvik, S. (2010b). *Tidsbruk blant professorer ved norske universiteter i et internasjonalt perspektiv* [The use of time among professors at Norwegian universities from a comparative perspective] (Det norske forsknings-og innovasjonssystemet-statistik og indikatorer). Oslo: NIFU STEP.

Kyvik, S. (2012). Trabajo en red, colaboración y publicaciones como medios de internatcionalisación de la investigación [Internationalization of research through networking, collaboration and publishing]. In N. Fernández Lamarra & M. Marquina (Eds.), *El futuro de la profesión académica: Desafíos para los países emergentes* [The future of the academic profession: Challenges for emerging countries] (pp. 318–328). Tres de Febrero: EDUNTREF.

Kyvik, S., & Vabø, A. (2012). La profesión académica en Noruega: tensiones entre procesos de homogeneización y diferenciación [The academic profession in Norway: Tensions between homogenisation and differentiation]. In N. Fernández Lamarra & M. Marquina (Eds.), *El futuro de la profesión académica: Desafíos para los países emergentes* [The future of the academic profession: Challenges for emerging countries] (pp. 237–248). Tres de Febrero: EDUNTREF.

Lamarra, F. (2011). *La profesión académica en América Latina. Situación y perspectivas* [The academic profession in Latin America. Situation and perspectives]. http://www.saece.org.ar/docs/congreso4/trab49.pdf

Lamarra, F., & Marquina, M. (2012). Introducción (Introduction). In N. Fernández Lamarra & M. Marquina (Eds.), *El futuro de la profesión académica: Desafíos para los países emergentes*. [The future of the academic profession: Challenges for emerging countries] (pp. 11–16). Tres de Febrero: EDUNTREF.

Leal, M., Robin, S. O., & Maidana, M. A. (2012). La tensión entre docencia e investigación en los académicos argentinos [The tension between teaching – research in the work of Argentinean academics]. In N. Fernández Lamarra & M. Marquina (Eds.), *El futuro de la profesión académica: Desafíos para los países emergentes* [The future of the academic profession: Challenges for emerging countries] (pp. 356–370). Tres de Febrero: EDUNTREF.

Ledic, J. (Ed.). (2012). *Promjene u akademskoj profesiji: odgovor na izazove u društvu?* [Changes in academic profession: Responses to societal challenges?]. Rijeka: Filozofski fakultet u Rijeci [EUROAC].

Leal, M., & Marquina, M. (2013) (forthcoming). Current challenges facing the academic profession in Argentina: Tensions between teaching and research. In J. C. Shin, A. Arimoto, W. K. Cummings, & U. Teichler (Eds.), *Teaching and research in contemporary higher education: Systems, activities, and rewards*. Dordrecht: Springer.

Lee, S. J., & Kim, Y. (2011). South Korea. The internationalization of universities in South Korea: Networking strategies and research performance. In RIHE (Ed.), *The changing academic profession in Asia: Contexts, realities and trends: Report of the international conference on the changing academic profession project 2011* (RIHE international seminar reports, Vol. 17, pp. 177–196). Hiroshima: Hiroshima University.

Li, Z. F., & Shen, H. (2006). Jiyu xueshu zhiye zhuanyehua de gaoxiao jiaoshi zhengce chuangxin [An innovation of policy for academic profession specialization in universities]. *Gaodneg gongcheng jiaoyu yanjiu* [Research in Higher education of Engineering], 5, 61–64.

Li, Z. F., & Shen, H. (2007a). lun xueshu zhiye de benzhi shuxing—gaoxiao jiaoshi congshi de shi yizhong xueshu zhiye [On the nature of academic profession – University teachers engaged in academic profession]. *Wuhan ligong daxue xuebao-shehui kexue ban* [Journal of Wuhan University of Technology-Social Sciences Edition], 6, 846–850.

Li, Z. F., & Shen, H. (2007b). Xueshu zhiye: Ouzhou zhong shiji shiqi de xingcheng yu xingtai [The academic profession: Its formation and morphology in medieval Europe]. *Zhongshan daxue xuebao-shehui kexue ban* [Journal of Sun Yatsen University-Social Science Edition], 4, 44–47.

Li, Z. F., & Shen, H. (2007c). Xueshu zhiye zhuanyehua de pingjia weidu [Evaluation dimensions on the specialization of academic profession]. *Daxue yanjiu yu pingjia* [Higher Education Research & Evaluation], *1*, 60–63.

Li, D., & Shen, H. (2009). Cong jingying gaodengjiaoyu shijiao kan xueshu zhiye fazhan [The development of academic profession from an angle of elite higher education]. *Jiangsu gaojiao* [Jiangsu Higher Education], *5*, 17–20.

Li, D., & Shen, H. (2010). Qianxi xueshu zhiye de lishi fazhan xingtai [A brief analysis on the historical styles of the development of the academic profession]. *Daxue jiaoyu kexue* [University Education Science], *1*, 74–77.

Litwin, E. (2012). Comentarios sobre gobierno, gestión y profesión académica [Coment about government, management and academic profession]. In N. Fernández Lamarra & M. Marquina (Eds.), *El futuro de la profesión académica: Desafíos para los países emergentes* [The future of the academic profession: Challenges for emerging countries] (pp. 411–412). Tres de Febrero: EDUNTREF.

Locke, W. (2007). *The changing academic profession in the UK: Setting the scene*. Research report. http://oro.open.ac.uk/11843/1/William_Locke_%282007%29_Changing_Academic_ Profession_-_Setting_the_Scene%2C_UUK_Research_Report.pdf. Accessed 18 May 2011.

Locke, W. (2008). The academic profession in England: Still stratified after all these years? In RIHE (Ed.), *The changing academic profession in international comparative and quantitative perspectives* (RIHE international seminar reports, Vol. 12, pp. 89–116). Hiroshima: Hiroshima University.

Locke, W. (2011). The international study of the changing academic profession: A unique source for examining the academy's perception of governance and management in comparative perspective. In W. Locke, W. K. Cummings, & D. Fisher (Eds.), *Changing governance and management in higher education: The perspectives of the academy* (The changing academy – The changing academic profession in international comparative perspective, Vol. 2, pp. 381–384). Dordrecht: Springer.

Locke, W. (2013a). Teaching and research in English higher education: The fragmentation, diversification and reorganization of academic work, 1992–2007. In J. C. Shin, A. Arimoto, W. K. Cummings, & U. Teichler (Eds.), *Teaching and research in contemporary higher education: Systems, activities, and rewards*. Dordrecht: Springer.

Locke, W. (2013b) (forthcoming). The Dislocation of teaching and research and the reconfiguring of academic work. *Review of Education* (London).

Locke, W., & Bennion, A. (2009). UK. Teaching and research in English higher education: New divisions of labour and changing perspectives on core academic roles. In RIHE (Ed.), *The changing academic profession over 1992–2007: International, comparative and quantitative perspectives* (RIHE international seminar reports, Vol. 13, pp. 231–252). Hiroshima: Hiroshima University.

Locke, W., & Bennion, A. (2010a). *Supplementary report to the HEFCE Higher Education Workforce Framework based on the international Changing academic profession (CAP) study*. Bristol: HEFCE. http://www.hefce.ac.uk/pubs/rdreports/2010/rd02_10/.

Locke, W., & Bennion, A. (2010b). *The changing academic profession in the UK and beyond*. Research report. London: CHERI. http://www.universitiesuk.ac.uk/Publications/Documents/ The%20Changing%20HE%20Profession.pdf.

Locke, W., & Bennion, A. (2011). The United Kingdom: Academic retreat or professional renewal? In W. Locke, W. K. Cummings, & D. Fisher (Eds.), *Changing governance and management in higher education: The perspectives of the academy* (The changing academy – The changing academic profession in international comparative perspective, Vol. 2, pp. 175–198). Dordrecht: Springer.

Locke, W., & Bennion, A. (2013). Satisfaction in stages – The academic profession in the United Kingdom and British Commonwealth. In P. Bentley, H. Coates, I. Dobson, L. Goedegebuere, & V. L. Meek (Eds.), *Job satisfaction around the academic world* (The changing academy – The changing academic profession in international comparative perspective, Vol. 7, pp. 223–238). Dordrecht: Springer.

Locke, W., Cummings, W. K., & Fisher, D. (Eds.). (2011). *Changing governance and management in higher education: The perspectives of the academy* (The changing academy – The changing academic profession in international comparative perspective, Vol. 2). Dordrecht: Springer.
Locke, W., & Kim, T. (2010). Transnational academic mobility and the academic profession. In Centre for Higher Education Research and Information CHERI (Ed.), *Higher education and society* (pp. 27–34). London: CHERI.
Locke, W., & Teichler, U. (2007a). Introduction. In W. Locke & U. Teichler (Eds.), *The changing conditions for academic work and careers in select countries* (Werkstattberichte/International Centre for Higher Education Research Kassel, Vol. 66, pp. 7–13). Kassel: Jenior.
Locke, W., & Teichler, U. (Eds.). (2007b). *The changing conditions for academic work and careers in select countries* (Werkstattberichte/International Centre for Higher Education Research Kassel, Vol. 66). Kassel: Jenior. http://www.gbv.de/dms/hebis-darmstadt/toc/190606959.pdf.
Lucarelli, E. (2012). Comentarios sobre carrera académica, trayectorias y condiciones de trabajo [Commentary about academic careers, paths and working conditions]. In N. Fernández Lamarra & M. Marquina (Eds.), *El futuro de la profesión académica: Desafios para los países emergentes* [The future of the academic profession: Challenges for emerging countries] (pp. 249–254). Tres de Febrero: EDUNTREF.
Marquina, M. (2012). La profesión académica en Argentina: principales características a partir de las políticas recientes [The academics profession in Argentina: main characteristics after recent politics]. In N. Fernández Lamarra & M. Marquina (Eds.), *El futuro de la profesión académica: Desafios para los países emergentes* [The future of the academic profession: Challenges for emerging countries] (pp. 126–147). Tres de Febrero: EDUNTREF.
Marquina, M., & Fernández Lamarra, N. (2008a). La profesión académica en Argentina: explorando su especificidad en el marco de las tendencias internacionales [Academic profession in Argentina: exploring particularities within international trends]. *Revista Alternatives* [Alternatives Journal], 49.
Marquina, M., & Fernández Lamarra, N. (2008b). The academic profession in Argentina: Characteristics and trends in the context of a mass higher education system. In RIHE (Ed.), *The changing academic profession in international comparative and quantitative perspectives* (RIHE international seminar reports, Vol. 12, pp. 363–388). Hiroshima: Hiroshima University.
Marquina, M., & Rebello, G. (2010). *The changing academic profession in Argentina: Personal characteristics, career trajectories and sense of identity/commitment*. http://ungs.academia.edu/documents/0068/4586/Argentina_paper_Personal_characteristics.pdf
Marquina, M., & Rebello, G. (2013). Academic work at the periphery – Why Argentine scholars are satisfied, despite all. In P. Bentley, H. Coates, I. Dobson, L. Goedegebuere, & V. L. Meek (Eds.), *Job satisfaction around the academic world* (The changing academy – The changing academic profession in international comparative perspective, Vol. 7, pp. 13–28). Dordrecht: Springer.
Meek, V. L. (2006). History and development of Australian higher education: An overview. In RIHE (Ed.), *Reports of changing academic profession project workshop on quality, relevance and governance in the changing academia: International perspectives* (COE publication series, Vol. 20, pp. 63–78). Hiroshima: Hiroshima University.
Meek, V. L. (2007). Internationalisation of higher education and the Australian academic profession. In M. Kogan & U. Teichler (Eds.), *Key challenges to the academic profession* (Werkstattberichte/International Centre for Higher Education Research Kassel, Vol. 65, pp. 65–80). Kassel: Jenior.
Melichar, M., & Pabian, P. (2007). Czech Republic – Shifting peripheries: A state of the art report on the Czech academic profession. In W. Locke & U. Teichler (Eds.), *The changing conditions for academic work and careers in select countries* (Werkstattberichte/International Centre for Higher Education Research Kassel, Vol. 66, pp. 39–56). Kassel: Jenior.
Metcalfe, A. S. (2008). The changing academic profession in Canada: Exploring themes of relevance, internationalization and management. In RIHE (Ed.), *The changing academic profession in international comparative and quantitative perspectives* (RIHE international seminar reports, Vol. 12, pp. 57–73). Hiroshima: Hiroshima University.

Metcalfe, A. S., Fisher, D., Gingaras, Y., Jones, G., Rubenson, K., & Snee, I. (2010). How influential are faculty today? Responses from the Canadian professoriate. *Academic Matters* (October–November), 16–20.

Metcalfe, S. A., Fisher, D., Rubenson, K., Snee, I., Gingras, Y., & Jones, G. A. (2011). Canada: Perspectives on governance and management. In W. Locke, W. K. Cummings, & D. Fisher (Eds.), *Changing governance and management in higher education: The perspectives of the academy* (The changing academy – The changing academic profession in international comparative perspective, Vol. 2, pp. 151–174). Dordrecht: Springer.

Mittelstrass, J. (2010). The future of the university. *European Review, 18*(Suppl. 1), 181–189.

Moraru, L. (2012). Academic internal stakeholder condition: A comparative approach. *Procedia – Social and Behavioral Sciences*.

Moraru, L., Praisler, M., Marin, S. A., & Bentea, C. (2013). The academic profession: Quality assurance, governance, relevance, and satisfaction. In B. M. Kehm & U. Teichler (Eds.), *The academic profession in Europe – New tasks and new challenges: The changing academic profession in international comparative perspective* (The changing academy – The changing academic profession in international comparative perspective, Vol. 5, pp. 141–162). Dordrecht: Springer [EUROAC].

Morshidi, S. (2007). Envisioning and imaging of the Malaysian universities towards achievement of 'Regional Hub' status: Are academics being marginalized and deprofessionalized in the process? In RIHE (Ed.), *Reports of COE international seminar on constructing university visions and the mission of academic profession in Asian countries: A comparative perspective* (COE publication series, Vol. 23, pp. 71–88). Hiroshima: Hiroshima University.

Morshidi, S., Ahmad Nurulazam, M. Z., Aida Suraya, M. Y., Haslina, H., Ibrahim, C. O., Kaur, S., et al. (2007). Malaysia: New and diversified roles and responsibilities for academics. In W. Locke & U. Teichler (Eds.), *The changing conditions for academic work and careers in select countries* (Werkstattberichte/International Centre for Higher Education Research Kassel, Vol. 66, pp. 147–161). Kassel: Jenior.

Moscati, R. (2011). Il lavoro accademico [The academic work]. In M. Rostan (Ed.), *La professione accademica in Italia. Aspetti, problemi e confronti nel contesto europeo* [The academic profession in Italy: Aspects, problems and comparisons within the European context] (pp. 63–76). Milano: Edizione Universitarie di Lettere Economia Diritto.

Muhamad, J., & Morshidi, S. (2008). Governance and decision-making related to academic activities: The case of higher educational institutions in Malaysia. In RIHE (Ed.), *The changing academic profession in international comparative and quantitative perspectives* (RIHE international seminar reports, Vol. 12, pp. 203–226). Hiroshima: Hiroshima University.

Murasawa, M. (2011). Hyōka [Evaluation]. In A. Arimoto (Ed.), *Henbō suru sekai no daigaku kyōjushoku* [The changing academic profession in the world] (pp. 275–290). Tamagawa: Tamagawadaigakushuppanbu (Tamagawa University Press).

Musselin, C. (2006). The French academic professions. In RIHE (Ed.), *Reports of changing academic profession project workshop on quality, relevance and governance in the changing academia: International perspectives* (COE publication series, Vol. 20, pp. 115–128). Hiroshima: Hiroshima University.

Musselin, C. (2007). Transformation of academic work: Facts and analysis. In M. Kogan & U. Teichler (Eds.), *Key challenges to the academic profession* (Werkstattberichte/International Centre for Higher Education Research Kassel, Vol. 65, pp. 175–190). Kassel: Jenior.

Naidoo, R., & Brennan, J. (2006). The higher education system in the United Kingdom. In RIHE (Ed.), *Reports of changing academic profession project workshop on quality, relevance and governance in the changing academia: International perspectives* (COE publication series, Vol. 20, pp. 45–62). Hiroshima: Hiroshima University.

Nanbu, H. (2011). Rōdō jōken [Labor conditions]. In A. Arimoto (Ed.), *Henbō suru sekai no daigaku kyōjushoku* [The changing academic profession in the world] (pp. 166–179). Tamagawa: Tamagawadaigakushuppanbu (Tamagawa University Press).

Nenninger, E., & Martinez Garcia, J. M (2011). *El peso de la docencia y la investigación desde la visión de los académicos de una universidad pública mexicana: El caso de la Universidad de*

Sonora [Teaching and research in the view of the academics at a public university in Mexico: The case of Sonora University]. Arizona State University. http://epaa.asu.edu/ojs/article/view/832

Neuber, D., & Kuroda, K. (Eds.). (2012). *Mobility and migration in Asian Pacific higher education*. New York: Palgrave Macmillan.

NIFU-STEP (Ed.). (2009). *Det norske forsknings- og innovasjonssystemet – statistikk og indikatorer 2009 (Norwegian research and innovation system - statistics and indicators 2009)*. Oslo: NIFU STEP.

Nishimoto, H. (2011). Sutoresu [Stress]. In A. Arimoto (Ed.), *Henbō suru sekai no daigaku kyōjushoku* [The changing academic profession in the world] (pp. 214–221). Tamagawa: Tamagawadaigakushuppanbu (Tamagawa University Press).

Norzaini, A. (2010). The impact of changing culture in Malaysian universities on the academic profession. In G. K. Sidhu & L. L. Fong (Eds.), *Transforming learning and teaching towards international practice* (pp. 347–365). Shah Alam: University Publication Centre UPENA UITM.

Norzaini, A., Muhamad, J., & Morshidi, S. (2009). The transformation of the academic profession in Malaysia: Trends and issues on institutional governance and management. *Journal of the World Universities Forum, 2*(5), 123–138.

Ntshoe, I. M., Higgs, P., Wolhuter, C. C., & Higgs, L. G. (2010a). Is quality assurance in higher education contextually relative? *South African Journal of Higher Education, 24*(1), 111–131.

Ntshoe, I. M., Higgs, P., & Higgs, L. G. (2010b). Policy reforms in higher education in South Africa: The changing academic profession project. In N. Popov, C. C. Wolhuter, B. Leutwyler, M. Mihova, & J. Ogunleye (Eds.), *Comparative education, teacher education, education policy, school leadership and social inclusion* (Vol. 8, pp. 209–214). Sofia: Bureau for Educational Services, University of Sofia. http://bces.conference.tripod.com/sitebuildercontent/sitebuilderfiles/8th.bces.conference.2010.book.vol.8.pdf.

Ogata, N. (2011). Akademiku karia [Academic career]. In A. Arimoto (Ed.), *Henbō suru sekai no daigaku kyōjushoku* [The changing academic profession in the world] (pp. 99–108). Tamagawa: Tamagawadaigakushuppanbu (Tamagawa University Press).

Padilla-Gonzalez, L., Metcalfe, A., Scott, P., Galaz-Fontes, J., Fisher, D., & Snee, I. (2011). Gender gaps in North American research productivity: Examining faculty publication rates in Mexico, Canada, and the U.S. *Compare: A Journal of Comparative and International Education, 41*(5), 649–668.

Padilla-González, L., Villaseñor Amézquita, M., Guzmán Acuña, T., & Moreno Olivos, T. (2012). La habilitación de los académicos mexicanos: una perspectiva desde la encuesta sobre la con figuración de la profesión academica en México [The habilitation of Mexican academics: A perspective of the changes in the Mexican profession according to the survey]. In N. Fernández Lamarra & M. Marquina (Eds.), *El futuro de la profesión académica: Desafíos para los países emergentes* [The future of the academic profession: Challenges for emerging countries] (pp. 262–272). Tres de Febrero: EDUNTREF.

Pang, L., & Shen, H. (2009). Kuayue jiaoyuxue he shehuixue xueke bianjie de xueshu zhiye yanjiu [Thoughts on the research of academic profession crossing pedagogy and sociology]. *Hongguo dizhi daxue xuebao-shehui kexue ban* [Journal of China University of Geosciences. Social Sciences Edition], *6*, 86–90.

Pang, V., Sirat, M., Yunus, A. S. M., Pandian, A., Taib, F. M., Shuib, M., et al. (2011). Malaysia. The academic profession in Malaysia 2010: A proposed study. In RIHE (Ed.), *The changing academic profession in Asia: Contexts, realities and trends: Report of the international conference on the changing academic profession project 2011* (RIHE international seminar reports, Vol. 17, pp. 149–160). Hiroshima: Hiroshima University.

Park, E. (2013). From academic self governance to executive university management – Institutional governance in the view of academics in Europe. In U. Teichler & E. A. Höhle (Eds.), *The work situation of the academic profession: Findings of a survey in twelve European countries* (The changing academy – The changing academic profession in international comparative perspective, Vol. 6, pp. 181–203). Dordrecht: Springer [EUROAC].

Pechar, H. (2012). *Karrierechancen für den akademischen Nachwuchs in Österreich* [Career chances of young researchers in Austria]. [EUROAC]. http://www.scribd.com/doc/94786764/Akademischer-Nachwuchs-in-Osterreich

Pekkola, E. (2009). Akateeminen professio suomessa: Valtakeskittymä vai kolmen luokan työntekijöitä? [Academic profession in Finland: Power entity or diversified workforce]. *Politiikka, 4*, 268–290.

Pekkola, E. (2010). Nuorten yliopistolaisten työn palkitsevuus ja sen vaikutus akateemisen uran houkuttelevuudelle [Is work of young academics rewarding and how does it affect the attractiveness of academic career?]. *Työelämän tutkimus - Arbetslivsforskning – lehti, 2*, 145–159.

Pekkola, E. (2011). Kollegiaalinen ja manageriaalinen johtaminen suomalaisissa yliopistoissa [Collegial and managerial management in Finnish universities]. *Hallinnon tutkimus, 1*, 37–55.

Perez Lindo, A. (2012). Comentarios sobre los casos de Sudáfrica, Malasia y China. [Comment about the cases South Africa, Malaysia and China]. In N. Fernández Lamarra & M. Marquina (Eds.), *El futuro de la profesión académica: Desafíos para los países emergentes* [The future of the academic profession: Challenges for emerging countries] (pp. 180–184). Tres de Febrero: EDUNTREF.

Postiglione, G. A. (2006). The Hong Kong special administrative region of the people's republic of China: Context, higher education, and a changing academia. In RIHE (Ed.), *Reports of changing academic profession project workshop on quality, relevance and governance in the changing academia: International perspectives* (COE publication series, Vol. 20, pp. 97–114). Hiroshima: Hiroshima University.

Postiglione, G. A. (2007). Hong Kong: Expansion, re-union with China and the transformation of academic culture. In W. Locke & U. Teichler (Eds.), *The changing conditions for academic work and careers in select countries* (Werkstattberichte/International Centre for Higher Education Research Kassel, Vol. 66, pp. 57–75). Kassel: Jenior.

Postiglione, G. A., & Shiru, W. (2011). Hong Kong: Governance and the-double-edged academy. In W. Locke, W. K. Cummings, & D. Fisher (Eds.), *Changing governance and management in higher education: The perspectives of the academy* (The changing academy – The changing academic profession in international comparative perspective, Vol. 2, pp. 343–368). Dordrecht: Springer.

Postiglione, G. A., & Tang, H. H. H. (2008). A preliminary review of the Hong Kong CAP data. In RIHE (Ed.), *The changing academic profession in international comparative and quantitative perspectives* (RIHE international seminar reports, Vol. 12, pp. 227–250). Hiroshima: Hiroshima University.

Probst, C., & Goastellec, G. (2013). Internationalisation and the academic labour market. In B. M. Kehm & U. Teichler (Eds.), *The academic profession in Europe – New tasks and new challenges: The changing academic profession in international comparative perspective* (The changing academy – The changing academic profession in international comparative perspective, Vol. 5, pp. 121–140). Dordrecht: Springer [EUROAC].

Quihui Andrade, A. (2009). *Rasgos de la actividad docente en la Universidad de Sonora, desde la perspectiva de sus académicos (Tesis no publicada de Maestría en Innovación Educativa)* [Traits of teaching at the University of Sonora from the perspectives of its academics].

Rebello, G., et al. (2012). Participación en el gobierno y la gestión universitaria: la mirada de los académicos argentinos. In N. Fernández Lamarra & M. Marquina (Eds.), *El futuro de la profesión académica: Desafíos para los países emergentes* [The future of the academic profession: Challenges for emerging countries] (pp. 440–452). Tres de Febrero: EDUNTREF.

RIHE (Ed.). (2006). *Reports of changing academic profession project workshop on quality, relevance and governance in the changing academia: International perspectives* (COE Publication Series, Vol. 20). Hiroshima: Hiroshima University. http://en.rihe.hiroshima-u.ac.jp/news_topic.php?id=198.

RIHE (Ed.). (2007). *Reports of COE international seminar on constructing university visions and the mission of academic profession in Asian countries: A comparative perspective* (COE publication series, Vol. 23). Hiroshima: Hiroshima University. http://en.rihe.hiroshima-u.ac.jp/news_topic.php?id=198.

RIHE (Ed.). (2008). *The changing academic profession in international comparative and quantitative perspectives* (RIHE international seminar reports, Vol. 12). Hiroshima: Hiroshima University. http://en.rihe.hiroshima-u.ac.jp/pl_default_1.php?c=RIHE+International+Seminar +Reports.

RIHE (Ed.). (2009). *The changing academic profession over 1992–2007: International, comparative and quantitative perspectives* (RIHE international seminar reports, Vol. 13). Hiroshima: Hiroshima University. http://en.rihe.hiroshima-u.ac.jp/pl_default_1.php?c=RIHE+Internation al+Seminar+Reports.

RIHE (Ed.). (2010). *The changing academic profession in international and quantitative perspectives: A focus on teaching & research activities: Report of the international conference on the changing academic profession project 2010* (RIHE international seminar reports, Vol. 15). Hiroshima: Hiroshima University. http://en.rihe.hiroshima-u.ac.jp/pl_default_1.php?c=RIHE+ International+Seminar+Reports.

RIHE (Ed.). (2011). *The changing academic profession in Asia: Contexts, realities and trends: Report of the international conference on the changing academic profession project 2011* (RIHE International Seminar Reports, Vol. 17). Hiroshima: Hiroshima University. http://en. rihe.hiroshima-u.ac.jp/pl_default_2.php?bid=105719.

Rončević, N., & Rafajac, B. (2010). *Promjene u akademskoj profesiji: komparativna analiza* [Changes in academic profession: Comparative analysis]. Rijeka: Filozofski fakultet u Rijeci [EUROAC].

Rončević, N., & Rafajac, B. (2012). *Održivi razvoj – izazov za sveučilište?* [Sustainable development- challenge for the university]. Rijeka: Filozofski fakultet u Rijeci [EUROAC].

Rostan, M. (2008). The changing academic profession in Italy: Accounts from the past, first insights from the present. In RIHE (Ed.), *The changing academic profession in international comparative and quantitative perspectives* (RIHE international seminar reports, Vol. 12, pp. 153–178). Hiroshima: Hiroshima University.

Rostan, M. (2010a). Challenges to academic freedom: Some empirical evidence. *European Review, 18*(Supplement 1), 71–88.

Rostan, M. (2010b). Teaching and research in a changing environment: Academic work in Italy. In RIHE (Ed.), *The changing academic profession in international and quantitative perspectives: A focus on teaching & research activities: Report of the international conference on the changing academic profession project 2010* (RIHE international seminar reports, Vol. 15, pp. 61–86). Hiroshima: Hiroshima University.

Rostan, M. (2011a). English as "Lingua Franca" and the internationalization of academe. *International Higher Education, 63*, 11–13.

Rostan, M. (2011b). Gli accademici e la ricerca [Academics and research]. In M. Rostan (Ed.), *La professione accademica in Italia. Aspetti, problemi e confronti nel contesto europeo* [The academic profession in Italy: Aspects, problems and comparisons within the European Context] (pp. 107–130). Milano: Edizione Universitarie di Lettere Economia Diritto.

Rostan, M. (Ed.). (2011c). *La professione accademica in Italia. Aspetti, problemi e confronti nel contesto europeo* [The academic profession in Italy: Aspects, problems and comparisons within the European Context]. Milano: Edizione Universitarie di Lettere Economia Diritto. http://www.ledonline.it/cirsis/index.html?/cirsis/home.shtml

Rostan, M. (2012). Beyond physical mobility: Other ways to internationalise the academic profession. In M. Vukasovic, P. Maassen, B. Stensaker, M. Nerland, R. Pinheiro, & A. Vabø (Eds.), *Effects of higher education reforms: Change dynamics* (pp. 239–258). Rotterdam: Sense.

Rostan, M. (2013) (forthcoming). Teaching and research at Italian universities: Continuities and changes. In J. C. Shin, A. Arimoto, W. K. Cummings, & U. Teichler (Eds.), *Teaching and research in contemporary higher education: Systems, activities, and rewards*. Dordrecht: Springer.

Rostan, M., & Vaira, M. (2011). Una professione che sta cambiando [A changing profession]. In M. Rostan (Ed.), *La professione accademica in Italia. Aspetti, problemi e confronti nel contesto europeo* [The academic profession in Italy: Aspects, problems and comparisons within the European Context] (pp. 7–50). Milano: Edizione Universitarie di Lettere Economia Diritto.

Rostan, M., Ceravolo, F. A., & Metcalfe, A. S. (2013) (forthcoming). The internationalization of academic research. In F. Huang, M. Finkelstein, & M. Rostan (Eds.), *The internationalization of the academy: Changes, realities and prospects*. Dordrecht: Springer.

Rostan, M., Finkelstein, M., & Huang, F. (2013) (forthcoming). A profile of the CAP countries and aggregated internationalization of academic activities in 2007–2008. In F. Huang, M. Finkelstein, & M. Rostan (Eds.), *The internationalization of the academy: Changes, realities and prospects*. Dordrecht: Springer.

Rostan. M., & Höhle, E. A. (2013) (forthcoming). The international mobility of academic staff. In F. Huang, M. Finkelstein, & M. Rostan (Eds.), *The internationalization of the academy: Changes, realities and prospects*. Dordrecht: Springer.

Rostan, M., Huang, F., & Finkelstein, M. (2013) (forthcoming). The internationalization of the academy: Findings, open questions, and implications. In F. Huang, M. Finkelstein, & M. Rostan (Eds.), The internationalization of the academy: Changes, realities and prospects. Dordrecht: Springer.

Sánchez Aparicio y Benítez, G. de, Jiménez Loza, L., & González Martínez, A. (2012). México: Entornos de cambio en la profesión académica. Diversificación de functiones y satisfacción laboral de los académicos mexicanos [Mexico: Environments and some patterns of change in the academic profession. Diversification and job satisfaction of the Mexican academics]. In N. Fernández Lamarra & M. Marquina (Eds.), *El futuro de la profesión académica*: *Desafios para los países emergentes* [The future of the academic profession: Challenges for emerging countries] (pp. 300–310). Tres de Febrero: EDUNTREF.

Sandoval, M. C. P. (2012). La profesión académica en Venezuela: pasado, presente y futuro [The academic profession in Venezuela: past, present and future]. In N. Fernández Lamarra & M. Marquina (Eds.), *El futuro de la profesión académica*: *Desafios para los países emergentes* [The future of the academic profession: Challenges for emerging countries] (pp. 168–179). Tres de Febrero: EDUNTREF.

Santiago, R., & Carvalho, T. (2011). Mudança no conhecimento e na profissão académica em Portugal [Changes in knowledge and in the academic profession in Portugal]. *Cadernos de Pesquisa [Research Journal], 41*(143), 402–426.

Santiago, R., Carvalho, T., & Vabo, A. (2012). Personal characteristics, career trajectories and sense of identity among male and female academics in Norway and Portugal. In M. Vukasovic, P. Maassen, B. Stensaker, M. Nerland, R. Pinheiro, & A. Vabø (Eds.), *Effects of higher education reforms: Change dynamics* (pp. 279–303). Rotterdam: Sense.

Santiago, R., Sousa, S., Carvalho, T., Machado-Taylor, L., & Amado, D. (2013). Teaching and research – Perspectives from Portugal. In J. Shin, A. Arimoto, W. K. Cummings, & U. Teichler (Eds.), *Teaching and research in contemporary higher education: Systems, activities, nexus, and rewards*. Dordrecht: Springer.

Schneijderberg, C., & Merkator, N. (2013). The new higher education professionals. In B. M. Kehm & U. Teichler (Eds.), *The academic profession in Europe – New tasks and new challenges: The changing academic profession in international comparative perspective* ([HOPRO], The changing academy – The changing academic profession in international comparative perspective, Vol. 5, pp. 53–92). Dordrecht: Springer [EUROAC].

Schwartzman, S., & Balbachevsky, E. (2009). Brazil. The academic profession in a diverse institutional environment: Converging or diverging values and beliefs? In RIHE (Ed.), *The changing academic profession over 1992–2007: International, comparative and quantitative perspectives* (RIHE international seminar reports, Vol. 13, pp. 145–165). Hiroshima: Hiroshima University.

Schwartzman, S., & Balbachevsky, E. (2013) (forthcoming). Research and teaching in a diverse institutional environment: Converging values and diverging practices in Brazil. In J. C. Shin, A. Arimoto, W. K. Cummings, & U. Teichler (Eds.). *Teaching and research in contemporary higher education: Systems, activities, and rewards*. Dordrecht: Springer.

Sevilla García, J., Galaz Fontes, J., Arcos Vega, J., Martínez Stack, J., & Alcántar Enríquez, V. (2012). La administración y gestión de las instituciones de educación superior mexicanas desde la perspectiva del profesorado: Resultados de la encuesta "la reconfiguración académica en México" [Administration and management of Mexican higher education institutions from the professoriate perspective]. In N. Fernández Lamarra & M. Marquina (Eds.), *El futuro de la profesión académica: Desafíos para los países emergentes* [The future of the academic profession: Challenges for emerging countries] (pp. 413–424). Tres de Febrero: EDUNTREF.

Shen, H. (2006). Academic profession in China: A focus on the higher education system. In RIHE (Ed.), *Reports of changing academic profession project workshop on quality, relevance and governance in the changing academia: International perspectives* (COE publication series, Vol. 20, pp. 79–96). Hiroshima: Hiroshima University.

Shen, H. (2007a). Bian48e zhong de xueshu zhiye—cong 14 guo/diqu dao 21 guo de hezuo yanjiu [Academic profession in reform – Collaboration research expanded from 14 countries/regions to 21 countries]. *Daxue yanjiu yu pingjia* [Higher Education Research & Evaluation], *1*, 49–52.

Shen, H. (2007b). Challenges on the academic profession development posed by the changing doctoral education in China. In M. Kogan & U. Teichler (Eds.), *Key challenges to the academic profession* (Werkstattberichte/International Centre for Higher Education Research Kassel, Vol. 65, pp. 125–142). Kassel: Jenior.

Shen, H. (2008). Progress of the academic profession in mainland China. In RIHE (Ed.), *The changing academic profession in international comparative and quantitative perspectives* (RIHE international seminar reports, Vol. 12, pp. 251–264). Hiroshima: Hiroshima University.

Shen, H. (2011a). lun xueshu zhiye de dutexing [The unique characteristics of academic profession]. *Beijing daxue jiaoyu pinglun* (Peking University Education Review), *2011(3)*, 18–27.

Shen, H. (2011b). Impact factors of faculty time and its allocation. *Journal of Higher Education Policy and Management, 3*, 59–67.

Shen, H., Zhiyuan, G., & Qian, L. (2011). Daxue jiaoshi gongzuo shijian he shijian fenpei de yingxiang yinsu: shizheng yanjiu [An empirical study on the influencing factors of faculty working time]. *Gaodeng jiaoyu yanjiu* [Journal of Higher Education], *9*, 55–63.

Shin, J. C. (2009). South Korea. Teaching and research across academic disciplines: Faculty's preference, activity, and performance. In RIHE (Ed.), *The changing academic profession over 1992–2007: International, comparative and quantitative perspectives* (RIHE international seminar reports, Vol. 13, pp. 213–230). Hiroshima: Hiroshima University.

Shin, J. C. (2010). Scholarship of service: Faculty perception, workloads, and reward systems. In RIHE (Ed.), *The changing academic profession in international and quantitative perspectives: A focus on teaching & research activities: Report of the international conference on the changing academic profession project 2010* (RIHE international seminar reports, Vol. 15, pp. 173–190). Hiroshima: Hiroshima University.

Shin, J. C. (2011a). South Korea: Decentralized centralization – Fading shared governance and rising managerialism. In W. Locke, W. K. Cummings, & D. Fisher (Eds.), *Changing governance and management in higher education: The perspectives of the academy* (The changing academy – The changing academic profession in international comparative perspective, Vol. 2, pp. 231–342). Dordrecht: Springer.

Shin, J. C. (2011b). South Korea. The Korean academic profession revisited: academic activity, performance, and governance. In RIHE (Ed.), *The changing academic profession in Asia: Contexts, realities and trends: Report of the international conference on the changing academic profession project 2011* (RIHE international seminar reports, Vol. 17, pp. 161–176). Hiroshima: Hiroshima University.

Shin, J. (2012). Foreign PhDs and Korean PhDs: How they differ in their academic activity, performance, and culture. In D. Neuber & K. Kuroda (Eds.), *Mobility and migration in Asian Pacific higher education*. New York: Palgrave Macmillan.

Shin, J. C., & Cummings, W. K. (2010). Multilevel analysis of academic publishing across disciplines: Research preference, collaboration, and time on research. *Scientometrics, 85*(2), 581–594.

Shin, J., Arimoto, A., Cummings, W. K., & Teichler, U. (Eds.). (2013). *Teaching and research in contemporary higher education: Systems, activities, nexus, and rewards*. Dordrecht: Springer.

Shin, J., & Cummings, W. K. (2013) (forthcoming). Teaching and research across higher education systems: A typology and implications. In J. C. Shin, A. Arimoto, W. K. Cummings, & U. Teichler (Eds.), *Teaching and research in contemporary higher education: Systems, activities, and rewards*. Dordrecht: Springer.

Shin, J., Jung, J., & Kim, Y. (2013) (forthcoming). Teaching and research of Korean academics across career stages. In J. C. Shin, A. Arimoto, W. K. Cummings, & U. Teichler (Eds.), *Teaching and research in contemporary higher education: Systems, activities, and rewards*. Dordrecht: Springer.

Sidhu, G. K., & Fong, L. L. (Eds.). (2010). *Transforming learning and teaching towards international practice*. Shah Alam: University Publication Centre UPENA UITM.

Sirat, M. (2012). Académicos malayos: ¿Quiénes son y por qué luchan? [Academic profession in Malaysia: More of the same?]. In N. Fernández Lamarra & M. Marquina (Eds.), *El futuro de la profesión académica: Desafíos para los países emergentes* [The future of the academic profession: Challenges for emerging countries] (pp. 185–198). Tres de Febrero: EDUNTREF.

Sirat, M., et al. (2012). Gobierno y administración de las instituciones de educación superior en Malasia: la perspectiva de los académicos [Government and management in higher education in Malaysia: A view from academics]. In N. Fernández Lamarra & M. Marquina (Eds.), *El futuro de la profesión académica: Desafíos para los países emergentes* [The future of the academic profession: Challenges for emerging countries] (pp. 425–439). Tres de Febrero: EDUNTREF.

Soares, M., Teichler, U., & Machado-Taylor, M. (Eds.). (2013). *Approaches to the academic career in Europe: Challenges, issues and developments*. Porto.

Song, X., & Shen, H. (2007). Xueshu zhiye zhong de xueshu ziyou yu xueshu zeren [Academic freedom and academic responsibility in academic profession]. *Daxue yanjiu yu pingjia* [Higher Education Research & Evaluation], *1*, 64–68.

Song, X., & Shen, H. (2008). Xueshu zhiye fazhan zhong de xueshu shengwang yu xueshu chuangxin [Academic prestige and innovation in the academic profession development]. *Kexuexue yu kexue jishu guanli* [Science of Science and Management of Sci. & Tech], *8*, 98–103.

Suasnábar, C. (2012). Comentarios sobre los casos de Chile y Venezuela (Comment about the cases Chile and Venezuela]. In N. Fernández Lamarra & M. Marquina (Eds.), *El futuro de la profesión académica: Desafíos para los países emergentes* [The future of the academic profession: Challenges for emerging countries] (pp. 148–152). Tres de Febrero: EDUNTREF.

Tai, H.-H., & Chen, C.-Y. (2011). Taiwan. The changing Taiwanese academic profession: From regulation to supervision. In RIHE (Ed.), *The changing academic profession in Asia: Contexts, realities and trends: Report of the international conference on the changing academic profession project 2011* (RIHE international seminar reports, Vol. 17, pp. 197–212). Hiroshima: Hiroshima University.

Taylor, J. S., Graça, M., de Lourdes-Machado, M., & Sousa, S. (2007). Portugal: Adapting in order to promote change. In W. Locke & U. Teichler (Eds.), *The changing conditions for academic work and careers in select countries* (Werkstattberichte/International Centre for Higher Education Research Kassel, Vol. 66, pp. 211–227). Kassel: Jenior.

Teichler, U. (2006). Principles of comparative higher education research. In RIHE (Ed.), *Reports of changing academic profession project workshop on quality, relevance and governance in the changing academia: International perspectives* (COE publication series, Vol. 20, pp. 267–277). Hiroshima: Hiroshima University.

Teichler, U. (2007). Germany and beyond: New dynamics for the academic profession. In W. Locke & U. Teichler (Eds.), *The changing conditions for academic work and careers in select countries* (Werkstattberichte/International Centre for Higher Education Research Kassel, Vol. 66, pp. 15–38). Kassel: Jenior.

Teichler, U. (2008). Academic staff in Germany: Per aspera ad astra? In RIHE (Ed.), *The changing academic profession in international comparative and quantitative perspectives* (RIHE international seminar reports, Vol. 12, pp. 131–152). Hiroshima: Hiroshima University.

Teichler, U. (2009). Biographies, careers and work of academics. In RIHE (Ed.), *The changing academic profession over 1992–2007: International, comparative and quantitative perspectives* (RIHE international seminar reports, Vol. 13, pp. 57–78). Hiroshima: Hiroshima University.

Teichler, U. (2010a). Teaching and research in Germany: Narrowing the gaps between institutional types and staff categories? In RIHE (Ed.), *The changing academic profession in international and quantitative perspectives: A focus on teaching & research activities: Report of the international conference on the changing academic profession project 2010* (RIHE international seminar reports, Vol. 15, pp. 41–60). Hiroshima: Hiroshima University.

Teichler, U. (2010b). The diversifying academic profession? *European Review, 18*(Supplement 1), 157–179.

Teichler, U. (2011). Germany: How changing governance management affects the views and work of academic profession. In W. Locke, W. K. Cummings, & D. Fisher (Eds.), *Changing governance and management in higher education: The perspectives of the academy* (The changing academy – The changing academic profession in international comparative perspective, Vol. 2, pp. 223–243). Dordrecht: Springer.

Teichler, U. (2012a). Cambios en el empleo y el trabajo de la profesión académica: la situación en las universidades orientadas a la investigación en los países económicamente avanzados [Towards career instability and employee-status of the academics?]. In N. Fernández Lamarra & M. Marquina (Eds.), *El futuro de la profesión académica: Desafíos para los países emergentes* [The future of the academic profession: Challenges for emerging countries] (pp. 17–30). Tres de Febrero: EDUNTREF.

Teichler, U. (2012b). Diversity of higher education in Europe and the findings of a comparative study of the academic profession. In A. Curaj, P. Scott, L. Vlasceanu, & L. Wilson (Eds.), *European higher education at the crossroads: Between the Bologna process and national reforms* (Vol. 2, pp. 935–959). Dordrecht: Springer.

Teichler, U. (2012c). La profesión académica en Alemania: cambios en el emplei y la situación laboral de 1992 a 2007 [The academic profession in Germany: changes from 1992 to 2007]. In N. Fernández Lamarra & M. Marquina (Eds.), *El futuro de la profesión académica: Desafíos para los países emergentes* [The future of the academic profession: Challenges for emerging countries] (pp. 226–236). Tres de Febrero: EDUNTREF.

Teichler, U. (2013) (forthcoming). Teaching and research in Germany: The notions of university professors. In J. C. Shin, A. Arimoto, W. K. Cummings, & U. Teichler (Eds.), *Teaching and research in contemporary higher education: Systems, activities, and rewards*. Dordrecht: Springer.

Teichler, U., & Bracht, O. (2006). The academic profession in Germany. In RIHE (Ed.), *Reports of changing academic profession project workshop on quality, relevance and governance in the changing academia: International perspectives* (COE publication series, Vol. 20, pp. 129–150). Hiroshima: Hiroshima University.

Teichler, U., & Höhle, E. A. (2013a). The academic profession in twelve European countries – The approach of the comparative study. In U. Teichler & E. A. Höhle (Eds.), *The work situation of the academic profession: Findings of a survey in twelve European countries* (The changing academy – The changing academic profession in international comparative perspective, Vol. 6, pp. 1–11). Dordrecht: Springer [EUROAC].

Teichler, U., & Höhle, E. A. (Eds.). (2013b). *The work situation of the academic profession: Findings of a survey in twelve European countries* (The changing academy – The changing academic profession in international comparative perspective, Vol. 6). Dordrecht: Springer [EUROAC].

Teichler, U., Arimoto, A., & Cummings, W. K. (2013). *The changing academic profession: Major findings of a comparative sutdy* (The changing academy – The changing academic profession in international comparative perspective, Vol. 1). Dordrecht: Springer.

Teichler, U., & Arimoto, A. (2013) (forthcoming). Teaching and research: A vulnerable linkage? In J. C. Shin, A. Arimoto, W. K. Cummings, & U. Teichler (Eds.), *Teaching and research in contemporary higher education: Systems, activities, and rewards*. Dordrecht: Springer.

Tierney, W. G. (2008). The shifting boundaries of the academic profession: The Malaysian professoriate in comparative perspective. *Kemanusiaan: The Asian Journal of Humanities, 15*, 1–12.

Trivellato, P., & Triventi, M. (2011). Gli accademici e la didattica [Academics and didactics]. In M. Rostan (Ed.), *La professione accademica in Italia: Aspetti, problemi e confronti nel con-*

testo europeo [The academic profession in Italy: Aspects, problems and comparisons within the European Context] (pp. 77–106). Milano: Edizione Universitarie di Lettere Economia Diritto.

Turk, M. (2011). Higher education in Croatia: Introduction. http://www.herdata.org/archives/383 [EUROAC].

Turk, M., Ćulum, B., & Ledić, J. (2011). Civilna misija sveucilista: element u tragovima? [University Civic Mission: An element in traces?]. *Društvena istraživanja, 20(4)* (Book Review), 1206–1210 [EUROAC].

Turk, M., Rončević, N., & Rafajac, B. (2013). Promjene u akademskoj profesiji: komparativna analiza [Changes in academic profession: Comparative analysis]. *Društvena istraživanja, 20(4)* (Book Review) [EUROAC].

Urata, H. (2011). Ryūdōsei – kenkyū katsudō wo kasseika shiteiruka? (Mobility — Are research activities being activated?). In A. Arimoto (Ed.), *Henbō suru sekai no daigaku kyōjushoku* [The changing academic profession in the world] (pp. 109–122). Tamagawa: Tamagawadaigakushuppanbu (Tamagawa University Press).

Vabø, A. (2007a). Challenges of internationalization for the academic profession in Norway. In M. Kogan & U. Teichler (Eds.), *Key challenges to the academic profession* (Werkstattberichte/International Centre for Higher Education Research Kassel, Vol. 65, pp. 99–107). Kassel: Jenior.

Vabø, A. (2007b). Norway: The principal-agent relationship and its impact on the autonomy of the academic profession. In W. Locke & U. Teichler (Eds.), *The changing conditions for academic work and careers in select countries* (Werkstattberichte/International Centre for Higher Education Research Kassel, Vol. 66, pp. 177–194). Kassel: Jenior.

Vabø, A. (2009). *Forskningsvilkår er mer enn tid til forskning* [Research conditions involve more than time for research]. Oslo: NIFU STEP.

Vabø, A. (2011). Norway: Between Humboldtian values and strategic management. In W. Locke, W. K. Cummings, & D. Fisher (Eds.), *Changing governance and management in higher education: The perspectives of the academy* (The changing academy – The changing academic profession in international comparative perspective, Vol. 2, pp. 263–280). Dordrecht: Springer.

Vabø, A. (2012). Gender and international research cooperation. *International Higher Education* (Boston/CIHE) 69.

Vabø, A., & Ramberg, I. (2009). *Arbeidsvilkår i norsk forskning. Working conditions within the Norwegian research community: Rapport 9/2009*. Oslo: NIFU STEP.

Vabø, A., Padilla-Gonzalez, L., Waagene, E., & Næss, T. (2013). Gender and faculty internationalization. In F. Huang, M. J. Finkelstein, & M. Rostan (Eds.), *The internationalisation of the academy: Changes, realities and prospects* (The changing academy – The changing academic profession in international comparative perspective, Vol. 9). Dordrecht: Springer.

Vaira, M. (2011). Gli accademici e l'organizzazione dell'università [Academics and the organization of the university]. In M. Rostan (Ed.), *La professione accademica in Italia. Aspetti, problemi e confronti nel contesto europeo* [The academic profession in Italy: Aspects, problems and comparisons within the European context] (pp. 131–150). Milano: Edizione Universitarie di Lettere Economia Diritto.

Van der Walt, J. J., Wolhuter, C. C., Potgieter, F. J., Higgs, P., Higgs, L. G., & Ntshoe, I. M. (2009). Die akademie in Suid-Afrika: 'n vervullende professie? [The academic profession in South Africa: a fulfilling career?]. *Koers, 74*(3), 409–436. http://www.koersjournal.org.za/index.php/koers/article/view/132.

Weinrib, J., Jones, G., Metcalfe, A. S., Fisher, D., Gingras, Y. R. K., & Snee, I. (2013). Canadian university academics' perceptions of job satisfaction – "the future is not what is used to be". In P. Bentley, H. Coates, I. Dobson, L. Goedegebuere, & V. L. Meek (Eds.), *Job satisfaction around the academic world* (The changing academy – The changing academic profession in international comparative perspective, Vol. 7, pp. 83–102). Dordrecht: Springer.

Wolhuter, C. C. (2012). South Africa: Job satisfaction for a besieged profession. In P. Bentley, H. Coates, I. Dobson, L. Goedegebuere, & V. L. Meek (Eds.), *Job satisfaction around the academic world* (The changing academy – The changing academic profession in international comparative perspective, Vol. 7, pp. 209–222). Dordrecht: Springer.

Wolhuter, C. (2013) (forthcoming). From teachers to perfect Humboldtian persons to academic superpersons: The teaching and research activities of the South African academic profession. In J. C. Shin, A. Arimoto, W. K. Cummings, & U. Teichler (Eds.), *Teaching and research in contemporary higher education: Systems, activities, and rewards*. Dordrecht: Springer.

Wolhuter, C. C., Higgs, L. G., & Higgs, P. (2007a). The South African academic profession: Rapid change and re-integration with the global community. In W. Locke & U. Teichler (Eds.), *The changing conditions for academic work and careers in select countries* (Werkstattberichte/ International Centre for Higher Education Research Kassel, Vol. 66, pp. 77–91). Kassel: Jenior.

Wolhuter, C., van der Walt, H., Higgs, L. G., & Higgs, P. (2007b). Die akademiese professie in Suid-Afrika se belewing van die huidige rekonstruksie van die samelewing en die hoër onderwys [How the South African academic profession experiences the current reconstruction of society]. *Tydskrif vir Geesteswetenskappe* [Journal of Humanities], *47*(4), 501–515. http://content.ebscohost.com/pdf19_22/pdf/2007/12KR/01Dec07/27981658.pdf?EbscoContent=dGJyMNXb4kSeqLA4v%2BvlOLCmr0qep7dSr624TLeWxWXS&ContentCustomer=dGJyMPHq43zz5OeOuePfgeyx7H312%2BKL3%2Bbn&T=P&P=AN&S=R&D=a9h&K=27981658.

Wolhuter, C. C., Higgs, P., Higgs, L. G., & Ntshoe, I. M. (2008). The academic profession in South Africa in times of change: Portrait from the preliminary results of the changing academic profession (CAP) research project. In RIHE (Ed.), *The changing academic profession in international comparative and quantitative perspectives* (RIHE international seminar reports, Vol. 12, pp. 389–400). Hiroshima: Hiroshima University.

Wolhuter, C. C., Higgs, P., Higgs, L. G., & Ntshoe, I. M. (2010a). Die tanende aantreklikheid van die akademiese professie in Suid-Afrika [The attractiveness of the academic profession in South Africa]. *Tydskrif vir Geesteswetenskappe [Journal of Humanities], 50*(2), 141–156. http://www.scielo.org.za/scielo.php?pid=S0041-47512010000200001&script=sci_arttext.

Wolhuter, C. C., Higgs, P., Higgs, L. G., & Ntshoe, I. M. (2010b). How affluent is the South African academic profession, and how strong is the South African academic profession, in the changing international higher education landscape? *South African Journal of Higher Education, 24*(1), 196–214.

Wolhuter, C. C., de Wet, C. N., Higgs, P., Higgs, L. G., & Ntshoe, I. M. (2010c). Die loopbaanbelewenis van akademiese personeel aan Suid-Afrikaanse universiteite [The career experience of academic staff in South African universities]. *Acta Academica, 42*(3), 145–168.

Wolhuter, C. C., Higgs, P., Higgs, L. G., & Ntshoe, I. M. (2011). South Africa: Recklessly incapacitated by a fifth column – The academic profession facing institutional governance. In W. Locke, W. K. Cummings, & D. Fisher (Eds.), *Changing governance and management in higher education: The perspectives of the academy* (The changing academy – The changing academic profession in international comparative perspective, Vol. 2, pp. 107–128). Dordrecht: Springer.

Wolhuter, C. C., Higgs, L. G., & Ntshoe, I. M. (2012). Sudáfrica: La delicada posición de la profesión académica en un país emergente [South Africa: The delicate position of the academic profession in an emerging country]. In N. Fernández Lamarra & M. Marquina (Eds.), *El futuro de la profesión académica: Desafíos para los países emergentes* [The future of the academic profession: Challenges for emerging countries] (pp. 199–208). Tres de Febrero: EDUNTREF.

Yamamoto, S. (2010). Foreword. In RIHE (Ed.), *The changing academic profession in international and quantitative perspectives: A focus on teaching & research activities: Report of the international conference on the changing academic profession project 2010* (RIHE international seminar reports, Vol. 15, p. i). Hiroshima: Hiroshima University.

Yamanoi, A. (2006). The Japanese academic marketplace and academic productivity. In RIHE (Ed.), *Reports of changing academic profession project workshop on quality, relevance and governance in the changing academia: International perspectives* (COE publication series, Vol. 20, pp. 21–36). Hiroshima: Hiroshima University.

Yan, F. (2010). The Academic profession in China in the context of social transition: An institutional perspective. *European Review, 18*(Supplement 1), 99–116.

Yan, F. (2011). China. The same term but different connotations: Cultural and historical perspectives on studying the academic profession in Asia. In RIHE (Ed.), *The changing academic profession in Asia: Contexts, realities and trends: Report of the international conference on the changing academic profession project 2011* (RIHE international seminar reports, Vol. 17, pp. 97–112). Hiroshima: Hiroshima University.

Yavaprabhas, S. (2011). Thailand. Connect ASEAN: Promoting regional integration in higher education in Southeast Asia. In RIHE (Ed.), *The changing academic profession in Asia: Contexts, realities and trends: Report of the international conference on the changing academic profession project 2011* (RIHE international seminar reports, Vol. 17, pp. 213–228). Hiroshima: Hiroshima University.

Zain, A. N. M., Shuib, M., & Abdullah, M. N. L. Y. (2010). Presenting Malaysian academics to the world: What's holding us back? In RIHE (Ed.), *The changing academic profession in international and quantitative perspectives: A focus on teaching & research activities: Report of the international conference on the changing academic profession project 2010* (RIHE international seminar reports, Vol. 15, pp. 159–172). Hiroshima: Hiroshima University.

Zavala Escalante, M. (2009). Satisfacción laboral, identidad y preferencias de académicos en una universidad pública estatal en México [Job satisfaction, identity and preferences of academics at the public state university]: *Tesis no publicada de Licenciatura en Psicología* [unpublished thesis in Psychology]. Hermosillo, Sonora.

Zhang, Y., & Shen, H. (2007a). lun xueshu zhiye rencai chubei zai woguo boshisheng jiaoyu zhong de queshi [Flaws of man power reservation of academic profession in Chinese doctoral education]. *Gaodeng gongcheng jiaoyu yanjiu [Research in Higher Education of Engineering], 2*, 71–78.

Zhang, Y., & Shen, H. (2007b). Xueshu zhiye: Gainian jieding zhong de kunjing [Academic profession: The predicament of its definition]. *Jiangsu gaojiao* [Jiangsu Higher Education], *5*, 26–28.

Zhang, Y., & Shen, H. (2007c). Xueshu zhiye: Guonei yanjiu jinzhan yu wenxian pingshu [Academic profession: Domestic research progress and literature review]. *Daxue yanjiu yu pingjia* [Higher Education Research & Evaluation], *1*, 54–58.

Printed by Printforce, the Netherlands